in a queer country

GAY and LESBIAN STUDIES in the CANADIAN CONTEXT

Edited by **TERRY GOLDIE**

ARSENAL PULP PRESS
VANCOUVER

ARSENAL PULP PRESS
103 – 1014 Homer Street
Vancouver, B.C.
Canada V6B 2W9
www.arsenalpulp.com

The publisher gratefully acknowledges the support of the Canada Council for the Arts and the B.C. Arts Council for its publishing program, and the support of the Government of Canada through the Book Publishing Industry Development Program for its publishing activities.

Design by Val Speidel
Cover photograph by Kevin Madill
Printed and bound in Canada

CANADIAN CATALOGUING IN PUBLICATION DATA

Main entry under title:
In a queer country

Includes bibliographical references.
ISBN 1-55152-105-9

1. Gays—Canada. 2. Lesbians—Canada. I. Goldie, Terry.
HQ75.16.C3152 2001 305.9'0664'0971 C2001-911290-4

CONTENTS

ACKNOWLEDGMENTS

Earlier versions of these papers, with the exception of the interview with Lynne Fernie and Terry Goldie's "Queer Nation?", were given at the "Queer Nation?" conference. Held in March 1997, it was sponsored by the Robarts Centre for Canadian Studies, York University. I would like to acknowledge the assistance provided by the acting director of the Centre, Carole Carpenter, the administrative assistant, Krystyna Tarkowski, and the graduate assistants, Michelle Power and Tamara Stieber. For the present volume I would also like to thank the energetic commitment of Robert Ballantyne and Mel McLean at Arsenal Pulp Press. Finally, I would like to thank various arms of York University for financial support for the conference and for this publication.

INTRODUCTION

Terry Goldie

In a Queer Country is a collection of extended and updated versions of papers given at the "Queer Nation?" conference, on lesbian and gay approaches to Canadian studies, at York University in Toronto in March 1996. As any reader might guess, there are many steps and missteps in the journey from the conference to the book. One part of that process has been the title. I thought the reference to the Queer Nation movement, quibbled by the question mark, was at once cute and informative. As well as the "nation," it might be seen to question "queer," which I was using primarily as shorthand for "gays and lesbians," but which of course is often used to include what has been called the alphabet soup of sexual diversity: bisexuals, transsexuals, intersexed, etc. Many, however, including several of the contributors, thought that it implied an acceptance of "queers" in Canada, which denies the homophobia most have experienced.

In a Queer Country: Gay and Lesbian Studies in the Canadian Context is a bit of a compromise, as is no doubt suitable. It offers possible suggestions of the compromising position that many political theorists have long asserted is the Canadian way of life. The title implies the contradictions of Canadian geography, in which our claims to the North are met by our tendency to live close to the southern border, in which our rural heritage is met by our tendency to live in cities, and in which our hardiness is met by our tendency to stay indoors. Yet perhaps *In a Queer Country* also implies something else. In old western movies, the cowboys always feel tremors of fear when they move into "Indian country." Native people in Canada now use that phrase to identify a state of mind, an epistemological territory that they control no matter how the nation-state decides land title. We who claim a different sexual identity might live in our own world, that indefinable space which could be called "queer country."

The conference itself was the result of a specific opportunity. In 1995–1996 I was privileged to hold the Robarts Chair of Canadian Studies. As part of this office, I held a series of seminars on gay and lesbian involvement in journalism, theatre, and the law, and also gave a public lecture, the original of the "Queer Nation?" article included here. These are part of the normal mandate of the Robarts Chair, but as the first person to hold the position who had an overtly "gay" project I wanted to do something new, to assemble a national meeting of those who wished to find the queer side of Canadian studies.

The idea of the conference was to examine gay and lesbian issues in Canada. There had been other gay and lesbian conferences in Canada but they had not to date had this focus. They either were less about academic analysis than about community activism or, as in the case of "La Ville en Rose" at the Université du Québec à Montréal in 1992 and "Queer Sites" at the University of Toronto in 1993, divided their attentions between Canadian and international matters. I had earlier been one of the organizers of a conference on "Theoretical Discourse in the Canadian Intellectual Community" and this could be said to be a "Queer Theory" version.

I have been involved in Canadian studies for some thirty years, and its response to theoretical developments and its attention to minorities might seem a stereotypical reflection of our position on the fringes of empire: innovation in most fields began elsewhere. There are exceptions. For example, Nicole Brossard's inventive combination of feminism, linguistics, and postmodernism led the world but most of the world did not realize that this creativity is not French but Québécoise. Most English Canadians who have heard of Brossard assume she is of only parochial importance. After all, she may be from Quebec but she is still just Canadian.

Most of the signature names of our disciplines—Gramsci, Foucault, Habermas, and so on—are not Canadians, and we would be very surprised if they were. Even the Canadian academics who have become markers of paradigm shifts in international thought have seldom made those shifts through the study of Canadian culture. Northrop Frye defined Canada's "garrison mentality" during off-hours from thinking about more important matters outside the ramparts, such as William Blake and the Bible. Marshall McLuhan saw the global village from his home in Toronto, but Canada seldom figured prominently in his work. His ironic and iconic appearance in Woody Allen's film *Annie Hall* has no interest in his place of residence.

The situation is somewhat similar for our interest in minorities. Canada was the location of many noteworthy events in the history of women's right, but women's studies as a field in Canada has developed after similar programs south of the border. African American studies were well established in the United States before we recognized similar needs here. As noted in various of the essays in this book, there have been many moments where Canadian society has been in advance of the American in changes in homophobic legislation and yet queer studies developed elsewhere and queer theory remains very much an American incursion, albeit in response to French thinkers such as Foucault and Lacan.

Not that the conference or this collection concentrated on the at times abstruse poststructuralist methods of queer theory. My intention was that the conference should incorporate developments in lesbian, gay, and queer studies but that they could follow a variety of paths. When the submissions came in, my primary concern was that those selected should be innovative, whether in theoretical method or in its application, and that they should have an interest in Canada beyond the usual veneer. Thus, the essays in this volume use many different methods to approach a wide range of specifically Canadian problems.

My own "Queer Nation?" offers an historical overview of gay and lesbian practices in Canada, with some suggestions that they reflect a national character. The approach of the article was shaped for its original general audience, its intention less to prove an argument than to posit a certain model. Histories of gay and lesbian cultures in Canada are scarce. The only one to try at least to glimpse the full range of Canadian experiences is Gary Kinsman's *The Regulation of Homo and Hetero Sexualities* (Montreal: Black Rose Books, 1996) but even that emphasizes less the history than Kinsman's thesis on social regulation. As the question mark suggests, "Queer Nation?" tests a possible Canadian homosexual tradition.

Both queer theory and Canadian studies have often been judged too literary. Both fields depend on textual methods and thus literature seems the most obvious example. This collection has less literary criticism than many in either field and yet the inclusions show how important are the cultural symptoms found in literature. Elaine Pigeon's "*Hosanna!* Michel Tremblay's Queering of National Identity" treats the literary but also considers theatrical elements of Tremblay's play. One central concern is the question of whether a minority can be hegemonic. Tremblay's characters seem to thematize Quebec through sexual orientation, but many Québécois sovereigntists have viewed homosexuality to be a particularly anti-national force. Still, perhaps in the twenty-first century, various liminalities are the ideal cultural forces.

The one interview in the collection is with Lynne Fernie, co-director with Aerlynn Weisman of the documentary, *Forbidden Love: The Unashamed Stories of Lesbian Lives*. The intention of this was not to suggest that *Forbidden Love* is above all others as a signature of gay and lesbian cinema but rather to address a gap in the collection, statements by gays and lesbians who are themselves theorist/creators. Fernie spoke at the conference and emphasized, as she does in the interview, that the film was intended as a multiple crossover. *Forbidden Love* uses the energies burgeoning in queer theory to depict the historical lesbian experience in a highly contemporary documentary.

Every conference is tortured by the attempts to cover as many elements of its area of concern as possible. There were no papers on Aboriginal issues, although there was a reading by the Delaware poet Daniel David Moses. Of the papers on what Canada has come to call "visible minorities," only one was available. In "Buller Men and Batty Bwoys: Hidden Men in Toronto and

Halifax Black Communities," Wesley Crichlow considers the various dynamics of closeting for black gay men from two cities and from a number of ethnicities. It is an example of contemporary developments in ethnographic studies, in which the participant observer is actually a member of the community, rather than an outsider temporarily moving in for his/her scholarly interests.

What one might call the "straight world" has particular impressions of life "in a queer country." Many gays and lesbians remark on the stereotype that our lives are represented by various aberrant examples instead of by the obvious truth that most of our existence is quite similar to that of any other Canadians and that recognition of our human rights will make this even more the case. Michelle K. Owen's " 'Family' as a Site of Contestation: Queering the Normal or Normalizing the Queer?" looks at what recently has become the most prominent aspect of this struggle for recognition. Like Crichlow's, Owen's response is informed and polemical, scholarship that wears its opinion proudly.

A quick glance at Pauline Greenhill's contributor's biography suggests her take on the world. One could speculate that this reflects her subject position, unusual in this volume, as what her essay describes as "token female heterosexual anthropological voyeur." In "Can You See the Difference? Queerying the Nation, Ethnicity, Festival, and Culture in Winnipeg," she examines, from a stance somewhat inside and somewhat outside but always sardonic, two specific examples in which gay and lesbian groups in Winnipeg provided ironic parodies of nationalist, touristic events.

One recurring problem for those who perceive themselves as in some sense identified by their sexuality is the multiple possibilities. When one adds to this other identity continua, such as race and ethnicity, the complexities become overwhelming. Zoë Newman's "The Bisexuality Wars: The Perils of Identity as Marginality" looks at differing views of sexual orientation, in particular the role of self-identified bisexuals in lesbian organizations, and how they might be compared to similar views of ethnicity, in this case the polarized interpretation of Jews, on the one side as a victim of discrimination and on the other as part of "white" hegemony.

The documentary, such as *Forbidden Love,* is usually given pride of place as depiction of a subculture but most of the wider society learns about that subculture through feature films. James Allan's "Imagining an Intercultural Nation: A Moment in Canadian Queer Cinema" explores three films of recent years which feature gay topics, *Kanada* by Mike Holboom, *Love and Human Remains* by Denys Arcand, and *Zero Patience* by John Greyson, the latter two seen quite widely in Canada. Allan examines a variety of ways questions of "queer" and "nation" intersect in these texts of a possible queer cinema.

Whether the discussion is of a queer nation or a queer country, citizenship must be a concern, but to follow the usual assumptions about the gay community, so must spectacle and display. bj wray's "The Elephant, the Mouse, and the Lesbian National Park Rangers" touches on all of these. As the rangers, Shawna Dempsey and Lorri Millan play with the lesbian as citizen, the lesbian as spectacle, the lesbian as endangered species, and even the lesbian as predator, all in a highly camp piece of performance art. wray problematizes the project and yet comes to the conclusion that they "reinvigorate the activist potentials of nationalism."

The most specifically literary essay is Andrew Lesk's "Having a Gay Old Time in Paris: John Glassco's Not-So-Queer Adventures." It is a common concern in literary studies of homosexuality to ascertain the sexuality of the author, but Glassco's autobiographical *Memoirs of Montparnasse* presents a special case. Much energy has been devoted by various scholars to prove that the published text of *Memoirs* was written much later than claimed, and thus than the events described. Lesk suggests that there is a similar distance between Glassco's homosexual experiences and the representation in *Memoirs*. Lesk believes that Glassco's needs as an author might have influenced his work as a writer.

Gordon Brent Ingram's list of publications in his contributor's biography suggests the range of his attention to actual geographical space, the "queer country" which we are all exploring. In this collection, he turns to a place in which gay men both define their identities through an assertion of territory and engage in the sexuality that makes them what they are. "Redesigning Wreck: Beach Meets Forest as Location of Male Homoerotic Culture & Place-making in Pacific Canada" considers Vancouver's Wreck Beach, one of the best-known spots in Canada for gay male cruising.

In "Challenging Canadian and Queer Nationalisms," Gary Kinsman takes issue with the very idea of the conference, that there could be a specific relationship between gays and lesbians and the country of Canada. Kinsman considers empirical research and interviews that show how much the Canadian state has done to oppress sexual diversity through treating homosexuals as *prima facie* risks to national security. He points to the ways that assertions of the importance of the nation reinforce restrictions on any minorities within the nation state.

In "Siting Lesbians: Urban Spaces and Sexuality," Catherine Nash discusses the complement to Ingram's study. He considers gay males seeking pleasure in the wide outdoors while Nash looks at lesbian daily life in the city. Her methodology is quite traditional sociological research, an assessment of the experience of various women who use businesses and resources that range from undefined to specifically lesbian. The approach might be traditional but the result has polemical potential. Nash suggests that lesbians seem to require specifically lesbian spaces for city living and that the configurations of those spaces are very different from the common gay ghetto, usually defined by gay male needs.

Andrea Frolic's work also might be compared to Ingram's. Those "aberrant examples" in the hegemonic view of queer cultures are often about flagrant sexual experience, as in Ingram, and flagrant sexual display, as in "Wear It With Pride: The Fashions of Toronto's Pride Parade and Canadian Queer Identities." There have been many studies that claim that homosexuals have long engaged in "reading" each other, in finding elements of presentation, which show "I am what you are." Frolic's essay discusses how dress is used for self-definitions for many different gay and lesbian identities and communities. Queer country has many different tribes and many different forms of national dress.

James Allan's study looks at only recent films, but Thomas Waugh's "Fairy Tales of Two Cities: Queer Nation(s)—National Cinema(s)" considers examples from a past when Canadian cinema in general was defining itself, in response to burgeoning nationalism in both English Canada and Quebec. Waugh examines a paradigm of four films, two from the sixties, two from the seventies, two from Quebec, two from Ontario, two with mainstream success, two little-known. Waugh suggests a few generalizations that might be made from this complex plot with four characters.

It is always tempting to acclaim such collections as "first." There have been other anthologies on Canada's sexualities, but arguably none pays such attention to scholarly issues in so many fields and contexts. This is a quite disparate collection, which moves in a variety of directions. Some pieces are overtly theoretical, some more empirical, some descriptive, and some polemical. Some combine all of these approaches. They show the possible range in academic studies of gay and lesbian cultures in Canada. The dimensions of those cultures are complex and varied. This collection reflects that diversity.

queer nation?

Terry Goldie

My title is first an ironic reference to the American organization of that name.[1] According to Lauren Berlant and Elizabeth Freeman, Queer Nation was founded at an ACT UP New York meeting in April 1990. It rapidly became a part of the gay and lesbian zeitgeist, in many directions, but it is worth noting that it began as a product of AIDS activism. While the demonstrations at Stonewall in 1968 are usually cited as the beginning of gay and lesbian liberation, it is generally agreed that it was the recognition of AIDS as a central and omnipresent problem that led to the greatest development of organization in the gay community.

AIDS is one of many issues given short shrift in this overview. This essay is a subjective version of who we are and of what the past tells us about who we are. Thus, AIDS is but one element of contemporary gay and lesbian life that deserves more consideration than I can offer. But one of the reasons purported for the creation of Queer Nation does affect my decision. Some felt that AIDS action was limited in two ways: first, it is an attack on a symptom, the disease, rather than the cause, homophobia; secondly, it is an emphasis on the negative rather than the positive, the power of difference shared by homosexuals.

Just as the cause for the birth of the organization was complex, so is the name. The "queer" part might seem the most complicated but it is just a reversal, in which a minority pridefully adopts a word that the majority has used pejoratively. However, it has become more troubled since Queer Nation first shouted: "We're here! We're queer! Get used to it!" Many gays and lesbians find the oppositional energy of the term off-putting. As well, it has been adopted by many people who are neither gay nor lesbian, who wish to embrace the anti-establishment possibilities of whatever their sexual practice might be. For most, however, "queer" remains just a collective term for gays and lesbians, albeit one which tends to be used by and applied to the younger part of the population.

On the other hand, the "nation" of Queer Nation has two rather opposed interpretations. One is a belief in a community that supersedes the traditional view of the nation-state. In this, the nation is a greater tie between two homosexuals than between a heterosexual and a homosexual of the same state. The other interpretation is what might be called a life of irony. This is the one explored by Berlant and Freeman, who consider the camp way that gay activists in the United States use symbols of patriotism such as the flag. The traditional American patriot stands in front of the Stars and Stripes, and he has a marine haircut and a gun. The queer nationalist is in the same position, with the same haircut, but has traded the gun for a dildo, and is quite likely a she. This is not so much a greater nation as the old one turned upside down.

The irony of the American Queer Nation becomes turned again in Canada. I do not mean to suggest that gay and lesbian culture in Canada constitutes a "queer nation." If anything, we are more disparate than the American homosexual community. But Canada in general is a strange nation, or "queer" in what at one time was the more common usage, and this in some ways enables the queers of Canada to function in a quite different way from that envisioned by Queer Nation in the United States.

As in almost any examination of "Canada," this discussion is caught by the inclusion or exclusion of Quebec. I choose exclusion because of an essential difference from the trajectory I am exploring. I make no comment on sovereignty as a movement when I say Quebec culture is not my culture. Michel Tremblay's play, *Hosanna,* represents a gay culture and a sense of nationalism which are alien to those experienced in the rest of Canada. Thus, when John Greyson makes *Lilies,* his film of Michel Marc Bouchard's play *Les Feluettes,* both director and writer are gay Canadians, but it is a cross-cultural creation. So the following is not of Quebec but of "English Canada," of "The Rest of Canada," or some other misshapen euphemism.

HOW TO BE CANADIAN

There are many similarities between the gay and lesbian cultures of different nations, but there are also many differences, which tend to reflect the overall characters of the nations. Canadians are at once less flamboyant and yet more respectful of variety than their American neighbours. The Canadian gay comic, Scott Thompson, is an interesting example. On the television program, *Kids in the Hall,* he often had the opportunity to do complex and subtle commentaries on gay culture, something he gave up to be the gay fixture in the corner of an American sitcom. Before he left, he often voiced a complaint typical of the Canadian artist: that locals failed to show him appropriate respect. This led *Xtra!,* Toronto's gay newspaper, to create its own version of *Where's Waldo?*: it put a photo of Thompson in every issue and offered a prize for picking him out.

One of Thompson's characters was Buddy, a flaming queen who tended a gay bar. In one episode, he reflected on what it means to be a Canadian by blowing his nose on a handkerchief that resembled a Canadian flag. He said, "Now you can't do that in the States." It would be difficult to reach all the layers of that joke: not only is Canadian nationalism ironic, its anti-nationalism is ironic, and both are ironic comments on American nationalism.

A few years ago in Guelph, at a conference of women playwrights, an organizer was giving the usual housekeeping announcements when a woman stood up in the audience and said, "I resent having this name tag which labels me as coming from the United States. I am proud to be a member of the lesbian nation. My tag should say 'lesbian.' And your name tag should say the same." The organizer replied, "But I'm a Canadian." This anecdote and Thompson's skit don't refuse homosexual difference from mainstream Canada, but do present an ambivalent respect for certain Canadian values, particularly tolerance.

Other Canadian values, however, have caused homosexual Canadians great trauma. In Canada, as in all other countries, sexuality is a physical fact that is organized in social terms. This is one of the reasons I refer here to gays and lesbians and not to other sexual possibilities, most notably bisexuals and the transgendered. My explanation—or excuse—is that my topic is not really sexual possibilities but rather the organization of same-sex relations. The majority of people whose lives provide the focus of this paper have had some activity that could be called heterosexual and are in that sense bisexual. Many have parts of their identity somewhere on the transgendered axis. But they are discussed here because of the part that could be called, which has been called, homosexual.

THE REGULATION OF DESIRE

This social organization through a basic division between heterosexuals and homosexuals provides the title of the best book on the subject in Canada, *The Regulation of Desire: Homo and Hetero Sexualities* (1996), by Gary Kinsman. Much of that regulation comes from elsewhere. Canada has its peculiarities as a remnant of British imperialism that is now part of the American economic empire. Canada's same-sex laws began with British statutes against sodomy. As Jonathan Goldberg points out in *Sodometries: Renaissance Texts, Modern Sexualities*, such laws were not simply proscriptions against same-sex practices but also attempts to control sexualities which were seen as endangering the state. As Canada became a nation and developed its own regulations, primarily shaped by changes in both British and American laws, the apparent religious impetus of anti-homosexual ordinances was always also part of a vision of the state.

This "Queer Nation?"—and the question mark seems to me essential—I am describing is a product of many factors. Thus, while there is nothing remotely close to a unified, broadly known gay history, a tradition of homosexuality passed on from generation to generation, our contemporary society has at least a family resemblance with moments of homosexuality in Canada's history. The variations between these examples suggest the gaps and connections of today's community. Scott Thompson's Buddy is a figure sewn from a cloth with more than a few threads.

FIRST NATIONS

The first European arrivals in Canada encountered extremely different orderings of same-sex sexualities, those of the First Nations. The usual response, as recorded in various missionary narratives, was revulsion at the apparent eruption of what they invariably saw as "sodomy." Of course, in those early years there was no specific Canada but rather the Americas, under various versions of colonization. The best source for research on homosexuality in the First Nations in general is found in the writings of Will Roscoe, an American. He has published several studies of specific cultural manifestations, but his broad analysis in "Was We'wha a Homosexual: Native American Survivance and the Two-Spirit Tradition" provides an excellent consideration of various ethnographic concerns. As Roscoe demonstrates, terms associated with Native homosexuality, such as "berdache," simply reflect the assumptions of the first Europeans who contacted them. "Berdache" itself came from a Persian term for a slave youth but by the Renaissance had come to mean a kept boy in a homosexual relationship. This has no resemblance to any Native traditions.

Some of the first significant scientific studies of homosexuality, published in the middle of the nineteenth century, viewed it as a third sex. In most cases this was a male homosexual, but some arguments suggested that the male and female homosexual should be grouped together. This was often based on assumptions of polarities, males at one end and females at the other. Gays and lesbians provided the middle. The third sex might fit some Native contexts, in which there were rules for males, rules for females, and rules for the berdaches. In some nations, males could not sleep with males nor females with females nor berdaches with berdaches, but any one of the three could marry any one of the other two. From my own limited research, this system was primarily organized with only one sex taking the role of the middle gender. Thus, in one culture there would be male berdaches and in another female.

In contemporary Native cultures, the common term is "two-spirited," which implies having characteristics of both male and female. This captures the essence of most Native traditions, which seem to work more in terms of cross-gendered behaviour than in same-sex desire. However, contemporary sociology and biology present profound differences between most transgendered persons and the homosexual. The homosexual, whether male or female, is not "deviant" in gender assignment but rather is "deviant" in the gender of desire.

Whether or not this distinction would have fit pre-contact Native cultures, it does provide some distinction between contemporary Native homosexual communities and what might be called the hegemonic gay and lesbian cultures. The latter play with cross-gendered behaviour but reject it as a deep meaning. Native gays and lesbians usually embrace the transgendered and have little attraction to the anti-drag queen, "straight-acting" gay culture so evident elsewhere. This is reflected in this portrait, from *Xtra!*, of Billy Merasty, the Native actor and writer (see Figure 1). The vitality of that Marilyn Monroe-like image, which seems to fly in the face of the Canadian norm, could be a contemporary manifestation of the berdaches who so frightened the first arrivals.

Still, contemporary Native cultures in general are just as homophobic as the mainstream. Regardless of their traditions of the berdaches, missionaries, government, and the general pressure of history have changed their social organization in many ways. For Native homosexuals, their two-spirited community has become a refuge much like Toronto's Church and Wellesley district for the rest of the gay and lesbian population. Although only one of the various gay areas in Canadian cities, it is often used as the generic Canadian sacred site, like the Stonewall-Christopher area of New York.

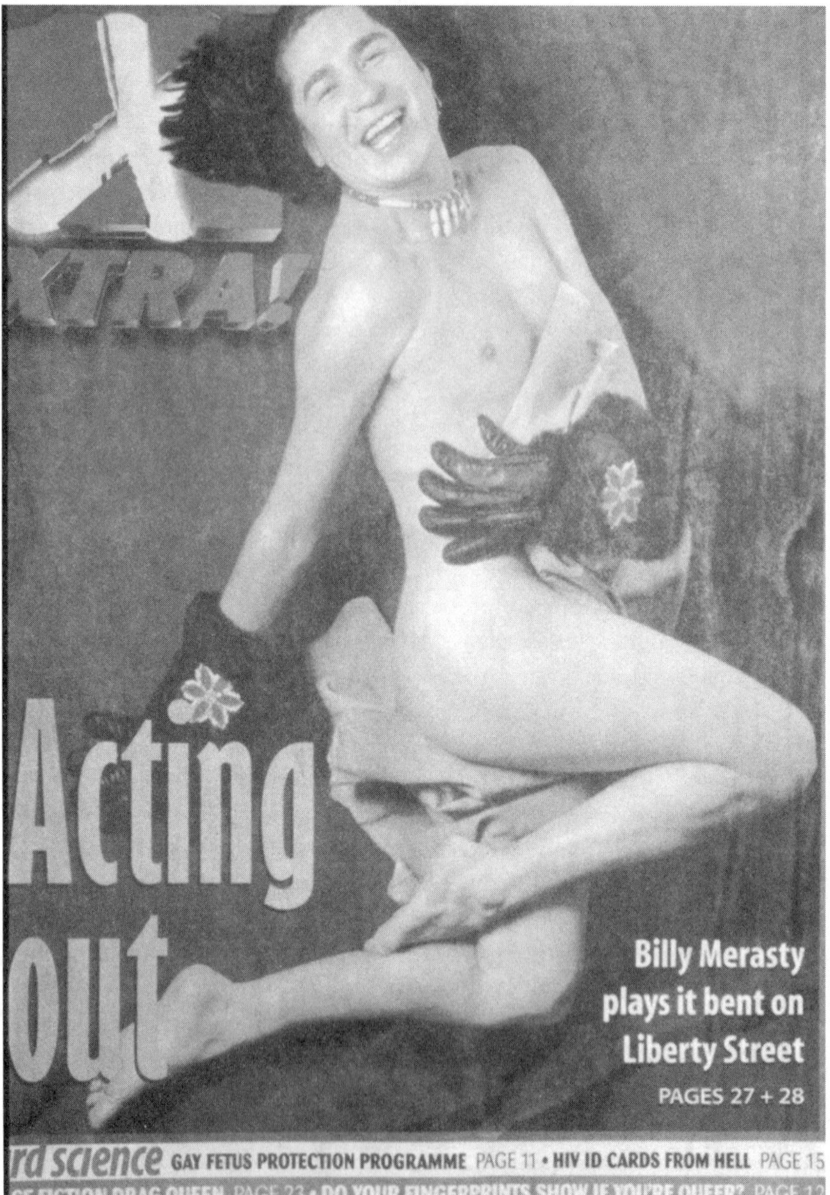

Figure 1. Billy Merasty. Courtesy of Photographer Tony Fong.

MOLLYWOOD NORTH

This essay is admittedly Toronto-centric. First, greater documentation exists for Toronto than for other places. Most Canadian analysis of gay culture has been done in Toronto on Toronto. Second, the tradition for gays and lesbians throughout the western world has been to gravitate to the metropolis, partly to escape pressures of conservative homes and partly to seek others like themselves who have made the journey before. Far more than other Canadians, the gay Canadian has treated Toronto as a mecca of opportunity.

Alexander Wood, who has left his name on two streets in the Church and Wellesley area, is the first figure in Canadian history who is generally acknowledged to be homosexual. Arriving as a young man, in 1793, from his native Scotland, he became a successful merchant and magistrate. In the latter position, however, he used the law to get himself in trouble with the law. He claimed that a young woman had accused various young men of rape and had said that she had scratched her assailant's genitals. In search of evidence, he examined the private parts of all of the suspects. Not surprisingly, in the small community of York, this held him up to ridicule, and he returned to Scotland. But two years later, in 1812, he was back and once more succeeded, again becoming a magistrate. His support of the Family Compact and particularly of Bishop Strachan maintained his position but his past continued to follow him, and a former friend, Judge Powell, made him the object of an attack in a pamphlet. Yet the *Dictionary of Canadian Biography* records, "At his death the *British Colonist* called him one of Toronto's 'most respected inhabitants.'"

Wood's prominence in our past partly reflects the system of history: those who were best known are now best remembered. But it is particularly interesting that he should have been such a combination of the sexually proscribed and the courtier of the powerful, a common position for the homosexual throughout history. Much like Buddy in the bar, gay men have recognized the various versions of guise needed to survive in a homophobic world. Given my little knowledge of Wood, I hesitate to make unfair comparisons, but his story is just a bit too close to Roy Cohn, the infamous homosexual homophobe.

This again fits the broader definition of sodomy. In Tony Kushner's play, *Angels in America,* the Roy Cohn character denies that he is homosexual because, as an assistant to Senator Joe McCarthy and associate of President Nixon, he was too much a part of state power to be such a deviant, regardless of his sexual practices. It seems likely that Wood was a somewhat similar figure, a sodomite redeemed by his governmental conformity. Of course this is not a view of Wood that Canadian gay culture especially wants. A play on his life, *MollyWood,* by John Wimbs and Christopher Richards, was produced in

1994, as the general Canadian nationalist interest in recovering a forgotten past extends to our gay ancestors.

The title itself suggests the flavour. As a pun on Hollywood, it implies the contrast between gay Tinseltown and the muddy York in which Wood found himself. The term "Molly" was used from the seventeenth century as a pejorative much as "faggot" is today, but it also was generic. Homosexuals congregated at what were called "Mollyhouses." In this sense, "Mollywood" is depicted in the play as a place, the equivalent of park sex for gay men today: an unsafe spot, potentially open to the world but avoided by the world in the hopes that the world might not see the anonymous acts of men hiding their sexuality. Thus Wood, whom the *DCB* records as a henchman of the oligarchy, which hanged Mackenzie's rebels in 1837, becomes in the play a gentle victim of a homophobic society. My only reply is: Why should gay culture any less than any other make the history that it needs?

CANADA AND THE AGE OF WILDE

The late nineteenth century marks the beginning of a figure which European society called the homosexual. The definitions were provided by Germany; the famous identities by Britain. Oscar Wilde is so profound a symbol, both in his age and today, that he was a focus for discussion of "that sort" on his brief trip to Canada. As in the other colonies, there was a sense that such behaviour had to be imported; it could not be a part of the hardy, pure colonial life. Wilde's own story provides a typically Canadian modification of that view. In *De Profundis,* Wilde states that his Canadian friend and former lover, Robert Ross, was the only person to acknowledge him publicly as he was taken away to prison. What a profoundly Canadian footnote to a famous story: at a time when a flamboyant Englishman became a world-wide icon of British state oppression of homosexuality, a Canadian homosexual overcame fears of revelations of association and instead embraced ethics to represent the possibility of a continued civility. Of course, it is also very Canadian that it may be an act *De Profundis* but it remains a footnote.

Throughout Canadian history, as my reference to Wilde suggests and as Kinsman describes, the Canadian experience was at times a part of, and usually at least similar to, the American and British ones. There are various figures, more or less closeted, such as Frances Loring and Florence Wyle, the Toronto sculptors known as "The Girls." A clearer picture is provided by a general excursion through legal records. Of course most of this is on male-male sexuality as Canada, like the rest of the English-speaking world, had a very clearly gendered version of closeted homosexuality. The generalization about same-sex relationships between women is that the "spinster" was in a couple known as a "Boston marriage," assumed to be just two women sharing. On the other hand the "confirmed bachelor" lived alone and found his sex where he could, thus being constant prey to the legal system.

THE GAY FIFTIES?

In 1972, when I was travelling in England, I met and stayed with a couple in Sussex. At the age of seventeen, the Canadian half of the pair had left Calgary for the war and had never returned. He is typical of one homosexual response to the Canada of mid-century: leave. While the metropolis of Toronto provided some space, it was still limited in comparison to life as an expatriate in Europe. The alternatives are explored in two films. One is *Jim Loves Jack.* Jim Egan began his activism with anti-homophobic letters and articles in 1949. He was often a lonely voice, an apparent crank who continued to confront Canadian heterosexism, usually in ways that the general populace ignored. In 1995, he became national news as he and his long-term partner, Jack Nesbitt, reached the Supreme Court with an attempt to gain the shared pension benefits available to heterosexual couples. While their claim was denied, the majority of the court agreed that the situation was discriminatory.

The film, *Forbidden Love: The Unashamed Stories of Lesbian Lives,* by Aerlyn Weissman and Lynne Fernie, follows the lesbian side of the story. The substance of the film is interviews with women who participated in lesbian life in the forties and fifties, using a number of striking clips and still photos. The documentation is very important, but I wish to point to the image on the poster, which represents almost all parts of this possibly queer nation. The illustration imitates those on the covers of the lesbian pulp fiction of the war and just after. I use the term "lesbian" although that is the subject rather than the audience. There is a scene in a Woody Allen film where someone sententiously says, "There are many types of love: a man for a woman, a father for a child, a priest for his god. . . ." and the Woody Allen character replies, "Don't forget my favourite: two girls!" Thus, this "lesbian" fiction was rather for heterosexual men seeking a look at the wild side of women.

But as the film shows, women seeking stories of same-sex desire snuck into the drugstores and bus terminals and bought these books. Some of the money-hungry publishers penetrated the Canadian hinterland so a woman might find one on a Sudbury newsstand. *Forbidden Love* presents an interview with a woman who recalls that these books convinced her that all the lesbians lived in Greenwich Village, and so one weekend she and her partner dressed in their best butch-femme gear and went to New York. This might be just the same as the proverbial journey from Kansas to sin city, but it seems a particularly Canadian paradigm. The deviant from the Canadian norm reads an American story of deviance and goes to the United States to find the other deviants.

The film extends this process in many ways. One of the most attractive elements is the narrative represented by this image. Between the interviews and documentary footage runs a sentimental lesbian romance, in which these pulp fiction covers dissolve into live action. The process seems to suggest that at the same time as the interviewees were struggling to live and love as lesbians in a homophobic Canada, there were images in books, but even more in their minds, which suggested the vision which could be. The basic source for these was male-oriented fiction, which was very soft core but which had what might be called a pornographic intent: it meant to be obscene. And it was just one small part of the continued dumping of American trash on the Canadian market.

Forbidden Love was produced by Studio D of the National Film Board of Canada (NFB). Canadians are often less impressed with the NFB than they should be, but in some American film schools there are complete courses devoted to the NFB as the quintessential producer of the documentary film. In many ways it has been the vehicle, much more than books or magazines, more than television, perhaps even more than radio, for telling Canadians who we are. The segment known as Studio D was set up as a reaction to the obvious absence of women behind the cameras. The larger impetus of Studio D was thus feminist, but it also had a significant part that was lesbian. So this film is an example of lesbians, in a sense, taking over as producer of the national image for their own purposes. A queering of the nation, perhaps.

But this specific image represents American trash, arguably American trash of a particularly bad sort, in which the perceived exoticism of a minority culture is reproduced in a stereotyped form for the majority: the equivalent of war bonnets and tomahawks in Banff. In this case, sophisticated cultural theorists, theorists who have declared feminist, lesbian, and nationalist agendas, have produced a film that makes this image of far greater value than it has ever had before, and have made it an intelligent part of Canadian lesbian history. Beyond the specifics of Kinsman's study, many have claimed that Canadian history in general is often not a line but a series of tangents: national events influenced more by world politics than by national events which preceded it. This claim is made still more emphatically in minority histories. Thus, an African Canadian is told to look to the Harlem Renaissance rather than Africville. But here, *Forbidden Love* has not only recorded Canadian lesbian history in the interviews, it has provided yet another reworking of American trash as a vehicle for Canadian sophistication, and it has done it by creating a line not through the trash, but through an earlier viable Canadian use of the trash.

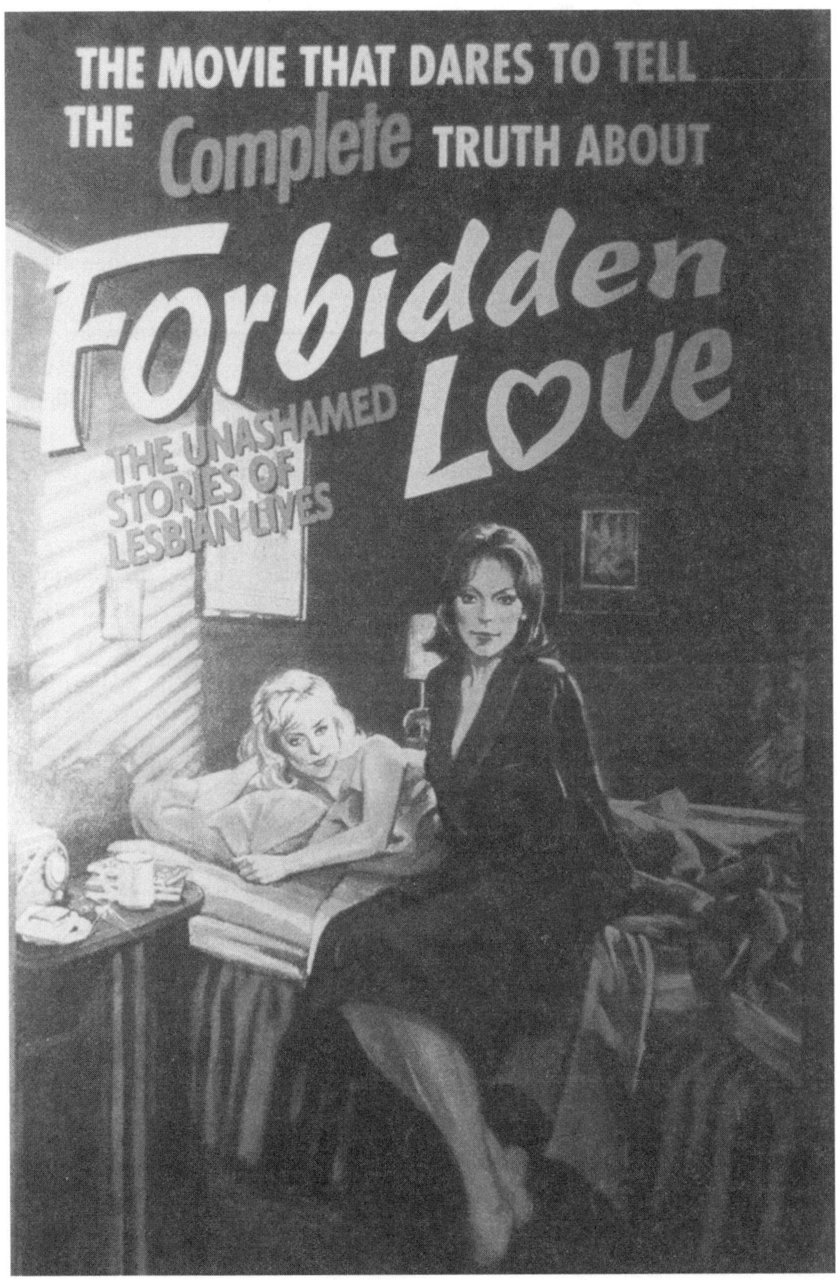

Figure 2. Image from *Forbidden Love: The Unashamed Stories of Lesbian Lives.* Courtesy of Illustrator Janet Wilson, and the National Film Board of Canada.

THE HOMOPHOBIC NATION

I am attempting to build a positive portrait of gay and lesbian moments rather than to document the negative, but there can be no question that the social position of gays and lesbians in this period—and much later—was negative. There were many persecutions. An extreme case was that of Everett George Klippert, who was declared a dangerous sexual offender in 1966. Many elements came together in this conviction, some quite specifically Canadian. Klippert was first arrested in the Northwest Territories. He lived in a region where extreme homosociality and extreme homophobia were uncomfortable bedfellows. All social contact tended to be intense and revealing because of the limited population. Social coercion on some problems, such as alcohol consumption, was lax, on others, such as sexual deviance, severe. The law was conservative, and the mechanics of legal process tended to be unsophisticated.

To this can be added class, in that Klippert was a mechanic's helper. This might seem rather ahistorical, but what might have happened to Alexander Wood had he been a mechanic's helper? Klippert lacked the skills or the finances to protect himself from the law. As well, he represented the class that bourgeois Canada believed to be rude and brutal, who must be controlled if society is to be protected.[2] Still, there seemed no question to many elements of society, even including the editorial writers of the *Toronto Star*, that sentencing Klippert as a dangerous offender represented extreme homophobia. This crystallized various energies that were already developing. The Association for Social Knowledge (ASK), one more example of Canada's attraction to provocative acronyms, began in Vancouver in 1964. Similar but usually less well-organized groups existed elsewhere, such as the Canadian Council on Religion and the Homosexual, but it was ASK that coalesced the most useful gay resources, including publicizing Klippert.

As Canada moved towards the law reform of 1969, which removed the most general proscriptions against homosexuality, Prime Minister Trudeau made the very quotable assertion, "The State has no business in the bedrooms of the nation." This is a particularly interesting phrase in the light of the tradition of sodomy laws. Renaissance European governments believed that the state was dependent on certain conformity in these bedrooms. Trudeau, however, was attempting to move Canada *as a nation* away from state control of such individual freedoms as are found in sexuality. Sexual morality was no longer to be a microcosm of governmentality.

AFTER STONEWALL?

In my reading, this shift in policy provides the tone for Canada's sexual coming of age. This limited sexual freedom was not a product of opposition and liberation demonstrations but instead a moving of the Canadian tradition of tolerance into statute. Groups such as ASK had made important statements, but the changes were arguably less from without than from within. Yet again the Canadian nation had adapted. But at the same time the Stonewall riots, a particularly American manifestation, were happening in New York. What seems like a coincidence, or at most a similar response to the zeitgeist of the sixties, once again led to an American event becoming the dominant metaphor in Canada. Thus the period of gay liberation throughout North America is "after Stonewall."

As someone who still feels very strongly the Canadian nationalism of the early seventies, I hesitate to accept an event so clearly American as a watershed in my culture, even my minority culture. I still don't want to accept that "the lesbians are in Greenwich Village." This period, the late sixties, was a time of massive disruption throughout the world, from the quiet revolution in Quebec through the Paris riots, through the velvet revolution in Czechoslovakia, through the release of *Sergeant Pepper's*. The times, they were a-changing. In its usual fashion, American culture seemed able to put its stamp on all of it.

Perhaps Canadian developments were linked to Stonewall, but it is certainly possible to find many Canadian events which offered sufficient definition, and in particularly Canadian ways. As Douglas Sanders has pointed out, the 1969 criminal code reform emphasized not the need to erase the perceptions of the deviance of same-sex desire nor the rights of those who identified as homosexual but rather the freedom of any Canadian to live as he or she wishes in the privacy of the home. Arguably, this attitude has created a different atmosphere in the Canadian community than that in the American, where such freedoms have always been assumed, and social coercion must be framed in other ways.

CENSORSHIP AND FEMINISM

There are a number of important moments in the early seventies, such as demonstrations, but the most important stems from a magazine. From 1971, *The Body Politic* developed a reputation for radical but also thoughtful analysis of gay culture. Many of its writers were new arrivals from the United States, some deserters and draft dodgers, but some just escapees from the

American system. They could be associated with the many agents of social change in Canada who have been Americans, very much including those supporters of William Lyon Mackenzie who magistrate Alexander Wood was trying to suppress.

This American presence is one reason why, regardless of its obvious low production values and limited distribution, *The Body Politic* had a continental and even wider influence. The magazine had various problems with censorship, but its most disastrous encounter was a result of Gerald Hannon's article on "man-boy love" in 1977. As Becki Ross records in her book on lesbian activism in Toronto in the seventies, *The House That Jill Built*, this was a particularly bad moment for the uneasy coalition between gays and lesbians.

The alliance of bourgeois homosexuals of both genders had existed at least since the late nineteenth century but rather than some "natural" bonding, it was primarily a mutual support network in the face of homophobia. As *Forbidden Love* shows, this was limited but important in Toronto. The rise of feminism in the sixties, however, raised questions about the validity of this association. While older lesbians felt more in common with other homosexuals than with the mass of women, the younger felt quite differently. Ross quotes Gillean Chase from 1974:

> I do not identify with the issue of homosexuality, I identify with the issue of gender. . . . Gay women know instinctively, even if not yet politically, that they are being oppressed, and that they are oppressed by their so-called homosexual brothers. (36)

The percentage of women writers for *The Body Politic* was small and apparently the proportion of female readers was smaller still, although there were prominent exceptions. One, Jane Rule, defined her contributions as opposition to homophobia and censorship. She records this in her aptly named collection, *A Hot-Eyed Moderate*:

> By writing for *The Body Politic*, I refuse to be a token, one of those who doesn't really seem like a lesbian at all. If the newspaper is found to be obscene, I am part of that obscenity. And proud to be, for, though my priorities and the paper's aren't always the same, I have been better and more thoughtfully informed about what it is to be homosexual in this culture by *The Body Politic* than by any other paper. . . . (64)

This is a period remembered by many, documented by few, and analyzed by fewer still. Still, Ross's portrait of radicalism and purity among lesbians in the seventies seems accurate. I was with a lesbian friend at a folk festival in

Toronto in 1976, and a few of her friends came up to her. She introduced me, but they refused to acknowledge me or even to look at me, apparently simply because I was male. In that moment, and in my friend's long apologies afterwards, I was seeing the crisis recorded by Ross.

This is by no means a specifically Canadian issue but it is sufficiently important that it is worth emphasizing here. The necessities of feminism led to assumptions and confusions enshrined in Ti-Grace Atkinson's famous dictum: "feminism is the theory and lesbianism is the practice" (Ross, 27). Many lesbian feminists thus sought an unadulterated life, first in as much separation from men as possible, but then in rejection of anything that might interfere with absolute woman-identification, including feminine clothing, Marxism, straight jobs, etc. On one hand, heterosexual feminists felt inadequate because they still associated with men, and on the other hand they were afraid that their coalition with lesbians would interfere with that association. So the very efforts of creating bonds with all women were also dividing them.

And dividing them from gay men, even from gay men's understanding, as this extremely important controversy at the nexus between lesbian and woman had no counterpart for the gay male. Male bonding at the level of the boardroom, the shop floor, or the hockey team had long been a fact of life for all men. Few wanted anything more, and many gay men did not want anything more except sex, although there were always those such as Jim and Jack, who sought a specific "long-term companion." Thus, it was not difficult for gay men to agree on homophobia and closeting as the issues. While the lesbians tended to see a profound difference between activists and "bar-women," often phrased in terms of feminism, the gays just saw this as a distinction between those who would work for the cause and those who wouldn't.

This creates an interesting comment on Gerald Hannon's most recent problems. Subsequent to *The Body Politic* scandal he became well-respected as a journalist on gay issues, including a number of pieces for the *Globe and Mail,* and he became a part-time journalism instructor at Ryerson University. In 1996, an old story resurfaced as claims were made that he had supported the National Association for Man-Boy Love in class. Soon after, the *Toronto Sun,* maintaining the tabloid tradition of homophobia, revealed that Hannon was a part-time prostitute, which led him to lose his teaching position. At this point, however, lesbians and gays were to a great extent united in their opposition to this discrimination and to anything which censured or censored gay and lesbian culture. The traditional belief has been that men are much more interested in objectifying sexuality and thus the pornography industry has been directed to a male market, whether straight or gay. Recently, however, an avant garde of the lesbian community has been creating its own images for itself. The title of the Kiss and Tell collective seems especially innovative in its inversion of female stereotypes. The first major anti-censorship academic study of the Butler decision on obscenity is by four women.

This does not of course mean that lesbians support pedophilia, nor does it mean that lesbians have abandoned feminist issues. For one thing, on issues such as spousal rights and adoption, lesbianism and feminism are once more enjoined. But today, for many, perhaps most, activist females in Canada, of any race or sexual orientation, feminism of a certain order is a given. Thus, for a lesbian activist to choose to emphasize discrimination on issues of sexual orientation, regardless of gender, is not surprising. Coalitions with activist gay men seem inevitable and often even comfortable. The connection is as it has not been since the early sixties, and in comparison with those days it is more considered and more substantive. And the boys in the bars? They're still in the bars.

TODAY: OUT OF THE MANY CLOSETS AND INTO THE ARTS

Although no one person could suggest the varieties of gay and lesbian cultures in Canada today, Svend Robinson is possibly their most significant symbol. An activist in mainstream politics, he represents his minority culture in both senses that Marx uses: he is there to take care of and also there in the place of. This is very different from the gay liberation demonstrations on Parliament Hill in the early seventies. And yet neither Robinson nor other gay and lesbian parliamentarians have been able to produce more than quite modest successes on adoption rights and human rights legislation. Still, the future might be quite different. The anti-same-sex marriage bills going through the various legislatures in the U.S. seem to be modified or even rejected in the face of even one or two gay or lesbian legislators.[3]

The arts have long been a place for gays and lesbians, but it depends on the category. A director or actor whose sexual orientation need not confront the audience is much less problematic than overt gay and lesbian material in writing, art, or music. Many important elements of Canadian theatre, such as the plays of Brad Fraser or the various productions at Buddies in Bad Times, have a prominent gay and lesbian component but they could be seen to be out of the mainstream. Thus, I wonder if it was safer that the first out lesbian in American popular music was a Canadian, kd lang, who presumably could be excused as really a foreigner.

As suggested by the comments on Robinson above, inclusion and exclusion are central questions for gay and lesbian cultures in Canada. A gay Native writer, Daniel David Moses, said that the mainstream "is pretty wide but it's spiritually shallow" (xiv). To extend the metaphor, however, the tributaries can offer some spiritual sustenance. Buddies is certainly not as "mainstream" as, say, the Canadian Stage production of *Angels in America*, but it is a constant figure in Toronto culture and provides the closest thing in the Canadian arts to a permanent gay and lesbian presence. The shift in artistic director, in 1997, from Sky Gilbert to Sarah Stanley, showed that it is both a gay and lesbian theatre.

The positioning of sexual orientation in the arts is arguably more successful and yet also more subtle in Canada than in some other cultures. One of Canada's best-known and best-loved authors, Timothy Findley, has long been known to be gay, his companion always prominent in his life. Some twenty years ago, he was to be profiled in a feature titled "A Day in the Life" in the Saturday newspaper supplement, *Weekend*, but the need to include his partner prevented this very good publicity opportunity. Still, the tenor of his fiction and his general demeanour seem to have deflected much of the homophobia felt by artists who are more overtly homoerotic, such as photographer Evergon and painter Attila Richard Lukacs. Evergon's reworking of homoerotic, anthropomorphic images of the classics and Lukacs' paintings of nude skinheads in imitation of Caravaggio have been deemed too overt for many. And yet they have also sold very well to mainstream buyers, as has Ashley MacIsaac. The popular fiddler's openness about his sexual practices apparently caused him to be removed from *Maclean's* magazine's list of honoured Canadians. However, he was still named Male Artist of the Year at the East Coast Music Awards. This might be the triumph of the regional over the national but perhaps it also comments on importance. As kd lang said, it seems as though once you achieve a certain status coming out doesn't hurt you but can actually make you even more prominent. It remains to be seen whether MacIsaac's revelations will destroy the usual Canadian acceptance of idiosyncracies which remain assuredly safe.

MULTICULTURALLY QUEER?

The House That Jill Built refers so often to "largely white, middle-class" it almost becomes a litany. But of course, this description applied to almost all social activism in Canada in the seventies. In recent history, there have been many struggles for change. Performance poets De Poonani Posse, like academic Wesley Crichlow and, perhaps most importantly, like writer and filmmaker Dionne Brand and writer and anthologist Makeda Silvera, situate themselves not just racially but also ethnically. They blend sexual orientation with their African and Caribbean ancestry. For them, the complications of the fight make the troubles of the lesbian feminists of the seventies seem like a cakewalk. De Poonani Posse refers to the racism of Canadian society, including gay and lesbian society, and the homophobia of both the immigrant community and the homes of their roots. To this Crichlow adds that, in North America, the small space given to be black and gay is defined by Joseph Beam and Essex Hemphill, the America of James Baldwin. De Poonani Posse have many fights and, with these and other colleagues, they are fighting them, as are Asian Canadians and South Asian Canadians and every other facet of Canada's many ethnicities. In 1999, Buddies in Bad Times made its own step in this direction with the appointment of David Oiye as artistic director. As Buddies thus notes, the multicultural nation is also a queer nation.

Many more names deserve mention, but I can't avoid the most famous Native playwright, Tomson Highway, and someone who has won awards for both plays and her novel, Ann-Marie MacDonald. But I must also turn to Daphne Marlatt, who represents a connection that is of particular interest given my opening comments. In her work with Nicole Brossard, Marlatt, published in the latter's *À tout regard,* has not only made a significant contribution to feminism, she has provided one of the few major blendings between English Canadian culture and Quebec. John Greyson's films and the translations of Michel Tremblay are of interest but they are not crossings, not hybrids. Marlatt and Brossard have offered a lesbian vision that embraces the "two nations."

Is it too much to see this strange nation as a queer nation?[4] When I was in England in the early seventies, I was surprised to find the term there was not inevitably pejorative but was generic among older homosexuals: "Do you think that young man is queer? . . . I have found England a good place to be queer. . . ." etc. It was a possible state of being, different from but not necessarily in opposition to. This might seem very different from the group who called themselves Queer Nation. And yet the work of the word "queer" recently has created still more confusion. Just a few short years ago it seemed a term that was at once strident and inclusive. All gays and lesbians who wished to think of themselves in oppositional terms could be queer. This was easily expanded to include the transgendered and bisexual. But the term queer seems ever more elastic, now extending to an array of possibilities, such as the Lesbian, Gay and Straight Teachers Network in the United States, or that delightful T-shirt, "Straight but not narrow." Or the PFLAG organization. You might guess that it is lesbians and gays who have dominated all gay activism, but there have been many instances where Parents and Friends of Lesbians and Gays have been the leaders in anti-discrimination actions.

Some years ago I wrote a piece in which I suggested that Native sovereignty in Canada is an impossibility which is a necessity. I wonder if this queer nation is the same thing. We are a queer nation, whether because of Quebec or because of many other things. I must repeat the words spoken by

Linda Hutcheon. She recalled a competition for the Canadian equivalent to "As American as motherhood and apple pie." The winner was "As Canadian as possible under the circumstances. . . ." If any nation is queer enough to accept a queer nation it must be this one. But as implied in Hutcheon's line, we should probably keep the question mark.

NOTES

1. The original version of this essay was given as the Robarts Lecture in March 1997 and was published as a pamphlet by the Robarts Centre for Canadian Studies, York University.
2. The recent sexual abuse scandal at Toronto's Maple Leaf Gardens seems one more example. The two men who were charged were working-class men with semi-skilled jobs. Society's general response has been phrased as obvious revulsion at the pedophilia, but whenever such people are accused of actions that might be seen to represent the eruption of primitive id-laden forces, bourgeois Canada quakes in its bankers' brogues.
3. A detailed analysis of both the Canadian and American contexts can be found in David Rayside's *On the Fringe: Gays and Lesbians in Politics* (Ithaca: Cornell University Press, 1988).
4. A specifically literary answer to this question is found in Peter Dickinson's *Here is Queer: Nationalisms, Sexualities and the Literature of Canada* (Toronto: University of Toronto Press, 1999).

WORKS CITED

Adkin, David. *Jim Loves Jack*. Toronto: David Adkin Productions, 1996.

Berlant, Lauren and Elizabeth Freeman. "Queer Nationality." *Fear of a Queer Planet: Queer Politics and Social Theory*. Ed. Michael Warner. Minneapolis: University of Minneapolis Press, 1994. 193–229.

Brossard, Nicole. *À tout regard*. Montreal: BQ, 1989.

Dickinson, Peter. *Here is Queer: Nationalisms, Sexualities and the Literatures of Canada*. Toronto: University of Toronto Press, 1999.

Egan, Jim. *Challenging the Conspiracy of Silence: My Life as a Canadian Gay Activist*. Compiled and edited by Donald W. McLeod. Toronto: Canadian Gay and Lesbian Archives, 1998.

Firth, Edith G. "Wood, Alexander." *Dictionary of Canadian Biography*. VII. 919–921.

Goldberg, Jonathan. *Sodometries: Renaissance Texts, Modern Sexualities*. Stanford: Stanford University Press, 1992.

Hutcheon, Linda. *As Canadian as—Possible—Under the Circumstances!* Toronto: ECW Press, 1990.

Jackson, Ed and Stan Persky, eds. *Flaunting It! A Decade of Gay Journalism from* The Body Politic. Toronto/Vancouver: Pink Triangle Press and New Star Books, 1982.

Kinsman, Gary. *The Regulation of Desire: Homo and Hetero Sexualities.* Toronto: Black Rose Books, 1996.

Maynard, Stephen. *Of Toronto the Gay: Homosexuality, Policing and the Dialectics of Discovery, Urban Toronto 1890–1930* (forthcoming from University of Chicago Press).

Moses, Daniel David and Terry Goldie, eds. *An Anthology of Canadian Native Literature in English.* Toronto: Oxford University Press, 1992.

Rayside, Morton David. *On the Fringe: Gays and Lesbians in Politics.* Ithaca, NY: Cornell University Press, 1998.

Roscoe, Will. "Was We'wha a Homosexual: Native American Survivance and the Two-Spirit Tradition," *Gay and Lesbian Quarterly: A Journal of Lesbian and Gay Studies* 2.3 (1995): 193–235.

Ross, Becki L. *The House That Jill Built: a Lesbian Nation in Formation.* Toronto: University of Toronto Press, 1995.

Rule, Jane. *Hot-Eyed Moderate.* Tallahassee, FL: The Naiad Press, 1985.

Weissman, Aerlyn and Lynne Fernie. *Forbidden Love: The Unashamed Stories of Lesbian Lives* [documentary]. Toronto: National Film Board of Canada, 1992.

hosanna! michel tremblay's queering of national identity

Elaine Pigeon

In 1968, Michel Tremblay made history in Quebec when he electrified audiences with his audacious play, *Les belles-soeurs.* No one had ever seen or heard anything like it before on the Quebec stage. Shock waves reverberated throughout the community, sparking unprecedented debate. There was also much cause for celebration: *Le théâtre Québécois* had finally been born. Tremblay's spectacular career took off, and for the next quarter of a century his work continued to arouse greater critical controversy in Canada than that of any other dramatist in or out of Quebec (Usmiani, *Michel Tremblay,* 2). Although his recent plays have lost their original political bite, to date Tremblay remains Quebec's most important playwright.

Les belles-soeurs introduced one of Tremblay's renowned theatrical innovations: his controversial use of *joual,* the term used to describe the particular variety of street French or slang commonly used in Quebec. By incorporating various Anglicisms and religious expressions, or "*sacres*"—such as "*crisse*" and "*tabarnac*" ("sacred"—such as "Christ" and "tabernacle")—along with the use of phonetic contractions, *joual* carries important religious and socio-political connotations. Renate Usmiani, who has written extensively on Tremblay, rightly points out that, at the time, young radicals "hailed the use of *joual* as a major step through which Québécois culture was finally asserting its independence from centuries-old bondage to the culture of France, the mother country, a partial liberation on the level of language which carried strong political overtones" (*Michel Tremblay*, 4). Clearly, Tremblay achieved a significant breakthrough in making the spoken language of his people acceptable as a dramatic idiom. But the initial effects of Tremblay's use of *joual* were of even greater import, for the cultural identity of a people had been galvanized. Consequently, the presentation of *Les belles-soeurs* can be viewed as a political marker, signifying nothing less than Quebec's first step towards decolonization and liberation (47).

Yet some critics were less than enthusiastic about Tremblay's use of *joual*, arguing that it was "a symptom of defeat: a language whose very texture expresses the alienation, lack of identity, inability to communicate and tragic impotence of Quebec society" (4). A heated debate over the correct usage of the French language in Quebec ensued, in which one writer, Jean Marcel, even went so far as to publish a book entitled *Le Joual de Troie* (*The Trojan Horse*), a pun on *joual*, the dialect pronunciation of *cheval*, meaning horse. For Marcel maintained that *joual* "constituted yet another pernicious instrument of colonization, encouraged by Anglophones to bring about the total destruction of Francophone culture" (Usmiani, *Theatre*, 97). Subsequently, some Quebec intellectuals began to insist that Québécois writers utilize a universal language—namely, standard French—in order to distance themselves from a regional dialect associated with underdevelopment and an illiterate working class. In part, their efforts succeeded.

Thus it is somewhat ironic that Tremblay's early plays—collectively known as *le cycle des belles-soeurs*—all depict members of the Quebec working class grappling with an oppressive family life: *la maudite vie plate* (the blasted boring life). But, in the sixtieés, the stereotypical Québécois was working class. Tremblay, moreover, was particularly vexed by the advent of a consumer society, one of the more insidious effects of Quebec's "Quiet Revolution." With the death of "*le chef*" (the boss), the autocratic Premier Maurice Duplessis, in 1959, Quebec rapidly underwent the final stages of modernization, shifting from an essentially agrarian culture to industrial urbanization, complete with a massive working class, the majority of whom were rural Québécois who had migrated to the cities in search of jobs and a better life filled with material prosperity. As Tremblay's plays so poignantly demonstrate, the good life that Quebec's modernization promised often translated into a tragic version of the American dream.

During this period, Quebec artists and intellectuals all began to focus on their unique social situation, summing up the problem as nothing less than total alienation on the political, economic, and cultural fronts. In 1963, the radical journal *Parti pris* was founded by a group of creative writers and political activists, including many Marxists. In the wittily titled "Fear of Federasty," Robert Schwartzwald—one of the few scholars who publishes in English on francophone Quebec culture—notes that the journal defined: "the specific tasks of Quebec's Quiet Revolution with a social program and a political objective that took its inspiration from the anti-imperialist and anti-colonial struggles of the period: national independence in Africa, revolution in Cuba, and the civil rights movement in the United States" ("Fear of Federasty," 177). The goal of *Parti pris* was nothing less than "an independent, socialist Quebec," but first the people had to be "free of political influence from the Catholic Church" (Forsyth,159).

Previously the Church had taught Quebec's agrarian nationalists "to be satisfied with a lesser lot in life, to believe that they had been '*nés pour un petit pain*'" (born for a little bread roll), which, Schwartzwald points out, is "a reference to the buns given out on the feast of Saint John the Baptist, the patron saint of French Canada" ("Fear of Federasty," 178; "Symbolic Homosexuality," 269). Under the old regime, "messianic ideology sought to turn Quebec's underdevelopment into a virtue," by which Quebec was to exemplify its "spiritual, Latin" ancestors in the New World ("Symbolic Homosexuality," 268). In contrast, modern nationalism sought to expose the self-deception behind this degrading subjugation, which further reinforced the collective sense of failure that had haunted Quebec's colonized consciousness ever since the "Conquest," the defeat of the French on the Plains of Abraham in 1759 ("Symbolic Homosexuality," 268–9; "Fear of Federasty," 176). Thus, the rise of Quebec's new nationalist movement also meant rejecting the second-class status of being Canada's Other, the so-called "French"-Canadians. So the task of Quebec artists, writers, and playwrights "became to denounce the past and to liberate—as well as create—a sense of identity" (Usmiani, *Michel Tremblay,* 13). In short, the Quiet Revolution finally "laid to rest the century-long ideological representation of Quebec as a piously Catholic, agrarian society" ("Fear of Federasty," 177) and thereby prepared the ground for the emergence of a new nationalist consciousness.

While the Quebec population discovered their "imagined community" or "nation-ness" through print culture—the process described by Benedict Anderson in his attempt to clarify the modern nation as a cultural formation—theatre audiences in Quebec also found their cultural identity reflected on the stage, which of course helped foster the construction of a new national identity. Therefore, to view Tremblay simply as a product of his time is not adequate; it is far more important to grasp how he participated in shaping Quebec's nationalist project, for Tremblay wrote in response to the momentous transformation that Quebec society was undergoing. By dramatizing individual efforts to break free of the family and to liberate the self from the repressive effects of the Catholic Church, Tremblay created allegories suggestive of national liberation. At the same time, he emphasized the pernicious influence of American consumerism on an emergent community, an issue that was then a major national concern, but even more pressing for a vulnerable Quebec.

Following *le cycle des belles-soeurs,* Tremblay went on to portray characters who had managed to escape from the tyranny of the family but were now surviving on the fringes of society, the social outcasts who frequent Montreal's *demi-monde* (fringe society), the downtown core locally known as "The Main." "The setting itself, and the choice of this particular milieu," Usmiani writes, "is a plea for marginality, for freedom of the individual from the pressures of society, as well as for the freedom of marginal societies," such as the Francophone community in North America (*Michel Tremblay,* 22). Tremblay's comments support this view. In discussing his predilection for marginal characters, Tremblay asserts: "If I choose to talk about the fringes of society, it is because my people are a fringe society" (Anthony, 283).

In *Hosanna,* Tremblay's most notorious play, he presents a vivid glimpse into the life of two homosexuals who have become part of that *demi-monde. Hosanna* was first performed at the Théâtre de Quat'Sous in Montreal in 1973. Initially its blatant homosexuality created such a sensation that the political implications of the play were largely overlooked. Because of its wild, exotic appeal, *Hosanna* was translated into English almost immediately, and the following year it was produced at the Tarragon Theatre in Toronto, where it instantly became a major success. *Hosanna* then opened on Broadway where, unfortunately, it achieved only a lukewarm reception; nevertheless, it went on to be staged in Vancouver, Amsterdam, Paris, London, Cologne, and Glasgow. In the early 1990s, a significantly modified version of the play was produced in Montreal in French; this version merits further consideration, since it also addresses nationalism's gender politics. While the original production bravely embraced homosexuality, by essentializing sexual identity, it reinscribed Quebec's marginal position, inadvertently replicating Quebec's feminization in relation to the rest of North America. Somewhat paradoxically, the 1991 production of *Hosanna* more readily lends itself to a queer reading of nationalism, since this version takes yet another step forward and attempts to deconstruct the heterosexual gender categories that privilege the masculine ideal.

HOSANNA IN THE SEVENTIES

Hosanna deals with the anguish of two aging homosexuals caught in the trap of identifying with heterosexually defined gender roles as a means of sustaining their relationship. By night, Claude, a hairdresser, transforms himself into the drag queen, Hosanna, while Raymond, a biker, complete with black leather and studs, is the macho lover who goes by the name of Cuirette. The play opens in Hosanna's cramped bachelor apartment on Halloween night. Cuirette and Hosanna, who is still in full drag, return from the annual costume party at Sandra's transvestite bar, where Hosanna had hoped to realize her lifelong dream and outdo Elizabeth Taylor's rendition of Cleopatra. As a transvestite, Hosanna wanted to emulate the most desirable of all women. However, to teach Hosanna a lesson for being such a bitchy queen—that is, for thinking herself better than all the other drag queens—Cuirette had them all show up dressed as Cleopatra as well. Of course, Hosanna was devastated. Hurt and humiliated, she has it out with Raymond, who wants Claude to stop pretending to be a woman. Finally, by the play's end, Claude declares that Cleopatra is dead; he removes all his makeup and strips down naked, boldly asserting: "Look, Raymond, I'm a man . . . I'm a man, Raymond . . . I'm a man . . ." (87). They passionately embrace and the lights fade.

One of the most remarkable aspects of the critical response to *Hosanna* is that the two primary interpretations tend to cancel each other out. On the one hand, numerous critics focused on the play's ostensive homosexuality, thereby eschewing a political interpretation. For example, immediately following *Hosanna*'s opening night in Montreal, Martial Dassylva, the theatre critic for *La Presse*, restricted his discussion to the play's homosexuality. He noted that this play offered the first time two of Tremblay's characters actually achieved a mutual understanding. While Dassylva expressly chose to defer a political analysis, a few days later, in *Le Devoir*, Albert Brie dismissed the possibility of any political message, claiming the play had no real theme: "*Il est à cent lieues du théâtre à these.*" Instead, Brie, in a gesture that appears to be an attempt to assuage his own sexual anxiety, clearly identified himself with straight audiences—"*Nous autres, normaux*" (We normal people . . .)—but encouraged them to see the play on the grounds that their assumptions about homosexuality would be dispelled. On the other hand, political readings of *Hosanna* see it as an allegory, but for the most part deny its homosexuality by interpreting Claude's feminization as a consequence of colonization by the English and his final declaration of manhood as an assertion of Quebec nationalism. Precisely because of the heterosexist bias that pervades western discursive practices, including nationalist discourse, the homosexuality intrinsic to the play simply vanishes.

An instance of such a reading can be found in Renate Usmiani's otherwise comprehensive study, *Michel Tremblay*. Rather than explore the significance of the play's homosexuality, she proposes that *Hosanna* also functions on a psychological level, in that "it offers a gripping insight into the complex workings of a lovers' relationship," which of course it does, but she then hastily concludes "that both happen to be male becomes irrelevant" (89)! To support her point, Usmiani quotes from an interview published in Geraldine Anthony's *Stage Voices*, in which Tremblay himself tends to privilege a political reading of the play:

> My play, *Hosanna*, deals in a symbolic way with the problems of Quebec. Although *Hosanna* concerns two homosexuals, one an exaggerated masculine character, the other a transvestite, it is *really* an allegory about Quebec. In the end they drop their poses and embrace their real identity. The climax occurs when Hosanna kills Elizabeth Taylor and at the end he appears naked on stage and says he is a man. He kills all the ghosts around him as Quebec did. We are not French but we are Québécois living in North America! (284, emphasis mine)

The play itself, however, shows that homosexuality is integral to *Hosanna*. As Schwartzwald remarks, in the second act, when Cuirette returns from his frustrating walk through Parc Lafontaine, he laments that "the newly installed floodlights have obliterated the shadows in which he used to cruise and have sex with other men. His response to this municipal act of moral zeal is a defiant one: 'From now on we're gonna do it in public, goddamn it!'" Schwartzwald deftly suggests that Cuirette's "refusal to seek new shadows and relegate his desire to the realm of the hidden sets the stage for Hosanna's own moment of enlightenment" ("From Authenticity," 499). Schwartzwald argues that *Hosanna* is a coming-out play, and in more ways than one, since on the level of political allegory, Claude is also coming out in terms of his cultural identity. In Schwartzwald's reading, homosexuality figures in the articulation of that identity, underscoring Quebec's position as a minority. While the repudiation of feminization still provides the key to a political interpretation of the play, Claude's avowed homosexuality significantly complicates his assertion of manhood and, by extension, Quebec's status within North America.

Even though Usmiani dismisses the play's homosexuality, she does offer some pertinent comments on Hosanna's transvestism and notes the prevalence of transvestite characters in Tremblay's work. She suggests that "these can be seen as inverted and caricatured versions of the sex symbol, a central element in the consumer society much hated by Tremblay. They also carry heavy overtones of political symbolism: the transvestite par excellence represents loss of identity, as well as impotence" (*Michel Tremblay*, 22). Indeed, Claude is powerless because of his marginal position as a Francophone in a Canada dominated by Anglophones. Culturally, however, Canada is marginal in relation to its more powerful neighbour, the United States. Thus, Claude's identification with Elizabeth Taylor, the British-born actor who became a major American movie star, brilliantly illustrates just how far removed Claude has become from his own cultural identity. Not only is Claude attempting to appropriate an English heritage—the cultural roots of the colonizer—his assumption of Elizabeth Taylor's star persona reveals the extent to which he has been overwhelmed by American culture. The fact that these identifications are played out under the guise of Cleopatra, the *femme fatale par excellence*, serves to highlight Claude's loss of a masculine identity. In this sense, Claude's feminization clearly signals his emasculation, his having been "conquered" by a dominant power.

However, Claude's sense of powerlessness is further exacerbated by his homosexuality, since it excludes him from heterosexual society, including Francophone Quebec, in which homophobic males dominate. In other words, Claude's feminization is pushed to the limit, so that drag becomes a means of empowerment, for, as Hosanna, Claude can assert his desirability by mimicking the heterosexual feminine ideal, even if he is restricted to society's margin. But in the process Claude is reduced to a sex object. Whereas the drag queen's often campy magnification of femininity highlights the performative aspect of gender, it also suggests how gender has been both reified and commodified. Yet, as a female impersonator, Claude takes his performance very much to heart, which signals the extent to which he has been alienated from his "true" or "essential" self. Usmiani suggests that as a theatrical device the transvestite embodies a universal archetype of alienation that exceeds the boundaries of any one nation or language (81). In her reading, Claude's final declaration of his manhood provides him with the strength necessary to assert his true cultural identity and thereby reclaim his humanity. But, in accordance with the humanist tradition upon which Usmiani draws, the subject is assumed to be a male heterosexual, constructed through the repression of the possibility of homosexuality.

What complicates a humanist reading of the play is that at the very moment Claude finally repudiates his feminization and asserts his manhood, he actually finds the courage to accept his homosexuality. By removing his makeup and stripping down naked, Claude reveals that he is indeed fully human, with needs and desires of his own: he is a man who loves other men. When viewed through a heterosexual lens, however, Claude's assertion that he is a man confounds the possibility of homosexuality precisely because "to be a man" is assumed to mean, "to be a heterosexual male." In *Sexual*

Dissidence, an illuminating study of homosexuality's symbolic centrality to modern society, Jonathan Dollimore states, "the opposition masculine/homosexual is a conflation of two other classic binaries: masculine/feminine; hetero/homosexual" (236). Homosexual relations are assumed to entail feminization for at least one of the males involved, since only one can physically penetrate the other, who must submit, thereby assuming the subordinate feminine role in relation to the dominant male. In terms of the binary logic that underpins this traditional definition of heterosexuality, the very logic that informs and drives the "violent hierarchies" of colonial discourse, the dominant male is privileged. That Raymond wanted to claim this role is made explicit by his macho posturing, even if it is an exaggerated masculinity suggestive of overcompensation. More to the point, however, by honestly confronting their homosexuality, Claude and Raymond are attempting to escape the trap of heterosexually-defined sex roles and to love each other as equals, in this case, as two human beings who are homosexual males. Tremblay himself maintains that as a political allegory his play means that the people of Quebec must "embrace their real identity," suggesting that despite their minority status within North America, Québécois, while different, are nevertheless entitled to full equality.

In his astute reading of the play, Schwartzwald is one of the few critics to explore Tremblay's convergence of discourses of sexual and national liberation, a convergence, Schwartzwald notes, that Tremblay makes appear *almost natural.* Precisely because Claude must accept that it is as a man that he desires other men before he can feel *bien dans sa peau* (comfortable in his own skin), "sexual desire is thus posed to perform as a more naturalized and radical arbiter of authenticity than gender, which for Tremblay is already encoded as more performative and therefore 'artificial' . . ." ("From Authenticity," 504). For despite Cuirette's macho posturing, it is he "who does all the cooking, cleaning, and housework and who is financially dependent upon '*her*'" (506); conversely, Hosanna, as the professional hairdresser Claude, is actually the breadwinner. Quite rightly, Schwartzwald argues that "the inconsistencies of Cuirette's gender performances, when compounded by their inevitable interaction with Hosanna's own, tend to underscore just how inoperative a category gender finally is for Tremblay" (506). In Foucauldian terms, Tremblay privileges sex as the measure of truth; in other words, it is the assertion of Claude's male sex, combined with the acceptance of his (homo)sexuality, that reveals the truth of his being—his essential, authentic identity.

Nevertheless, the deployment of the category of the homosexual as a means of stabilizing cultural identity proves problematic, since it creates a seeming paradox: as Schwartzwald notes, Claude's "rapprochement with his homosexual essence permanently marginalizes him as a sexual minority even as it authenticates him" (504). It was, moreover, the intolerably oppressive minoritizing dynamic of Quebec's relation to the rest of Canada and Quebec's vulnerable position within North America that fuelled the nationalist argument in the first place. Is Tremblay then suggesting that Quebec embrace its uniqueness, its inherent "*Québécité*," and accept its marginal status, even as this minority position stubbornly reinscribes Quebec's feminization in relation to the rest of North America? Or, as Schwartzwald puts it: Does Hosanna's reconciliation with the authenticity of his sexual desire imply that Quebec "was to be a permanently countercultural society, and consequently excluded from easy integration into the extended family of modern nations"? ("Symbolic Homosexuality," 265) Conceptions of the modern nation rely on the heterosexual model of the patriarchal family as a means of naturalizing nationalism.

In his study of French nationalism during the first half of the twentieth century, David Carroll observes that if "organic unity" is to characterize the form of the modern nation, "the origin of the nation and its model is the *patrie* conceived as the primal family, the original and natural community or society" (84). As nationalism gained prominence over the course of the nineteenth century, the rhetoric of empire building replicated the rigid gender divisions that privileged heterosexual men. Mary Louise Pratt concisely sums up the predicament of women by pointing out that their "value was specifically attached to (and implicitly conditioned on) their reproductive capacity. As mothers of the nation, they are precariously other to the nation. They are imagined as dependent rather than sovereign. They are practically forbidden to be limited and finite, being obsessively defined by their reproductive capacity" (51). While women were relegated to the domestic or private sphere, men presided over the public sphere, which included business, the military, and of course politics, a realm in which they sought to consolidate and expand the power of the nation. Most significantly, men's privileged position was predicated on the maintenance of homosocial relations; to transgress this social code meant to lose the privileges of heterosexual male entitlement and, hence, to be excluded from society, becoming, like women, other to the national project. Ideologically, even as it exists today, nationalism is closely imbricated with what Adrienne Rich has adroitly called "compulsory heterosexuality." Thus, the figuration of a national entity as homosexual as a means of authenticating its identity virtually excludes it from "the extended family of modern nations."

While Benedict Anderson claims that "in the modern world, everyone can, should, will 'have' a nationality, as he or she has a gender" (14), it is vitally important to recognize that national identity is already imbued with gendered significance. In an engaging analysis of queer belonging in Quebec, Elspeth Probyn astutely notes that what is less evident in Anderson's "formulation is that the type of nationality one will 'have' is dependent on the way in which gender is locally articulated" (36). For the centre and its margins are conceived as respectively masculine and feminine through the interpretative grid of heterosexuality. For instance, traditionally Canada has figured as feminine in relation to the United States; in addition, prior to the Quiet Revolution, Quebec figured as a marginal female in relation to the rest of Canada. It was precisely this oppressive configuration that Tremblay drew on for *Les belles-soeurs*. Usmiani, who aptly describes the play as "a contemporary domestic tragedy," notes that when read as a political allegory, Tremblay's presentation of an all-female society, "a powerless, exploited and almost marginal group in traditional society, effectively parallels the position of Quebec as a whole versus the rest of the North American continent" (*Theatre*, 45). However, to further complicate things, Probyn reminds us that "the French 'minority' comprises, in actual fact, 82% of the population within Québec which then allows some anglophone rights groups to position themselves as marginal and in need of protection. This then produces a discourse of anglophones as 'emasculated' in relation to the Québécois strongman" (50).

More relevant though is Probyn's observation that "the general troping of national identity as gendered and heterosexual can break down" (50). For the shifting power relations between various nations or "imagined communities" that give rise to the figuring of gendered positions illustrate how heterosexual binary categories are not stable, since the dominant masculine position can collapse into the feminine, while the feminine can assume a masculine position of dominance. By exposing the absence of an immutable essence around which each of these binary opposites can cohere, these transformations highlight the abstract conceptions on which traditional definitions of gender have tenuously been grounded. At the same time, the persistent articulation of nations in terms of their gendered positions betrays the extent to which a heterosexist bias shapes nationalist discourse, which of course continues to privilege the heterosexual male.

In asserting its difference, homosexuality radically challenges conceptions of the nation based on the traditional familial model. As Schwartzwald remarks, it is not difficult to see how Tremblay's "construction of homosexual and national identity as adequate metaphorical substitutions for each other could seem scandalous to those nationalist ideologues who saw independence as the goal in a developmental narrative deployed around a trope of infantilism and maturity" ("From Authenticity," 504). In Freudian terms, maturity means the assumption of male heterosexuality: identification with the father; Freud considered homosexuality "to be a variation of the sexual function produced by a certain arrest of development" (Dollimore, 196), identification with the dreaded mother. Burdened with the mark of effeminacy, homosexuality perturbs the link between traditional notions of masculinity and postcolonial conceptions of the nation that derive from a normalizing or regulatory model of the patriarchal family. As a stigma, effeminacy, or feminization, further suggests just how far removed we remain from accepting the sexes as equal. During the not-too-distant nineties, western nations consistently devalued democratic ideals traditionally associated with the "feminine," such as the notion that society is responsible for its disaffected, since in western discursive practices the feminine continues to be equated with frivolousness, weakness, and subservience. Indeed, for women to be taken seriously, they must deny their difference and conform to the masculine "norm." In contrast, because the feminine has been so denigrated in the western imaginary, when it "penetrates" the heterosexual male ideal, it contaminates it, rendering it abject. That the feminization of the masculine systematically evokes abhorrence demonstrates how misogyny drives homophobia, thereby revealing how the two are intimately related. By differing from the norm, the white heterosexual male, *all others* are deemed inferior, even if they comprise a majority. Yet, despite its privileging of the male, what was so remarkable about the original production of *Hosanna* was Tremblay's attempt to counter the devaluation of difference by having two men accept and love each other with dignity and mutual respect. Significantly, this only becomes possible once Claude and Raymond drop their heterosexual posturing and its attendant power dynamics, a move which enables them to recognize each other's sameness, their essential equality.

In *Epistemology of the Closet*, Eve Kosofsky Sedgwick brilliantly argues that "thought and knowledge in twentieth-century Western culture as a whole are structured—indeed, fractured—by a chronic, now endemic crisis of homo/heterosexual definition, indicatively male, dating from the end of the nineteenth century," when the category of the homosexual first emerged in medical discourse. As a result, "an understanding of virtually any aspect of modern Western culture must be, not merely incomplete, but damaged in its central substance to the degree that it does not incorporate a critical analysis of modern homo/heterosexual definition" (1). While not unique, Quebec nationalists have proven particularly resistant to just such incorporation. Their analyses of the failure of the nationalist project evince a typically homophobic response, which however provides valuable insight into their underlying assumptions and projections.

However, as Schwartzwald points out, "One of the most salient features of modern intellectual (self-)representation in Québec turns out to be that the homophobic elements of its *learned* discourse on identity are largely inconsistent with both liberal legal discourse and popular attitudes" ("Symbolic Homosexuality," 266). Ironically, "Québec was the first state jurisdiction in North America to adopt anti-discrimination legislation on grounds of sexual orientation, and this was done by the *nationalist* Parti Québécois government," which was elected in 1976 ("Fear of Federasty," 180). Far from stigmatizing homosexuals as emblematic of "national alienation," at that time, the government, under the leadership of the late René Lévesque, "spoke of wanting to protect and further the interests of all communities in an inclusive figuration of the nation" (180). Nevertheless, following the defeat of the 1980 referendum on sovereignty-association, the analytic trend of Quebec nationalists proved to be especially sensitive to "homosexually inflected articulations of identity, which [were] compulsively read for clues that might explicate the identitary impasse of the Québécois subject-nation" ("Symbolic Homosexuality," 267). Drawing on the coming-of-age trope common to postcolonial discourse, "a developmental narrative in which Québec's independence would be the culmination of a process leading from 'infancy' to 'maturity'" was consistently produced (265). Consequently, Quebec nationalists all too readily assumed "the homophobic assignation of homosexuality as *arrested* development" in support of their "explanations of Québec's long, halting progress toward self-determination" (267).

While "the formation of a viable Québécois nation implicitly depended upon the forging of a new, emancipatory social contract," which was "one of the most powerful discursive ruptures initiated by the Quiet Revolution," Schwartzwald concludes that:

> the overarching persistence of a developmental model for nationhood within this contractual paradigm and its particular claims to modernity reveals an enduring reliance upon heterosexually ordered and ultimately archaicizing familial models when constructing the national 'body' itself. Subjecting contractual models to pressures as great as the defeat of a popular referendum on sovereignty is perhaps a sad but effective way of demonstrating how the attendant figures of a familial model never entirely disappear, but are instead held 'in reserve' until a disastrous conjuncture resuscitates them. (270)

In his analysis of the discursive practices of Quebec nationalists, Schwartzwald goes on to show how homosexuality persistently figures as central "to the identitary matrix of the subject-nation" but becomes "the repressed whose return portends only disruption and signifies failure" (270). It is, however, the heterosexually ordered familial model of the nation/state that is doomed to failure. Precisely because heterosexuality is predicated on the denial of homosexuality, the latter underpins the very foundation on which masculine identity is precariously constructed, creating an unstable structure. Whereas homosexuality is an internally repressed difference, for the insecure or threatened heterosexually identified male, through the process of unconscious projection, homosexuality is perceived as an external threat, an unsettling recognition of denied otherness. In his book, *Homos*, Leo Bersani suggests that "homophobia may be this fearful excitement at the prospect of becoming what one already is" (28). Of necessity, a successful model of the modern nation must dispense with heterosexual rigidity. A new, more inclusive national configuration is now needed; such a model must be expansive and diverse in its conception, allowing for difference rather than assimilation, which only leads back to the reinstatement of an exclusive, self-defeating norm. While the appropriation of a heterosexual model inflects the queering of nationhood with developmental failure, in order to arrest this interpretive trend, it is imperative to recognize how homophobic anxiety inevitably undermines the very model it seeks to impose.

Dollimore determines that the "associations of sexual deviation and political threat have a long history sedimented into our language and culture" (236–237). By way of example, he cites the term "buggery," the origin of which apparently "derives from the religious as well as sexual nonconformity of an eleventh-century Bulgarian sect that practised the Manichaean heresy and refused to propagate the species. The *Oxford English Dictionary* tells us that it was later applied to other heretics, to whom abominable practices were also ascribed" (237). In addition, Dollimore finds that "social and political crisis provokes renewed urgency in the policing of sexual deviance" (237). He then refers to Arthur N. Gilbert, who reports that in England "[d]uring the Napoleonic wars the numbers of prosecutions for sodomy increased. To understand why," he continues, "we need to understand the construction of the sodomite, his association at that time with evil, rebellion, and insurrection, and the belief that to tolerate his sin was to court the possibility of divine revenge (as with Sodom and Gomorrah)" (237). During this period the mythology surrounding the sodomite found an immediate focus: he "was perceived as an internal deviant who refigured a foreign threat, in this case the threat from the French" (237). The displacement of non-sexual fears onto the sexual deviant, Dollimore concludes, "are made possible because other kinds of transgression—political, religious—are not only loosely associated with the sexual deviant, but 'condensed' in the very definition of deviance"; that this process of displacement succeeded attests to "the paranoid instabilities at the heart of dominant cultural identities (237).

In "Fear of Federasty," Schwartzwald explores the homophobic tropes deployed by Quebec nationalists during the 1960s and 1970s, tropes that evoke the mythology that connects sexual deviance with political threat. He suggests that for these nationalists, "homosexuality signifies metonymically . . . that is, as the *presence* of an earlier intellectual élite composed of or tied to the clergy that entered into a compact with Anglo-Canadian capital to divide supervision over the colonized body of the Québécois. . . ." (180). In their attempts to effect a radical break with the conservative nationalism of the past, the homophobic anxiety of the new nationalists was articulated by characterizing "those found to be traitors or sell-outs to the cause of national revolution . . . as passive/seductive men" (179). Such a man was labelled a *fédéraste*, a play on *pédéraste*, the French word used to signify homosexuality, although its primary definition concerns the love of men for boys. For to be called a *fédéraste*, Schwartzwald duly notes, meant to be one of those who are "first the victims, then the corrupted perpetrators of what is figured as a permanent violation by a salacious 'fully grown' Canada against the waifish, innocent Québec" (179). Because the term *pédéraste* is not usually used in Quebec, "its foreignness as a continental French signifier for homosexuality underlines the 'exotic' or unrooted personality of the traitor/violator"; in addition, "the activity to which *fédéraste*s give themselves over is compulsive, repetitious, and unproductive" (180). Thus, the figuring of Quebec as a homosexual came to assume a doubly vexed position. As a consequence, even those who considered themselves among the most progressive of the new breed of nationalists were primarily interested in reasserting conventional gender definitions, in which Quebec would assume the position of a dominant heterosexual male.

Schwartzwald cites an essay that appeared in *Parti pris* in 1964, tellingly titled "The Colonial Oedipus," in which Pierre Maheu, in a fit of blatantly sexist rhetoric, urged fellow nationalists "to accept that we are sons of women. This will lead us to make of women both our lovers and wives while we liberate ourselves from the Mother by surging forth once again from her breast, well armed for a new combat, a new confrontation: that of the free man who attacks concrete enemies head on . . ." (188). Quebec's nationalist project was not unique; rather it situated itself "within the universalizing discourse of all the great anti-colonial movements of the epoch in question" (179). Schwartzwald proposes that it was "the preoccupation with unified subjectivity that led to a profound sexual anxiety in Québec's anti-colonial discourse, an anxiety which is *already* borne within the attempted synthesis of Marxist, existentialist, and Freudian theory that underlies the anti-colonial writings of the post-war period" (178).

Freud's writings, given their complexity and contradictions, offer various possibilities for a counter-discourse. Of particular relevance is Freud's acceptance of Wilhelm Fliess's view that human beings are inherently bisexual. In

The Ego and the Id, Freud maintains that the most important way in which bisexuality influences the vicissitudes of the Oedipus complex is in its complete form, which is two-fold, both positive and negative, meaning both same-sex identification and opposite-sex identification. Surprisingly, Freud then suggests that the positive or "simple Oedipus complex is by no means its commonest form . . ." (279). The more complete Oedipus complex, he writes:

> . . . is due to the bisexuality originally present in children: that is to say, a boy has not merely an ambivalent attitude towards his father and an affectionate object-choice towards his mother, but at the same time he also behaves like a girl and displays an affectionate feminine attitude to his father and a corresponding jealousy and hostility towards his mother. It is this complicating element introduced by bisexuality that makes it so difficult to obtain a clear view of the facts in connection with the earliest object-choices and identifications, and still more difficult to describe them intelligibly. (279)

Freud's characterization of the boy's affection for the father as feminine is a key. As Judith Butler points out, "for Freud *bisexuality is the coincidence of two heterosexual desires within a single psyche*. The masculine disposition is, in effect, never oriented toward the father as an object of sexual love, and neither is the feminine disposition oriented toward the mother. . . . Hence, within Freud's thesis of primary bisexuality, there is no homosexuality, and only opposites attract" (61). While this highlights a fundamental flaw in Freud's thinking, which of course reflects the much larger problem in western conceptual systems, Freud's reinscription of heterosexuality is symptomatic of his own sexual anxiety and evidence of the regulatory pressures of compulsory heterosexuality. Freud acknowledges these pressures elsewhere, indicating that the predominance of heterosexuality is driven by cultural attitudes.

For instance, in 1915, Freud added to his *Three Essays on the Theory of Sexuality* an extraordinary footnote that extends over four pages, in which he argues against "separating off homosexuals from the rest of mankind as a group of a special character" (56). To support his argument, he makes the astonishing statement that heterosexuality is *also a problem* that is not fully understood:

> [F]rom the point of view of psychoanalysis the exclusive sexual interest felt by men for women is also a problem that needs elucidating and is not a self-evident fact based upon an attraction that is ultimately of a chemical nature. A person's final sexual attitude is not decided until

> after puberty and is the result of a number of factors, not all of which are yet known; some are of a constitutional nature but others are accidental. . . . But in general the multiplicity of determining factors is reflected in the variety of manifest sexual attitudes in which they find their issue in mankind. (57)

In recognizing the limits of his knowledge, Freud makes a generous allowance for cultural determinants and their diverse manifestations.

Although Dollimore maintains he is not interested "in recovering the authentic voice of psychoanalysis," he is particularly interested in Freud's "deconstructive assault on normality" (182). Dollimore argues how, via Freud, "we can see that the concept of perversion always embodied what has now become a fundamental deconstructive proposition: whatever a culture designates as alien, utterly other, and incommensurably different is rarely and perhaps never so" (182). Drawing on Freud's concepts of repression, disavowal, negation, and splitting, Dollimore elaborates on what he calls "the perverse dynamic": how perversion "destroys the binary structure of which it is initially an effect" (183). Freud recognized that the development of culture inevitably led to the production of the effects it sought to repress (188). As Dollimore remarks, at this point Freud anticipates Michel Foucault.

In *The History of Sexuality*, Foucault makes his now famous argument that the intensification of the regulation of sexuality over the course of the eighteenth and nineteenth centuries did not lead to the repression of same-sex activity; on the contrary, it led to the production of the category of the homosexual. "Homosexuality," Foucault writes, "appeared as one of the forms of sexuality when it was transposed from the practice of sodomy onto a kind of interior androgyny, a hermaphrodism of the soul. The sodomite had been a temporary aberration; the homosexual was now a species" (43). While the end product may appear to be qualitatively distinct, Robert May points out that "analysis shows that the determinants are only different in degree" (163). Citing Freud's remarkable footnote, May draws attention to Freud's admission that there are no "constitutional peculiarities" that can be attributed to the homosexual that are not present, "though less strongly, in the constitution of transitional types and those whose manifest attitude is normal" (163). In other words, for Freud, heterosexuality and homosexuality are not discrete categories, but overlap, thus destroying their binary structure. So, if masculinity and femininity are merely elaborate cultural fictions deployed to promote heterosexuality in the interests of empire building, what then does it mean to be a man or a woman? But even more disturbing, can the differences between the sexes and sexual difference be articulated without recourse to the heterosexual matrix?

HOSANNA IN THE NINETIES

Within its specific historical context, the deployment of sexual binaries provided Tremblay with a unique means of authenticating Claude's cultural identity. In 1991, however, a new production of *Hosanna* was staged in Montreal, in which the emphasis on an essentialized conception of sexual identity shifted to foreground gender roles and their performative character. As previously noted, while discussing the original production of the play, Tremblay stated, "*Hosanna* concerns two homosexuals, one an exaggerated masculine character, the other a transvestite . . ." (Anthony, 284). In a note in the 1991 program, Tremblay proceeds to describe the play as an exploration of the crisis of "*two* transvestites, not only Hosanna but her lover Cuirette . . ." ("From Authenticity" 502). Tremblay's comment, Schwartzwald observes, "reminds us that these issues were present in the original version, but remained largely illegible when set against the overarching, virtually compulsory reading of *Hosanna* at that time as an allegory of national oppression" (502). In addition, in the 1991 stage production, Claude is no longer in drag; instead, Hosanna's bright red dress glares out at us from the open closet, and Cuirette's macho posturing is also exposed as an exaggerated gender performance. Even Claude's final line, "I'm a man," no longer resembles an affirmation of an authentic identity; rather it has become a profound interrogation charged with ambivalence, creating a gaping uncertainty ("From Authenticity" 501). The new version of *Hosanna* engages a Quebec that has undergone profound cultural changes, including a confrontation with the developments of French feminism and deconstruction. "To those who yearn to be part of a stable, homogeneous majority," Schwartzwald concludes, the new "*Hosanna* responds with another allegory, this time mocking the self-delusion that underwrites the self-confident 'putting on' of gender roles that appear more natural, but whose performative character is denied" (505).

In *Gender Trouble*, Butler argues that while there is no abiding substance or immutable gender core that derives from morphological sex, gender is not a set of free-floating attributes that can be assumed at will, but "the substantive effect of gender is performatively produced" over time by the demands of a regulatory discourse that encodes masculinity and femininity within the heterosexual matrix (24). Because gender categories have been organized to coincide with and promote heterosexuality, for a male to become a "man" requires the repudiation of an identification with the feminine, a repudiation which "becomes a precondition for the heterosexualization of sexual desire and hence . . . its fundamental ambivalence" ("Gender Melancholy," 26). It is this fundamental ambivalence—a haunting doubt that must constantly be appeased—that produces sexual anxiety for the heterosexual male. While the misogyny underpinning the privileging of male heterosexuality fuels homophobia, leading to aggression, intimidation and even violence, it also perpetuates the oppression of women, who, in assuming the masquerade of femininity, obediently conform to the inferior position and thus provide a mirror that enables masculine dominance.

As a homosexual attempting to assert his desirability, Claude emulates the ultimate woman, but once he removes his costume and makeup—as Hosanna presents himself to the audience in the 1991 production—he reveals himself as a male, and as such, from an already gendered position. It is precisely at this point that Butler's analysis becomes most relevant, for she points out that there is no one prior to this *naturalized* performance of gender. Gender itself proves to be performative, "that is, constituting the identity it is purported to be" (25), even if its performative character is not evident. As Hosanna laments, "the show must go on . . . and on . . . and on . . . and on . . ." (62). The question now becomes where to go from here: Once the masks have been removed, how are Claude and Raymond to articulate their identities as gay men?

In rethinking gender performativity, Butler refers to Jacques Derrida, who emphasizes that it is necessary to understand performativity "*as* citationality, for the invocation of identity is always a *re*invocation" (Rajchman, 132). This means that a subject can be produced only "through the citing of a norm, a citing which instantiates and institutes the norm" (134). How then can gay men articulate their masculinity and not efface their homosexuality? It seems that a specifically gay male identity can be produced only by queering the norm, by marking it with an exaggerated expression of femininity or masculinity. This of course is not to suggest blind adherence to heterosexual gender positions, the positions which Cuirette and Hosanna initially tried to inhabit before accepting their homosexuality. Rather, the self-conscious re-invocation of these gendered markers can be used with deliberation, to signal the incoherence of heterosexual gender binaries while simultaneously producing a queer subject position.

Since the emergence of queer theory in the late 1980s, the term "queer" has taken on new significance. Embraced as a site of resistance, "the desanctioning power of the name 'queer' is reversed to sanction a contestation of the terms of sexual legitimacy" ("Critically Queer" 18). Butler's translation of queer theory into praxis envisions a new form of political activism. She elaborates:

> Paradoxically, but also with great promise, the subject who is 'queered' into public discourse through homophobic interpellations of various kinds *takes up* or *cites* that very term as the discursive basis for an opposition. This kind of citation will emerge as *theatri-*

> *cal* to the extent that *it mimes and renders hyperbolic* the discursive convention that it also *reverses*. The hyperbolic gesture is crucial to the exposure of the homophobic law which can no longer control the terms of its own abjecting strategies. (18)

Not only does the performance of queerness enable the articulation of a specifically homosexual subject position, it also provides the ground on which to develop an oppositional movement. By mocking the incoherence of its antagonists' position, queerness undermines the very ground from which the attack was launched. Thus queer politics instantiates what Dollimore defines as the "perverse dynamic," for the queer dynamic activates the deconstruction of the binary structure that not only produced it, but also attempts to contain and oppress it.

Even though queer theory is anti-essentialist, queer politics remains a form of identity politics since the modern political realm is dominated by the notion of a coherent or essential self. Nevertheless, it is identity politics with a difference: its potential lies in queerness as a political identity. As Jeffrey Weeks puts it, in its broadest sense, the organizing principle of queer politics "is not an assumed sexual identity based on orientation or practice, but identification with the forms of politics and patterns of transgression that define queerness" (112). In addition, Michael Warner argues that queerness "rejects a minoritizing logic of toleration or simple political interest-representation in favor of a more thorough resistance to regimes of the normal" (xxii). Specifically, it is the privileging of the white heterosexual male that is being contested. This makes for a potentially inclusive political movement, one which covers a broad spectrum, including gays and lesbians, bisexuals, transsexuals, single mothers, feminists, sympathetic heterosexuals, and ethnic minorities. Indeed, it covers all who embrace the ambiguity of culturally produced identities and want actively to challenge the ways in which categories such as gender, sexuality, race, and nation are constructed by powerful cultural narratives in order to protect and promote the existing norm by marginalizing difference.

Bersani questions queer theory's effectiveness as praxis and thus proposes an alternate strategy—what he calls "homo-ness"—arguing that it is a more radical possibility, since "*it necessitates a massive redefining of relationality*" (76). Bersani remarks that "[i]t is not possible to be gay-affirmative, or politically effective as gays, if gayness has no specificity" (61). He then reminds us that in a heterosexual society women have played an important role in teaching gay men how to frame and stage their sexuality (61). Referring to Kaja Silverman's *Male Subjectivity at the Margins*, Bersani reiterates her queer argument that "the gay man's deployment of signifiers of the feminine may be a powerful weapon in the defeat of those defensive maneuvers that have defined sexual difference. This goal," he adds, "is also served by the instability of the deployment" (61). But, as he sees it:

> The gay man's identification with women is countered by an imitation of those desiring subjects with whom we have been officially identified: other men. In a sense, then, the very maintaining of the couples man-woman, heterosexual-homosexual, serves to break down their oppositional distinctions. These binary divisions help to create the diversified desiring field across which we can move, thus reducing sexual difference itself—at least as far as desire is concerned—to a merely formal arrangement inviting us to transgress the very identity assigned to us within the couple. (61)

In other words, the assumption of heterosexually defined roles *at will*—alternating between mimicry and reversal—will inevitably strip these roles of their power.

Quite rightly, Bersani proposes that we can also all learn something from the experience of homosexuals. Rather than privilege difference, which the dominant power perceives as the inferior term, he recommends we begin to privilege our "*near-sameness*" or, as he prefers to call it, our "homo-ness," which, however, does not mean "the perfect identity of terms" (146). For, "identities," Bersani adds, *always* "spill over." So, instead of focusing on difference, he suggests we first acknowledge our likeness, not necessarily the essentialized sameness of gender, sexuality, or race, but shared characteristics, such as the fact that we are all living, breathing, feeling, thinking beings, in short, equal. "To recognize universal homo-ness," Bersani writes, "can allay the terror of difference, which generally gives rise to a hopeless dream of eliminating difference entirely. A massively heteroized perception of the universal gives urgency to a narcissistic project that would reduce—radically, with no surplus whatsoever of alterity—the other to the same" (146). Bersani's proposal is worth considering, for its implications are far reaching.

For instance, the 1991 production of *Hosanna* suggests that we can extend the questioning of heterosexual gender categories to that of national identity; specifically, we can ask what it means to be a Québécois or a Canadian. In an attempt to rewrite the narrative of the nation, the postcolonial theorist Homi K. Bhabha effectively argues that the ambivalence that haunts the articulation of gender positions parallels the ambivalence that haunts the idea of the modern nation. According to Bhabha's timely argument, in the discursive production of the nation, "there is a split between the continuist, accumulative temporality of the pedagogical," the people as an *a priori* historical presence, an ideal, and the people constructed in the performance of narration, the enunciatory present (297–9). In Quebec, the pedagogical ideal of a homogeneous mass, the people as one deriving from old Québécois stock—*la souche*—creates the imaginary boundary that marks the nation's selfhood: "the people as 'image' and its signification as a differentiating sign of Self, distinct from the Other or the Outside" (299). But within the postmodern context of mass migration, the pedagogical narrative is disrupted, introducing a temporality of the "in-between," what Bhabha defines as a liminal "space of representation that threatens binary division with its difference" (299). The opening up of this "in-between" space, where the external threat of the other is now perceived as having infiltrated the nation/state, creates intense anxiety, often leading to xenophobia. However, the enunciation of cultural differences within a nation, Bhabha points out, can only be agonistically articulated. Although it is doubtful that the agony of this postmodern articulation can be avoided, as Bersani suggests, the terror of difference can be allayed by privileging our "near-sameness." It is here that his concept of "homo-ness" reveals its broadest applicability.

While heterogeneous figures now proliferate on the streets of Montreal, the obsession of Quebec nationalists with *la souche*, Probyn pointedly remarks, "continually threatens to asphyxiate their movement" (63). Referring to C. Philo, Probyn adds, "it is deeply insufficient to think that we can comprehend forms of belonging by seeking to refer them to an underlying structuring principle, a stable and guaranteeing referent" (17). As she notes, when the Parti Québécois resumed power in 1994, one of the first statements Premiere Jacques Parizeau made was "that it is now time to make Quebec into a normal country" (n65), meaning of course a patriarchal nation-state based on the white male norm. Sadly Parizeau's response to the failure of Quebec's 1995 referendum confirms Bhabha's assertion that such a model is no longer viable within a postmodern context. For Parizeau, overcome with bitterness, firmly placed the blame on "money and the ethnic vote," money here referring to the English minority in Quebec, who are for the most part no longer wealthy, since the money migrated west. And why immigrants would vote for a sovereign Quebec that bars them from participating in that society poses a serious question these nationalists must now address. As Bhabha concludes:

> Once the liminality of the nation-space is established, and its 'difference is turned from the boundary 'outside' to its finitude 'within,' the threat of cultural difference is no longer a problem of 'other' people. It becomes a question of the otherness of the people-as-one. The national subject

> splits in the ethnographic perspective of culture's contemporaneity and provides both a theoretical position and a narrative authority for marginal voices or minority discourse. (301)

Somewhat ironically, in Quebec, the narrative authority of marginal voices has actually succeeded in asserting its presence. But here, as elsewhere, the issue of identity remains an ongoing preoccupation. Perhaps, then, in rethinking the Canadian experiment in the face of the "perplexity of living," there remains the possibility of imagining a new, postmodern community.

WORKS CITED

Anderson, Benedict. *Imagined Communities: Reflections on the Origin and Spread of Nationalism.* London: Verso, 1983.

Anthony, Geraldine, ed. *Stage Voices: Twelve Canadian Playwrights Talk about Their Lives and Work.* Toronto: Doubleday, 1978.

Bersani, Leo. *Homos.* Cambridge, MA: Harvard University Press, 1995.

Bhabha, Homi K. "DissemiNation: time, narrative, and the margins of the modern nation." In *Nation and Narration.* Ed. Homi K. Bhabha. New York: Routledge, 1990. 291–322.

Brie, Albert. "Tremblay joue et gagne." *Le Devoir* (15 mai 1973): 10.

Butler, Judith. "Critically Queer." In *Playing with Fire: Queer Politics, Queer Theories.* Ed. Shane Phelan. New York: Routledge, 1997. 11–29.

———. *Gender Trouble: Feminism and the Subversion of Identity.* New York: Routledge, 1990.

———. "Melancholy Gender/Refused Identification." In *Constructing Masculinity.* Eds. Maurice Berger, Brian Wallis and Simon Watson. New York: Routledge, 1995. 21–36.

Carroll, David. *French Literary Fascism: Nationalism, Anti-Semitism, and the Ideology of Culture.* Princeton, NJ: Princeton University Press, 1995.

Dassylva, Martial. "Des éclaircies de tendresse." *La Presse* (11 mai 1973): 12A.

Dollimore, Jonathan. *Sexual Dissidence: Augustine to Wilde, Freud to Foucault.* Oxford: Clarendon Press, 1991.

Forsyth, Louise H. "Beyond the Myths and Fictions of Traditionalism and Nationalism: The Political in the Work of Nicole Brossard." In *Traditionalism, Nationalism, and Feminism: Women Writers of Quebec.* Ed. Paula Gilbert Lewis. Westport, CT: Greenwood Press, 1985. 157–72.

Foucault, Michel. *The History of Sexuality: An Introduction.* Vol. 1. Trans. Robert Hurley. New York: Vintage Books, 1990.

Freud, Sigmund. *On Sexuality: Three Essays on the Theory of Sexuality and other Works.* Vol. 7. Trans. James Strachey. London: Penguin Books, 1977.

———. *The Ego and the Id.* Excerpt in *Freud on Women: A Reader.* Ed. Elisabeth Young-Bruehl. New York: W.W. Norton, 1990. 274–282.

May, Robert. "Re-reading Freud on Homosexuality." In *Disorienting Sexuality: Psychoanalytic Reappraisals of Sexual Identities.* Eds. Thomas Domenici and Ronnie C. Lesser. New York: Routledge, 1995. 153–165.

Pratt, Mary Louise. "Women, Literature, and National Brotherhood." In *Women, Culture, and Politics in Latin America: Seminar on Feminism and Culture in Latin America.* Eds. Emilie Bergmann et al. Berkeley: University of California Press, 1990.

Probyn, Elspeth. "Love in a Cold Climate." *Queer Belongings in Québec.* Montréal: GRECC, 1994.

Rajchman, John, ed. *The Identity in Question.* New York: Routledge, 1995.

Schwartzwald, Robert. "Fear of Federasty: Québec's Inverted Fictions." In *Comparative American Identities: Race, Sex, and Nationality in the Modern Text.* Ed. Hortense J. Spillers. New York: Routledge: 1991. 175–195.

———. "From Authenticity to Ambivalence: Michel Tremblay's *Hosanna.*" In *American Review of Canadian Studies* 4th ser. 22 (1992): 499–510.

———. "'Symbolic' Homosexuality, 'False Feminine,' and the Problematics of Identity in Québec." In *Fear of a Queer Planet: Queer Politics and Social Theory.* Ed. Michael Warner. Minneapolis, MN: University of Minnesota Press, 1993. 264–299.

Sedgwick, Eve Kosofsky. *Epistemology of the Closet.* Berkeley: University of California Press, 1990.

Tremblay, Michel. *Hosanna.* Trans. John Van Burek and Bill Glassco. Vancouver: Talonbooks, 1991.

Usmiani, Renate. *Michel Tremblay.* Vancouver: Douglas & McIntyre, 1982.

———. *The Theatre of Frustration: Super Realism in the Dramatic Work of F.X. Kroetz and Michel Tremblay.* New York: Garland Publishing, Inc., 1990.

Warner, Michael, ed. *Fear of a Queer Planet: Queer Politics and Social Theory.* Minneapolis, MN: University of Minnesota Press, 1993.

Weeks, Jeffrey. *Invented Moralities: Sexual Values in an Age of Uncertainty.* New York: Columbia University Press, 1995.

talking forbidden love: an interview with lynne fernie

Terry Goldie

Lynne Fernie co-directed and wrote, with Aerlyn Weissman, *Forbidden Love: The Unashamed Stories of Lesbian Lives*, a feature-length documentary film of lesbian oral histories of Canada in the 1950s and 1960s, produced by Studio D of the National Film Board of Canada (NFB) (executive producers: Rina Fraticelli/Ginny Stikeman; Producers: Ginny Stikeman/ Margaret Pettigrew). It premiered at the Festival of Festivals in Toronto in 1992. *Forbidden Love* received various awards including the Genie for best feature-length documentary in Canada (1993); Best Documentary, 15th International Film Festival, Durban, South Africa (1994); and Best Documentary, Turin Gay and Lesbian Film Festival, Italy (1995). It was broadcast on public or cable television in: Canada (CBC & WTN), Finland, Ireland, England (Channel 4), Germany, Switzerland, Slovak Republic, France, Barbados, Mexico, Australia, Japan, Italy, Trinidad & Tobago, Panama, Nicaragua, and Jamaica.

TG: *How did you get started with the project?*

LF: I was doing research for an international lesbian history film being produced by Studio D at the National Film Board of Canada in 1987, and I met Aerlyn Weissman, who was recording sound for that film, on its first shoot at the Michigan Womyn's Music Festival. About eight months later, Aerlyn and I were asked to submit a proposal for a lesbian film to Studio D. The international film had a very broad agenda, so we wanted to focus on Canada.

TG: *It was very much a Canadian project from the beginning.*

LF: Yes. The documentaries I'd seen on gays and lesbians were mostly American or British and tended to be big survey documentaries. In *Before Stonewall*, for example, the filmmakers had the necessary burden of representing a vast and complicated history that hadn't been filmed before. Aerlyn and I talked about our proposal, and decided—because these survey films had been done and were in distribution—that we could take a narrower focus and try to tell an evocative story of a specific time. We realized that we didn't even know how lesbians had lived in Toronto thirty years ago, much less in earlier decades. We decided to make a documentary about women who were still alive, and could tell their histories in their own voices. We began with very simple questions: What was it like to be a Canadian lesbian in the fifties and sixties, before the current lesbian and feminist movements? How did you meet other women? Where did you go? What did you read?

TG: *Did you plan to concentrate on certain places? Because obviously you centred on Toronto, Vancouver, and Montreal.*

LF: We chose to focus on lesbians whose need for each other and some sense of community led them to the few seedy beer parlours or bars where women could be openly lesbian at the time. We felt that these women were confronting the social and sexual regulation of all women by having the courage to occupy these spaces, and we wanted to be able to show the edges where lesbian desire and the policing of that desire conflicted. We concentrated on three large cities because they were more likely to have such bars. Also, we felt the anonymity of a large city would make it more likely to find women who would agree to be on film. We weren't trying to do a comprehensive Canadian history of lesbianism because, of course, most lesbians lived intensely private and hidden lives.

TG: *Did you think of this as a Studio D sort of film? One often reads about Studio D as a certain kind of environment.*[1]

LF: We were invited to do this project while Rina Fraticelli was the head of Studio D. I believe the international history documentary and ours were the first specifically lesbian documentaries the studio was producing. We had wonderful support from Ginny Stikeman, our initial producer, and Margaret Pettigrew who became our producer when Ginny became head of the studio. Aerlyn and I were not staff directors; we were on contract. Studio D was in Montreal and we worked on the film in Toronto, mostly out of my studio on Queen Street West. We were only at Studio D for brief periods of time. The lesbians we were interviewing for the film had such incredible energy, humour, and storytelling abilities, that we knew we had to construct the film around that energy. We wanted the histories to unfold dramatically, with no "expert" documentary voice-overs.

TG: *One of the interesting things in the film is the balance between the women that you meet, the documentary photographs, the illustrations, and the narrative. Were all four things there at the beginning?*

LF: Strangely enough, when I look back—Becki Ross has my only copy left of the original proposal somewhere out in B.C. and I wish she'd return it—I believe we submitted our proposal with all of these elements, including the drama, very early on. We may have omitted the drama in the proposal we first submitted to the Studio, figuring that once we were funded for the documentary, we could sneak it in during the treatment phase. But it was always our desire to do the drama. It took enormous work to find the stills, newspaper clippings and stock footage at that time. We had the privilege of working with a stock and stills researcher, but Aerlyn and I did a lot of it ourselves. I remember she and I going through every single stock shot in the NFB archives indexed with the word "police." You have to remember that very little in most archives was categorized by "gay," "lesbian," or "homosexual," so we had to search through categories like "crime" or "police" for traces, and read contaminated sources like crime reports and homophobic gossip paper columns for information.

TG: *Do you remember why you wanted all of these elements in the film?*

LF: Interviews combined with photographs and stock footage are conventional documentary materials, but there hadn't been this level of visual research done for Canadian lesbian history and that was very exciting. Still, the drama and how we dealt with it were more unusual for documentary and made the film a "hybrid." I was working in the non-profit, artist-run art world, in the middle of intense debates about the politics of representation, art, sex and gender, racism, the relationship between filmmaker and audience, the lesbian imaginary, hybridity, etc. I also edited *Parallélogramme*, a national arts magazine that published contemporary art, video, and film criticism. I wanted to reflect the complexities of all those issues in the film. Aerlyn was a highly respected sound recordist in the industry, had been one of the directors of *A Winter Tan,* and wanted to move into directing. We both fell in love with the pulp novel covers, and knew we'd use them in the film. I was into the cross-pollination of popular culture with lesbian history, feminist art and film theory, and she was extremely knowledgeable about documentary filmmaking, so we made a very good team. It was an excellent collaboration.

TG: *So did you use lesbian pulp novels as a base?*

LF: Besides *The Well of Loneliness,* the lesbian pulp novels were often the first things women found with lesbian content. Paperback novels were a significant part of popular culture in the forties and fifties, and the lesbo pulp books were a sub-genre. They were displayed on book racks in drugstores and dime stores, along with westerns and detective stories. They were soft porn written for men, and the illustrations were to attract men. But women also found them, and read them for their own pleasure—even with the horrible endings. We read a lot of these novels because we wanted to find typical scenes, scenes repeated so often that they could be the representational stages of a typical coming out story. We then hijacked them for our own pleasure. We inserted them into our lesbian context, used them to make a direct address to viewers, and included those viewers in the joke of interrupting fictional desire as it is usually constructed in a feature film.

TG: *The characters, the dark-haired woman and the blonde woman?*

LF: Very typical. On a typical book cover, the butch is dark haired, the femme is blonde; there is always a bad sofa and bad table lamps. I did quite a bit of research on the illustrations. In fact, I found our illustrator through a meeting with an art editor for Harlequin Romance!

TG: *Were these books important to a lot of women?*

LF: Yes, because it was all they could find. And whether you read them or not, those books were a primary way in which stereotypes about lesbians, queers, and perverts circulated. They functioned a bit like schoolyard gossip today. Whether or not a child has ever watched *Geraldo,* the content on *Geraldo* hits the schoolyard and becomes a current of information—mostly misinformation!

TG: *Does it make any difference that they were American pulp novels? That people thought of being lesbian as a big city thing?*

LF: Yes. We found that different women had different relationships with what they read. Some of the more naïve would certainly believe that Greenwich Village was the only place lesbians lived. In the film there is a story where Reva and her lover dress in butch and femme clothes, as described in the novels, and set off to Greenwich Village to find the lesbians. They never find them—probably, Reva laughs, because they were dressed so oddly. But there are a lot of other ways that those novels, being American, inflected, probably misinformed, through details we don't even notice, readers in other countries. People might watch American programs such as *Law and Order*, and think Canadians have the same legal rights, and it's not until you get in trouble that you discover the differences.

TG: *There is a real undercurrent of class in the film, which is not emphasized, although it is suggested in the way the women talk.*

LF: Women from all classes would go to these beer parlours, but they had a working-class, even a white trash or skid row, aesthetic, so they had that rough-and-ready aspect to them. Lois is probably the most middle- to upper-middle-class woman in the film, although I don't think she comes across that way. Class is evident through the women's stories. I like that it's embedded in the fabric of the film rather than a didactic imposition.

TG: *Wasn't it her who talked of having parties with men, in hotels? Because that seemed very middle-class.*

LF: No, that was Carol. She describes a Toronto scene where gays and lesbians went to the theatre and then to snazzy hotel bars, but they went elegantly dressed and were, really, in the closet. Everyone in a certain scene might know which bar elegant gay people met at, but it wouldn't have been known outside. And this was more of a men's scene, I think, because women could not go drinking to a high-class bar without a man. They'd likely be turfed out for being prostitutes.

TG: *Well, I suppose like anyone else you move according to where you want to go. But to get back to the narrative of the film, you mention that the dark one is the butch, but she doesn't look that butch.*

LF: No, but the models didn't look like diesel dykes on those covers. Some wanted us to depict a diesel dyke, but that character was such a subgenre we didn't do it. The dark-haired woman in pants was considered and read to be butch at the time. In the post-World War II period, women were being re-contained back into skirts and very feminine clothes. So the pants were definitely a signal of butch at the time. Also, those book covers were created to attract a male readership, so both women had to look somewhat "sexy." If the butch looked too butch, it might challenge the gender power of the male reader, rather than increasing it. A woman in our research interviews reminded us that the way women commonly dress today, in jeans and a sweatshirt, was considered butch in the 1950s.

TG: *I had the impression from books such as Leslie Feinberg's* Stone Butch Blues *that women in the bars were really butch.*

LF: Some of them were, and some of them weren't, as depicted in the stories the women tell in our film. *Stone Butch Blues* is about particular American bar scenes, but we know that there were passing women and what were called "downtown" butches in some of the beer parlours and bars in Canada. But in the drama, we were playing with popular culture representations and melodrama films of the fifties, not attempting to counter them with true-to-life characters. We were thinking of an imaginary lesbian reader in the fifties picking up one of those novels and reading it, except that we gave it a happy ending for audiences in the nineties. There were reasons for that. The first was a kind of historical restitution, providing erotic pleasure for lesbian and gay viewers in the context of our historical period. We could play with these clichés or conventions, even disrupt them through the context in which the drama was placed. We wanted to distinguish the documentary reality described by the women from the popular culture characters represented in the books. We also felt that in order to represent a really tough butch character from the past in 1989, we would need more than a three-minute episodic structure. We would have reproduced a homophobic stereotype because we didn't have the time to develop character.

TG: *I'm forgetting that back in the late eighties, the lesbian culture was quite alienated from butch-femme ideas.*

LF: Joan Nestle had just published *A Restricted Country*, her ground-breaking book on butch-femme culture in New York City, and that was the beginning of a re-owning of that history. Certainly the women in the documentary describe that history—the pleasures, the contradictions, and some of the difficulties. Every decision we made was based on our privileging of a lesbian and gay audience, so we didn't whitewash stories—we felt we needed to know our history. But we also felt responsible to the people in the film and the audiences. It's different now, of course, and such a butch might work. A great many more films and images have circulated in the past ten years, and queers of all types are being commercialized, if not mainstreamed.

TG: The Forbidden Love *images look so accurate. They really look just like a pulp novel. And your ability to bleed them back and forth into the narrative is brilliant.*

LF: It looks very simple, but we pounded around about it, how it was going to read, how we were going to do it. We shot the drama last, so we could code references from the documentary into the script. We thrashed around quite a while before it came together.

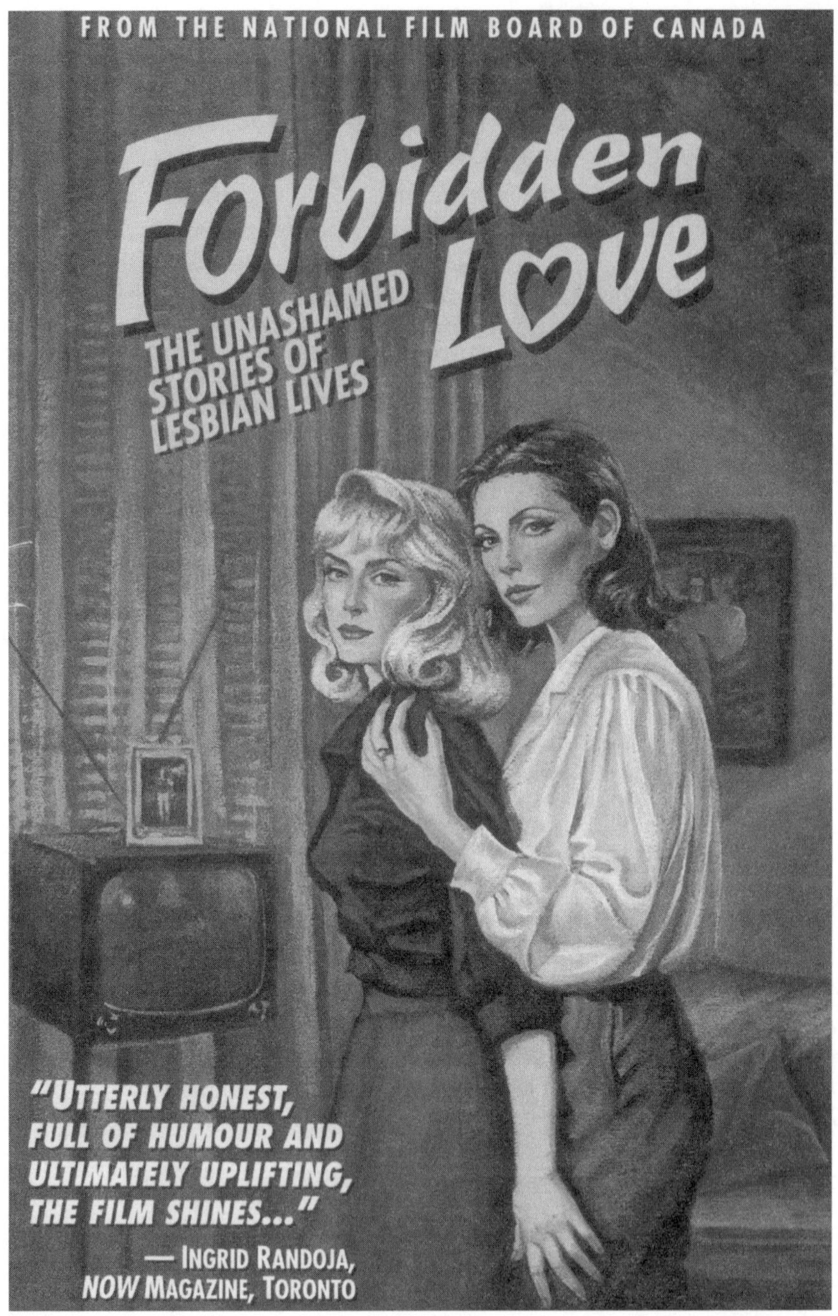

Figure 1. Image from *Forbidden Love: The Unashamed Stories of Lesbian Lives.* Courtesy Illustrator Janet Wilson, and the National Film Board of Canada.

TG: *The illustrator then went directly from the stills to see what you were after?*

LF: She's wonderful—Janet Wilson. We had choreographed the final pose of each scene to resemble a typical book cover, then had to direct the actors into the pose and freeze frame it later in the lab. We gave Janet the last frame of the drama to work with. Everything had to match exactly, but the film board had world-class people working in opticals and technicals in the lab. We were able to take advantage of these skills.

TG: *I think the balance works really well.*

LF: There was a fear at the studio that the drama would overwhelm or belittle the women's stories in the documentary. But when we shot the drama, we had seen our documentary rushes, and we knew that nothing but nothing was going to overpower the personalities and storytelling of the women in the documentary.

TG: *How did you choose them? You must have had an awful lot of women that didn't make it to the film.*

LF: We did. We did about forty or forty-five research interviews. We talked with a lot of women to get as broad a picture of the history as possible, and also looked for people who could tell the different aspects of people's experience that would, together, construct that history. They chose us as much as we chose them, in some ways, because some women couldn't be on film because of their jobs, or they didn't feel they could handle it. We never said, "It's only going to be seen in a few gay venues." We said that we didn't know but we hoped it would be on television, be seen widely, everywhere, so you have to be prepared and feel comfortable with being in it.

TG: *I have two children and I'm never sure whether I'm going to say something publicly with which they would just as soon not be associated. I don't want to do that if it can be avoided.*

LF: Many of the women shared those concerns and more. It took courage to agree to appear in the film because they would be vulnerable and recognizable to neighbours, Also, many had lived double lives. For example, Lois ran for the NDP and she has been very active in politics. She knows Bob Rae, she knows everybody—she's a lefty.

TG: *She seems as though she would be to the left of the NDP.*

LF:: The current NDP, perhaps, but not the NDP as it was twenty or thirty years ago. When *Forbidden Love* was on CBC television a year after it was released, Lois had calls from all these stunned NDP people who had no idea she had a double life in the lesbian bar while she was helping them with their campaigns. She enjoyed the notoriety of it all. But these women were very brave. Different women had different reasons for wanting to be in the film. Jean Healy, who is not a public person at all, agreed to be in the film because she wanted younger lesbians to understand what it had been like without a public movement or community.

TG: *Which one was she?*

LF: She's very droll, she used to rent a piano booth at Heintzmans to drink rye and make out with her girlfriend. She is the intellectual of the group, really. And a brat—she and a pal used to go up to the really butch butches in the bar and ask, "Are you a butch or femme? Because we are looking for a femme." This would give the butches a conniption, to be mistaken for a femme!

TG: *The one that really surprised me was the very femme woman, Ruth, the blonde. She struck me as exactly the kind of woman I would expect from having read things like* Stone Butch Blues, *but I've never met one. The femmes today are much less natural; they understand all the levels of irony.*

LF: Ruth was very much a femme in the fifties sense. She liked butches in a similar way a hetero femme fatale can seduce and manipulate her man. There is an element of that erotic pleasure in her sexuality. Femme-identified women today are not so much less "natural," as more aware of the politics of gender being different from the erotics of gender.

TG: *Have you been in touch with any of them since or have they been in touch with you?*

LF: I stayed in touch with almost all of the women for a number of years, and I've just fallen away a bit in the past three or four years. Unfortunately, Nairobi died a few years ago from a complication due to her heart transplant. Lois checked herself, and her husband Walter, into an old age home behind the Eaton's Centre. Jean is in an apartment in the east end with Phoebe, one of a batch of kittens born in my garage. Keeley is living with a new lover on some other ranch in B.C. Ruth moved to the States to be a blackjack dealer for a few years, but I think she's back in Burnaby or White Rock. I haven't heard from Reva for a number of years; she was in Victoria doing photography. Amanda is doing amazing work with First Nations youth in Vancouver, and I see her whenever I'm there. I had a couple of perfect martinis with Carol a few years ago. Stephanie is with a new lover; her daughter had a baby last year so she's a very happy grandmother.

TG: *How did you find Keeley?*

LF: We found her through a Vancouver artist named Cornelia Wyngaarden, who had done a video installation with Keeley called "As a Wife has a Cow." Cornelia had come out at the end of the era of those beer parlours and, just as we were doing research, Cornelia went to a Vanport reunion and reconnected with Keeley and Ruth. She also met a number of women she'd known in the beer parlour and helped us to do research interviews with them. A woman named Alaine Blais did the same thing for us in Montreal. And, in Toronto, Amy Gottlieb and Maureen Fitzgerald, of the Lesbians Making History group, were enormously generous with their contacts and resources.

TG: *What did you think of your relationship with history? Were you trying to get it as it was, as the women remembered it to be, as it would make the best film?*

LF: All of those things. Not "the way it really was," in a definitive sense. It's hard to do that in a 2000–page book, much less in a seventy-five-minute film. We were interested in how lesbians negotiated the different attitudes, laws, and pressures regulating sexuality, and how they remembered their experiences. So yes, it is an oral history with the pleasures and restrictions that an oral history film entail. We had a complex relationship with the notions of history, more complex than are shown in the film. We cut to convey the truth of the women's experiences and stories in film. There are details, which you would never omit in a text with a footnote structure, which we omitted in the film, as long as the "truth" of the experience wasn't misrepresented. For example, the police raid is constructed from different women's experiences of being raided at different times, and we used stock footage. An academic historian might say, well, that footage is from Montreal and that is from Toronto and that is from Vancouver! It's not historically accurate. But it is emotionally accurate, and that is also history, and we respected the ability of film to convey what these raids felt like to the women who described them.

TG: *A lot of people who do oral histories say that they're trying to get the consciousness of a person who has been there, who is now recounting it, so, in other words, it is the documentation of the mind of the person who experienced it rather than of the events.*

LF: Absolutely. That is integral to oral histories, film or text. There are issues of memory and subjectivity, and their relationship to the history of events. If you are doing oral history, you have to deal with the vicissitudes of selective memory and subjective interpretation. We researched photographs, newspaper headlines, criminal legislation, and other kinds of texts and presented them as historical context for the women's stories. But those sources are extremely homophobic, and reek of the social and moral prejudices of the time. The oral histories might not be one hundred percent accurate in factual terms, but they are accurate responses to the political temper of the times—and to the fears and the pleasures that mark women's memories.

TG: *So the research didn't contradict what these women were saying?*

LF: For example, we researched the liquor laws and how they affected social spaces. We found the photographs of a lot of bars in the B.C. Liquor Control Board archives. We used the Canadian Lesbian and Gay Archives to determine events and reports. We went through as much legal history as we could. We were in a sea of conflicting historical documents and, even more difficult, historical absences. I had a sticker with a quote from Tolstoy on my research binder that said, "History would be an excellent thing if only it were true."

TG: *Does the idea come up in the film that if you were cross-dressed, you had to wear two items of clothing of your own sex?*

LF: Yes. I forget how many items of clothing.

TG: *As I understand it, that has never been a law anywhere.*

LF: It was a law in Florida, because Robin Tyler, the lesbian comedian, was arrested under it. So it was a law in some cities and states, but it might have been used, extra legally, by the police to threaten and harass people. We never found a concrete example of that law.

TG: *That is what I understand it was, a law that police said existed but didn't exist. So the police would say, "Well, I'll arrest you." But you were not allowed to cross-dress to perform an illegal act, and if homosexuality was illegal, then they had you there anyway.*

LF: Certainly various American states had such ways of harassing queers. Most of the women we talked to were harassed for petty things, such as jaywalking. The police would hang around outside the beer parlours and harass women at the end of the night for not having enough money. When I left Vancouver in the sixties, there was a law that if you didn't have a certain amount of money on you could be considered an indigent and be arrested. The cops would use laws like this to hassle women because they were lesbian.

TG: *And as I understand it, a lot of these bars were pretty shady. The kinds of people who would allow gays and lesbians into their bars were pretty shady so there probably would have been illegal acts going on anyway.*

LF: Absolutely. Most of those bars, except a couple of clubs in Montreal, were seedy bars, and there was everything going on in there that you could imagine.

TG: *It must have been hard for some of these women just to handle that.*

LF: Some of the women we did research interviews with said they went to one of these bars and found them so dangerous, disgusting, and dirty that they never went back. Jane Rule said no working class woman who wasn't already rebelling would have been allowed to set foot inside those bars.

TG: *This is right at the end of my youth, but the bars were either "Men Only" or "Ladies and Escorts," so for gays it was easy in that sense: everywhere was a man's bar.*

LF: I think the lesbian and gay social scene really changed when the liquor laws licensed cocktail lounges. When I went to the Parkside on Yonge, most of the gay men were on the "Men Only" side. The women were in the "Ladies and Escorts" side because they didn't have "Ladies Only." So lesbians were more likely to sitting with down-and-out straight guys than with gay men.

TG: *Well, the bar in your narrative is an ideal cocktail lounge.*

LF: That is a representational bar from the books. It really is not the seedy beer parlour where the women would have met in a Canadian city. It's based on the "Greenwich Village" bar women fantasized about when they read a pulp novel.

TG: *Even the boyfriend at the beginning of the narrative, he is certainly a "representational" cowboy.*

LF: Yes, he's the typical, small-town, clean-cut boy who rescues his girlfriend from a lesbian friendship, while the "real" lesbian leaves for the city and "her own kind." We had the privilege of working with wonderful actors and a great production crew from the NFB. And we shot on 35mm film, which makes the drama look great.

TG: *What did you think was your relationship with your subjects, with the women?*

LF: There are some reasons why those women opened up to us in this particular film. It was very important that we were also gay because it assisted us in developing trust with them. These are women who lost jobs, who lost family members, who lost a lot for being lesbians—they're not the lesbian in-your-face feminist of the seventies and eighties. So we had to build up a trust factor for a number of reasons. First, people who are queer, or in marginalized groups, know that even the liberal media uses them as spectacles and victims, as shown in those pathetic documentaries about gays in the 1960s and 1970s. Second, they wanted to know how the subject would be treated. We didn't do sociological-type interviews with a set list of questions and answers during our initial research. We had our questions, but we engaged in wide-ranging conversations. We contributed our own stories in those early interviews, and women talked about a lot of things we hadn't realized were important. We had a lot of respect for them. So we got along really well with the women. We developed a relationship with Amanda for over a year before she felt okay to appear in the film.

TG: *She looks very young.*

LF: She was younger but she was at the tail end of that scene as a young woman. A number of older First Nations women who were around at that time were unavailable. Some had died; but some were doing healing work in their communities and didn't want to be outed. They just said, "It's not my issue right now." And Amanda thought a lot about whether it would be healing for young Aboriginal gays and lesbians if she were in the film, or difficult for the community. The responses she received from her father and other community members about being in the film turned out to be very positive ones.

TG: *Did you make any choices that you thought your subjects might not like? Did you worry about that when you were putting the film together?*

LF: You always do because you are taking these fabulous forty-minute interviews and cutting them down to five minutes of screen time. But we had a good relationship and could talk with our subjects about what we were up to. We felt quite allied with our subjects. On the other hand, we were responsible for presenting an oral history that was as honest and accurate as we could make it. We tried to respect the women's contributions within that framework. For example, Lois did not like the drama when she first saw it. She did not like having a sex scene in it, and she did not like Stephanie's story about being in a violent relationship. And there were some test viewers who said, "Why do you have to go into that?" But once it was all finished, and she was at the premiere, she loved it.

TG: *Stephanie's story is to my mind one of the most alive ones. She is such a vital character and you really understand why she has done what she has done. More than others who seem less visceral.*

LF: All the women seem very visceral to me! Every person I've talked to has a different woman they relate more with. Stephanie is the woman who became the minister.

TG: *All the characters are very separate. You don't get a sense of connection except that they're all of the same era.*

LF: Yes, we did that on purpose. We wanted to have people who entered the scene from different places, different life stories and backgrounds, and different opinions. But all Canadian. I experienced a particular pleasure, almost a subversive pleasure, in the women's use of Canadian street names, of wanting to hear the names of the cities, especially after reading all those pulp novels and having seen lesbian films made in the States. There has always been this thing in feature films: "We must set it in New York or Chicago because Americans won't look at it and it won't be successful outside of Canada." Aerlyn comes from Chicago—she's been here many years and Canada is her home—but I think I was

Figure 2. Lynn Adams (*Left*) as "Mitch" and Stephanie Morgenstern as "Laura" (*Right*) in *Forbidden Love.* Courtesy the National Film Board of Canada.

particularly sensitive to seeing those subtitles and hearing geographic names. I'm not sure if you notice their presence unless you've experienced the tsunami of their absence.

TG: *Have you had much of an American audience?*

LF: Huge.

TG: *Do they notice that it's in Canada?*

LF: Some people are very sensitive to it. Others, even critics and reviewers, assume that we're the fifty-first state. There was a review written about in an American academic history journal, and it was a good review, and she mentioned that it was set in Canada, but then raised all the flashpoints in American lesbian history that we hadn't covered. She clearly wasn't aware that we had beer parlours with their own peculiar regulations. She wasn't aware that although there was some influence of returned servicewomen on lesbian communities in Canada in post-World War II years, it wasn't as much as it was in the States. It happened here, and we talked with women who had military experiences, but we didn't uncover a history that showed it as a primary influence. However, if you focussed your research only on women who had been in the military, another lesbian history might emerge.

TG: *I think they had army units in the States where lesbians pretty well took over the entire battalion.*

LF: The absence of certain strands of American history bothered a few people. It was a Canadian rather than American history. The problem was more an ignorance about Canada than anything else. But in the main, American audiences loved the film and it is widely taught in film studies classes in the U.S. Women Make Movies, the U.S. distributor, is still selling a lot of videotapes.

TG: *I found Nairobi very interesting because she represented a black presence in the Montreal bar system that is still difficult for Canadians to understand but very different from the American context.*

LF: Nairobi is amazing in that sense. She is from Costa Rica and did show biz all over the world, went to Winnipeg to do a gig, and ended up in Montreal. Nairobi arrived in Canada just before increased immigration from the Caribbean and Haiti, so she was a singular presence in the lesbian bars in Montreal.

TG: *Were you self-conscious about having a Black woman, a Native woman, that kind of thing?*

LF: It was very important to us, not because women of colour were in the beer parlours or bars of the time in great numbers, but because the reasons for their absence are so important to our contemporary understanding of discrimination and inclusion. We were making the film in the early 1990s, at a time when critiques were exposing the mechanisms that reproduce conditions of racism, homophobia, and privilege. We were engaged in these issues in our work, and it was important they be addressed in the film. There is a Black lesbian history film to be made, but with the exception of a few individual stories, it's not going to be about women going to those beer parlours. It's going to be somewhere else. We tried to bring out certain stories or issues that pointed to more areas of research than the scope of our film would allow us to pursue.

TG: *Have you done a lot of Q and A's?*

LF: Not so much now, but I did. Although I still do a few.

TG: *First, what did you find in terms of reactions to Q and A's when the film was first released and secondly, what do you think the effects of the film are now, both for you personally and for the rest of the community?*

LF: The screenings at universities and festivals were fabulous when the film came out and remain so. I think it's because audiences really get pleasure from the women's stories, but also because even though women recount a certain amount of pain, we did not portray them as victims. They are, if anything, ordinary heroines, in the sense that they dealt with their lives with courage and with a great sense of humour.

TG: *Did you have victims and leave them out or did you not meet victims?*

LF: Victims are often constructed by the way you portray people's lives in a film. We all have bad things happen to us. If you focus on that one experience, instead of on a person's broader life, you will have turned her from a person who has been victimized into a "victim." Filmmakers who turn people into "victims" for audience consumption drive me nuts. This genre of pseudo-compassionate documentary disguises a politics of privilege, power, and representation; they often ooze with a smarmy kind of pity, and are built on a relation between privileged filmmaker and privileged spectator over the body of the represented "victim." I know that there are people who become victims, and it is tragic. The women in *Forbidden Love* were victimized, but they are survivors. Did we meet women who were victims? Of the forty-five we originally interviewed, I would say not. We met women who were scarred. But their lives carry on.

TG: *Stephanie was obviously scarred but she came through in a pretty tough fashion.*

LF: If you survived that era you had to be pretty spunky. In fact if you survived those bars you had to be pretty spunky. I still do Q and A's a couple of times a year and the audience has changed in ten years in what you can assume people know. For example, when I show the film in universities these days, people assume that all those pulp novels were written *for* lesbians. Ten years ago, students knew that the pulp novels were part of a seedy, male-oriented literature that women appropriated for their own pleasure even though dykes always suffered terrible things in the last chapter. Young students now don't know that. I have to mention it because otherwise people go away thinking the forties and fifties were a real golden age of lesbian literature. A lot of history books, articles, and films exist which were not available in the late 1980s, and there's a tendency for people to forget the historical moment during which we made the film. Overall, though, people still seem to enjoy the film. Students are as embarrassed by the sex scene now as they were ten years ago, and there is a big silence at the end of the film. People are not used to seeing explicit sex in a university lecture hall. So there is always a little bit of coughing and stuff. I always tell the audience that if they don't stay for the Q and A, we all know they've rushed out to rent a hotel room. Which usually causes laughter, and I think relaxes students enough to ask questions.

TG: *What do you think about the film as a statement for you?*

LF: It was a kind of gift to work on the film at that time, a confluence of timing, energy, funding, and the right fabulous people. I'm pleased that

Figure 3. Stephanie Morgenstern (*Left*) as "Laura" and Lynn Adams (*Right*) as "Mitch" in *Forbidden Love.* Courtesy the National Film Board of Canada.

Aerlyn and I were able to collaborate so well, to bring our respective strengths to the film, and to have a lot of fun doing it. And I'm grateful to have had the resources from Studio D to accomplish that level of filmmaking, and to be able to contribute it to lesbian and gay history. I guess what I personally feel best about is that we were able to take quite complex historical, political, and representational ideas and embed them in the film. My personal artistic struggle was to incorporate some of those issues in the film as essential threads of storytelling, without having people function as illustrations of them.

TG: *What issues?*

LF: There were the issues of history and oral history that we have talked about, which intersected with gay and feminist histories, and then contemporary politics: Do we leave in negative stories which might reproduce homophobic stereotypes for a mainstream audience? Who was our primary audience? We privileged lesbian and gay audiences and made our decisions in the cutting room on that basis. How do we make issues of race and class completely integral to the film, without saying "Class is . . . Race is . . ."? For example, Amanda and Nairobi had very different backgrounds than the white women in the film, and we showed more of their personal histories so that the differences in their lives would be very clear to audiences, so they weren't simply conflated with the experiences of white women. What are the ethics of making a film like this with women who are not sophisticated media critics? Are they going to be shown as victims? What are we going to leave in the cut? And, with the drama, we played with theories of spectatorship that Laura Mulvey and other feminist film theorists were debating. If women were situated as the object of the "male" gaze in cinema, as they certainly were marketing tools for men on the covers of the pulp novels, then could we disrupt this? Could we hijack those images of women on the covers and make them come alive as the subjects of their own desires, and thus make a different relationship with spectators? Will the audience share in the joke of us interrupting narrative desire with a pose that mimics a direct address and yet returns the characters to representation? How can we treat the drama to evoke melodrama, but avoid nostalgia? How do we balance the strength of the documentary with the conventions of dramatic film? I remember us thrashing each one of these issues out numerous times—and issues that I don't even remember now.

TG: *Do you feel that you left things out?*

LF: There are as many good stories on the editing room floor as there are in the film. Our favourite cut was about three-and-a-half hours.

TG: *The characters that are in the film, you didn't leave things out that might be harmful to them?*

LF: Actually, there was only one thing that someone talked about during filming and then asked that it not be used. It was an explicit statement she made about her life as a prostitute. We had material which talked about her street life, and that was okay with her, but she'd made a very explicit statement that she asked us not to use. We respected that because it was difficult enough coming out to her community. These issues are part of the ethical decision-making process in documentary filmmaking. But we certainly didn't leave anything out on the grounds that an individual would hate it, or disagree with it; we weren't collaborating in that sense, nor consulting editorially with our subjects. No one saw the film until it was completely finished. We were committed to making as strong an oral history—within the limits of the film's focus—as we could. I think one of the most important things for Aerlyn and me was not to create a nostalgia for that time as if it were perfect. And so while we wanted the energy and the spunk and the rebellion, we wanted to show some of the painful experiences the women had, too.

TG: *Did you feel a responsibility to the Canadian lesbian community, whatever that might be?*

LF: Absolutely. That's what I was saying. We felt enormously responsible to Canadian lesbians to do as good a job as possible, to make a history which was alive with desire as well as present the complex ways different women reacted in those times.

TG: *Some people talk about our communities trashing each other. Have you had any reactions that you should have made a tougher film or a more pleasant film? You mention the abuse issue.*

LF: In the world of lesbian and gay theory, I knew where it could be critiqued at the time—but you can't do everything in one film, and you can critique yourself out of doing a project if you try. We made this film as complex as we could. For example, we didn't have everyone saying, "Yeah, butch/femme was perfect." Women told different stories about their relationship to it: someone had an ironic relationship to it, someone only lived it when she went to the bar, someone who started a femme and became a butch, so we were able to bring a kind of fluidity, those multiple voices into the film. I know that one of the effects of *Forbidden Love* in Canada, and even in the States, it's become a code, to have the poster in the set of a film, as in *Better than Chocolate*. Which feels great. When I go to talk about the film at universities, etc., the students feel that they are getting in touch with their elders, who they don't have a chance to meet. Our film evokes the past. Those students tell me there is an historical need and we did a little bit to answer it.

NOTE

1. See Elizabeth Anderson's "Studio D's Imagined Community: From Development (1974) to Realignment (1986–1990)." In *Gendering the Nation: Canadian Women's Cinema*. Ed. Kay Armatage et al (Toronto: University of Toronto Press, 1999), 41–61.

buller men and batty bwoys: hidden men in toronto and halifax black communities

Wesley Crichlow

INTRODUCTION

In Jamaica, women engaging in same-sex relationships are called sodomites and/or "man royal," a term peculiar to that country. Makeda Silvera says of these labels: "Dread words. So dread, that women dare not use these words to name themselves. They were names given to women by men to describe aspects of our/their lives that men neither understood nor approved" (14).

So I would say of buller men and batty bwoys.

This project is personal, situated in my own life, but also collaborative and dependent on the assistance of other buller men and batty bwoys living in Canada. My goal is to interrogate the ways in which these names and the associated experiences shape the daily realities of English-speaking African Caribbean men living in Toronto and African Canadian men born or raised in Halifax who engage in sexual practices with other men.[1] The general *lacunae* of sociological—or any other—studies of these men necessitate this attempt to establish a framework, one which will describe the complexities of their lives, produced by intersections of race, nationalism, identity, and sexuality. This framework must discover the structures that inform and signify the indexical relationship between categories of social life and the experiences of those whom these categories seek to characterize. More particularly, how do historically specific categories of sexualized identities, interwoven with assumptions of race and nation, shape the experience of men with such identities? There are correspondences among the politico/sociocultural structures of my research subjects, myself, and the text: we need to understand, name, experience, and negotiate heterosexism and create survival spaces in various Black communities.

The complex issue of signifying a racialized and sexualized identity is raised by Audre Lorde (1994) in her critique of the application of "lesbian" as a term for Black women who engage in same-sex relationships. She asserts the cultural and historical specificity of a Caribbean same-sex identity, an identity that requires its own linguistic self-identification. Lorde suggests an alternative word: zami.[2] Remembering her Grenadian mother's life on a small island called Carriacou, Lorde states that zami is a Carriacou name for women who work together as friends and lovers. The word comes from the French patois for "Les amies," lesbians. For Lorde, "zami" signifies a cluster of meanings, associations, issues, concerns, and structures of identifications that differ from those associated with "lesbian," a term with distinct origins and associations in white Western culture. This is not to say that zami is a mono-referential term without differences. However, Lorde argues that those Black women with Caribbean and African Caribbean backgrounds who engage in same-sex relationships articulate a sexual identity different from that designated by the term "lesbian." Zami, therefore, is not just the Black equivalent of "lesbian" (a white concept) but a historically specific term that makes visible hidden experiences and newly acknowledged Black same-sex communal realities.

For Carol-Boyce Davies, the name zami implies ". . . a similar move to find new language and new starting points from which to express a reality, as is, for example, Alice Walker's definition of 'womanist' as another term of meaning for Black Feminist" (121–22).[3] Madiha Didi Khayatt also questions the universalizing assumptions behind the concept of lesbian. She states, "the incompleteness of the conceptual framework currently in use to discuss 'lesbian' identity has meant that the experiences of women whose cultures have produced different identities but similar desires are not fully recognizable under the term" (3). In other words, using a word that reduces the complex forms of social regulation and resistance that have evolved to only one, modelled by European traditions, excludes the experiences of those women it claims to describe. This critique of white Western lesbian politics by Lorde, Davies, and Khayatt is the starting point for my project on English-speaking African Caribbean and African Canadian men who engage in same-sex relations and practices. Like these authors, I am seeking appropriate language to begin to theorize Black men's same-sex practices from a non-Western viewpoint.

In this project, Black men who engage in same-sex relations will be defined as "buller men" and "batty bwoys." According to Richard Allsopp's *The Dictionary of Caribbean English Usage*, Buller man is a derogatory term used to describe same-sex male relations in Trinidad & Tobago, St. Lucia, St. Vincent, and Barbados (120). "To be a bugger; to be (male) homosexual. G said that he heard M say that C 'bulled his way through the Gold Coast in St. James'. G said that he understood the word 'bull' to mean to be a homosexual. Thus it is also to gender with the male cow. The word appears to have a different history in Barbados. Sir Denys Williams, Chief Justice of Barbados, stated in a judgement dated June 17, 1987, 'that the natural and obvious meaning those words [he bulled his way to success] to a Barbadian audience is that the plaintiff engaged in homosexual activity . . . that the plaintiff . . . had . . . committed the offense of buggery." Batty bwoy/man is used in Jamaica, Antigua, and Guyana (qtd. in Allsop, 84), to describe men who engage in same-sex relations. I have not been able to discover its etymology as I have been able to do with buller man, but an adequate history of the genesis of the term might help to enable its use in contemporary theories of African Caribbean and Black same-sex sexuality. For the purposes of this work, the terms buller man and batty bwoy will be used interchangeably to define the living, social, and political conditions of these Black same-sex men in Canada.

The vernacular character of the terms reflects the cultures. The life stories of buller men and batty bwoys are not perfect records but rather fables, or fabulous strategies, which represent selective memories of the past that they wish to share with us. Their life stories show the very notion of a sexual identity to be suspect. In this condition, in a mixed diasporic space such as Black Toronto, with its amalgam of cultures, terminology varies and even conflicts. For African Canadian men in Halifax these terms are at least at first external, learned through popular cultural musical forms (rap, reggae, hip hop, movies) and socialization with people from the Caribbean living in Halifax. African Canadian men in Halifax do not have the same associations with these terms as men with a Caribbean heritage. Still I choose to apply these terms to both the African Caribbean Canadians from Toronto and the African Canadians from Halifax in order to define a Black same-sex identity. Something concrete and significant is evoked by representing the experiences of these men as buller men and batty bwoys.

This is a group of men whose heritage is an integral part of the history, geography, political economy, and culture of the colonized English-speaking Caribbean. How they live amid the relations of the family, the workplace, and community, how they engage others for purposes of pleasure and utility, must be recognized as historically instantiated and culturally specific. In search of safety, these men negotiate their relationships within the structure of dominance that exists within Black heterosexual and homophobic communities. Heterosexist violence takes place against individuals in same-sex relations in many communities, not just Black ones, but there is a specificity to that violence in Black communal settings. The act of identifying oneself as a buller man or batty bwoy places an individual, historically and geographically, in proximity to a specific set of narratives, images, and values. This naming ties identity to the history of the people in the Caribbean, to a historical, cultural, collective, and personal sense of ancestral heritage, language, body gestures, and memory that is specific to African Caribbean men engaging in same-sex relations. To recall Lorde's zami, not "gay" or even homosexual—but buller men and batty bwoys.[4]

THE INVISIBLE MEN

The lack of literature by or about buller men and batty bwoys in Canada marks the buller as analogous to the *Invisible Man* in Ralph Ellison's 1947 classic novel of the same name. A buller is not seen or heard, even though he exists. In Canada, bullers experience a triple form of oppression: racism and heterosexism within white society; racism and the sexualization of racism within the white gay community; and heterosexism within the Black community. Given the paucity of written literature, little is known about how buller men negotiate their identities within Canadian societies. Denial of heterosexist privilege, combined with white racial privilege, has led to a void in social science literature. There have been few opportunities in Canada for bullers and batty bwoys who are cultural workers to publish. Like their heterosexual brothers, white gay academics continue to write as if they have access to everybody's experience and emotions, instead of offering bullers an opportunity to depict us. In our ethnic communities, where the subject of same-sex relations is treated as taboo or a form of gender inversion, we are denied the luxury of writing and researching.

As C. Chan has observed, while studies of lesbian and gay experience in North America have expanded in the last two decades, they have most often been studies of the white, middle-class experience (16–18). Instead, studies such as B. Green note the complex interrelations between racial identity and the many factors that create sexual orientation, many of which surface in language (243–251).[5] Blacks and Whites have different epistemologies and therefore language signifies differently for each. For Mikhail Bakhtin, language has its own embedded history and memory. He states:

> Language has been completely taken over, shot through, with intentions and accents. . . . All words have the "taste" of a profession, a genre, a tendency, a party, a particular work, a particular person, a generation, an age group, day and hour. Each word tastes of the context and contexts in which it has lived its socially charged life; all words and forms are populated by intentions. (293)

To define oneself as a buller man or batty bwoy accepts a set of communicative relationships in which the parties share a history and parlance that define a mutual place within a shared linguistic culture. These terms are full of specific intentions, suggesting picaresque constructions and surreal scenes. They arise from a mother tongue, a language with a history that is instituted before our birth and remains after our death. Its patterns can be filled with one's own motivation and cultural context. Speakers fill language with intentions, occupy it for the span of their lives and leave it for other users. In essence, there is a historical, cultural, linguistic, collective, and personal sense of ancestral heritage and memory for men of English-speaking, African Caribbean heritage, which appears in their conduct. There is a need to reframe sexualized identity through a language that incorporates some historical specificity and that makes visible who people are. Jean Bernabe, Patrick Chamoiseau, and Raphael Confiant, writing on the importance of oral inscriptions and the ethnic self as it pertains to Creole language, argue that:

> Taking over oral tradition should not be considered as a backward mode of nostalgic stagnation. . . . To return to it, yes, first in order to restore this cultural continuity . . . without which it is difficult for collective identity to take shape. To return to it, yes, in order to enrich our enunciation, to integrate it and go beyond it. . . . We may then, through the marriage of our trained senses, inseminate Creole in the new writing. In short, *we shall create a literature,* which will obey all demands of modern writing while taking roots in the traditional configurations of our orality. (896)

"Buller man" and "batty bwoy" have not yet been reworked by their objects in Black communities to connote positive affirmations and identities as words such as "queer," "fag," and "gay" have done in the White communities. This project attempts to do just this by expanding the theoretical tradition established by Audre Lorde, Madiha Khayatt, Cherrie Moraga, Gloria Anzaldua, Kobena Mercer, Isaac Julien, and other "gay and lesbian" activists and academics, and also to make buller men and batty bwoys subjects, not objects, of the sexualized exotic—dangerous and violent, but still visible in only two dimensions. Examples of the Black male as exotic and sexually racialized can be easily found in most male same-sex magazines or in Robert Mapplethorpe's photographs of Black men. Isaac Julien and Kobena Mercer argue that Mapplethorpe shows Black + Male = aesthetic, erotic object. Regardless of the sexual orientation of the artist or spectator, this system of images suggests that the essential truth of Black masculinity lies in the domain of sexuality (143). Within the process of show and tell, the Black male body loses human agency and is diffused by a process of commodification that strips it of dignity, self-worth, and voice.

SHIFTING THE GAYS

For many Black men engaged in same-sex relationships in the Caribbean and in North America, the terms "gay" and "queer" conjure stereotypical images of a population that is characteristically White, effeminate, weak, and affluent. These descriptors can actually efface, rather than affirm, the socio-political and cultural history they experience, such as the interrelations of colonialism, racism, sexism, and imperialism that play an underlying role in social construction. Essex Hemphill comments that:

> The post-Stonewall white gay community of the 1980's was not seriously concerned with the existence of Black gay men except as sexual objects. . . . It has not fully dawned on white gay men that racist conditioning has rendered many of them no different from their heterosexual brothers in the eyes of Black gays and lesbians. (xviii)

Same-sex activism within white western society has embraced "queer" as a term that signifies political activism, identity, and social practice. Queer has become a way of renaming and re-appropriating a historically negative concept and affirming same-sex identifications. It has also posited same-sex practitioners in Western societies as an ethnic group, using arguments that support the creation of a flag, language, and community. These claims are similar to those that have been used historically to define ethnic minority groups through language, custom, and food. Commenting on the use of the word queer as a style of "Americocentrism"[6] in gay politics, queer activism, and social justice, Michael Warner posits that the term is "thoroughly embedded in modern Anglo-American culture, does not translate easily and is a politically unstable. Queer dates from the George Bush, Margaret Thatcher, and Brian Mulroney era" (xxi). I became familiar with the concept of queer after migrating to Canada and socializing primarily with White gays and lesbians in this country. I cannot recall how many times I was confused when they (my White friends) would use North American political and cultural expressions to talk about their gay and lesbian lives.[7] In Trinidad, the word "gay" was used only in the less specific version employed in standard English, to express a sense of happiness, or people having a fun time, as is demonstrated in Trinidadian writer Raoul Pantin's 1990 book *Black Power.* Pantin, writing on the aftermath of the February, 1990 Black power revolution, states, ". . . and for all the Black Power Rhetoric, the crowd still seemed in a gay, lighthearted mood" (58). Further, Samuel Johnson, in *The Economist,* June 29, 1996, captioned a cartoon with the following: "Avoid unwanted Carnival Babies. A few days of gay abandon can mean a lifetime of regret. Go to your family planning clinic!" (88). In the Caribbean, it was usual to hear our parents use the terms "gay" and "queer" to describe the behaviour of people who behaved "happily," "partied it up," or were "crazy" or "insane." But the inappropriateness of these terms for bullers, including those living in or leaving from the Caribbean, Africa, and Asia, has not been a concern for members of the White gay and lesbian movement.

The inapplicability of North American, Western or European homosexual concepts such as "queer," "fruit," "lesbian," and "gay" to Caribbean and other Black identified bullers is an important distinction to make in establishing the political, cultural, and racial grounding of Black same-sex loving. Questions of class and colonial discourses are also important elements in this debate. The writer James Baldwin, although born a Black American, often spoke of his discomfort with the term "gay." When asked if he felt like a stranger in gay America, Baldwin responded:

> Well, first of all I feel like a stranger in America from almost every conceivable angle except, oddly enough, as a Black person. The word "gay" has always rubbed me the wrong way. . . . I simply feel it's a word that has very little to do with me, with where I did my growing up. I was never at home in it. (150)

Interestingly, his insistent rejection of this label closely parallels what the Black men interviewed expressed. The literature used by many theorists and activists in North America does not address the Americocentrism and colonialism inherent in the gay and lesbian movement. Neither does the literature produced by Black American gay activists address the concerns of bullers and batty bwoys in the Caribbean or non-American parts of the Diaspora.

SHAME AND CONTRADICTION IN BLACK CULTURAL FRAMEWORKS

While renaming social-sexual practices within Black cultural frameworks is an important aspect of affirming a self-identification, the rejection by those very frameworks is an ever-present problem. The renaming, in the form of "coming out," can be a humiliating and a contradictory experience. Black male nationalists such as Amiri Baraka, Louis Farrakhan, and Eldridge Cleaver are obsessed with "gayness" as a "white man's disease."[8] Dr. Llaila O. Afrika, in his book *African Holistic Health,* views "gayness" as a disease. He also argues that " 'western man' " (white man) is the victim of AIDS" and further that "those Black men who follow western sexual perversions are AIDS victims" (32). According to this Black nationalist, not only is the buller man diseased, he is also AIDS-ridden. Furthermore, for some, "gayness" is interpreted as a sign of European decadence or of weak masculinity. In this context, men who participate in sexual relationships with other men are often regarded as race traitors. It is important to note that this oppressive view held by some Black intellectuals and leaders has been a major influence in creating shame and contradiction in the psyches of the censured and in marginalizing their lived realities in same-sex relationships. These leaders appeal to a fairly large percentage of Black populations in North America and the Caribbean, and their ideas are circulated and embraced by many who believe in their work.

The negative connotations associated with the terms buller man and batty bwoy still remain in Black Caribbean communities. While men may identify with these terms, if they are culturally unspeakable, they may not want to be publicly identified as such. There is no question that the Caribbean origins of buller man and batty bwoy contain venomous connotations. As lesbian activist and scholar Jewelle Gomez, has written, "it's very difficult to cleave to that negativeness" (qtd. in Clarke, 63). So why do some men still desire to be identified as bullers and batty bwoys? The refusal of erasure attempts to change the semantic and affective meanings of the terms and provides culturally specific Black and Caribbean language consistent with lived reality. In addition, these terms provide a point of self-reference. As linguistic markers, they specifically identify a particular set of associations that define the parameters for many men from English-speaking African Caribbean backgrounds. More specifically, these terms have historical, cultural, and linguistic contexts and identities. These words, when used against a person suspected of practicing same-sex loving and sexual relations, carried and asserted a certain public and familial shame. This shaming often results in feelings of uncleanness, guilt, and isolation. But the acceptance of the terms by bullers overcomes the isolation and helps to overcome the shaming.

In Black communal settings particular bodily practices are morally regulated. A part of this regulation leads to Black nationalist labelling of the buller man as "diseased," "a race traitor," "feminine," and "sick," but religious practices play similar roles. Black nationalism and Christianity have marked these sexual inscriptions as evils embedded within Black communal structures. These two Black guiding ideological principles offer powerful signifiers about appropriate sexuality, about the kind of sexuality that presumably imperils the race/nation and about the kind of sexuality that is beneficent to Black families, the Black nation, and Black nationalism. [9] Shame, then, is grounded in Black ideological logic that gets translated into claims of what constitutes "a good Black nationalist" or "good Black Christian." However, it ranges still wider than that. In a January 1993 article in *The Village Voice* on buller men and batty bwoys in New York City, Peter Noel states that: "Legend has it that the Buller man is cursed with a Jumbie, an evil spirit sent by the Obeah man. Bullers can only become 'straight,' so the legend goes, when the Obeah man himself is lured with bark, calabash, Julie mango and angel hair trapped in a rum bottle under a silk cotton tree."

In Trinidad, Jumbie is an evil spirit of the dead that assumes human forms and sheds its skin at night in order to raid the abode or steal the voice of living persons, an operation which it must complete before daybreak comes, when it must hide (Allsopp, 317–18). The Jumbie is supposed to be a ghost, a misçhievous or malevolent spirit, creature or person that functions at night (Mendes, 71). In some Caribbean islands, the Obeah man or woman is seen as a person to be feared, dealing with evil spirits, the "Jumbie," opposed to God, Christianity, and biblical teachings. White colonialists failed to understand religious practices (Obeah and Shango) brought to the Caribbean from Africa by enslaved Africans. They Christianized (or in their terms "civilized") the Africans so that they could understand Black slaves' forms of resistance to white domination. John Mbiti, in *Traditional African Religions and Philosophies*, for example, argues that terms such as superstition, witchcraft, and magic are often applied to African world-views:

> Most [traditional] peoples . . . believe that the spirits are what remains of human beings when they die physically. This then becomes the ultimate status. . . . Man [or a woman] does not and need not, hope to become a spirit: [s]he is inevitably to become one, just as a child will automatically grow to become an adult. (69)

Mbiti states that African religions reject the socially constructed dichotomies between sacred and secular, spiritual, and political, which are prevalent within western societies.

While there are many negative views of these African-descended beliefs, Obeah and the Obeah man are often reaffirmed in Black Caribbean culture as associated with spiritual evils but are also able to cure them. According to Allsopp, "Obeah is a system of secret beliefs, in the use of supernatural forces to attain or defend someone from evil." It uses herbs, candles, incense, and poisons aimed at mystical healing, harming or charming. The Obeah man or woman is a person (*who wo'k's obeah)* "who carries out the practice of Obeah as a secret profession and has paying clients" (412). To be cured from being a buller, you must pay the Obeah man a fixed sum of money, for which this spiritual healing is done over a couple of days or weeks. Its unusual power is often sought in any situation in which there is some deviation from normal behaviour that can be seen as demonic. The Obeah man or woman, then, is the ultimate force that could cure a buller or batty bwoy from evil temptations. Thus, the shaming of buller men and batty bwoys is embedded within specific referential cultural markers and practices that emanate from collective memories of African Caribbean religion.

BLACK COMMUNAL STRUCTURES ENTERING THE CRITIQUE

It is often hard to sustain meaningful dialogue between members of heterogeneous Black communities, heterogeneous in terms of various views of family history, class, and sexual orientation. Even in the absence of overt homophobia, men who engage in same-sex practices are overlooked or forced into the homogeneity of the Black nation, Black family, and Black communal structure, leaving no room for difference or visibility. Hence the reference to "hidden men" in the subtitle of this essay. Giving these men a voice might make Black communities more accepting of buller men's and batty bwoys' lived conditions.

It is not my intention to represent Black communities as more heterosexist and barbaric, lacking in logic, compassion, social justice, and sensitivity to human rights, than other communities. Rather, I wish to recognize that, at present, bullers and batty bwoys are *persona non grata* and instead must push the community to revise the "normative frames of reference of Black identity" that allow the buller-bashing rhetoric presented by performers Buju Banton and Shabba Ranks and religious leader Minister Louis Farrakhan. This will take the form of what Paulo Freire calls "a social praxis . . . [t]hat is helping to free human beings from the oppression that strangles them in their objective reality" (125). The oppressiveness of racism, sexism, classism, and heterosexism are intricately linked for buller men and batty bwoys. Despite the different patterns oppression takes, many of its machinations follow the "blame the victims" syndrome. All of these "isms" deny bullers and batty bwoys their human agency. They regulate, oppress, deny, and suppress the fantasies, differences, desires, and practices of bullers. Institutions such as the Black church, Black nationalism, and the Black family are the triple pillars obstructing progress on the issue of Black same-sex loving. As Lorde states, compulsory heterosexuality ". . . operates from the premise that heterosexuality is the 'norm' or privileged practice and any other form of human sexual, or emotional existence is deviant, sick or abnormal" (*Sister*, 28). The "othering" of same-sexers by the Black community is often interpreted by other communities as an indication that we are more heterosexist and homophobic than they are. But Black heterosexist analysis is based on race first, which, in essence, is reductive politicking. The ongoing debate about race, racism, sexuality, and gender within various Black communities continues to view race as absolute, while all other identities such as gender, age, ability, and sexual orientation are put aside or completely ignored. The argument made is that "the white man" (racism as gender specific) sees colour and does not see sexual identity or orientation. Here, race and racism are manipulated to subsume Black same-sex desires, and made to blur and suppress all interplay between same-sex desires, gender, and racism. Craig Owens has argued that "homophobia is not primarily an instrument for oppressing a sexual minority; it is, rather, a powerful tool for regulating the entire spectrum of male relations" (221). The male sex-role ideology, Charles Socarides argues, "embodies the competitive egocentricity of the capitalist market system, that further militates against the solidarity of the homoerotic bond which threatens the atomizing methods of domination" (228). The regulatory forces of heterosexism, as lived through racism, deny Black men the opportunity to be affectionate, emotional, or compassionate with their women and their children, much less with each other. This is a power paradigm firmly ensconced in a heritage of brutality.

Many of the men I interviewed voice the pain of having been silenced or excluded because they were perceived as "being different," "not masculine enough," or "not Black enough." Black structures of dominance are felt in many ways, including public shame, loneliness, and exclusion from Black communal living. In using the phrase "structures of dominance," I am referring to the myriad ways in which bullers and batty bwoys are marginalized in epistemic, if not physical, violence. Nikki Giovanni reminds us of the symptomatic and cathartic violence that must be challenged in order to transform Blacks from victims into active subjects. Structures of dominance are created by the hegemonic discourses of a well-articulated Black cultural formation, produced by Black consciousness and collective struggle. "Collective struggle" is a set of practices that are organized to solve historic problems in the struggle for self-determination through Black community life, especially attempts to promote Black liberation, nationalism, and decolonization. Within these processes, social forms become projects of moral regulation, which establish norms of what is "proper" within Black communities (27–28).

Michel Foucault suggests that structures of dominance and oppressive conditions are always locally contested within discursive fields:

> The power to control a particular field resides in claims to scientific knowledge embodied not only in writing but also in disciplinary and professional organizations, in institutions (hospitals, prisons, schools, factories) and in social relationships (doctor/patient, teacher/student, employer/employee, parent/child, husband/wife). Discourse is thus contained or expressed in organizations and institutions as well as in words; all of these constitute texts or documents to be read. (67)

In Black communities, a variety of "discursive fields of force" compete with one another for legitimacy, but the Black church and groups devoted to promoting a Black nationalist identity dominate the discursive fields which act as moral regulators of everyday life. As Philip Corrigan states:

> Moral regulation through its reproduction of particular (proper, permitted, encouraged) forms of expressions fixes (or tries to fix) particular signs, genres, repertoires, codes, as normal representations of 'standard' experiences which represent human beings as far more standardly 'equal' than they can be in fact. (111)

In Toronto's Black communities, "moral regulation" is articulated and legitimated by a heterosexist alliance that includes not just intellectuals, activists, and religious leaders, but entertainers and clothing designers. They assume that "the Black political project" requires a Black national identity that silences sexual difference to produce a common identity into which all Blacks must fit. In this context, "Black Masculinity," under the disguise of a universal Black culture, will always erase Black male same-sex eroticism. Community activists and academics, like Molefi Kete Asante, seek the legitimization and celebration of Kwanzaa as a sharing for all Black people, but it asserts a unity for Black heterosexual nuclear families, with Black heterosexual men and women loving each other in procreative ways.[10] Same-sex practices are represented as part of the external, a white man's disease.

CONCLUSION

If, as Foucault claims, nothing is pre-discursive, then it is essential that the recognized discourse of Black culture incorporate all possibilities within that discourse. H. Nigel Thomas's novel *Spirits In The Dark* begins to address a discourse of exclusion based on "normative" ways of Black sexuality, by developing a language derived from anti-imperial discourses, violence, post-coloniality, and sexuality, while critiquing contemporary Caribbean homophobic communal societies. This study extends that beginning, but it also joins and extends other discourses, such as those by dissenting same-sex and anti-heterosexist writers such as Lorde, Gomez, B. Smith, Hemphill, Mercer, Cheryl Clarke, bell hooks, E. Hardy, and Baldwin; and filmmakers like Marlon Riggs, Parbita Parmar, Issac Julien, and Cheryl Dunyne. They have challenged and informed my understanding of Black same-sex identities, difference, and nationalism and have influenced my attempts to develop a non-hierarchical approach to Black nationalism and Black consciousness. Riggs, for example, suggests that a hierarchy of identities on Black issues is problematic, since all characteristics can be "both nurturing and nourishing of your spirit. You can embrace all of that lovingly equally" (191).

I join Audre Lorde's exhortation to:

> Commit ourselves to some future that can include each other and to work toward that future with the particular strengths of our individual identities. And in order to do this, we must allow each other our differences at the same time as we recognize our sameness. ("Sister" 142)

For some African Canadian and African Caribbean men, engaging in same-sex relations involves a denial of self and sexuality in order to be accepted in or become a part of Black communal solidarity and Black familial expectations. They—or rather we—suffer the public and communal violence that is associated with being labelled "weak," "buller man," "batty bwoy," "feminine," or "race traitors." These men's negotiations are not free from the gender trappings of sexism and sexual oppression, because sexual oppression is about traditional roles. I am a buller man who affirms a Black, same-sex, nationalistic politic attempting to make sense of how Black men experience domination through Black nationalistic political discourse. This discourse is not simply abstract politics, but implicates Black men in the process. This needs to be radically challenged and transformed.

By us.

NOTES

1. English-speaking African Caribbean here refers to Caribbean peoples from Trinidad & Tobago, Jamaica, Guyana, Barbados, Bahamas, St. Lucia, and Grenada. Absent in fact, but not in spirit, from this project are the Spanish, Dutch, French and Papiamento-speaking Caribbean peoples.
2. *Zami: A New Spelling Of My Name.* Freedom, CA: The Crossing Press, 1994.
3. For Alice Walker, "Womanist" embraces a spiritual function while acknowledging same-sex love among women. She thus attempts to avoid isolating same-sex practices from the signification of the term "woman." Alice Walker, *The Color Purple* (New York: Simon & Schuster, 1992).
4. Some might see the word "homosexual" as scientific and thus not ethnocentric. Still, it has a particular origin in the study of sexuality, used to define a particular sexual practice as a pathological identity. Michel Foucault, using Carl Westphal's 1870, *Archiv Fur Neurlogie,* argues that the very construct of the word homosexual comes from the medical community constituted as a disease and then is transformed legally and politically into a crime (Foucault, 43). These connections show the social specificity of this word that most people in the West take for granted as having a universal meaning. That specificity erases its applicability in the present context.
5. Sexual orientation, according to Simpson (1994), refers to an individual's predisposition to experience physical and affectional attraction to members of the same, the other, or both sexes. Established early in life, it is the result of a little understood but complex set of genetic, biological, and environmental factors.
6. I borrow this concept from Paul Gilroy's article "It's a Family Affair" (1992). As Gilroy suggests, America sees itself as the centre of the universe and thus able to set the frames of reference for everyone else. In this case, Black same-sex subjectivity must develop a politic through white American gay political frames of reference.
7. None of the typical terms such as "queer," "fruit," "diesel dyke," "drag queen" or "gay" was used by my friends or me when I lived in Trinidad during the 1970s and 1980s.
8. According to Wahneema Lubiano, Black nationalism, in its broadest sense, is a sign, an analytic, describing a range of historically manifested ideas about Black American possibilities that include any or all of the following: racial solidarity, cultural specificity, religious, economic, and political separatism. (This last has been articulated as a possibility both within and without U.S. territorial boundaries.) (234).
9. Nation here derives from the Latin word *natio* meaning birth, race, people, nation, or to be born. Hence Black nationalism and the Black nation may not be geographically specific but rather are used to refer to Africa as "motherland," the place of birth to which Blacks must turn for salvation.

10. Kwanzaa is an African American celebration, celebrated from December 26 through January 1. It is based on the agricultural celebrations in Africa called "the first fruits," which were times of harvest, requiring reverence, commemoration, recommitment, and celebration. There are seven principles to Kwanzaa: Umoja (unity), Kujichagalia (self determination,) Ujima (collective work and responsibility,) Ujama (cooperative economics), Nia (purpose), Kuumba (creativity), and Imani (faith). These constitute a moral code that is perceived to oppose same-sex practices.

WORKS CITED

Afrika, Llaila. *African Holistic Health.* New York: A&B Publishers, 1989.

Allsopp, Richard. *The Dictionary of Caribbean English Usage.* London: Oxford University Press, 1996.

Anzaldua, Gloria. *Borderlands/La Frontera: The New Mestiza.* San Francisco: Spinsters/Aunt Lute, 1987.

Asante, Molefi. *Afrocentricity.* Trenton, NJ: Africa World Press, 1988.

Bakhtin, Mikhail, M. "Discourse in The Novel." In *The Dialogic Imagination.* Eds. Michael Holquist and Caryl Emerson. Austin: University of Texas Press, 1981.

Baldwin, James. *Nobody Knows My Name: More Notes of a Native Son.* New York: The Dial Press, 1961.

Baraka, Amiri. *Home: Social Essays.* New York: Morrow, 1966.

Bernabe, Jean, Patrick Chamoiseau and Raphael Confiant. "In Praise of Creoleness," trans. Mohammed B. Taleb Khyar, *Callaloo 13* (1990): 895–900.

Chan, C. "Asian Lesbians: Psychological Issues in the Coming Out Process." *Asian American Psychological Association Journal* 12 (1987): 16–18.

Clarke, Cheryl. "Lesbianism: An act of Resistance." In *This Bridge Called My Back.* Eds. Cherrie Moraga and Gloria Anzaldua. New York: Kitchen Table, Women of Color Press, 1983.

Clarke, Cheryl, Jewel Gomez, Evelynn Hammonds, Bonnie Johnson, and Linda Powell. "Black Women on Black Women Writers: Conversations and Questions," *Conditions* 9 (Spring 1983): 130–140.

Cleaver, Eldridge. *Soul on Ice.* New York: McGraw-Hill, 1968.

Corrigan, Philip. "Social Forms: Human Capacities." In *Essays in Authority and Difference.* New York: Routledge, 1990.

Crichlow, Wesley. "Buller Men and Batty Bwoys: Hidden Men in Toronto and Halifax Black Communities" Dissertation. Toronto: OISE, 1999.

Davies, Carol-Boyce. *Black Women, Writing & Identity: Migrations of the Subject.* New York: Routledge, 1994.

Ellison, Ralph. *Invisible Man.* New York: Vintage Books, 1947.

Farrakhan, Louis. Public Speech on The Nation of Islam and Blacks In The United States. Buffalo Convention Center, Buffalo. New York, 1990.

Foucault, Michel. *The History of Sexuality: Volume 1.* New York: Vintage Books, 1980.

Freire, Paulo. *The Politics of Education: Culture, Power and Liberation.* South Hadley, MA: Bergin & Garvey, 1985.

Gilroy, Paul. "It's A Family Affair." In *Black Popular Culture.* A Project by Michelle Wallace. Ed. Gina Dent. Seattle: Bay Press, 1992.

Giovanni, Nikki. "The True Import of Present Dialogue: Black vs. Negro." *Black Graphics International* 3 (1969): 27–28.

Green, B. "Ethnic-Minority Lesbians and Gay Men: Mental Health and Treatment Issues." *Journal of Consulting and Clinical Psychology* 62 (1994): 243–251.

Hemphill, Essex. *Brother To Brother: New writings by Black Gay Men.* Boston: Alyson Publications, 1991.

hooks, bell. *Race Looks: Race and Representation.* Boston: South End Press. 1992.

Johnson, Samuel. *The Economist.* June 29th, 1996.

Julien, Isaac and Kobena Mercer. "Race, Sexual Politics and Black Masculinity: A Dossier." In *Male Order: Unwrapping Masculinity.* Eds. Rowena Chapman and Jonathan Rutherford. London: Lawrence and Wishart, 1988.

Julien, Isaac. *Looking For Langston.* Courtesy of the British Film Institute, London, 1989.

Khayatt, Madiha-Didi. Work in progress unpublished paper on Egyptian Women's Identity. 1995.

Lee, Don (Haki. R. Madhubuti). *Don't Cry, Scream.* Detroit: Broadside Press, 1969.

Lorde, Audre. *Sister Outsider.* Trumansburg, NY: Crossing Press, 1984.

———. *Zami: A New Spelling of My Name.* Freedom, CA: The Crossing Press, 1994.

Lubiano, Wahneema, ed. *The House That Race Built: Black Americans, U.S. Terrain.* New York: Pantheon Books, 1997.

Mbiti, John. *Traditional African Religions and Philosophies.* London: Heinemann, 1969.

Mendes, John. *Cote Ce Cote La: Trinidad & Tobago Dictionary.* Port of Spain, Trinidad: The College Press, 1985.

Mercer, Kobena. *Welcome to the Jungle: New Positions In Black Cultural Studies.* New York: Routledge, 1994.

Noel, Peter. "Buller Man and the Obeah." *Village Voice* 38.2 (January 1993).

Owens, Craig. "Outlaws: Gay Men in Feminism." In *Men In Feminism.* Eds. Alice Jardine and Paul Smith. London, Methuen, 1987.

Pantin, Raoul. *Black Power Day: The 1970 February Revolution, A Reporter's Story.* Santa Cruz, Trinidad & Tobago: Hautey Productions, 1990.

Riggs, Marlon T. *Tongues Untied.* San Francisco: Frameline, 1989.

———. "Interview." In *Brother to Brother: New Writings by Black Gay Men.* Ed. Essex Hemphill. Boston: Alyson Publications, 1991.

———. *Black Is Black Ain't.* A Presentation of the Independent Television Service: California Newsreel, 1995.

Silvera, Makeda. "Man Royals and Sodomites: Some Thoughts on the Invisibility of Afro-Caribbean Lesbians." In *A Piece Of My Heart: A Lesbian Of Colour Anthology.* Ed. Makeda Silvera. Toronto: Sister Vision Press, 1991.

Simpson, B. "Opening Doors: Making Substance Abuse and Other Services More Accessible to Lesbian, Gay and Bi-sexual Youth." Central Toronto Youth Services, 1994.

Socarides, Charles W. *Beyond Sexual Freedom.* New York: International Universities Press, 1975.

Smith, Barbara, ed. *Home Girls: A Black Feminist Anthology.* New York: Kitchen Table Press/Women of Color Press, 1983.

Thomas, H. Higel. *Spirits In The Dark.* Toronto: House of Anansi Press, 1993.

Walker, Alice. *The Color Purple.* New York: Simon and Schuster, 1982.

Warner, Michael. *Fear of a Queer Planet: Queer Politics and Social Theory.* Minneapolis: University of Minnesota Press, 1993.

"family" as a site of contestation: queering the normal or normalizing the queer?

Michelle K. Owen

LET THEM EAT CAKE

"It's normal to be queer."

This heading appears above one of the feature articles in the January 6, 1996 issue of *The Economist* on "the global emergence of ordinary gayness." The article characterizes homosexuality as an orientation, and a neutral, even banal, one at that, i.e., the sexual equivalent of being left-handed.[1] Furthermore, the article portrays same-sex relationships in a positive, albeit mundane, light. The cover of the issue, which bears the title "Let Them Wed," portrays two white male figurines wearing tuxedos and holding hands on top of a wedding cake. In many respects, it is astonishing that a prominent right-wing British journal chose to devote so much space to the topic of lesbian and gay relationships. The editors go so far as to call for an end to the exclusively heterosexual nature of marriage ("Moreover," 68–69).

In response to the conservative charge that "marital anarchy" may ensue if same-sex marriage is legalized, another article in the issue assures readers that "countless homosexual couples, especially lesbian ones, have shown that they are as capable of fidelity, responsibility and devotion as heterosexual couples. . . ." Furthermore, this article states, "permitting gay marriage could reaffirm society's hope that people of all kinds settle down into stable unions." The article concludes that same-sex partnerships are neither frivolous nor dangerous. Rather, they must be encouraged by the state because they benefit society. For example, stable unions provide people (especially women) with a more secure economic base, keep people happier and healthier, and are a "great social stabilizer of men" ("Leader," 13–14). One of the great effects of marriage is that it keeps people from depending on social assistance. So, therefore, queers are normal, and could become even more normal if their relationships received official recognition, especially in the form of marriage.

In this essay, I interrogate the notion that families headed by same-sex couples "normalize the queer," and ask whether such relationships do not also "queer the normal."[2] My focus will be on current contestations of "family" in political and theoretical realms. To this end, I will examine the Canadian legal landscape, critically review assimilationist/anti-assimilationist debates, and contrast works that strive to disrupt heteronormative family discourse.

NORMALIZING THE QUEER

In the 1990s, Canadian lesbian and gay activism was primarily centred on making same-sex relationships the legal equivalent of heterosexual common-law relationships. In the year 2000, this has been achieved, and the floodgates are open for same-sex marriage. In what follows, I will trace some of the events that posed challenges to "family." The Ontario New Democratic Party (NDP) introduced omnibus legislation in 1994 designed to change the definition of "spouse" in the provincial Human Rights Code (HRC) and over fifty Acts. In this historic moment, a governing body attempted to argue that families headed by same-sex couples were normal and as such worthy of family rights and responsibilities. The Equality Rights Statute Amendment Law (Bill 167) was defeated on second reading.[3]

The government as a whole was not supportive of the proposed legislation, and a number of Members of Provincial Parliament (MPP), including some from the NDP, actively opposed what they perceived as an attack on "the traditional family." Anxiety ran particularly high in regard to adoption.[4] Moreover, many people both within and without the political realm believed that Bill 167 threatened the sanctity of marriage. This misconception took hold despite the fact that the Attorney General emphasized that legal matrimony was outside the bounds of the legislation. Despite the backlash, and the subsequent defeat of the bill, the introduction of same-sex spousal recognition legislation proved to be significant on a number of levels. The existence of same-sex headed families, for instance, confronted the mainstream on a daily basis by way of the mass media. And, as Becki Ross notes: "[T]hese fiercely competing positions approach the character of an informal referendum on homosexuality, sexual liberation, and the family" (226).

In the aftermath of Bill 167, activists turned to the courts to fill the void left by politicians. One year later, in 1995, four lesbian couples in Toronto won the right to apply for adoption of the children they were co-parenting. The judge ruled that the couples were "spouses" and "parents" as defined in the Child and Family Services Act (CFSA) and the Family Law Act (FLA).[5] This judgment was endorsed by a higher court a few months later.[6] In the same period, the Supreme Court of Canada ruled in *Egan v. Canada* that sexual orientation was a protected analogous ground under Section 15 of the Charter of Rights and Freedoms, and that this protection extends to same-sex partnerships. According to barbara findlay, this judgment was significant, because it meant that governments would have to justify all legislation that excluded lesbians and gay men and their children.[7]

In 1995, another case regarding the definition of "spouse" was heard in an Ontario court. The issue in *M. v. H.* revolved around support. The plaintiff ("M.") wanted the right to sue her ex-partner ("H.") and argued that the definition of "spouse" found in section 29 of the FLA was exclusionary and unconstitutional.[8] The courts ruled in "M."s favour in 1996, and she was permitted to bring forward a claim, which she subsequently won. This ruling was upheld later that year, when "H." launched an appeal. Also in 1996, the federal government passed Bill C-33, adding "sexual orientation" to the list of prohibited grounds of discrimination in the country's HRC. When a Conservative government was elected in Ontario, it also sought to reverse the decision in *M. v. H.* In 1997, the Supreme Court of Canada agreed to hear the case.

That same year, British Columbia passed legislation (Bills 31 and 32) that changed the definition of "spouse" in a number of key areas.[9] Prior to this, in 1996, the Adoption Act had been amended by Bill 51, and same-sex couples were granted the right to joint adoption. With the amendments to the Family Relations Act and the Family Maintenance Enforcement Act, B.C. became the first jurisdiction in Canada to offer same-sex couples many of the same rights and responsibilities as heterosexual common-law couples.[10] Same-sex partners became "spouses" for the purposes of laws governing family support, child maintenance, access, and custody. In contrast to the strategy employed by the NDP government in Ontario, the NDP government in B.C. chose to proceed incrementally.

In 1998, the two women involved in the *M. v. H.* case reached an out-of-court settlement; nonetheless, the Ontario government continued with its appeal. The next year a suit was launched against the federal government by the Foundation for Equal Families.[11] The organization of lesbian and gay lawyers demanded that fifty-eight statutes be amended in light of recent judicial decisions in the area of same-sex spousal recognition. Later in 1999, in a landmark decision, the Supreme Court of Canada ruled that Ontario's definition of "spouse" violated the Charter. The provincial government was ordered to rewrite the sections of the FLA pertaining to support payments so that same-sex couples would be treated the same as common-law heterosexual couples. Ironically, while previous legislation would have entrenched same-sex family rights and responsibilities firmly outside of matrimony, the Supreme Court decision (brought about by the appeals of the Ontario government) opened a space for challenges to the laws governing marriage.[12]

The Ontario government responded to the Supreme Court ruling in 1999 by making changes to sixty-seven provincial statutes (Bill 5), albeit avoiding a redefinition of "spouse" by creating a new category of "same-sex partner." Given that the ruling came from the country's highest court, the ramifications of the decision in *M. v. H.* extended beyond Ontario.[13] The National Assembly of Quebec adopted Bill 32 in a unanimous vote, changing the definition of "spouse" to include same-sex couples in thirty-nine laws and regulations. The Definition of Spouse Amendment Act was introduced in B.C. to extend the term "spouse" to same-sex couples who have lived for two years in a "marriage-like relationship." The provincial government has also promised to introduce omnibus legislation. In Alberta the government amended its Child Welfare Act to allow people involved in same-sex relationships to apply for stepparent adoptions.

In 2000, the Canadian government passed legislation, The Modernization of Benefits and Obligations Act (Bill C-23), which recognized same-sex couples as common-law partners and provides equality in over sixty-eight federal statutes. The intent of this omnibus legislation is to standardize the laws pertaining to same-sex couples across the country.[14] Despite the objections of activist groups, an amendment was added to Bill C-23, one that reserved marriage for heterosexual couples. Critics have denounced this move as offensive and unnecessary, stating that the amendment will only serve to make the legislation vulnerable to constitutional challenge.[15] The City of Toronto has asked the courts to rule on applications by same-sex couples for marriage licenses.[16] In addition, the B.C. government has commenced a legal challenge to overturn the laws that restrict the rights of same-sex partners to marry.[17]

WE ARE "FAMILY"?

For better or for worse, Canadian lesbians, gay men, bisexuals, and transgendered people in same-sex relationships are now subject to the same non-voluntary dependency model of family as heterosexuals.[18] At the same time, laws are being changed in such a way that common-law relationships are becoming increasingly like marriage, and legal matrimony for same-sex couples is closer to becoming a reality. In this country, as in many western nations, families of all kinds proliferate even as conventional notions of "family" are challenged. As Margrit Eichler writes, "The very ground on which families are built has shifted" (1). However, despite a decline in the number of heterosexual nuclear families, and a conceptual shift away from the patriarchal model of family, an idealized notion of "family" remains powerful. According to Shelley Gavigan, "The ideology of the patriarchal nuclear family provides a prism through which relationships are examined, the ideal to which many aspire and the measure against which we all are judged. . . ." (105). It is within this context that lesbians in particular, as well as some gay men, bisexuals, and transgendered people, have formed, or hope to form, families.[19] Many are pleased that their relationships with partners and children are officially recognized. Others are wary of such legal rights and responsibilities, while some have mixed feelings. Therein lies the tension. "Are gay [same-sex] families inherently assimilationist," as Kath Weston asks, "or do they represent a radical departure from more conventional understandings of kinship?" (2). A related, but less popular, query is whether queers should be affiliated with "family" discourse at all. Are queers "family"? Could queers be "family"? Should queers be "family"?

The bulk of lesbian parenting literature, grounded in the experiential, takes the value of "family" as a given. This thrust is just as strong in newer texts such as *Lesbian Parenting: Living with Pride and Prejudice* as in pioneering works like *Politics of the Heart: A Lesbian Parenting Anthology*. Ultimately the lived reality of lesbian mothers emerges as an epistemologically and politically privileged site. It is not difficult to imagine why this is the case. Lesbians are often in a defensive position as they struggle to form and maintain families in the face of great adversity. Hence lesbian mothers are more likely to argue that their families are "normal," especially when they are threatened, rather than openly challenge the ideological underpinnings of "family." In other words, as Julia Brophy states, "[a] custody dispute is not the forum in which to mount a feminist critique of the family" (385).

Lesbian families are also posited as inherently (and subversively) radical. Lesbians challenge the concept of "family" by having and raising children, particularly when men are involved only as sperm donors. The very act of lesbian procreation poses a threat to "the (heterosexual, nuclear) family." Interestingly, then, "pro-family" lesbian parenting literature holds in tension two seemingly contradictory convictions, namely that lesbian families are at once both mundane and menacing. While female-headed same-sex families go about their everyday lives, sometimes looking and acting a lot like heterosexual families, they disrupt heteronormative assumptions by their very existence.

By contrast, writers such as legal theorist Ruthann Robson position themselves against the trend to refigure families and "family" (975–976). Rather than attempting to liberalize legal definitions of "family," Robson asserts that lesbians should resist such categorization, and she means lesbians exclusively, not gay men or bisexuals. She insists on gendering the category of "sexual orientation" because lesbians are marginalized in a very particular manner (975). Instead, the entire notion of "family" must be deconstructed. As she puts it, "family must be problematized as a nonessential, cognitive, and contested category rather than [as] an unproblematized 'reality' of 'lived experience' " (979).

Carol Allen is also suspicious of the extension of "family" status to lesbians (and gay men). Like Robson, Allen maintains that lesbian families do not necessarily change the repressive nature of the institution. Allen brings an awareness of difference to her analysis, which is missing in much of the literature, by arguing that the legal category "family" only offers protection to some by excluding others. When "equality" is interpreted as "sameness," only a relatively elite group prospers, namely "professional, white, middle-class, able-bodied lesbians and gays, whose family form looks very much like the traditional heterosexual ideal" (103). Benefits that depend on spousal status leave out queers who live in non-nuclear arrangements, for instance in collective households or non-monogamous relationships. Moreover, people who are multiply disadvantaged, such as poor lesbians on social assistance, will be penalized by a redefinition of "spouse." Allen was correct when she speculated that low-income same-sex couples would see a reduction in their standard of living with a redefinition of "spouse." This is part of the trend to shift responsibility away from the state and download care of people into families. Allen insists that all of these factors be taken into account by lesbians who want to be "family" (105).

INCLUSION VS. REVOLUTION

In *Lesbian Motherhood: An Exploration of Canadian Lesbian Families,* Fiona Nelson presents a study of thirty lesbian women involved in parenting. She prefers to use the term "lesbian women" to highlight the fact that lesbians, like gay men, have other/many identities. According to Nelson, the lesbian family "is a revolutionary force in our understanding of motherhood and the family—a force that has implications for family-focused policies and programs" (137). One of her most striking observations is that the presence of a second/an other/a non-biological mother throws into question the entire concept of "motherhood." Unlike heterosexuals, lesbian women cannot take for granted what a mother is and what a mother does. For instance, lesbians who choose to conceive a baby together by donor insemination (d.i.) do not (indeed, cannot) become mothers without a great deal of planning and forethought (83).[20] Lesbian partners who form a blended family with children from previous (predominantly heterosexual) relationships struggle with how to parent together.

Nelson outlines a hierarchy of motherhood which places married middle-class heterosexual women at the top, single poor, and/or young heterosexual women in the middle, and lesbian mothers at the bottom. Nelson argues that placement in this hierarchy is determined by more than one's sexual orientation and family status. Rather, "a woman is evaluated as a mother less on the basis of her own merits than on the basis of the social position of the father and the relationship she has with him." She continues on to say that:

> In this sense lesbian motherhood can be seen as a truly subversive activity that poses more than a conceptual threat. . . .[I]t is a structural threat to patriarchal power in Canadian society. A subculture of women is not only living with little regard for males and male authority, but its members are also reproducing themselves! Moreover, they are doing so, as much as possible, without men. (136–137)

Unfortunately, Nelson does not bring a critical race perspective to her work, although she does acknowledge that her research participants comprised a homogeneous group. All the women she spoke with were white, and most were middle-class, well educated, and identified themselves as feminist. She outlines in this regard the difficulty she had finding lesbian mothers to interview, and surmises that women with privilege are most likely to parent openly with another woman (17–19). This is an interesting point which Nelson raises, but does not pursue. Hence her research suffers because of the absence of race analysis. For example, the hierarchy that she describes might make sense when all the women are white, but what about the impact of racial difference on mothers' status? Certainly a middle-class, able-bodied, white lesbian mother is in many respects privileged in a racist society such as ours compared with a poor black heterosexual mother. Likewise, for racially non-dominant women, qualifications for motherhood have at least as mu if not more, to do with race as the social position of the father.[21]

Furthermore, neither Nelson nor the women in her sample challenge the notion of "family" beyond replacing a man and a woman and kids with two women and kids. This model is, of course, shaped by race and class. Nevertheless, I would not want to deny the very real difficulties that these lesbian women face in a heterosexist society. For instance, the lesbian mothers describe in vivid detail the problems in deciding when to come out, who to come out to, how to explain the role of the non-biological mother, how to prepare their children to face prejudice, when to attempt to educate others, etc. The focus, however, is always on reform, expanding the definition of "family." Nelson describes this situation as such: "What this means for lesbian families is that to live a 'normal' family life, they must constantly tell people that they *are* a normal family" (127). But I would argue that, because the value of the so-called "normal family" is never challenged, heteronormativity is reinscribed even though the subject matter is lesbian-headed families.

In *The Neutered Mother, the Sexual Family and Other Twentieth Century Tragedies* American law professor Martha Albertson Fineman argues for the primacy of the Mother-Child dyad in conceptions of the family for the purpose of formulating social policy. While her argument is not specifically about lesbian mothers, it has implications for lesbian mothers and for alternative definitions of "family" that would accommodate lesbian motherhood.[22] Fineman proposes a new model of "family" premised on the care of dependents such as children rather than on sexual relations between adults, be they opposite or same-sex couples.[23] I should clarify that she means Mother-Child to be taken up as a metaphor (although there is some slippage). In other words, it is not the exclusive domain of women and children, but could be occupied by men, the elderly, people with disabilities, etc. The problem, from Fineman's perspective, is not that the state has been slow to recognize alternative family structures, but rather that the concept of "Mother" has been decontextualized within legal and political systems.

Fineman is not suggesting that differences such as gender, race, and class are inconsequential. On the contrary, she emphasizes that American culture is misogynist and racist. Fineman's point is that Mother has been rendered gender (as well as race and class) neutral in legal discourse and hence ineffectual (67–69). Mother has become a symbol and is no longer a person. "Equality," Fineman writes, "makes Mother an empty legal category, robbing real-life mothers of the protection of their specificity."[24] Hence, nurturing and caretaking roles, traditionally associated with Mother, are considered suspect. Fineman uses the term "caretaking" instead of "caregiving" to emphasize that the work is real, and should not be regarded as a gift (9,69).

According to Fineman, the metanarrative of the "natural family" premised upon the monogamous romantic sexual affiliation of one man and one woman is powerful and cuts through many discourses, including law. Idealized notions of "family" are cast as sacred and beyond critique. She states:

> The shared assumption is that the appropriate family is founded on the heterosexual couple—a reproductive, biological pairing that is designated as divinely ordained in religion, crucial in social policy, and a normative imperative in ideology. (145)

Moreover, marriage, which enshrines the man as the head of the household, serves to reinforce patriarchy. Fineman goes on to explain that although this institution is generally experienced as "horizontal" intimacy (one man and one woman), "vertical" intimacy (intergenerational relationships, i.e., children, elderly) can also be accommodated. But either way, "[t]he dominant paradigm . . . privileges the couple as foundational and fundamental" (145).

So, although the law has had to change in the face of challenges from common-law heterosexual couples as well as lesbian and gay couples, Fineman maintains that these so-called "alternative" family arrangements are not as revolutionary as they may appear. As she puts it:

> To a large extent, the new visions of the family merely reformulate basic assumptions about the nature of intimacy. They reflect the dyadic nature of the old (sexual) family story, updating and modifying it to accommodate new family "alternatives" while retaining the centrality of sexual affiliation to the organization and understanding of intimacy. This process of reiteration and reformulation reveals the power of the metanarrative about sexual affiliation and the family. The paradigm structures and directs the debate about alternatives. (147)

In contrast to Nelson, Fineman regards single motherhood as the ultimate threat to patriarchy. I appreciate Fineman's idea that lone female parents are marginalized and thus empowered in a particular way because they are raising children without a partner. However, an analysis of race, class, and difference in ability is strikingly absent. How, for instance, does the social positioning of a poor woman of colour or a disabled woman with children compare with that of a white, middle-class, able-bodied mother?[25] Partnered lesbian women and gay men, unlike sole-support mothers, can be made to fit into the legal model of sexual-romantic coupledom, although not everyone will accept them. "Single" motherhood (and presumably fatherhood), on the other hand, "is deviant because it represents the rejection of the sexual connection as the core organizing familial concept" (147–8). Significantly, Fineman notes that this is the only form of motherhood that is qualified by reference to a woman's marital status.[26] Single mothers—and here it is interesting to note that, unlike Eichler, Fineman retains the term "single"— the group most removed from Mother, are regarded by politicians and social workers as both "dangerous" and "pathological" (71). In order to contain this element, the law attempts to (re)attach men to mothers and children.[27] Some examples of this "egalitarian" thrust include increased cases of joint custody between "parents" and the economic punishment of single mothers.[28]

Ultimately, whereas Nelson maintains the primacy of sexual ties, Fineman advocates the abolition of legal marriage and emphasizes care of dependents. While I perceive Fineman's as the more revolutionary vision, in that she thinks the concept of "family" should be justified, as opposed to simply claiming lesbian relationships as "family," her proposal contains some shortcomings. For one, despite the fact that the Mother-Child dyad is meant metaphorically, Fineman does, at points, romanticize and essentialize the relationship between actual mothers and actual children. She does not address, for instance, problems such as abuse and neglect. Secondly, the "new family line" which she draws invokes another legal category of family, albeit without marriage (231). Thirdly, this new unit (also a dyad) revalorizes privacy and individualism. Lastly, Fineman's model points to, but does not seriously reckon with, the fact that women (especially less privileged women) will still be responsible for the majority of caretaking. Despite these critiques, Fineman's work, while not specifically about lesbians, offers an insightful feminist (de)(re)construction of "family." Nelson's study, on the other hand, focuses exclusively on lesbians but does not trouble "family" beyond inclusion.

QUEERING THE NORMAL

There is a feminist adage that goes something like this: women who want to be as good as men lack ambition. This saying sums up much of what I feel in regard to the struggle for the legal recognition of same-sex couples and their children. On the one hand, it only seems fair that these families receive the same benefits as units formed by heterosexuals.[29] And yet this vision of equality is inherently limited and limiting. Here is where I get stuck. Ironically, for all my critical thinking, I find myself caught up in yet another binary opposition, namely the assimilationist/pro-family stance ("we are family") versus the anti-assimilationist/anti-family position ("we are not, nor do we want to be, like the patriarchal heterosexual family"). The work of Brenda

Cossman has been useful in helping me to navigate this rocky terrain. She argues that "family" is always more complicated than these strategies would suggest or can allow for.

Cossman identifies the "choice" which emerges between challenging exclusion from the family and challenging the discourse of family itself as false ("Same-Sex Couples," 229).[30] The debate needs to be opened up so that it becomes possible for queers to both embrace and deconstruct "family." The problem is not that "family" is a site of contestation, but rather that legal and political systems demand that people choose a side ("Inside/Out," 124). Thus, when same-sex couples present themselves as "normal" in pursuit of formal recognition, the polarization of "family" and "not family" is effectively cemented. Since the concept of "family" is not a simple one, political strategies must also embrace complexity. In her words, "To move beyond the opposition, the either/or, the inside/out, we have to recognize that we are family, and we are not; we are inside and we are out" (139). Carole-Ann O'Brien and Lorna Weir concur that queers' relationship to family is not an easy one. They state that "family" and "homosexuality" have traditionally been posited by English and French Canadians, unlike some Aboriginal peoples, as dichotomous. In "Lesbians and Gay Men Inside and Outside Families," they cite the existence of "two-spirited" Aboriginal people, who are believed to embody both male and female elements and permitted to engage in same-gender (their terminology) sexual activity. Being "two-spirited" was and is regarded as fortunate and continues to be respected within some First Nations communities despite European Christian colonization (112–115). Unfortunately, the field of sociology has served to support and reinforce this harmful, and artificial, binarism, and in doing so has perpetuated a heterosexist stance. Lesbians and gay men are either left out of sociological analyses of family altogether, or they are labelled "deviant." O'Brien and Weir argue that to the contrary, most Canadians, regardless of sexual preference or orientation, do not exist independently of families. In their words, "The ideology that constructs lesbians and gay men as outside of and dangerous to families denies as well that gay men and lesbians are born to mothers and fathers: gay men and lesbians are *inside* families" (114–115). Many do go on to form families of their own, as witnessed by the "lesbian baby boom" which has occurred as mothers who came out as lesbian become lesbians who are becoming mothers.

In the current Canadian situation, the legal rights and responsibilities of same-sex partners are seen through an entrenched formal model of equality. Coupled queers and their children are "family," (almost) like heterosexuals. But this does not mean that there is no room left for queers to resist "family." Apart from not living in arrangements that the government recognizes as family, it is worth looking to alternative visions such as Margrit Eichler's social responsibility model (124–144). In brief, she replaces the household with the individual as the unit of administration. The result would be that every citizen and permanent resident would be entitled to a basic level of care regardless of her or his attachment to a particular familial constellation. This holds great potential for disentangling the legal function of family from the social functions.

Deconstructing the totalization and stabilization of identity, Carl Stychin strives to complicate equality rights. This presents another way to envision "family" by asserting that Canada may be the first postmodern state. According to Stychin:

> . . . the Canadian national imaginary displays an instability which leaves it particularly open to contestation. The contingency of the national sign facilitates the articulation of competing identities deploying the language of nationalism. (107)

Stychin sees the opportunity for diverse sexual identities to insert themselves into the social-political-judicial discourses of our country. This is an exciting and inspiring thought. Queers can engage the conundrum of "family" through the gaps, the absences, and the spaces.

HAVING YOUR CAKE AND EATING IT, TOO

In conclusion, families headed by same-sex couples signal both a "normalization of the queer" and a "queering of the normal." It is not enough to simply deconstruct or valorize "family," thereby allowing the assimilationist/anti-assimilationist binarism to remain intact. Moreover, it is important to recognize that some queers are considered "more normal" than others. Lesbian mothers, for instance, especially those who are white, middle-class, and live in nuclear-type arrangements, have attained some level of respectability. While lesbians are not immediately equated with the virtues of motherhood, being mothers makes lesbians somewhat more acceptable. In other words, queers who most closely resemble the heterosexual ideal are deemed the most "normal." As to whether or not it is desirable for queers to be considered normal, opinion remains divided.

Nonetheless, being queer is not yet entirely ordinary, despite what is written in *The Economist* or enshrined in Canadian law. Heterosexism and homophobia are, unfortunately, still a source of oppression in our society, and same-sex partners and their children face a number of hurdles on a daily basis. It remains to be seen what will become of the latest struggle over marriage. Will lesbians, gay men, bisexuals, and transgendered people be permitted entrance to this most sacred of heterosexual institutions? And if they are, what effect will this have on matrimony? On queers? And so the contestation of "family" continues.

NOTES

1. Throughout this essay I use the somewhat legalistic term, "same-sex," to signify couples who are deemed by society to be both "female" or both "male." This is problematic, because sex refers to biology rather than social roles, and I view sex and gender (and sexuality) as existing on a continuum. However, "same-sex" is generally understood, and "same-gender" seems even less accurate to me. For instance, a "butch" woman and a "femme" woman have very different gender identities. Moreover, simply writing "lesbian and gay" is too restrictive, and "bisexual" and "transgendered" do not work in every context. Finally, I employ "queer," acknowledging that this term has a long and varied history. See Gary Kinsman, *The Regulation of Desire: Homo and Hetero Sexualities*, second Edition (Montreal: Black Rose Books), 1996.
2. When more than two adults decide to form a family of one or more "sexes," the challenges are enormous. The topic of multiple partner families is important and deserves to be researched separately. See Kevin Lano and Claire Parry, eds., *Breaking the Barriers to Desire: Polyamory, Polyfidelity and Non-*Monogamy—*New Approaches to Multiple Relationships* (Nottingham: Five Leaves Publications, 1995). For the purposes of this paper, I have limited my scope to same-sex relationships between two people, primarily women.
3. For a detailed account of Bill 167, see David Rayside, *On the Fringe: Gays and Lesbians in Politics* (Ithaca: Cornell University Press, 1998), and Michelle K. Owen, "'We Are Family?': The Struggle for Same-Sex Spousal Recognition in Ontario and the Conundrum of 'Family,'" Ph.D. Thesis (University of Toronto, 1999).
4. Susan Ursel, "Bill 167 and Full Human Rights," in Katherine Arnup, ed., *Lesbian Parenting: Living with Pride and Prejudice* (Charlottetown: gynergy books, 1995), 350.
5. *K. et al.* (1995), in *Consolidated Ontario Family Law Statutes and Regulations* (Toronto: Carswell, 1995), 2.
6. *Re: Catherine Elizabeth G. and Linda Kathleen G.* (No. 1). See "The Spousal Collection, October 1989–May 1999," compiled by C.M. Donald for the Coalition for Lesbian and Gay Rights in Ontario, 41.
7. barbara findlay, "All in the Family Values: An examination of the construction of 'family' and the impact of law on the lives of lesbians and gay men," paper prepared for a course on family law in Vancouver, British Columbia (July 1995), 13–14.
8. This case had previously been heard in 1993 and 1994. The Ontario NDP had intervener status, and asked that the provincial FLA be declared unconstitutional. See

Kelly Gervais, "Are We Family? A House Divided: The 'M. v. H.' Spousal Support Case," *Siren* (June/July 1996), 3–4.

9. Jim Beatty, "Family-support laws extended to BC gays," *Vancouver Sun* (July 23, 1997), A4.
10. Hungary became the first country to recognize same-sex unions under common-law in 1996. However, adoption was excluded from this legislation. "The Spousal Collection," 36.
11. EGALE (Equality for Gays and Lesbians Everywhere), "Gay Community Launches Historic Federal Challenge to Recognize Same-Sex Families." Press Release (January 7, 1999).
12. Kirk Makin, "Legal marriages for gays may be next: Line now drawn could be quickly erased," *The Globe and Mail* (May 1999), A8.
13. See EGALE, "Submissions to the House of Commons Standing Committee on Justice and Human Rights (Bill C-23)," undated.
14. At the time of this writing, provincial governments are responding in a variety of ways to the federal act. The hope, of course, is that inconsistencies between jurisdictions will be smoothed out. This has yet to be realized.
15. Foundation for Equal Families, "Fed's Legitimate Discrimination in Equity Bill on Same-Sex Rights," undated.
16. Paul Moloney, "City Wants Same-Sex Marriage Review," *Toronto Star* (May 20, 2000), B1.
17. Paul Willcocks, "Murray Warren Doesn't Want to Wait Much Longer for a Marriage Licence," *Vancouver Sun* (July 21, 2000).
18. And, as a result of the Supreme Court decision in the 1999 Bracklow case, a healthy spouse now has an obligation to support an ailing ex-spouse. See Brenda Cossman, "The full monty: Spousal rights mean you'll be on the hook for years to come," *Xtra!* no. 377 (April 8, 1999), 11.
19. It is estimated that between twenty and thirty percent of lesbians are mothers. See Katherine Arnup, "In the Family Way: Lesbian Mothers in Canada," in *Feminism and Families*, 80. Not surprisingly, then, the majority of research on same-sex headed families is centred on lesbians. As well, there are numerous books written by, about, and for lesbian parents. By contrast, it is difficult to find materials pertaining to other types of families.
20. Interestingly, Nelson observes that lesbian women tend to conceive male babies at a much higher rate than female babies due to the timing of insemination.
21. Patricia Monture, for example, writes about the devastating effects that the Canadian government's residential schools have had on Native families and communities. See "A Vicious Circle: Child Welfare and the First Nations," *Canadian Journal of Women and the Law* 3, no. 1 (1989): 1–17.
22. But not lesbian couples without children.
23. Fineman is critical of the gendered and privatized nature of care of dependents.

She notes that women end up doing the vast majority of such work, and in doing so relieve the state of responsibility for children, the elderly, and people with disabilities. See Fineman, 161–163.

24. She does not mention that this same "specificity" can be dangerous for mothers who are women of colour and/or lesbians. See Fineman, 67

25. On the topic of disability in regard to families, see Karen A. Blackford, "A Different Parent," *Healthsharing* (Summer 1990): 20–25, and J. Ridington, *The Only Parent in the Neighbourhood: Mothering and Women with Disabilities* (Vancouver: Disabled Women's Network, 1989).

26. This point is debatable. I would argue that the signifier "lesbian mother" also says a great deal about (legal, heterosexual) married status.

27. In terms of same-sex couples, the legal system has been more concerned with the rights of male sperm donors than those of the non-biological lesbian parent in the recent past.

28. The OSAP (Ontario Student Assistance Program) rules, which disallow people who are receiving student loans to collect Family Benefits, are a case in point. In order to fund their education, poor, single parents, the majority of whom are women, are forced to incur large debts. For an analysis of the Social Assistance Reform Act (Bill 142), see Ontario Social Safety NetWork, Backgrounder: "Welfare Reform and Single Mothers" <welfarewatch.toronto.on.ca/wrkfrw/singlemo.htm>.

29. The argument that it will cost too much to recognize same-sex headed families is not sustainable. And, as Bruce Ryder writes, the law has traditionally created material inequality in two ways: lesbians and gays pay more taxes than heterosexuals and in turn they receive fewer public benefits. "In other words, gays and lesbians are being forced to subsidize heterosexual privilege." Bruce Ryder, "Equality Rights and Sexual Orientation," *Canadian Journal of Family Law* 4 (1990): 48. Of course, the situation is a little more complicated than this as how much one pays depends on which tax bracket one is in. The main point, however, is well taken.

30. While I appreciate the way that Cossman holds together the "inside" and the "outside," I am disconcerted by what I perceive as a collapse of the legal and social functions of the family.

WORKS CITED

Allen, Carol. "Who Gets to be Family?: Some Thoughts on the Lesbian and Gay Fight for Equality." In *And Still Rise: Feminist Political Mobilizing in Contemporary Canada*. Ed. Linda Carty. Toronto: Women's Press, 1993. 101–107.

Arnup, Katherine, ed. *Lesbian Parenting: Living with Pride and Prejudice*. Charlottetown: gynergy books, 1995.

———. "In the Family Way: Lesbian Mothers in Canada." *Feminism and Families: Critical Policies and Changing Practices.* Ed. Meg Luxton. Halifax: Fernwood Publishing, 1997. 80–97.

Beatty, Jim. "Family-support laws extended to B.C. gays." *Vancouver Sun* (July 23, 1997): A4.

Blackford, Karen A. "A Different Parent." *Healthsharing* (Summer 1990): 20–25.

Brophy, Julia. "New Families, Judicial Decision-Making, and Children's Welfare." *Canadian Journal of Women and the Law* 5 (1992): 484–497.

Consolidated Ontario Family Law Statutes and Regulations 1996. Toronto: Carswell, 1995.

Cossman, Brenda. "The full monty: Spousal rights mean you'll be on the hook for years to come." *Xtra!* no. 377 (April 8, 1999), 11.

———. "Same-Sex Couples and the Politics of Family Status." In *Women and Canadian Public Policy.* Ed. Janine Brodie. Toronto: Harcourt Brace and Company, 1996. 223–278.

———. "Family Inside/Out." *Feminism and Families: Critical Policies and Changing Practices.* Ed. Meg Luxton. Halifax: Fernwood Publishing, 1997. 124–141.

The Economist. "Let Them Wed" Issue (January 6, 1996).

EGALE (Equality for Gays and Lesbians Everywhere), "Gay Community Launches Historic Federal Challenge to Recognize Same-Sex Families." Press Release, January 7, 1999.

———. "Submissions to the House of Commons Standing Committee on Justice and Human Rights (Bill C-23)," undated.

Eichler, Margrit. *Family Shifts: Families, Policies, and Gender Equality.* Toronto: Oxford University Press, 1997.

findlay, barbara. "All in the Family Values: An Examination of the Construction of 'Family' and the Impact of Law on the Lives of Lesbians and Gay Men." Paper prepared for a course on family law (July 1995).

Fineman, Martha A. *The Neutered Mother, the Sexual Family and Other Twentieth Century Tragedies.* New York: Routledge, 1995.

Foundation for Equal Families, "Fed's Legitimate Discrimination in Equity Bill on Same-Sex Rights," undated.

Gavigan, Shelley A. M. "Feminism, Familial Ideology and Family Law." In *Feminism and Families: Critical Policies and Changing Practices.* Ed. Meg Luxton. Halifax: Fernwood Publishing, 1997. 98–123.

Gervais, Kelly. "Are We Family? A House Divided: The 'M v. H' Spousal Support Case." *Siren* (June/July 1996): 3–4.

Kinsman, Gary. *The Regulation of Desire: Homo and Hetero Sexualities.* Second Edition. Montreal: Black Rose Books, 1996.

Lano, Kevin, and Claire Parry, eds. *Breaking the Barriers to Desire: Polyamory Polyfidelity, and Non-monogamy—New Approaches to Multiple Relationships.* Nottingham: Five Leaves Publications, 1995.

Makin, Kirk. "Legal Marriages for gays may be next: Line now drawn could be quickly erased." *The Globe and Mail* (May 21, 1999): A8.

Moloney, Paul. "City Wants Same-Sex Marriage Review." *Toronto Star* (May 20, 2000): B1.

Monture, Patricia. "A Vicious Circle: Child Welfare and the First Nations." *Canadian Journal of Women and the Law* 3.1 (1989): 1–17.

Nelson, Fiona. *Lesbian Motherhood: An Exploration of Canadian Lesbian Families.* Toronto: University of Toronto Press, 1993.

O'Brien, Carol-Anne and Lorna Weir. "Lesbians and Gay Men Inside and Outside Families." In *Canadian Families: Diversity, Conflict and Change.* Eds. Nancy Mandell and Ann Duffy. Toronto: Harcourt Brace, 1999. 111–139.

Ontario Social Safety NetWork, Backgrounder: "Welfare Reform and Single Mothers." Inactive site. <welfarewatch.toronto.on.ca/wrkfrw/singlemo.htm>.

Owen, Michelle K. "We Are 'Family?': The Struggle for Same-Sex Spousal Rights and the Conundrum of 'Family.'" Ph.D. Thesis. University of Toronto, 1999.

Pollack, Sandra, and Jeanne Vaughn, eds. *Politics of the Heart: A Lesbian Parenting Anthology.* New York: Firebrand Books, 1987.

Rayside, David. *On the Fringe: Gays and Lesbians in Politics.* Ithaca: Cornell University Press, 1996.

Ridington, J. *The Only Parent in the Neighbourhood: Mothering and Women with Disabilities.* Vancouver: Disabled Women's Network, 1989.

Robson, Ruthann. "Resisting the Family: Repositioning Lesbians in Legal Theory." *Signs: Journal of Women in Culture and Society* 19.4 (Summer 1994): 975–996.

Ross, Becki L. *The House That Jill Built: A Lesbian Nation in Formation.* Toronto: University of Toronto Press, 1995.

Ryder, Bruce. "Equality Rights and Sexual Orientation: Confronting Heterosexual Family Privilege." *Canadian Journal of Family Law* 4 (1990): 30–97.

"The Spousal Collection: October 1989–May 1999." Compiled by C.M. Donald for the Coalition for Lesbian and Gay Rights in Ontario. Toronto.

Carl Stychin. *Law's Desire: Sexuality and the Limits of Justice.* London: Anchor Books, 1995.

Ursel, Susan. "Bill 167 and Full Human Rights." In *Lesbian Parenting: Living with Pride and Prejudice.* Ed. Katherine Arnup. Charlottetown: gynergy books, 1995. 341–351.

Weston, Kath. *Families We Choose: Lesbians, Gays, Kinship.* New York: Columbia University Press, 1991.

Wilcocks, Paul. "Murray Warren Doesn't Want to Wait Much Longer for a Marriage Licence." *Vancouver Sun* (July 21, 2000).

can you see the difference?: queerying the nation, ethnicity, festival, and culture in winnipeg

Pauline Greenhill

> You don't have to be a ravingly straight suburbanite to think that a festival devoted to bizarre sexual imagery has little purpose beyond entertaining a few radicals in the sexual wars. Many mainstream gays and lesbians, closeted or otherwise, don't like the members of Queer Culture Canada, whom they see as a handful of youthful provocateurs who will only bring grief to an already embattled community. This view contains more than a grain of truth. But it doesn't mean that the Festival du Voyeur should be treated with contempt. Voices from the fringe often sound hysterical, but their messages can be profitably heard. Goodness knows, Winnipeg is grown up enough to withstand this minor assault on its puritan sensibilities. (Walker, D8)

In this *Winnipeg Free Press* article, columnist Morley Walker takes on The Festival du Voyeur, a forty-day and forty-night celebration of visual arts and writing, primarily by gay, lesbian, and bisexual artists. I use the term "queer" to refer to these folks, mainly because it was the one chosen by Winnipeg, Manitoba's Queer Culture Canada, who presented the Festival. On the down side, "queer" has problematic associations with gay male culture, but to its credit it can avoid the gendering and culturing associations of the terms gay and lesbian particularly, and can include transgendered, transsexual, and other populations. The latter use—the inclusive "queer"—is intended here.

Held January 22 to March 6, 1993, the Festival du Voyeur was organized primarily by the Plug In Gallery, an internationally known artist-run contemporary arts gallery. However, collaboration between many artists and galleries in Winnipeg allowed the festival to showcase local, national, and international queer materials, including painting, photography, videos, poetry, and performance. Relatively well funded by both the Canada Council and the Manitoba Arts Council, the festival became a focus and signifier for queering artistic creation and experience in the city, as Culture (in anthropological senses of expression of social group identities), and as culture (in aesthetic senses as expression of individual creativity). But Voyeur also posed a pervasive question, a que(e)rying about Culture/culture's forms and meanings, their limitations as well as their possibilities.

Intrigued by the event's name and aims, and welcomed by its organizers, I entered into this inquiry/investigation representing myself as the "token female heterosexual anthropological voyeur" (Greenhill 1993). I have continued to occupy this political position and social location, but not without some uneasiness. Shane Phelan's cautioning about cultural marginality and centrality can be at times too comforting. She says, "The fact of marginality does not make one an expert on the culture any more than hegemony does. It provides one with access to truth that is invisible to hegemonic groups unless they actively seek it out" (157–158). I happen to agree, but this doesn't let me off the hook. I wouldn't do this work—indeed, I probably wouldn't conduct research as an anthropologist—if I thought only "insiders" have the right to look at, talk about, and write up their own culture. As critical theory suggests, inside and outside are not so easily located. No individual is ultimately reducible to a single defining identity—male or female, gay or straight, inside or out, and so on.

Nevertheless, my position as a political and personal outsider to the queer communities I am studying, indeed anthropologizing, can mean I may be less sensitive to the very real dangers of outing, exoticizing, and othering that my work can allow. Since anthropologists have tended to study the distant and unfamiliar, studying any group as an anthropologist can have the effect of distancing and defamiliarizing them—quite the opposite of my intentions with this research.

I have not resolved some of the inherent problems of the power position of researcher to my own satisfaction—or to that of many in the queer communities I work in, in Winnipeg and beyond. Thus, my work focuses primarily on public figures and public knowledge—indeed, on public culture. I'm not telling you any secrets, ferreted out in the anthropological mode of long-term, discreet observation; it's no surprise that anthropology and espionage are often confused by both the observers and the observed! And part of my research involves actively fostering my discomfort about my own hegemony, homophobia, and heterosexism, particularly by dialoguing with queers who are not wholly convinced of the intrinsic value or necessity of my work.

These concerns are not entirely a simple reflection of the joke about the postmodern anthropologist, who says to his informant—"Enough about you; let's talk about me." [1] The issues pertain to the inside/outside problematics of much queer culture. (Such as: Is a closeted lesbian a "real" lesbian? How many same sexual experiences must a man have to be considered gay? Does it really take one to know one?) But they also refer to the implicit position of one attending any event with a name like the Festival du Voyeur, in which the spectator, as much as the spectacle, is always being celebrated—and implicated. Voyeurs like to watch. But they're not the only kinky ones. So are anthropologists.

Parodying/travestying the concurrent Franco Manitoban Festival du Voyageur, the Festival du Voyeur's rigorous questioning of ideas of cultural production in a festival context had a predecessor. It was the Multi-Culti-Queer Pavilion, held the previous summer (1992) as a (counter)part of the multicultural showcase Folklorama. The notion that the Festival du Voyeur and the Multi-Culti-Queer Pavilion were attempts to present or represent a culture or cultures was essential to reactions by both straight and queer audiences, both in support and in opposition. That the metaphor of ethnicity could apply to queer culture, and that sexuality could be a mode for cultural pluralism, raised significant issues for the events' audiences, which I will explore.[2] The implications, however, go beyond a mere catalogue of responses, from the enthusiastic to the homophobic. Queer Culture Canada's application to the Canada Council referred to "an emerging queer culture," and stated: "No one can know in advance where the limits of a gay/lesbian centred inquiry are to be drawn" (Baerwaldt et al). Thus, these events created Queer Culture as much as they reflected it. Perhaps more.

These two statements of queer nationhood, the Festival du Voyeur and the Multi-Culti-Queer Pavilion, were constructed playfully as parodies/travesties in order to highlight the sameness/difference that characterizes mainstream Canadian attempts to understand cultures. And they succeeded in this. The official reaction of Folklorama was to emphasize sameness, and that of the Festival du Voyageur to assert difference. Yet neither could stay comfortably within these easy oppositions; nor could media representations. Similarly, any attempt to construct and articulate queer nationhood should take into consideration the pluralism of queer communities—just as constructions of other cultures cannot rely on ideal types and representatives. All cultures are plural and contain their own differences and contradictions, so no individual or group can give the whole picture.[3]

And such articulations should understand pluralism not solely in terms of recognizing the non-whiteness, non-Christianity, etc., of many lesbians and gays. The queer community also differs in that while some appreciate overt performances of difference, others would prefer to fit into the mainstream and confine those performances to the metaphorical bedroom.[4] So in a sense, Morley Walker's statement that opened this piece is right—these events don't reflect a lot of queer Winnipeg. But they do reflect one of the central tasks of contemporary art—to provoke, at the very least, a voyeur's double take. What the heck is going on here? The answers implicate the underlying subjects being examined, parodied, travestied—in these cases Folklorama and the Festival du Voyageur—just as much as they do the Multi-Culti-Queer Pavilion and the Festival du Voyeur.

FOLKLORAMA/THE MULTI-CULTI-QUEER PAVILION

Folklorama has been held in Winnipeg for two weeks every August since 1970. It combines local boosterism with big corporate sponsorship to create a tourist event. Various venues throughout the city—mainly ethnic society halls, community centres, and public education buildings—represent ethnic, linguistic, national, and/or geographical groupings. In the words of its own promotion, "Folklorama takes you down the street and around the world." It bills itself as "Canada's greatest cultural celebration" and "the world's largest multicultural festival." In fact, it's quite similar to festivals held in other major Canadian cities—Toronto's Caravan, for one.[5]

These ethnic, linguistic, national, and/or geographical groups are represented in a "pavilion"—or, in many cases, in more than one pavilion, such as the "Ireland/Irish Pavilion" and "Isle of the Shamrock-Ireland Pavilion." One might suspect that the presence of two pavilions indicates political discord, or at the very least some heterogeneity in cultural presentation.[6] But Folklorama is structured to ensure that contrasts within and between groups are masked by common presentation of three elements. So although their website suggests that "Folklorama gives every group a chance to release whatever they want to express to everyone about their culture" (summer 1996), in fact, expressions are limited almost exclusively to music/dance, food/drink, and the display and sale of crafts. Thus, similarities and differences within and between groups are presented in discreet, separate locations. Only a few venues, like the Centre Culturel Franco-Manitobain, host more than one pavilion. And all are circumscribed within the aforementioned common structure of performances, edibles, and crafts, but also within one city.

Information distributed by the Plug In Gallery prior to the opening of the Multi-Culti-Queer Pavilion suggested that:

> . . . a queer cultural voice can best be heard when Winnipeg audiences are geared to thinking of the Other, the marginalized or invisible ethnic cultures that are usually devalued the rest of the year. Queer Pavilion organizers are keen to explore notions of difference in art produced by gay, lesbian, or bisexual artists, notions not represented in the predominantly heterosexual cultures assumed by the other ethnic pavilions of Folklorama. (n.d.)

Paralleling this discourse of difference was one of identity and sameness, at least in structural terms. Drawing upon the three touchstones for Folklorama pavilions, the Multi-Culti-Queer Pavilion had queer food (Cheezies, freshly squeezed orange juice, and Fruit Loops with homo milk), queer performances (including one literally "phoned in" from Toronto by artists Shawna Dempsey and Lorri Millan), and queer craft exhibitions (like demonstrations of "totally queer hair-doos"). Thus, organizers constructed a correspondence with, and provided counterparts to, the patterns of its ostensible object, which they termed "Faux-klorama." Further, they issued a proclamation, not unlike those routinely issued by the Winnipeg mayor's office:

> We, the people of Winnipeg, hereby proclaim the Multi-Culti-Queer Pavilion as a participant in the city's ethnic celebrations. As well, we proclaim the establishment of a multicultural Queer Nation as a sovereign state within the medieval walls of the city of Winnipeg.

> Your silent servant,
> Will Gough,[7]
> Mayoral candidate '93.

Of course, a location within the medieval walls of the city of Winnipeg is nowhere, and the fictitious Will Gough was hardly in a position to make such a proclamation. But Folklorama was not amused. Their governing body the Folk Arts Council's first reaction was a letter from their lawyers, demanding "an immediate follow-up release disclaiming any association of these activities with Folklorama so that the public will not be under any misconception that your event is part of the Folklorama festival" (letter to Plug In Gallery solicitors, 1992). Their interlocutors complied:

> In response to overwhelming desire and pressure from the organisers and counsel for Folk Arts Council and Folklorama, the lovely and health-conscious Multi-Culti-Queer Pavilion . . . would like to issue the following press release regarding the association of their conceptual art installation with the annual multicultural celebration calling itself Folklorama:
>
> *The planned Multi-Culti-Queer Event is not sponsored by, or associated in any [way] with, Folklorama or any of its activities and is not a Folklorama Pavilion.*
>
> *Plug In Gallery or any one or group organising this event has never applied for a Pavilion licence nor have they ever been a member of Folklorama Inc. or applied for membership.*
>
> In light of this press release we would like to repeat that the Multi-Culti-Queer Pavilion will be open to the public come hell or high water. No passports are necessary, only a sense of dismay and wonder. . . .[8] (August 1, 1992)

Folklorama's concern with sameness may have been well-founded, particularly given the Multi-Culti-Queer's parody of its structure. But the greatest success of the spoof was its possibility for moving into locations beyond its own art gallery venue, and for restructuring Folklorama's prototype discourse. For example, the Folklorama brochure's evocation of desire and pleasure uncomfortably becomes something different, something no longer "family-oriented" in the conventional sense, when juxtaposed to queer culture: "Become *one* with the culture of the world . . . you are guaranteed to experience the wonderful cultural diversity that makes Canada, indeed the world so magnificent . . . *one* exciting festival . . . *one* sizzling summer show." (Brochure 1993, emphases mine)

Ultimately, Folklorama argued that the problem with the Multi-Culti-Queer pavilion was infringement of copyright. They requested that the sponsoring gallery, Plug In, be restrained from using the name 'Folklorama,' and, they said, "in particular, from displaying the name 'Folklorama' on any wearing apparel or any printed or other material advertising or displaying the Multi Culti Queer event . . . from holding and sponsoring a Miss/Mr Queer 'Folklorama', etc." (Court Order, 1992). The last matter to be resolved was that of the T-shirts, which were surgically altered to comply with Folklorama demands.[9]

Folklorama apparently feared an inevitable reaction of shock and horror by their straight, middle-aged and older, mainstream Canadian and American tourist and local audience, and thus, damage to their reputation via a queer infection of their body politic. It was, however, extremely unlikely that any real confusion might ensue. The Plug In Gallery is located in a part of the city with no Folklorama venues. No other pavilion was domiciled in an art gallery. And since the Multi-Culti-Queer was not part of official Folklorama, and thus not on the map, in the passport, nor on any of the tours, the possibility of an "innocent" bystander's mistaking it was minimal. I never heard of any such confusion occurring.

Folklorama's organizers claimed that the problem was that no application had been made to become the official Folklorama queer pavilion. Queer Culture Canada immediately requested an application for the following year. They were told the forms were being redesigned and that one would be sent as soon as they were ready. Last time I spoke to the organizers, Queer Culture Canada was still waiting.

Perhaps Folklorama chose the copyright (sameness) issue because to make a damage-to-reputation argument would have necessitated more frank statements of homophobia than Manitoba's public culture of niceness could readily accommodate. After all, our license plate says "Friendly Manitoba." Indeed, lawyers might have had some difficulty arguing a case that defamed a group that was even then protected in part by the Manitoba Human Rights Code's ban on discrimination according to sexual orientation. (Federal anti-discrimination laws' inclusion of lesbian and gay rights followed much later.)

But this fear and loathing was by no means an univocally heterosexual response, as columnist George Stephenson pointed out. His consideration began with the question, debated in feminist and queer theory as well, of the value of using nation as a metaphor to describe what may in fact be a more migrant, nomadic, homeless culture:[10]

> Many gays were not amused by the so-called pavilion, wondering just what nation—country—they were supposed to represent. These would

> be gays who would settle for being accepted as normal, everyday, boring members of society, whose contributions are not centred on their sexual orientation. You like vanilla, I like strawberry. Who cares? But no. Instead, they are portrayed as a bunch of quiche-and-salad-eating, fruit-shake-drinking folks who like to encourage being called queers. This isn't the image appreciated by gay friends of mine, who, aside from their dating preferences, consider themselves the same as anyone else. . . . Of course the Queer Pavilion is making sport with stereotypes, showing it has, one assumes, a sense of irony or humor—or something. Just what this accomplishes is far from obvious. We don't see the real pavilions advancing the cause of ethnic minorities by making fun of themselves. Watermelon served at a pavilion set up by blacks? No. Polish jokes told at a pavilion celebrating Poland? No. Minorities of any kind have enough trouble with stereotypes created by others. It hardly advances human rights when they do it to themselves. (5)

In fact, as recent work by my research team on Folklorama shows, many official pavilions are by no means beyond representing themselves stereotypically—or parodically. Yet many resist such portrayals, and enact a realism that seems contrary to the "light family entertainment" ethos of much of the festival. Anthropologist Cynthia Thoroski has noted, for example, the 1996 Ireland/Irish pavilion's acknowledgement of "the devastation of conflicts in Northern Ireland . . . within the context of a cultural poster display," but also their refusal to create faked Irish accents and their presentation and enjoyment of "English drinking [and other] songs of dubious Irish descent" ("Adventures in Ethnicity" 1997).

Nor are the Folklorama pavilions beyond employing irony; this trope was not exclusive to Queer culture's depictions. Thoroski also comments upon the very popular Africa/Caribbean pavilion. In addition to its "wonderful spicy food . . . dramatic and energetic stage shows featuring the Uganda dancers, drumming displays and the spectacular flaming Jamaican limbo dancer/fire eater Neville Johnson," it had, in her words:

> a cultural display [which] mirrored the souvenir-style tourism of all the other pavilions. . . . [It presented] dubious cultural artifacts such as fabric banners with the names of countries or regions printed on them, shell necklaces, and t-shirts. . . . [but also] a book on how to make money selling souvenirs to tourists. On the cover of this exposé was a white man in full rasta attire, selling the same sorts of items which were visible in the cultural display for the Africa/Caribbean pavilion. ("Adventures in Ethnicity" 1997)

Like these satirical comments and the Ireland/Irish pavilion's resistance to expectations, the Multi-Culti-Queer pavilion questioned the comfortable notion that ethnicity and culture are not only fundamentally unthreatening, but also fundamentally "foreign." These interventions highlight the uncommon in the common, and the everyday in the exotic.[11]

But for too many Canadians, ethnicity and culture are not only the exclusive property of others, but they must also at all costs be kept explicitly separate from the economic and political spheres of "real life." An ironic stance toward *any* cultural representation, in this perspective, becomes problematic. Culture, in this framework, is an authentic reified truth. Stereotypes may be dismissed as both partial and negative, but they nevertheless refer to the others being stereotyped, rather than to the selves who use them to other. The resisting pavilions, and the Multi-Culti-Queer pavilion, show that exoticism is constructed by the mainstream, not by the margin. And so, raising what was for some the spectre of a Queer Nation in our very midst, the Folklorama's sameness discourse could not help making a useful political point: there is here; they are us.

THE FESTIVAL DU VOYAGEUR/ THE FESTIVAL DU VOYEUR

The initial touchstone of the Festival du Voyeur was the partly concurrent Festival du Voyageur. A web page promises:

> a truely [sic] family orientated atmosphere [where] most of the city is transformed into a winter wonderland, with giant snow sculptures being erected at most of the city's main intersections and many community centers being converted into what we call 'trading posts' . . . where one can sample local and heritage foods and, take part in an old fashion [sic] way in the joie de vivre of the old time voyageurs. Everybody dawns [sic] thier [sic] ceinture flecher [sic] (or sach [sic]) red touque and moccasins for this ten day celebration which starts off with a huge street party. . . . The atmosphere at this event has been likened to the great feasts of the wintering partners of the fur trade in the 18th and 19th centuries. During the festival week you can partake in the voyageur games to test your strengt [sic] and agility, or, in the worlds [sic] largest beard growing contest, or maybe take a dog team for a ride on the river. All this happens during the second week of Feburary [sic] every year to celebrate our Native, French, Scotish [sic], and Irish heritages in a uniqly [sic] canadian [sic] way and to relive our past so that our children can get a sense of roots. (Beaudry 1996)

Franco Manitobans, who are the Voyageur's primary subject, are contingently a marginalized group in the context of the Anglophone mainstream, but this event clearly invokes explicitly colonialist scenes and rhetorics. British curator Simon Herbert commented:

> Whilst the frozen river banks of the Assiniboine hosted beard-growing contests, dog-sled trials and huge carved ice sculptures, the Plug In Gallery hosted three freezers which, when opened, contained small ice sculptures such as Sondra Haglund's "Lick Me, Lick Me, Lick Me" and Richard Dyck's "Please Taste." As the buck-skin voyageurs would say, "plus ça change . . ." (Herbert 1993)

If Folklorama's reaction to the Multi-Culti-Queer pavilion was "people could think we're the same," the Festival du Voyageur's reaction to the Voyeurs was "people shouldn't think we're not different." Semantically, voyageurs and voyeurs could be very different creatures; morphologically and phonetically, they're very easy to confuse.[12]

This play of sameness/difference is nowhere more clearly articulated than in a *Winnipeg Sun* article entitled "Can You See the Difference?" which compares and contrasts the two events. It opens with a comparison between my own essay for the Festival du Voyeur catalogue (Greenhill 1993) and the message from the Prime Minister of Canada included in the Voyageur program—strange bedfellows! And they continue:

> [Voyageur] Program has message from the Office of the Mayor/[Voyeur] Program mentions that the mayor is on the verge of declaring Pink Triangle Day, along with German Shepherd Week [Despite annual requests, then Mayor Susan Thompson NEVER declared Pink Triangle Day, but you will be happy to know that she did declare German Shepherd Week.] . . .
>
> [Voyageur's] Winter Galleries features ice sculptures of Voyageurs, buffaloes, historical figures; [Voyeur's] Deep Freezer ice sculpture installations feature artworks that, according to the program, "reflect on the 'voyeur' in queer culture and aspects of a 'winter paradise.'" . . .
>
> [Voyageur's] Maple Sugar Shack serves maple syrup snow cakes; In [Voyeur's] show Mermaid In Love[13] Shawna Dempsey crushes a cake between her thighs. . . .
>
> [Voyageur's] Band at the La Fame de Nuit Trading Post includes country cajun band Prairie Fire; [Voyeur's] film program . . . includes the gay cult film Flaming Creatures. (King, 31)

Reporter Randall King's strategic choices construct more similarities between the two events than the actual Voyeur program might suggest. In fact, the main reference to the Voyageur festival in displays and events was in the Voyeur's Deep Freezer Ice Sculptures (parodying Voyageur's monumental, public, uncloseted ice sculptures). However, the original grant application asserted:

> Festival du Voyeur . . . addresses some of the gaps in [Voyageur's] presentation of a closed and whole sense of history. Our Festival intends to highlight the ill-informed notion of a universal history applied to the Voyageur Festival that ignores questions such as: "What was the structure, function, historical surround of same-sex love in and for the voyageur (lesbian or gay) or aboriginal peoples (lesbian or gay)?" We propose that this question is central to the almost infinite elasticity that suggests no one can know in advance where the limits of a queer-centred inquiry are to be drawn, or where a queer theorizing of and through even the hegemonic high (or low) culture of the European tradition may need or be able to lead. . . . Collectively speaking the artists and writers in our Festival plan to take imagery and subject matter identified with the Voyageur (some of it sexist, historically incorrect and exclusionary) turning it on its head. (Baerwaldt et al)

Despite these intentions, in fact, the materials represented—including paintings by Attila Richard Lukacs, photography by Pierre Molinier, a public lecture by Eve Kosofsky Sedgwick, a performance by Tim Miller, and so on—actively explored the issue of voyeurism much more than they referenced the Franco Manitoban Festival.

The "Can You Tell the Difference" article also began by asserting that "Festival du Voyageur is comfortable enough with its masculinity/femininity to be good natured about the competition" (King 31). Even leaving aside the implied definition of masculinity and femininity in exclusively heterosexual terms, this assertion was quite untrue. In 1993, Voyageur president Lucille Cenerini wrote a letter to Allan Gottlieb, chair of the Canada Council, Voyeur's major funder, in which they asked for an apology from Plug In. They asked that the gallery cease to promote activities threatening their images. They wanted the Canada Council to open a review and demand that Plug In stop using the name Festival du Voyeur; and stop its aggressive action against the Festival du Voyageur, including using symbols and logos which seek to mock the organization and its activities, before any further subvention be advanced. The fulcrum of Cenerini's argument was that the Festival du Voyeur, unlike the Festival du Voyageur, was a political event—that they were essentially, fundamentally different. She asked:

> How can the Festival du Voyageur maintain its cultural integrity if it must compete with organisations which receive funds for artistic work, but in which the art is in part a façade for political objectives? The kind of intervention and resources necessary to act in this socio-political scene is not always available to cultural groups, so that organisations which promote art and culture become the targets/butts ("les cibles") for those which are political. This is not about suggesting intervention against artistic groups with political missions, but this should not be done at the expense of cultural organizations and especially not with public funds (translation mine).

The "no politics here" argument advanced by organizations like Voyageur and Folklorama is a pillar of mainstream thought, and contributes to the disappearing of queer culture.[14] As I've suggested,[15] this viewpoint sees ethnicity in terms of display, colour, and quaintness—as it does sexuality in terms of specific practices in the bedroom—and eschews the political dimensions of both.

In any case, the construction of difference in Cenerini's letter is voiced as a fear of sameness; people might think Voyageur is political too. But underlying this concern may be another fear, that Voyeur's presence makes Voyageur's implicit politics of colonalization explicit, just as the Multi-Culti-Queer pavilion forced a reinterpretation of Folklorama.

Canada Council chair Allan Gottlieb's response expressed sorrow that the Voyeur organizers hadn't taken the initiative to make Voyageur aware of their intentions, and the hope that they would do so. He strongly reaffirmed the Council's decision on the basis of quality of the artistic programming, support by the arts community, and quality of the work of the artists involved. His reaction, of course, equally side-stepped the issue of the politics of art and culture, and reframed it in the more comfortable terms of peer review and excellence.

But the politics of art and culture—what Plug In curator Wayne Baerwaldt called "going beyond your own bedroom"—was in fact the Festival's fulcrum. When we go beyond our own bedrooms, clearly, identity and self—gay against straight; Winnipegger or not; youth versus experience—become potently meaningful. Queer culture can be mainstream legitimate only in limited terms; it must remain in the realm of the aesthetic cultural, and never intrude into "real life"—economics, politics, and so forth. When it does, as Cenerini's letter makes clear, it's a betrayal not only of ideology, but also of Canadian nationhood. It becomes, in Phelan's prescriptive terms, identity politics:

> Identity politics [means] building our public action on who we are and how that identity fits into and does not fit into our society. This is and must be the basis for political action that addresses nonjuridical, non-state-centred power. . . . If we are to be free, we must learn to embrace paradox and confusion; in short, we must embrace politics. Identity politics must be based on an appreciation for politics as the art of living together. Politics that ignores our identities, that makes them "private," is useless; but nonnegotiable identities will enslave us whether they are imposed from within or without. (170)

REMAINING QUEERIES

And there have been further moves in this direction. Perhaps inspired at least in part by the Multi-Culti-Queer pavilion and the Festival du Voyeur, Winnipeg artist Michael Olito has more recently taken on what he calls the "ethnic posturing" of Folklorama and Voyageur. His group, "Zapatistas del Norte," infiltrated the Festival du Voyageur in 1996 with an alleged plan to construct a snow sculpture depicting a Métis riding a buffalo. Olito's periodical publication, *Under the Machete*, reports that "what emerged from the snow block after five hours of furious attacks was Emiliano Zapata riding a rhinoceros." (Olito himself was a "rogue Rhino" candidate in several federal elections.) [16]

Olito followed this with a "High Noon" raid on the new Louis Riel[17] statue at the Manitoba Legislature, which replaced a controversial predecessor. He asserted that "depicting [Riel] as a staid bureaucrat rather than a tortured rebel is an insult not only to the Métis of Canada but to all rebels. . . . History cannot be made right simply by making Riel larger than Queen Victoria."[18] "Louis Gets His Hat" reports that "accompanied by Spanish music played on a guitar and violin, [the Zapatistas Del Norte] place a huge sombrero of willow sticks on the head of the Louis Riel statue." And the group warned, "See you at Folklorama."

To the opening of Folklorama 1996, the Zapatistas took their own cultural display, music, and food in their "mobile pavilion," a pick-up truck "decorated with flowers, masks, banners, and armadillos. Mariachi music blared from the old tape deck and Zapatistas in authentic Mexican costume offered ethnic food, beans, to the people." Olito reported to me that Folklorama security's response was to threaten to call the police, slash the truck's tires, and beat up the musicians. Nevertheless, the pavilion drove away peacefully, and once the official party had entered the Pantages theatre, the Zapatistas "drove around town, becoming the only float in our own Folklorama parade."

And finally, an ice sculpture of an armadillo wearing a sombrero emblazoned with a Z appeared at Provencher Park in 1997. Olito notes that "[t]he

Central Committee of the revolution chose an armadillo because it more closely resembled a rhinoceros than any other Mexican animal did, although some exaggeration in size was necessary."

I profoundly appreciated the humour and commitment displayed in these festival spoofs. But can I, the token female heterosexual anthropological voyeur, have citizenship in these countries? My place in these events, like that of many who do not share their queer—or artistic—identity, was to wander about, and wonder about, the limits of culture. Anthropologists' invocations of concepts of self and other may be useful for the groups anthropologists have actively othered, and for anthropologists who need to recognize their privilege and colonial status. Anthropologists have proved time and time again that, as my activist friends would say, knowing how to talk the talk does not necessarily mean that you actually walk the walk. Perhaps I have in this reflection been guilty of some of the excesses for which I criticize anthropologists and institutions alike. I have created a couple of straw festivals—Folklorama and the Festival du Voyageur—and then bashed them with a queer stick. I have invoked heroes and villains; exemplars of truth and exemplars of false consciousness. I am in danger of establishing and reinforcing a mainstream and a margin, rather than of critiquing the processes which create those divisions.

As researcher Lisa Hagen-Smith suggests, the politics of festivals and of festival parodies needs further scrutiny. She says "while the [Multi-Culti-Queer] performers may think they are challenging the mainstream view of Folklorama, it *feels* like they are offering up our culture to be consumed in the very same way as other ethnicities, a dish from the multicultural feast of sexuality. And, as we have already discovered, this does not necessarily bring with it a lessening of homophobia, any more than an Aboriginal pavilion lessens racism in Winnipeg" (personal communication, 1997). This happens, at least in part, because of the class location of the objects of Queer Culture Canada's parodies. Specifically, as Hagen-Smith says, "Many at the Multi-Culti-Queer pavilion were inhabiting elite spaces at the same time as their queer spaces. . . . There is more than one fringe here, and the fringe is not always the most marginal space."[19] In choosing to parody Folklorama, Queer Culture Canada made fun of the kind of polyester, bus tour, French-fries-and-gravy culture that is too easy a target because we middle-class folks know it's tacky, and we're supposed to laugh at it.

To some, any criticism of Folklorama, the Festival du Voyageur, or other expressions of ethnicity runs the risk of racism.[20] The intended parody in the events under discussion here was not of marginalization, but instead of attempts to create readily consumable, mainstream, legitimate commodities out of cultural difference. Yet it is clear that many people—queer and nonqueer—mistook the Multi-Culti-Queer and the Festival du Voyeur as ethnic and racial slurs, or even as insults against queers. Because of their marked objects, such interventions can be dismissed as inappropriate or wrong-headed—but of course it's possible to dismiss any intervention, no matter how politically focused. And it's more difficult to take on the mainstream because of its slipperiness, its lack of definition.

Further, it's hard to imagine that the organizers and supporters of the Festival du Voyageur, as members of a socially and politically embattled marginal linguistic and cultural group, *really* think their actions are apolitical. My research team cannot ascertain if this is truly their position, because the Executive Directors of both events have declined to work with us. But a stance of such wide-eyed innocence seems fairly implausible. Simultaneous with the 1998 Festival du Voyageur was some public lobbying to get "Bienvenue" added to Manitoba's "Friendly" license plate, as well as considerable fur advertising and anti-fur protest. A questionnaire, administered by the public opinion research group Viewpoints, asked Voyageur visitors if they were attending because they were looking for winter entertainment, because they supported French and English culture, or because they supported French culture. Politics and political concerns, albeit somewhat muted, were present. The constraints of multicultural and heritage funding make the kind of culture criticism and advocacy in the Voyeur event impossible for the Voyageur. Voyeur as an arts event is subject to peer review by artists, but Voyageur's funding—contrary to its own protestations—responds to political concerns. Hagen-Smith suggests Voyageur organizers could have been "'performing' ignorance of political agendas because they are also trapped by the mainstream culture of 'no politics here' for their own agendas" (personal communication, 1997). If they want to keep their grants, any resistance must be covert and coded.[21]

But some might suggest that the situation in Winnipeg and in Canada has changed drastically since the beginning of the last decade of the twentieth century when the Voyeur Festival and the Multi-Culti-Queer Pavilion took place. After all, in 1998, Winnipeg elected Canada's first openly gay mayor, Glen Murray. Some queer activism and artistic expression in Winnipeg has become more carefully circumspect as a result of Murray's election. Artists Shawna Dempsey and Lorri Millan are pursuing a Human Rights case against Mediacom for refusing to display their "Winnipeg—One Gay City" posters in 1997,[22] but are concerned that currently, public display of these artworks might be interpreted as a reflection on Murray. Yet these artists and other groups, like the Radical Cheerleaders who perform at rallies, on Pride Day, and at fundraising venues throughout the city, and the activist group Queer Invasion, do not feel that Murray's election signals the actual formation of a gay paradise. In fact, at least one local radio talk show aired on the evening of the Winnipeg civic election unleashed a torrent of rampant homophobia and hate speech. Several callers threatened to move out of the city because of Murray's election.[23]

Since the Multi-Culti-Queer Pavilion and the Festival du Voyeur, lesbians and gays have been granted named and specific protection under the Canadian Charter of Rights and Freedoms. Yet, if mention in the Charter actually guaranteed equal treatment, there would be no more discrimination against the differently-abled, women, or people of colour. Sadly, that is not the case.

And so I hope there will be other events as simultaneously engaging, amusing, and perplexing as the Multi-Culti-Queer Pavilion and the Festival du Voyeur. Even if they leave the viewers with more queeries than straight answers, I guess that's as it should be.

ACKNOWLEDGMENTS

It is a pleasure to thank those whose help with this work was literally indispensable. Noam Gonick, President of Queer Culture Canada, who first welcomed me; Wayne Baerwaldt and Thea Demetrakopolous at Plug In, who echoed that welcome; and all those other participants and observers who've helped me to see their understanding of the Festival du Voyeur, Multi-Culti-Queer, and related phenomena by agreeing to be interviewed or just talking it over: Don Belton, Di Brandt, Karen Busby, Nathalie Cohen, Shawna Dempsey, Alison Gillmor, Bob McKaskell, Lorri Millan, Jay Mirus, Mike Olito, Pat Onysko, and Robert Taylor. Comments from Doug Arrell, Lisa Hagen-Smith, and Cynthia Thoroski helped me to think through the issues. I also gratefully acknowledge funding for my work from a Social Sciences and Humanities Research Council of Canada (SSHRC) research grant.

NOTES

1. Yes, this individual is gendered male as evident in Clifford and Marcus.
2. See Sedgwick and Lisa Hagen-Smith, 113–121.
3. A useful discussion of the problematics of the idea of representation can be found in Findlay.
4. See Lisa Hagen-Smith for a discussion on rainbow flag symbolism in Pride parades.
5. For more on Folklorama, see Greenhill (1999), Thoroski (1997), and Thoroski and Greenhill (2001).
6. Many in the ethnic organizations feel that profit provides a more reasonable explanation for pavilion pluralism (see Thoroski and Greenhill, forthcoming).
7. Pronounced "will go."
8. For some years, Folklorama visitors could buy a "passport" with which they were

entitled to unlimited entries into all pavilions. This mode of payment was recently discontinued as financially unfeasible.

9. Thea, Noam, and I sat in the Plug In lawyer's office and cut the word "Folklorama" out of the T-shirt. All the shirts, and all the "Folkloramas," were counted before the shirts were returned to the gallery. I don't know what happened to the "Folkloramas."
10. For more on contemporary nomadic culture, see Braidotti, 245–257.
11. I discuss this and other manifestations of the tension between the exotic and the everyday in Greenhill (1994).
12. As I have proved several times when presenting this paper, and said "Voyeur" for "Voyageur," and vice versa. Similarly, a University of Manitoba law professor, who assigned the voyeur/voyageur copyright issue as a case study for her students, recounted to me how one of them, arguing the case for the "Voyeur" side, began, "No one could ever confuse voyeurs with voyageurs," but throughout the presentation frequently substituted one for the other.
13. This is an error, the cake squish was part of Dempsey and Millan's piece "Mary Medusa" (see Greenhill 1998).
14. As discussed, in other contexts, in Sedgwick.
15. For example in Greenhill (forthcoming).
16. With the disbanding of the surrealist/anarchic Rhinoceros party, Olito could not run as an official Rhino, hence his "rogue" status.
17. Métis leader Louis Riel is generally considered the founder of the province of Manitoba. He was found guilty of treason and hanged in 1885.
18. The statue of a seated Queen Victoria directly in front of the Manitoba Legislature is quite imposing. Size doesn't matter, of course, but perhaps placement does—Louis Riel is at the back.
19. For a discussion of the problematic risking of protection against discrimination in litigation concerning sexual orientation, see Carol Allen.
20. Though one might wonder whether or not such accusations are in fact attempts to reinscribe the status quo. For example, not all people of colour experience racism in the same way—class and a secure economic position can provide a substantial buffer against many forms of discrimination. And not all individuals with white privilege can access that privilege directly or on an everyday basis.
21. For discussions of queer and feminist coding, see Radner.
22. Oakley discusses the transformation of this project from posters to postcards.
23. To which we might reply, "Good riddance!"

WORKS CITED

Allen, Carol. "Who Gets To Be Family?" In *And Still We Rise: Feminist Political Mobilizing in Contemporary Canada*. Ed. Linda Carty. Toronto: Women's Press, 1993. 101–108.

Baerwaldt, Wayne, et al. Explorations Program Grant Application, Queer Culture Canada, Festival du Voyeur, September 14, 1992.

Beaudry, F. "Festival du Voyageur." 1996. [Cited 1996] <cyberplus.ca/~jembree/festival.htm>.

Braidotti, Rosi. *Nomadic Subjects: Embodiment and Sexual Difference in Contemporary Feminist Theory.* New York: Columbia University Press, 1994.

Clifford, James and George E. Marcus. *Writing Culture: The Poetics and Politics of Ethnography.* Berkeley: University of California Press, 1986.

Findlay, Sue. "Problematizing Privilege: Another Look at Representation." In *And Still We Rise: Feminist Political Mobilizing in Contemporary Canada.* Ed. Linda Carty. Toronto: Women's Press, 1993. 207–224.

Greenhill, Pauline. "Rethinking Festival." *Festival du Voyeur: Canada's Most Thrilling Art Album*, Winnipeg, Manitoba, 2, 1993.

———. *Ethnicity in the Mainstream: Three Studies of English Canadian Culture in Ontario.* Montreal: McGill-Queen's University Press, 1994.

———. "Lesbian Mess(ages): Decoding Shawna Dempsey's Cake Squish at the Festival du Voyeur." *Atlantis* 23.1 (1998): 91–99.

———. "Backyard World/Canadian Culture: Looking at Festival Agendas." *Canadian University Music Review* 19.2 (1999): 37–46.

———. "Folk and Academic Racism: Concepts from Morris and Folklore." *Journal of American Folklore.* Forthcoming.

Hagen-Smith, Lisa. "Politics and Celebration: Manifesting the Rainbow Flag." *Canadian Folklore canadien* 19.2 (1997): 113–121.

Herbert, Simon. "Festival du Voyeur." Unpublished manuscript, 1993.

King, Randall. "Can You See The Difference?" *Winnipeg Sun* (February 12, 1993), 31.

Oakley, Janice. "Postcards from the Edge: Decoding Winnipeg's 'One Gay City' Campaign." *Ethnologies* 21.1 (1999): 177–192.

Phelan, Shane. *Identity Politics: Lesbian Feminism and the Limits of Community.* Philadelphia: Temple University Press, 1989.

Radner, Jo. "Gay Talk in Straight Company: Strategies of Complicit Coding By Lesbians and Gay Men." Paper presented by the "Gay and Lesbian Coding" panel at the American Folklore Society meetings, Eugene, Oregon, 1993.

Sedgwick, Eve Kosofsky. *Epistemology of the Closet.* Berkeley: University of California Press, 1990.

———. "Nationalisms and Sexualities in the Age of Wilde." In *Nationalisms and Sexualities.* Eds. Andrew Parker, Mary Russo, Doris Sommer, and Patricia Yaeger. New York: Routledge, 1992. 235–245.

Stephenson, George. "Folklorama stunt irks gays most." *Winnipeg Sun* (August 9, 1992), 5.

Thoroski, Cynthia. "Adventures in Ethnicity: Consuming Performances of Cultural Identity in Winnipeg's Folklorama," presented at Folklore Studies Association of

Canada/Canadian Women's Studies/Association for Canadian Studies meetings, Learned Societies, St. John's, Newfoundland, 1997.

———. "Adventures in Ethnicity: Consuming Performances of Cultural Identity in Winnipeg's Folklorama." *Canadian Folklore canadien* 19:2 (1997): 105–113.

———. and Pauline Greenhill, forthcoming. "Putting a Price on Culture: Ethnic Organizations, Volunteers, and the Marketing of Multicultural Festivals." *Ethnologies.* 23.1 (2001): 189–210.

Walker, Morley. "Firing at MTN benefits gay fest." *Winnipeg Free Press* (January 29, 1993), D8.

the bisexuality wars: the perils of identity as marginality

Zoë Newman

What I will describe in the next few pages is something I suspect many of us will unfortunately recognize from political work. This is an account of how a group of white women created a community around what were assumed to be common cultural identities and political goals, and how this same group reached an impasse—"the bisexuality wars"—and eventually disbanded in the course of disputes about identity. [1] To understand how identity can be both a catalyst for and an impediment to political struggle, I have looked at the various constructions of identity at work in the group referred to here by the pseudonym Jewish Feminist Action (JFA). More than a discussion of bisexuality, this essay is a reflection on the perils of identity constructed as marginality, an identity constructed in defiance of the multiply constituted subject.

In the fall of 1992, a dozen or so white women gathered in a living room in downtown Toronto. They were politically engaged and progressive—women who were students, artists, activists, professionals. They had assembled to discuss the possibility of starting a political organization that would allow them to be active as both Jews *and* feminists. This desire, I'm told, arose from a growing sense of alienation in work with other politically progressive groups. Apparently one story became emblematic as it was repeated by the women assembled: having experienced anti-Semitism while doing work on antiracism. The women I interviewed all described the first meeting as intense and exciting: everyone was telling stories they'd "never shared" before. These stories were greeted with reactions of delight and dismay and surprise. The women in the room kept exclaiming they'd never known others felt the way they did. There was a sense of sameness and commonality and of having found a political home. Out of this came JFA, and meetings a couple of times a month, and demonstrations, and pamphlets, and much discussion.

Two years later, JFA was organizing an annual commemoration of Jewish resistance during the Holocaust, when one woman pointed out that something had been left out in two places in a pamphlet created for the event: in the section titled "who is JFA," bisexual women were not mentioned as members, and where JFA declared what it existed to combat, biphobia was equally absent. In response, someone said, "We haven't had the bisexuality debate yet," and she was then accused of being biphobic by the first woman. Thus began the bisexuality debate or the bisexuality wars,[2] with JFA effectively divided along two lines: "Bisexual oppression does not exist as a separate category," and "Bisexual oppression does exist and so do bisexuals." Along with their opposing attitudes towards bisexuality, the two contingents were divided on the politics of identity. The former camp, which I'll refer to as the gatekeepers, argued that for specific historical and political reasons, it is necessary to keep identity categories clear, at least in relation to the line between bisexuals and lesbians. The second camp, the boundary-blurrers, maintained that categories are only useful strategically, and that self-identification and complicating categories are called for in various present-day political contexts.

Many versions of bisexuality were mobilized in the course of the bisexuality wars. Among them: that bisexuality does not exist, but is only the intermediate identity adopted by those who a) are just coming out as lesbians; b) are *really* lesbians but are afraid to say so; and c) are lesbians but wish to preserve for themselves some fragment of "heterosexual privilege." Alternately, another view was that bisexuals do exist, but they're not to be entirely trusted because they fraternize/sleep with the enemy, and as a result won't always defend their lesbian sisters in times of need; an offshoot of this is that bisexuals are a problem because usually, when they claim discrimination, they say it is by the lesbian/gay community (otherwise, it is argued, bisexual women actually face discrimination as *de facto* lesbians). It was also argued that bisexuality is an identity that is distinct and separate from both homosexuality and heterosexuality and one that is doubly oppressed by mainstream society, which fears/dislikes ambiguity, and by gay/lesbian communities for the same reason. Bisexuality is a separate and more highly advanced identity which is not bound by the sexed binary system; bisexuality is no more of a distinct category than any other, and is only an artificial name given to a constellation of beliefs and behaviours, recognizing the artificiality of all categories is a valuable political project.

According to the boundary-blurrers, bisexuality was contentious for the gatekeepers because it rendered murky the divide between lesbian and hetero sexuality. However, the blurrers felt that what the keepers rejected most strenuously was the notion that lesbians can discriminate against bisexual women on the basis of their sexuality. The keepers did raise questions about naming bisexuality as a separate category: what does it mean if a woman who is involved in a long-term relationship with another woman calls herself bisexual and not lesbian? What about a woman in a long-term relationship with a man who identifies as bisexual, thus complicating notions of heterosexual privilege? The keepers seemed to be arguing that if sexual connection between women is no longer the sole domain of lesbians, and if lesbians are no longer the only women excluded from the benefits of heterosexuality, then what remains unique about lesbians? Central to these concerns seems to be the desire for identity to be unambiguous and consistent. Ideas about power and the parameters of community—specifically, that one is either exclusively privileged or oppressed, not both—are also implicitly contained in these notions of identity.

The gatekeepers objected to the notion of biphobia because it implicates gays and lesbians in the oppression of bisexual people. Biphobia as a category separate from homophobia suggests that bisexual people are discriminated against not just for their difference from dominant culture, but also for their difference from gay and lesbian cultures. This aspect of the conflict clearly involved differing power analyses: gatekeepers maintained that if you are lesbian, you are an oppressed person, and as such are powerless and incapable of oppressing anyone else; the position of boundary-blurrers was that in places where lesbians form the majority, lesbians are in a position to wield power against bisexual women, and further, that bisexual people are not only discriminated against for being attracted to people of the same sex, but are universally regarded with suspicion for their sexual ambiguity or plurality.

As the debate continued, in all-day meetings and with moderators, people grew defensive and hostile. Women who had been friends felt betrayed by each other, and ultimately, though unofficially, the group came apart. For months, I wondered why the argument had become so personal, and what had fueled it to persist so long. I was initially struck by the similarity between what had happened in JFA, and the political debates within gay and lesbian organizations that Joshua Gamson examined in "Must Identity Movements Self-Destruct? A Queer Dilemma." He characterizes a particular set of conflicts as arising when competing understandings of identity and power meet in the same activist movement. Gamson writes of the results as:

> ... "border skirmishes" over membership conditions and group boundaries ... [which] spotlight the possibility that sexual and gender identities are not the solid political ground they have been thought to be—which perhaps accounts for the particularly frantic tone of [disputes]. (398)

However, I realized that at least in JFA, there was another dynamic at work: an identity dispute predating the bisexuality wars that might very well have triggered the conflict in JFA.

During the winter of 1993–94, just a few months before the bisexuality wars, JFA was working in coalition with other antiracism activists—both women of colour and white women—to develop some educational materials on antiracism.[3] The coalition had agreed at the outset that anti-Semitism would be named as a form of racism in these materials. However, as the materials were created, anti-Semitism was not mentioned, and it began to be clear that racism as it was defined in these texts only referred to skin colour. When the omissions were pointed out by JFA representatives in the coalition, the material was modified to reflect experiences of Jews and Arabs. But when a subsequent coalition document was produced, racism was again defined as a form of oppression on the basis of skin colour. Once more a member of JFA disputed this definition, and once more a change was made, to include the naming of racial minorities as marginalized people. Throughout this process there seems to have been goodwill on all sides, and willingness to compromise and reformulate positions. However, at a general meeting of the coalition, someone—not a member of JFA—made a statement that combating anti-Semitism was not a mandate of the group. When the member of JFA in the coalition questioned this statement, she was told that this had been the coalition's mandate from the beginning, and that JFA had agreed to participate on those grounds. At that point, according to a letter JFA wrote, another member of the coalition got up and said that JFA had been "manipulative" at the last meeting, consequently convincing the coalition to include anti-Semitism, and that JFA was trying to destroy the coalition. During that meeting, it was also suggested that anti-Semitism is not a form of racism. JFA responded with a letter requesting the following: a commitment from the coalition to address anti-Semitism in its mandate and work; acknowledgment that certain of the coalition's acts were anti-Semitic and an apology for same; and reassurances that members of the coalition would educate themselves about anti-Semitism. There was no response to the letter, either in coalition meetings or their minutes, or directly to JFA. Eventually, JFA withdrew from the coalition. It later turned out that the coalition had approached other Jewish women's organizations to continue discussions about the relationship between anti-Semitism and racism.

That these remarkable parallels were not apparent to me when I started to work on what had happened with JFA points to my own inability to recognize how issues in JFA were "raced." Nor did anyone I talked to from JFA note a parallel between the competing marginalities of lesbian and bisexual identities with debates about the relationship between racism and anti-Semitism—and here I'm mindful not only of the specific example above, but also of the earlier stories of alienation that women recounted at JFA's inception. The struggle for Jews about acknowledging anti-Semitism as a form of racism represents the possibility that Jews are not only complicit with racist systems, but also similarly victimized by them. What gets slippery is whether definitions of racism that include anti-Semitism produce an understanding of how identity is marked by shifting moments of privilege and subordination, or whether such inclusive definitions are incorporated into identity positions as confirmation that Jews, in this example, experience discrimination and therefore cannot be responsible for racism. My conjecture about how and why this displacement—from the conflict about anti-Semitism as a form of racism, to the debate about bisexuality and biphobia—manifested itself is best answered with a dissection of identity constructions.

I imagine the formulation of identity operative in JFA as a series of assumptions, or a chain of logic. The logic goes like this: first, the subject is coherent, stable, and knowable—both to itself and to others; second, identity is a manifestation or representation of the subject's self-knowledge, and as such is similarly stable and autonomous; third, political identification is born of experiences of marginalization and homelessness, which suggests from a psychoanalytic perspective that identity is then always, at some level, about marginalization; and finally, marginalized subjects, once they have publicly identified themselves, will be able to come together and work towards liberation.[4]

This chain of logic affords a view of how the construction of identity operates within a framework of interlocking narratives; identities of marginality are always premised on what dominant culture has deemed abject or has romanticized as forbidden. Even when those demonized categories have been resisted and reappropriated, marginal identities still constitute the outer boundaries of what is considered normative in dominant culture. As Sander Gilman says, "in reversing the idea of 'race,' we have not eliminated its negative implications, we have only masked them" (171). Even when we have transformed epithets into proud slogans, we are still engaged in a system that depends upon absolute boundaries, between self and other, and between two marginalized identities which claim independence from each other, despite the ways they are comprehensible only in relation to each other. Within that system, there is little room to assert an identity composed of otherness and dominance, or of shifting culpability and innocence. Once marginality premised on undistorted self-knowledge and innocence are embraced as an identity and a place of even equivocal safety, it must be policed in order to maintain that notion of selfhood.

And yet Judith Butler reminds us that the process of identification is always ambivalent and unstable, so the job of policing mandates not just external vigilance, but self-monitoring. [5] And it is a job without end. Thus, what I have come to suspect is that this identity chain is as responsible for making possible our political projects as it is for rendering them unworkable. I will therefore attempt to trace the workings of this chain, and the moments at which it binds us, through JFA's bisexuality wars.

Analyzing systems of oppression as interlocking narratives serves to uncouple one of the links in my chain by disrupting the idea that identities are autonomous and freestanding. Further, what becomes apparent is that the relationship between identities is not only interdependent but hierarchically ordered.[6] To say that systems of oppression are interlocking or symbiotic refers not only to the ways in which social discourses, such as race and gender, draw on each other for coherence; an analysis of how systems interlock also applies to the internal logic of race and gender separately. In the first case, whiteness as a social identity requires a circumscribed otherness. Similarly, lesbian identity depends on a very static and monolithic definition of bisexual identity for its meaning, and white and Jewish lesbian identity are constructed in relation to a colonial notion of women of colour. Rather than identity as a freestanding, singular representation of a true self, identity is constructed as contingent, as a game of dominoes, where shifting one piece—the difference between lesbians and bisexuals—causes a ripple in the entire chain. The crucial relationship revealed in the bisexuality wars is that identities premised on marginality and thus on innocence cannot withstand charges of complicity in oppression.

Sander Gilman makes use of nineteenth-century medical and artistic representations of white and black women to illustrate another version of how systems interconnect. He traces the symbolic installation of interconnections between stereotypes, specifically how the deviance, which is mapped onto one body, is transferred to another. Of particular importance is his thesis that the interactions between stereotypes continue to adhere long after the association has been made.[7] These ideas theorized in his work are suggestive of the older dynamics at play in JFA.

That JFA's bisexuality wars took place in the wake of a disagreement with antiracist women of colour and white women about Jewish identity as marginality makes manifest the constitutive presence of women of colour. The relationship with women of colour in the coalition, and the claims made about who is radicalized, threatened to strip us of our claim to innocence. Yet the actual absence of women of colour in JFA, and JFA's disagreement with the coalition's claims about what "counts" as racism, allowed us to continue to imagine ourselves as marginalized subjects.[8] It was then in the context of JFA that we did battle for a place on the margins in relation to each other.

It is clear from my interviews that JFA came into being for two reasons: to be a political force from a marginalized identity standpoint, and to provide community for its members. Because of anti-Semitism in Toronto, safety in the shape of community was desirable, but the expectation of safety is also related to privilege. I would argue that white middle-class women, challenged about the privileges of white skin, experience a profound threat to our sense of belonging and entitlement, our sense of community and identity. Shaken by this, we sometimes reassert our marginality as a lack of safety. The illusion of sameness or common experiences, and with it the expectation of safety and acceptance, was one of JFA's strongest attractions for people, and was to become one of our greatest stumbling blocks. Similarly, the assumption embedded in the promise of JFA as community was that this group would be the one place where we could reveal and act from all facets of ourselves, as if we could finally be our *true selves.* The equation of identity with self-knowledge had proved attractive, and yet would contribute to the impasse we arrived at.

The model that brought people together in the first place—individuals, their common identities, and the expression of these identities—was the same one that derailed the enterprise in the end. What became contested was which identities are acceptable or innocent, what those identities should look like, why, and when they cease to be recognizable. At work here are three problematic assumptions. First, that there is such a thing as a stable, common identity. Second, that those people who identify the same way—as lesbians—will act the same way. Third, that identity provides sufficient basis for community. The problem is that the "capital L" Lesbian is a fantasy, the creation of pathologizing and romanticizing discourses. And identity is always unstable—because it is constructed through a repetitious performance, and ambivalent because, as Stuart Hall says, it involves "an internalization of the self—as—other," a doubling of fear and desire (255).

Even as everyone extolled the virtues of JFA—feeling accepted, understood, connected—one of the women I interviewed signaled a less apparent uniting element that she found problematic: Jewish identity informed principally by anti-Semitism. This brings us back to the idea of identity as always founded on a sense of marginality. Identity, as marginality, is *a priori* premised on victimhood, which equals a claim of innocence and a denial of dominance. While all the women in JFA were there as Jewish activists, the suggestion that experiences of anti-Semitism are interconnected with needing a Jewish feminist/lesbian community provides another clue to the conflict that ensued.

If the existence of anti-Semitism is an integral part of being Jewish, then that identity will always be ambivalent and premised on victimhood. It is ambivalent because it is the result of internalized anti-Semitism alongside pride; for some of us this ambivalence also resides in not feeling "authentic"—which is anyway a feature of the unattainable ideal of identity. Ashkenazi Jewish identity is also ambivalent because of the possibility for some of passing as white and Christian, which symbolically is an erasure of identity, and materially can produce benefits—though historically, passing has had distinct limits. This erasure of Jewish identity is a double loss of innocence: erasure of the identity of marginality, and replacement with the identity of oppressor. These two elements of identity—ambivalence and innocence, as well as the idea of stability—in one way or another contributed to our dispute.

What is not always explicit is in whose company JFA women had felt alienated in the time before JFA was formed. I suspect that the succor provided by JFA was defined against the difference of unnamed, absent women of colour. Yet, the fragility of the JFA community was also in relation to women of colour. The foundations of that community were unsettled by encounters with some women of colour, who told us at various times that we were being racist, that Zionism is a form of racism, and that anti-Semitism is not racism. If we are capable of being racist, then we are not innocent. If we can be oppressive, then how can we be oppressed? If we are like other white people—oppressive and dominant—then what is unique to being Jewish? This questioning of our individual and community claims, an unsettling that emerged in our relations with women of colour, then prefigured the bisexuality conflict, which pressed all the same buttons: if lesbians can be biphobic, then we are sometimes dominant, not exclusively oppressed; if lesbians can be oppressive, then we are not innocent; if bisexual women have long-term relationships with women, then what is distinct about being lesbian? As Jo Eadie points out:

> So much disavowal suggests a very strong anxiety. And the anxiety is, very simply, this: if there is not a discrete group of people who only ever experience homosexual desire, then *what if we are not so different from the straight world after all?* (153, emphasis mine)

The two debates are analogous in the threat they posed to our identity claims, specifically our claims to being innocent of oppressiveness, and able to self-determine our identities.

We constructed identity not just as marginality, but also as a form of self-knowledge.[9] This identity construction was characterized by the kind of soul-searching that requires significant cultural capital, a further example of how our whiteness was a precondition for the bisexuality wars. The North American liberal ideal is that we come to know ourselves by expanding our horizons, by consuming foreign culture which leads to an appreciation of the superiority and civility of home. To borrow from bell hooks's discussion of young white men experimenting sexually with Black women:

> . . . one dares—acts—on the assumption that the exploration into the world of difference, into the body of the Other, will provide a greater, more intense pleasure than any that exists in the ordinary world of one's familiar racial group. And even though the conviction is that the familiar world will remain intact even as one ventures outside it, the hope is that [the explorer] will reenter the world no longer the same. (24–25)

For some middle-class, white women, feminism and activism are extensions of this same journey towards self-fulfillment and knowledge. This "journey" evokes the colonial quest to travel, conquer, and come to know oneself in relation to foreign bodies who are imagined as all that you are not. The colonial figure, like its present-day descendant, the global citizen, assumes the right to go anywhere. In the economy of the liberal subject, claiming a public political identity is one more manifestation of the search for the true self, a self that is rendered distinct in relation to a constellation of Others.

The search for self is not just a mental activity, but requires material resources, as well as a view of oneself as *entitled* to freedom. Patricia Williams reminds us that "freedom is . . . a relation. On whose back does my freedom rest?" (qtd. in Fellows and Razack, 1065). For libratory projects such as JFA to operate with an understanding of subjectivity and identity categories as stable and as the basis on which to build a politics is tenuous and even self-defeating. Identity as marginality and as self-knowledge rendered it problematic, if not impossible for us in JFA to accept that we occupy a dominant position in relation to women of colour. Mary Louise Fellows and Sherene

Razack describe this situation as "the difference impasse": "Presuming innocence, each of us is consistently surprised when we are viewed by other women as agents of oppression" (1048). I suspect that people who have experienced marginalization sometimes conceptualize a rigid split between the powerful and the powerless, with ourselves on the latter side, in service of a denial of responsibility for oppression—because there are indeed places in our lives when we are subjected to discrimination. Yet to quote Fellows and Razack again, "we have to pay careful attention to the multiple ways in which our listening and speaking are regulated . . . to the moments when we are simultaneously powerless and powerful" (1077). It was perhaps the concrete example of that dual status, as Jewish and white, both "powerless and powerful," that contributed to an unsettling of our identities, and thus predetermined the dispute about bisexuality.

Not only did the bisexuality wars push all the sensitive buttons that set off a challenge to identity and to the self but they stirred up other similar challenges to Jewish lesbian and bisexual identities. Charges that we—Jews—are racist have the same effect as suggestions that lesbians are biphobic and bisexual women have "heterosexual privilege": they disrupt identity posited on marginality, and reveal the coexistence of innocence and complicity. Being told we are not innocent is in effect being told we are not who we thought we were. So we react with great consternation and protest. We make essentialist statements, about ourselves and about what a lesbian is/a bisexual is not. And we race to the margins, where we might find our innocence intact, and our identity stabilized. These moves are triggered by the chain that builds from the subject as coherent, all the way along to the marginal identity and its claims, to the community founded on sameness. However, I do not mean to deny the political and emotional necessity of essentialism. Being fragmented is not mentally comfortable, nor is it strategically astute when under attack. We have only to think of Stuart Hall's statement about the essential black subject, once "a necessary fiction" (254). It is not only at certain historical junctures that we need to present ourselves as coherent, but throughout time there are sites where we virtually cannot, and for our own well-being should not, operate except as some version of the liberal subject. But the dispute in JFA was neither such a moment nor such a place. It may, however, have been a relatively safe place to oppose challenges to our identities constructed as marginality.

There was safety in JFA, which represented home and acceptance to its members. Home and acceptance—in other words, an absence of difference—though it is difference that delineates the limits of identity. The riddle of identity is laid out in one of Eve Kosofsky Sedgwick's axioms: that to identify *as* something implies a process of identification *with*, not to mention identification *against* (61). As Biddy Martin and Chandra Mohanty point out:

> "Being home" refers to the place where one lives within familiar, safe, protected boundaries; "not being home" is a matter of realizing that home was an illusion of coherence and safety based on the exclusion of specific histories of oppression and resistance, the repression of differences even within oneself. (196)

The construction of home, then, is an attempted externalization of the idealized, coherent, singular self. Perhaps we come together in community precisely to obscure our differences and deny the fragility of our individual identity claims. Yet like the illusory coherent subject, premised on a denial of the other within, the desired "safety" of community will always require us to find and expell some new enemy within the group.

The blurring of identity categories unsettles a whole series of assumptions, and throws into question principles that appear foundational. As Kobena Mercer says, "Identity only becomes an issue when it is in crisis, when something assumed to be fixed, coherent and stable is displaced by the experiences of doubt and uncertainty" (259). Bisexuality, like the apparently anti-category queer, does represent the possibility of blurring and/or exploding categories. Yet in other respects, bisexuality and queer strategies are only another enunciation of a familiar desire for self-knowledge, self-definition, for a community of people who are like-minded if not similarly identified. When I started this research, I imagined ending with a discussion of "queer" as a kind of solution. But I have begun to suspect that "queer" is fraught with some of the same problems as identity as marginality, as self-knowledge, as innocence. Let me briefly suggest what is transformative, and retrograde, about queer as a strategic concept.

In the words of Helen (charles), "Queer posture is transgressive, rude-positive, non-accommodationist, risky" (100). Queer is an anti-assimilationist, defiant, "in your face," aggressive, unapologetic celebration of difference, as in the by-now trite "We're here, we're queer, get used to it." The potential of queer seems to be that we do not come together around an assumption of sameness, but around a critique of "the normal." But there are ways in which this approach remains embedded in a problematic discourse.

What is brought to the fore by "queer" is how much stasis is required for the development and survival of identity—any identity. It could be argued—and likely has been argued—that the birth of queer is the death of identity. On the other hand, is queer really such a challenge to current practices? For all its flashy glory, queer politics may be not that unlike the politics in JFA: Allan Berube and Jeffrey Escoffier suggest that queer is sometimes employed "'to affirm sameness by defining a common identity on the fringes'" (qtd. in

Gamson, 396). And according to Joshua Gamson, queer does not contest the model of family, only who is allowed in. What happens when one person's position on the fringes is challenged? When there is jockeying for a spot furthest on the outskirts, closest to the presumed innocence of marginality? Doesn't queer erase power difference by saying we're all equally weird? (charles) raises this same worry:

> The way I see the direction of Queer is that it is not only aimed at mainstream gay and lesbian peoples. It has "perversion" as a reverse-discourse strategy sitting next to it, and this title is being used to attract *anybody*. . . . If this is going to break down the barriers of racism, sexism and homophobia, fine. If it is merely glossing over difference(s) and inequality, not fine. (101)

The limitless limits of queerness may amount to no more than a mask of relations of power. And where there is denial of difference, there are the exclusionary politics we know so well from white, middle-class feminism.

In sameness is a denial of difference; paradoxically, installing difference as the norm ultimately amounts to demands for sameness. When power relations are left out of the equation, difference is leveled. Yet asserting difference for the sake of difference does not allow us to comprehend how we are positioning ourselves, and on what we are premising our communities. As I have attempted to demonstrate, even as we become political and join together to organize for social change, we sometimes reproduce the systems and beliefs—the autonomous individual, identity as self-knowledge, fixed categories—that are implicated in our servitude. These same systems may also support our privilege. And it is privilege dependent on the subordination of others. Despite differences in how power was conceptualized, and what the function of categories was perceived to be, it seems to me that everyone in the JFA conflict was motivated by a similar concern: that is, defense of the self and fending off upheavals to identity.

According to Fellows and Razack, identity as marginality leads to a "difference impasse" and encourages people to try to create communities that stand as external monuments to our desire for solidity and sameness. It is in these communities that we perform our "border patrols" (1048). If what we are policing are our claims to marginality, as well as the fixedness of our identities, the question we need to consider is how do we think about marginality differently. What is at stake is becoming able to acknowledge complicity in the subordination of one another. The authors assert that we will not be able to manage this shift with an approach that ignores the power wielded by individuals, in favour of deconstructing the power of institutions, and that conceptualizes difference as nothing more than variety. Rather, we need to map our complicity in structures of domination in order to "move out of the subject position we claim on the margins and into the shifting and multiple subject positions of oppressed and oppressor" (1075–76). Gayatri Spivak gives an analogous piece of advice: "I would say that the major project for me is to *unlearn our privilege as our loss*" (10, emphasis mine). This strategy, of constructing identity on an understanding of ourselves as multiply constituted by marginality and complicity, is by no means simple. We will continue to find ourselves marginalized at times, we will continue to need comfort and to band together with others to fight for social change. But once we are there, with our difficult histories, how do we conduct ourselves? Where do we go for support, and what do we expect when we get there?

The best hope is to avoid constructing a system whereby we try to cast off the ways in which we have power, in the belief that to have power is to be oppressive. For as Michel Foucault has taught us, even the act of shedding power is born of power; power circulates throughout our relations, it enables and it restricts (92–96). We are all sometimes more and sometimes less powerful. Sometimes we are undeniably oppressed, and sometimes we benefit from the domination of others. What is so critical, and yet so confusing, is that these moments may not look the way we expect them to: taking into account the workings of interlocking systems, we must consider that there will be times when our freedom is contingent on absent, unfree bodies. We will perhaps not even be aware that we are at that moment requiring someone else to be enslaved so that we might know ourselves as self-determining, or autonomous, or free.

This is what I believe happened in Jewish Feminist Action. Our "discovered" marginality brought us to an identity, and then brought us together, to a place we hoped would provide the safety and sameness we were longing for. Because of a series of disruptions to Jewish and sexual identity claims, we were threatened and we responded defensively. There were the direct challenges implicit in the bisexuality wars: that lesbians can oppress; that bisexual women have privilege; that there is no clear consistent difference between the two categories. And, there were the underlying, older unsettlings from our work in coalition, which found a forum in this safer debate: are Jews oppressed, or oppressive? How are Jews distinct from other white people? We fought to maintain our positions, but as our individual subjectivities were threatened, so too was the unity and purpose of the group. As we came apart, so did JFA.

NOTES

1. Of course, not all Jews are white-skinned. Ashkenazi Jews, or Jews who settled Europe, tend to be able to pass. However, there are Ashkenazi Jews who have very Semitic features. Most of the women in JFA, and all those I interviewed, are Ashkenazi. As well, there are dark-skinned Sephardic Jews (from Spain and North Africa), Jews in India, Ethiopia and China. For an example of stereotypical response to a dark-skinned Jew, see Kyla Wazana, "JEW, JEWISH, KIKE, J.A.P., COLOURED, THIRD WORLD...," *Fireweed: A Feminist Quarterly* 35 (1992), 26–27. For a historical account of the racialization of Ashkenazi Jews, and the representation of Jews as Black, see Sander Gilman, *The Jew's Body* (New York: Routledge, 1991), especially Chapter 7, "The Jewish Nose: Are Jews White? Or, The History of the Nose Job."
2. Alex (a pseudonym for one of the JFA members I interviewed) first coined this phrase.
3. Although I was not part of the coalition, I was a member of JFA at the time and recall discussion of these events. I am, however, drawing not on my memory, but on minutes and a detailed letter JFA wrote to the coalition to tell "our" side of the story after we had withdrawn from the coalition, as well as drawing on other correspondences to and from the coalition.
4. Consider that Lacan maintains that "loss is a condition of signification." See Julia Creet, "Anxieties of Identity: Coming Out and Coming Undone." In *Negotiating Lesbian and Gay Subjects*. Eds. Monica Dorenkamp and Richard Henke (New York: Routledge, 1995): 188.
5. Butler writes that "if the 'I' is a site of repetition, that is, if the 'I' only achieves the semblance of identity through a certain repetition of itself, then the 'I' is always displaced by the very repetition that sustains it. In other words, does or can the 'I' ever repeat itself, cite itself, faithfully, or is there always a displacement from its former moment that establishes the permanently non-self-identical status of that 'I' or its 'being lesbian'? ... for if the performance is 'repeated,' there is always the question of what differentiates from each other the moments of identity that are repeated." Judith Butler, "Imitation and Gender Insubordination." In *inside/out: Lesbian Theories, Gay Theories*, Ed. Diana Fuss (New York: Routledge, 1991): 18.
6. Sherene Razack, *Looking White People in the Eye: Gender, Race and Culture in Courtrooms and Classrooms* (Toronto: University of Toronto Press, 1998): 13.
7. Sander Gilman, "Black Bodies, White Bodies: Toward an Iconography of Female Sexuality in Late Nineteenth-Century Art, Medicine and Literature." In *"Race," Culture & Difference*, Eds. James Donald and Ali Rattansi (London: Sage, 1992). There is, however, a significant problem with Gilman's work: it has been pointed out that he does harm by employing some of the images he does (in particular that of the Hottentot woman) without discussing the physical and psychological

violence done to black bodies in the nineteenth century. He also fails to make the connection between representation and material realities. However, Gilman remains useful in tracing how certain bodies have been pathologized and demonized. Specifically, those bodies are the black female servant, the white female prostitute, and the lesbian. Many thanks to Anodyne Chablis-Clark for this insight on Gilman.

8. See note 2 above.

9. Diana Fuss suggests a psychoanalytic reading of the identity as self-knowledge cluster. She writes of identification, the internal process that is made public as identity, as "the psychical mechanism that produces self-recognition." Though she isn't addressing the vicissitudes of public or political identity, she lends some insight into why identity is not a stable entity: identification, the mechanism that produces identity, is fraught with paradox, ambivalence, and reversals. Diana Fuss, *Identification Papers* (New York: Routledge, 1995): 2.

WORKS CITED

Butler, Judith. "Imitation and Gender Insubordination." In *inside/out: Lesbian Theories, Gay Theories* Ed. Diana Fuss. New York: Routledge, 1991. 13–31.

(charles), Helen. "'Queer Nigger': Theorizing 'White' Activism." In *Activating Theory: Lesbian, Gay, Bisexual Politics.* Eds. Joseph Bristow and Angelia R. Wilson. London: Lawrence & Wishart, 1993. 97–106.

Creet, Julia. "Anxieties of Identity: Coming Out and Coming Undone." In *Negotiating Lesbian and Gay Subjects.* Eds. Monica Dorenkamp and Richard Henke. New York: Routledge, 1995. 179–99.

Eadie, Jo. "Activating Bisexuality: Towards a Bi/Sexual Politics." In *Activating Theory: Lesbian, Gay, Bisexual Politics.* Eds. Joseph Bristow and Angelia R. Wilson. London: Lawrence & Wishart, 1993. 139–70.

Fellows, Mary Louise, and Sherene Razack. "Seeking Relations: Law and Feminism Roundtables." *Signs: Journal of Women in Culture and Society* 19.4 (1994): 1048–83.

Foucault, Michel. *The History of Sexuality. Volume I: An Introduction.* New York: Vintage, 1990.

Fuss, Diana. *Identification Papers.* New York: Routledge, 1995.

Gamson, Joshua. "Must Identity Movements Self-Destruct? A Queer Dilemma." *Social Problems* 42.3 (1995): 390–407.

Gilman, Sander. *The Jew's Body.* New York: Routledge, 1991.

———. "Black Bodies, White Bodies: Toward an Iconography of Female Sexuality in Late Nineteenth-century Art, Medicine and Literature." *In "Race," Culture & Difference.* Eds. James Donald and Ali Rattansi. London: Sage, 1992. 171–97.

Hall, Stuart. "New Ethnicities." In *"Race," Culture & Difference.* Eds. James Donald and Ali Rattansi. London: Sage, 1992. 252–9.

hooks, bell. *Black Looks: Race and Representation.* Toronto: Between the Lines, 1992.

Martin, Biddy, and Chandra Talpade Mohanty. "Feminist Politics: What's Home Got to Do with It?" In *Feminist Studies/Critical Studies.* Ed. Teresa de Lauretis. Bloomington: Indiana University Press, 1986. 191–12

Mercer, Kobena. *Welcome to the Jungle: New Positions in Black Cultural Studies.* New York: Routledge, 1994.

Newman, Zoë. "Coming Together, Coming Apart: Identity, Community and Political Struggle" dissertation, University of Toronto, 1996.

Razack, Sherene. *Looking White People in the Eye: Gender, Race and Culture in Courtrooms and Classrooms.* Toronto: University of Toronto Press, 1998.

Sedgwick, Eve Kosofsky. *Epistemology of the Closet.* Berkeley: University of California Press, 1990.

Spivak, Gayatri Chakravorty. *The Post-Colonial Critic: Interviews, Strategies, Dialogues.* New York: Routledge, 1990.

Wazana, Kyla. "JEW, JEWISH, KIKE, J.A.P., COLOURED, THIRD WORLD...," *Fireweed: A Feminist Quarterly* 35 (1992): 26–7.

imagining an intercultural nation: a moment in canadian queer cinema

James Allan

Canadians make some rather queer movies. Whether they are gay or straight, a bewildering array of Canadian filmmakers (David Cronenberg, Patricia Rozema, Atom Egoyan, Lynne Stopkewich, Thom Fitzgerald, and others) are famously intrigued by unusual, atypical sexual practices and identities. But is there such a thing as a Canadian queer cinema? This question is not a simple one. To even consider discussing queer Canadian film is to start with a number of assumptions: about nations, about queers, about national film traditions. How can we articulate and delineate a national film tradition in the late twentieth century, a period of well-publicized international travel, multinational co-productions, and perhaps even of post-national identities? [1] And, keeping in mind both the recent expansion of the concept of "the nation" and the political demands being made by various subaltern groups around the world, what counts as a "nation" in this discussion? Who is the Queer Nation, and can this community claim a group of texts as its national body of film? And if so, what happens when this queer body gets in bed with a Canadian?

These questions will require some detailed explorations of nationhood, the role of cultural production in the creation and propagation of nations, and the ways in which such ideas can be applied to the tenuous collective known as the Queer Nation. But such explorations are vital if we are to think clearly about queer cinema, Canadian or otherwise, as a distinct body of work.

These considerations are becoming both more important and more complicated as this collection of films becomes larger. Since the international emergence of the so-called New Queer Cinema in the early 1990s, there have been an ever-increasing number of films featuring gay/lesbian/bisexual/trangenered (GLBT) characters appearing on screens around the world, emerging from a variety of countries.[2] Created within national contexts of production and reception, these queer films engender links between international queer audiences and national queer subjects, links that ideally might foster an international, cosmopolitan queer identity, promoting an awareness of the multiplicity of queer lives and the productive similarities between them. At the same time, however, such trans-national film cultures may simply encourage a vast sea of narrative clones, representing and replicating a single vision of queer identity across borders and cultures, overshadowing local practices and traditions.

With these stakes and possibilities in mind, the remarkable variety of Canadian queer films provokes an enormous question. Is there some kind of cultural affinity between Canadian and queer subjects or positions, or is there a shared history of outsider status, of indefinable identity that makes Canadian film and queer subjects such frequent bedfellows? In order to investigate such ideas, I will address three rather queer Canadian films that were released during 1993 and 1994, immediately following the emergence of the New Queer Cinema internationally. Specifically, I will consider *Love and Human Remains* by Denys Arcand (1994), *Kanada* by Mike Hoolboom (1993), and *Zero Patience* by John Greyson (1993), a trio of films that runs the gamut from big-budget to experimental to art-house.

NATIONS AND NATIONALISMS, QUEER AND OTHERWISE

Theoretical discussions of nations and nationalism have become increasingly complex as established definitions of "nation" come under scrutiny from various subaltern populations. Political groups and activist organizations such as

Queer Nation attempt to recast the old definitions in their own terms and for their own goals, picking and choosing from among the established streams of thought on "the nation." Meanwhile, the meanings and ramifications of "the nation" as an entity are changing, even within more traditional circles of thought. To understand these processes and the resulting situation, a consideration of some of the major theoretical positions is a useful starting point. Benedict Anderson, in his 1991 book, *Imagined Communities: Reflections on the Origin and Spread of Nationalism,* famously defines a nation as "an imagined political community" (6). This definition is an important intervention in the debates around nationalism, shifting attention from the existence of nations themselves to the power of their imaginations. According to Anderson, nations are communities constructed primarily through the imagination because the members of even the smallest nation will never meet, hear, or know even a portion of their fellow members; yet these members still consider themselves attached to all the others in a powerful communion (6). He suggests that the key issue for scholars of nationalism is thus not the genuineness of a nation—i.e., whether or not it is a "real" nation by some predetermined definition—but *how* such attachments are formed: how a political community continually imagines itself into a coherent existence that is both social and political. Importantly, he is interested in the *means* of such an imaginary feat.

Anthony Smith echoes this change in emphasis by suggesting that explorations of nationalism and nationalist sentiment must focus less on the common characteristics and cultures shared among those who feel themselves to be part of a community, and more on the "myth-and-symbol-defined boundaries [of such a community] and the communicators who codify these differentiating perceptions" (453). Such national symbolic work, often embodied in mass-mediated texts like film, can operate in a multitude of ways: from simply representing a previously unrepresented group or perspective; to creating complex networks of in-jokes and cultural references which foster a feeling of belonging for those skilled enough to understand; to clearly demarcating the nation's boundaries, stating who and who does not belong.

Both prompting and capitalizing on these theoretical changes, various subaltern groups have made a wide variety of demands on both the concept of nation and on recognized nation-states themselves: GLBT groups, civil rights organizations, women's movements, and a multitude of diasporic linguistic and cultural communities. James Tully addresses these wide-ranging demands in his book, *Strange Multiplicity: Constitutionalism in an age of diversity.* Foregrounding the ways in which cultures and movements develop through interaction and interdependence—feminists can be members of minority language groups, civil rights activists embody a number of social positions other than "activist"—Tully asserts that: *"The modern age is intercultural rather than multicultural"* (11, emphasis mine). This concept of the intercultural is particularly germane for considerations of queer community: no one, after all, is simply queer, but is also queer and male and black and Canadian, or queer and female and Jewish and German. This surfeit of identity-positions promotes a politics of *identification,* rather than of simple identity. Self-definition becomes a process that is contextual, that the subject must negotiate in a variety of situations, rather than in a given, fixed reality. Such a process is never truly free, however; an individual rarely has the luxury of choosing his or her identifications and identities but may have various labels attached and affixed, without much choice in the matter. Still, the shift from the notion of identity to one of identification is an important one for considerations of nations and communities. If both nations *and* individuals are imagined, where does that leave the relationship between the two?

Tully attempts to grapple with this question by arguing that, "Due to the overlap, interaction and negotiation of cultures, the experience of cultural difference is *internal* to a culture" (13, emphasis in original). Cultural difference is not experienced simply between supposedly homogeneous nations but within the nation as well: any community harbours as much difference as it does similarity, and thus its existence as a community depends on individual associations, identifications, and imaginations—which may or may not be voluntary, depending on circumstance. This conception of difference as internal and integral to all cultures/nations stands as one of the most useful elements of Tully's work, but since his interest is more political than cultural, he does not address the important question of how. *How* do we experience this internal cultural difference? Where? With whom? And who are "we," anyway? These questions are often the driving forces behind both "Canadian culture" and "queer culture," for in many respects the types of nationhood and nationalism under discussion in these two very different-seeming debates are remarkably similar. Such similarities provoke questions about the intersections of nationalism and queer culture, questions that are central to Lauren Berlant and Elizabeth Freeman's work on the activist group Queer Nation. In their article "Queer Nationality," Berlant and Freeman chronicle the different ways that Queer Nation attempted to engage with ideas of nationhood and sexuality. Such an engagement is absolutely necessary, they argue:

> as long as PWAS (Persons with AIDS) require state support, as long as the official nation invests its identity in the pseudoright to police nonnormative sexual representations and sexual practices, the lesbian, gay, feminist, and queer communities in the United States [or anywhere else] do not have the privilege to disregard national identity. (197)

Queer Nation began the process of addressing the connection between sexuality and the nation-state by foregrounding the ways in which the nation's underlying, unspoken sexuality is always heterosexuality. At the same time, Queer Nation disputed this linkage between the national and the heterosexual by inflecting national symbols and tropes with queer meanings, by simulating "'the national' with a camp inflection." Such a strategy goes beyond the specifics of Queer Nation as an organization: many queer organizations and individuals have long connected their queerness to their perceived national home. For years the Montreal queer community held its Pride celebrations on the same weekend as Quebec's nationalist holiday, St. Jean Baptiste Day; around the country, T-shirts and car bumpers displayed a rainbow version of the Canadian flag throughout the year. These moments, as limited as they are, would seem to fulfill one of Berlant and Freeman's key demands: not just safety from bashing, but "safe[ty] *for* demonstration, in the mode of patriotic ritual, which always involves a deployment of affect, knowledge, spectacle and, crucially, a kind of banality, ordinariness, popularity" (198).

Queer visibility thus becomes a nationalist project. From the action of a Queer Night Out where Queer Nationals move into "straight space" and perform kiss-ins and dance-ins, to the poster campaign "We're Here. We're Queer. Get Used to It." (Berlant and Freeman, 201; 205–207), the Queer Nation agenda asserts the need to be visible, to be unwilling to be shunted to the shadows. Queer Nation, as Berlant and Freeman articulate it, attempts to demonstrate that the "boundedness of heterosexual spaces is also contingent upon the (enforced) willingness of gays to remain invisible" (207). Film, as an evocative narrative form that moves easily across national and cultural boundaries, represents one opportunity for queer visibility, while also proving to be a powerful tool for constructing and reaffirming queer communities and nations. Both developing and relying on Smith's "myth-and-symbol-defined boundaries," queer films are made in and articulated to specific national and cultural contexts. Queer cinema thus represents a nationality which is always multiple.

CANADIAN QUEER CINEMA: INTERNAL DIFFERENCES, ETERNAL CONFLICTS

The idea of "national cinema" is on one hand rather simple: it generally refers to a body of films that were produced in a specific country. Yet Andrew Higson, in his article, "The Concept of National Cinema," suggests that we need to look beyond a film's country-of-origin (even as such origins are becoming increasingly complicated in this age of international co-production) to think about other ways in which we can define a film's nationality. He outlines three criteria for re-conceptualizing the idea of national cinema:

economic/production criteria, which link the "national cinema" to the domestic film industry; *textual criteria,* which address a pattern of filmic subjects and styles; and, finally, *consumption-based criteria,* which address what national audiences are actually watching (36–37). Each of these criteria is differently applicable to the double-nations under discussion here.

In the Canadian nation, the Canadian Radio-television and Telecommunications Commission (CRTC), in an effort to support the Canadian film industry, requires that films fulfill certain remarkably detailed production criteria to qualify as Canadian Content: this industry, so the theory goes, will then naturally produce Canadian stories and culture. [3] Things operate somewhat differently in the queer nation: although the community has no official bodies like the CRTC to govern "Queer Content," media watchdogs such as the American Gay and Lesbian Alliance Against Defamation (GLAAD) concentrate most of their efforts on media products which feature GLBT characters or subjects, regardless of whether the programs were produced by queers. For the purposes of this essay, I will thus use *both* production and textual criteria in order to investigate possible textual patterns central to a Canadian queer cinema. I will address three films that are directed by Canadians, set in Canada, and considered by CRTC regulations to "be Canadian," and that also feature GLBT characters and are considered by the wider GLBT community to "be queer."[4] I realize that these rather conventional delineations have very powerful effects. I would produce a very different notion of the queer Canadian canon if I focused instead on the films that queer Canadians actually watch—likely straight Hollywood fare for the most part, except perhaps among Francophone Quebeckers. Yet this is not primarily an audience-oriented study: I am currently most interested in Canadian filmmakers and their interactions with queer subject-material, and so it makes more sense to use these production/content criteria.

Echoing Anderson and Smith, Higson points out that the articulation of a national filmic tradition is always an act of discursive production. He writes:

> To identify a national cinema is first of all to specify a coherence and a unity . . . the process of identification is thus invariably a hegemonising, mythologising process, involving both the production and the assignation of a particular set of meanings, and the attempt to contain . . . other meanings. (37)

Identifying a national cinema is thus an instance of national imagining, one that helps to form and shape the nation itself, and so my project here becomes part of an attempt to identify and solidify a Canadian queer nation. Yet such an attempt to create a coherent national image may prove problematic.

R. Bruce Brasell, in his article "Queer Nationalism and the Musical Fag Bashing of John Greyson's *The Making of 'Monsters,'*" suggests that formulating a queer nation is in fact impossible. He asserts:

> Queer cultures as the basis for a nationalism provide an inherently unstable foundation because queer identity seeks to contest and break down sexual boundaries while the intent of nationalism is to establish boundaries. (28)

Perhaps the conflict here emerges from clashing assumptions. Brasell's statement assumes that national boundaries are always fixed and permanent, and that national membership is certain. This might be acceptable if we consider only the traditional idea of the political nation-state but if, following Anderson, Smith, and Tully, we postulate instead that the nation is by definition uncertain, intercultural, eminently permeable, and contextual, it seems to resonate powerfully with Brasell's concept of queer identity and Berlant and Freeman's work on Queer Nation. In fact, the clichés of Canadian identity—which is always uncertain, impossible to identify, existing only in opposition to other identities, primarily American—also resonate deeply with Brasell's concept of queer identity. It seems very Canadian to be queer, and very queer to be Canadian.

Denys Arcand's 1994 film, *Love and Human Remains,* is the best known and most widely distributed of the films under discussion here, and thus will function as a useful starting point. An internationally acclaimed French Canadian director, Arcand, whose films include the critically acclaimed *Jésus de Montréal,* is not particularly known for his gay-themed work, yet homosexuality and queer relationships form the core of *Love and Human Remains.* At the same time, *Love and Human Remains* represented another departure for Arcand: the film was the director's first English-language project, based on the play "Unidentified Human Remains and the True Nature of Love," by Edmontonian playwright Brad Fraser. The film, positioned as a Generation-X ensemble comedy/drama, tells the story of seven urban twentysomethings, living their lives in a vaguely pan-Canadian landscape as a serial killer dominates the news and questions of love and sexual relationships dominate their lives. At the same time, *Love and Human Remains* consciously plays with many of the questions of identity, sexuality, and intercultural difference that characterize our discussion of the nation, both queer and Canadian.

Queerness is certainly a permeable, multifarious category for Arcand's characters. Both of the avowedly queer characters in the film, the gay actor-turned-waiter David (Thomas Gibson) and the lesbian schoolteacher Jerri (Joanne Vannicola), have had past heterosexual relationships. In a period of heterosexual frustration, Candy (Ruth Marshall), David's straight roommate and ex-girlfriend, begins to experiment with lesbianism by dating Jerri. Unsatisfied, she returns to heterosexuality with Robert (Rick Roberts). Kane (Matthew Ferguson), David's seventeen-year-old busboy from the restaurant, considers himself straight but is clearly romantically infatuated with David. At the same time, he continues to date women, saying "Sometimes I just wanna get laid."[5] Importantly, these sexual and identity shifts are not necessarily portrayed as crises, but are also the subjects of jokes and play. When Candy tells David that she's considering relationships with women, he says, "I don't know Candy. I can't see you as a dyke," to which she replies, in a mock-hurt tone of voice, "Please! I'd be a *lesbian*. . . ." When David and Jerri finally meet, they joke together about their common queerness ("So, Candy tells me you're a dyke!") thus playing up the fact that a shared sexuality does not guarantee any social connection. Such a jocular sensibility extends even to homophobia. After discussing her divorce and shift to a lesbian identity, Jerri says to Candy, "Some people are freaked out by gays and lesbians," to which Candy replies, "Yeah, well, some people wear polyester." A complicated, fluctuating factor in these characters' lives, queerness represents a vast array of identity positions and cultural perspectives; Arcand's queers make up an intercultural community that does not present a unified front.

Compared to queerness, Canadian-ness seems to play a rather small role in the film, barely registering even in its *mise en scène*. Although shot in multilingual, multicultural Montreal, the film is set in an anglo-Canadian urban anywhere. This vagueness of geography seems ironic, considering that the film was made in Quebec by a Quebec filmmaker, in a city with a distinctive architectural style and a vibrant queer community. The film was originally supposed to be both set and shot in Edmonton, where the play on which it was based had been set, but problems with Alberta granting agencies necessitated a move by the producers to refinance the film without the aid of the Alberta government, and to relocate the shoot to Montreal (Rice-Barker, F5). Perhaps the film's bland every-city setting emerged from this mid-production shift of locations. I would suggest, however, that it may also have been motivated by a desire to make the film more acceptable to American audiences, who are notoriously known for preferring American settings. By downplaying the film's Canadian-ness, the producers may have hoped to garner a larger American box office. Unfortunately, this means that the film cannot actively engage with the complexity of Canadian identity: instead, all of its major characters are white (except perhaps for Jerri, whose physical appearance suggests a different ethnic background), Anglophone, and largely uninvolved with any sort of national culture. This unexamined and uncomplicated Canadian-ness stands in sharp contrast to the remarkably complex and fluctuating sexual identities described above: the Canadian nation is not what's at stake here.

Interestingly, the few markers of Canadian-ness that exist within the film are mainly media texts. Except for the occasional reference to Toronto as a scorned and distant locale, the characters themselves do not articulate any sort of Canadian identity or belonging; this task is left to the media products that exist within the characters' lives. Newspapers glimpsed in grocery stores feature a small Canadian flag next to the mastheads; in a number of scenes, David flips through the television channels, scanning past weather-report maps of Canada and news reports about events in Toronto. These rather innocuous indicators of Canadian-ness set the stage for a self-reflexive narrative comment on identity and Canadian media. The seventeen-year-old Kane is obsessed with David's childhood acting career and his status as an ex-television star: midway through the film, Kane shows David a credit-sequence from the actor's childhood television series, "The Beavertons." This fictional piece of Canadian Content, with its gee-whiz patriotic title and its lumber camp setting, seems to be loosely modelled on "The Beachcombers," a successful CBC television drama, which ran for an impressive nineteen seasons during the 1970s and 1980s. "The Beavertons," which David wants to forget, appears designed both to mock a certain variety of Canadian cultural production as hokey, rural, perky, historical, and straight, and to demonstrate how far we as a nation have come. [6] With this moment of self-conscious cultural play, Arcand demonstrates how different his film is from much of the Canadian Content canon. Unlike "The Beavertons," *Love and Human Remains* is hip, urban, sardonic, contemporary, and queer: Canada, as a nation defined by its media products, is shifting and changing.

Still, despite the shifting nature of both sexual identity and Canadian culture, some boundaries remain uncrossed. Bernie (Cameron Bancroft), appears to have strong feelings for his straight best friend, David, but never expresses them in any form other than that of heterosexualized friendship. The film's most obviously homo-romantic shot is of Bernie—the "straight man"—gazing at David, shirtless in athletic underwear, as the light and shadow play across his chest and face. He awkwardly says "David? When you were away, I missed you." The film thus places Bernie in a homoerotic gaze, despite his supposed straight-ness.[7] The viewer is left with two possible options: either Bernie is not so straight after all, or anyone can be the object of the homoerotic gaze, regardless of his/her own sexuality. Perhaps both. When Bernie later reveals himself to be the serial killer, attacking first David's friend Benita (Mia Kershner), and then Candy, the viewer is left to wonder about Bernie's possible sexual frustration. In one of the final scenes, after admitting openly that he has been killing women throughout the city, Bernie confronts David, almost blaming him: "I changed when you left me. . . . You left me here all by myself." The viewer is left to ask: Was Bernie driven to kill by his inability to admit that he loves David?

Leaving this question unanswered, *Love and Human Remains* nevertheless demonizes the inability to cross boundaries and valourizes the openness and confusion of a society in which boundaries of identity and sexuality are frequently crossed. The film complicates the very concept of a queer nation, echoing Brasell's arguments about nations and queerness. Does Candy belong to such a community because she slept with Jerri? Does Kane belong to it because he is in love with David? Does Bernie belong, despite his disavowal of his love for David? These questions, however, become less important when we consider the nation as intercultural, multivalent, and contextual; as Anderson suggests, the matter becomes one of how such a community imagines itself, rather than of its validity. Arcand's queers move and shift and learn and grow within a community, coming together, at their best, to help each other, to form and maintain powerful bonds of love and friendship. This community, this nation, is thus imagined into being through friendship, sex, and love; and yet, while this act of imagination has political implications, it does not actively engage in Canadian politics.

Mike Hoolboom's film, *Kanada,* which he wrote and directed, is both more experimental than Arcand's film and more directly concerned with Canadian politics and nationhood. Hoolboom's first narrative film, *Kanada* is set in a near-future Kanadian dystopia and features four distinct threads: a newscaster in a death mask (Hoolboom) reads the often-horrific news of an increasingly violent and chaotic Kanada while surreal images flash on the screen behind him; Prime Minister Wayne Gretzky[8] (Andrew Scorer) and his aide (Sky Gilbert) discuss economics, plot against Quebec sovereignty, and eventually launch a civil war; two women, Charlie (Babs Chula) and Bobbie[9] (Gabrielle Rose), fall in love, move in together, and then break up in a violent encounter; and the image of a young bride in her wedding gown (Kika Thorne) appears over and over again, seemingly unconnected to any of the narrative elements of the film. In addition to this already-complex structure, the film makes use of a disjointed soundtrack, first person voice-overs, intertitles, non-narrative sequences, and image layering. The resulting disjointed nature of the film evokes the experience of television (which is an important thematic element in the film), except that writer/director Hoolboom is the one flipping the channels; the viewer has little control, a situation that seems pandemic in the film. At the same time, such formal complexity speaks to a filmic version of Tully's concept of interculturalism. Black-and-white sequences, which owe a great debt to German Formalism, are interlaced with gritty, overexposed *cinéma-vérité* sequences reminiscent of British documentaries; the film is a riot of different visual styles, seeming to defy any single mode of representation. Hoolboom's *Kanada* thus exists as a filmic mosaic, seeming to mimic or mock, on a formal level, one of the defining metaphors for the Canadian government's approach to national complexity.

The film opens with a series of quick cuts, accompanied by a voice-over, spoken by Bobbie:

> It's one country, Kanada, made up of hamlets, farms, cities and villages. When we try to come together, we do it in the only way we know how. We declare war. War on the natives, the French, the English, on each other. The force of the union. Sometimes I feel it like a physical thing. Like love.

The connections between nationhood, intercultural difference, love, and violence established here are presented again and again throughout the film. At the same time, the film foregrounds the complexity and uncertainty of the Kanadian nation at every turn: queers, straights, French, English, middle-class suburbanites and working-class hookers—coming together, tearing themselves and their country apart. The bride-figure sequences echo this chaos on a metaphoric level. The bride—often a symbolic representative of the Canadian nation in nineteenth- and early twentieth-century political cartoons—dances down a set of railroad tracks, runs panicked through a decaying city, and spray-paints graffiti on a brick wall. This juxtaposition of images of Canadian unity (like the railroad with its almost mythical place in the history of Canadian nation-building) with images of vandalism and social action problematizes the very concept of nation-building: what can be built can also be destroyed.

The film also problematizes Queer Nation's goal of visibility. In many of the shots during the Bobbie and/or Charlie sequences, the camera is placed as if it were behind a mirror, or inside a television. Bobbie and Charlie stare directly at the camera, often distorted in extreme close-up, putting on makeup or watching a tennis match. The viewer, uncomfortably close to the action, becomes a secret observer hiding within their domestic life, watching them from behind the mirror, or from within their television. The reference to George Orwell's *1984* is obvious; the viewer here is voyeur, watcher, Big Brother.

The state holds an important place in *Kanada*, a film concerned with deficits, referenda, and civil war, but the (traditional) nation is a concept held up for ridicule. Reporting on the launch of Parti Quebécois leader Lucien Bouchard's campaign for Quebec independence, the newscaster reports that Bouchard demonstrated the French method of walking, eating, talking, driving, and shitting before he "closed his address with a French kiss." This contempt for ethnic nationalism is matched by a contempt for the state itself. Partway through the film, Prime Minister Gretzky declares war on the now-sovereign Quebec, as intercultural difference becomes intranational conflict: then to reduce the massive Kanadian deficit, he sells the TV broadcast rights to the American Sports Network, which will broadcast the war live, twenty-four hours a day. Hoolboom clearly has little faith in politicians, who appear to be both ridiculous and malicious. For example, early in the film Prime Minister Gretzky titles his federalist referendum campaign "I'm Okay. You're Okaybec," but during the post-sovereignty war he launches irresponsible military offensives, calculated to earn Kanada money from the Sports Network's dollar-per-body policy. This remarkable cynicism permeates the film: arriving home from her work as a prostitute, Charlie says, "If voting made a difference they'd make it illegal."

At the same time, however, *Kanada* displays an intensity of emotion, a remarkable belief in the value of emotional expression and communication across differences. Charlie and Bobbie are Hoolboom's heroines, finding love and solace before eventually losing it throughout the course of the film. Amidst the escalating war, they talk eloquently and frankly, about their pasts, their loves, their politics, and their experiences. Importantly, these experiences mark them as coming from very different worlds: Charlie is a prostitute from a working-class background who comes home from her job "smelling of man-cock," whereas Bobbie grew up comfortably middle class and works as a writer and social worker. Such differences provide both fodder for conversation—the bulk of their dialogue and interactions involve the two women relating stories from their pasts—and for arguments: Bobbie hates that Charlie works as a prostitute; she likens the job to factory work, which makes her feel like just another one of Charlie's tricks. Charlie, in turn, resents Bobbie's job, saying:

> I sell my cunt, that's what I do. It's no big deal. You, you sell the words you say. You say 'I love you,' 'Move in with me,' 'Don't ever leave me.' They're the same words you say at work. They're the same words you say when we come home together. They're the same words you say when we cum.

Despite these conflicts, which complicate the distinctions between sexual and linguistic monogamy, and the separation between work and love, the lovers manage to maintain a playful, sardonic, and loving relationship for a period of time, in part by building moments of understanding and empathy through their storytelling: cultural differences are bridged by the power of narrative.

Such storytelling, however, does not remain on a purely personal level. In one powerful sequence, Charlie and Bobbie stare directly into the camera, reliving the Montreal Massacre of 1989, speaking first as two individuals but eventually becoming two separate voices of a single consciousness: [10]

BOBBIE:	He asks the men to stand on one side of the room.
CHARLIE:	And the women on the other.
BOBBIE:	And he raises the gun.
CHARLIE:	And I see him looking at me for the first time.
BOBBIE:	And I see him looking at me for the last time.
CHARLIE:	And the woman next to me drops to the floor.
BOBBIE:	And then I drop to the floor.
CHARLIE:	And then I see the blood.
BOBBIE:	And then I see it's coming from me.
CHARLIE:	And then he's gone.

This speech, although intensely stylized, creates a directness of affect in this sequence that contrasts with the alienation—from politics and from one's country—that dominates the film as a whole. At the same time, this sequence creates a powerful remembrance of a national tragedy, reminding us that moments of national unity are often rooted in violence. Such a remembrance, performed by a lesbian couple, also asserts queer claims to, and involvement in, national events: Berlant and Freeman's arguments about the importance of queering the national resurface here, although Hoolboom's tone is not the playful, mocking one which Queer Nation often adopted.

Still the film as a whole is a narrative of dissolution. Kanada self-destructs in war due to implacable internal differences, demonstrating that the intercultural is not always a mode of national harmony. Even Charlie and Bobbie, although they come together for a brief time, cannot make their relationship work. Torn apart by national stresses and class differences, the lovers eventually declare war on each other; they fight, both emotionally and physically, and then separate. Overall, Hoolboom's vision of the Canadian queer nation is one that is dark, unstable, and unable to contain its intercultural conflicts.

John Greyson's film *Zero Patience*, although set in Canada and featuring many GLBT characters, is not particularly concerned with the permeable boundaries of Arcand's queer community, nor does it directly question Canadian nationhood. Instead, Greyson's subject is the AIDS nation, a community that nevertheless intersects in powerful and often-contentious ways with both the nation-state and the queer nation. In this nation, it is not just sexual identities or nation-states that are unstable, but the truth itself.

A musical complete with numerous song-and-dance sequences, *Zero Patience* was Greyson's first big-budget feature film, a "mainstream" debut for the self-identified queer filmmaker. Such an audacious debut did not go unnoticed. Unlike either *Love and Human Remains* or *Kanada, Zero Patience* has received some attention in film criticism, much of it negative. Canadian film critic Robin Wood was particularly critical of the film, asserting that "nothing was good enough" and that the film was "misguided on the levels both of conception and execution" (11). Wood writes that he put the film to the "most stringent test" (he saw the film when "one of the most important people in [his] life . . . was in the final stage of AIDS"), but he seems to have put it to the wrong test, and understandably so (13). The film's subtitle, "A Movie Musical About AIDS," is misleading. The film is not a typical drama about AIDS or people with AIDS; instead, it is an often-irreverent look at *the social and cultural ramifications* of the syndrome, about life in the AIDS nation. The story also foregrounds the ways in which that life is complicated by confusing and conflicting discourses about AIDS itself.

The opening moment of the film fades into a block of text which reads: "In 1987, newspapers around the world accused a Canadian flight attendant of bringing AIDS to North America. They called him Patient Zero." This is quickly followed, during the credits sequence, with a seeming non-sequitur: a school child translates a sentence about the fictional character Scheherezade from French into English: "If she could tell a story, a story that would please the king, her life would be saved—her life would be spared, until the next night." These two sequences foreground the practices of naming and identifying, the difficulties of translating and the importance of storytelling for survival.

The film revolves around two main characters: Sir Richard Burton (John Robinson), the noted Victorian scientist, translator, and sexologist who, according to the playful premise of the film, is still alive and working as a taxidermist at the Museum of Natural History, and Patient Zero (Normand Fauteux), who returns to earth as a ghost and searches for a way to come back to life, a way "to appear." Burton, who is working on an exhibit called "The Hall of Contagion," begins to research AIDS and the stories around Patient Zero. Zero, who is invisible to all except for Burton, eventually encounters Burton and they begin to work together, and eventually fall in love. The importance of naming and the media are apparent from the very beginning, starting with Zero's name. The opening text asserts that "the newspapers" called him Zero, and that functions as his name throughout the entire film; his mother (Charlotte Boisjoli) is even listed in the telephone book as "Zero, Mrs. Patient." The actual name of the flight attendant has become obliterated by the power of his named status. But this process of naming is inherently problematic, a fact of which Greyson is well aware. A voice-over segment similarly observes that the various historical accounts of Burton portray very different individuals: in one account he is named a swashbuckling sexual libertine, and in another a sexually troubled misogynist.

This discursive instability occurs throughout the film, particularly around the issue of AIDS drugs, research, and treatment. George (Richardo Keens-Douglas), who is HIV-positive, is conflicted because his doctor has suggested that he take the new drug "ZPO," even though his friends have heard from other sources that it is useless. Moreover, ZPO is produced by Gilbert-Sullivan Pharmaceuticals, a large corporation making record profits from its AIDS drugs. The film thus emphasizes that, while the medical, social, and economic consequences of treatment decisions are important, reliable answers are rare. George sings, "They're positive that I'm positive. They're sure that these doubts are a curse. I'm supposed to be certainly certain. Well, I'm sure I'm getting worse." Later in the film, George brings his inner conflict over ZPO to his ACT UP companions, and the discussion becomes a heated argument. When they discover Burton taping the argument, the ACT UP crew seizes his tapes, saying that they must present a visibly united front; they cannot let the world know that PWAS actually argue. George, however, denies that such simple ideas of unity are necessary. He criticizes the group's actions and expresses frustration at the idea of enforced solidarity.

At the same time, such complexity and uncertainty are not always negative characteristics in Greyson's story. One of the over-arching themes throughout the film is the need to move away from a quest for certainty organized around blame. Burton "discovers," over the course of the film, that Zero was not the first person to bring AIDS to North America, and that the history of the syndrome is far more complicated than a single point of origin. More importantly, Burton learns that the search for a "first case" is neither productive for research, nor helpful to those living with AIDS. In that spirit, the film's ending intercuts two sequences: one in which a young schoolboy comes to visit and comfort George, who has gone blind, in the hospital, and the other in which ACT UP activists sabotage the museum exhibit that blames Patient Zero for bringing AIDS to North America. In the face of medical uncertainty around AIDS treatments, compassion, care, and action are the most important responses.

Just as he problematizes any single overarching idea about AIDS and promotes a multiplicity of discourse, Greyson mocks received stereotypes of Canadian identity. Because Patient Zero was French Canadian—a factor which makes him appealing as an AIDS scapegoat to the Anglo Canadian museum head—Greyson constructs him as a Francophone stereotype: Zero is sexy and libidinal, a party boy, living by instinct and for sex, yet he is a boy who loves his *maman*. Similarly, Burton is the archetypical Englishman: intellectual, eccentric but sexually restrained (he "lies back and thinks of England"), and he "talks too much." With such a move, Greyson attempts to deal with intercultural difference through humour and irony, casting two stereotypes of

Canadian identity into the roles of reluctant gay male lovers, thereby queering the nation and sexing the conflict. But such a tactic is always a risk. By creating Burton and Zero as heavily stereotyped characters, Greyson may obviate the clichés and thus deconstruct some of the conflicts between English and French Canada. The success of this gambit, however, depends as much on the audience as on the performer. To a Canadian audience, these stereotypes may be familiar enough to be recognized as such. To an international audience, the sly, self-mocking jokes likely would not register at all. However, as though aware of this danger, Greyson juxtaposes these Canadian types against the complexity of both the AIDS community and the Canadian nation itself. The rest of Greyson's cast of characters is drawn from a wide variety of racial, ethnic, linguistic, and sexual communities, reflecting the multitude of social and political actors who are affected by AIDS, a community of people who come together to work for progress in the fight against AIDS.

CONCLUSIONS: CREATING CANONS AND COMMUNITIES

These films, differing as they do in formal style, narrative structure, budget, market, and critical reception, all share a notable emphasis on the intercultural. Although each filmmaker deals with such experiences of internal cultural difference on different registers and in markedly different ways—Arcand and Greyson with a certain degree of hope, Hoolboom with a much more pessimistic perspective—together they foreground the difficulties involved in attempting to forge a community, a "nation." Such difficulties draw on and echo many of the political problems that have dogged various models of Canadian federalism and nationalism, as the country attempts to grapple with the complexity of its nationhood.

Although Tully argues that the experience of cultural difference is internal to *all* cultures and nations, many nationalisms emphasize shared histories, shared ideologies, shared origins. The accepted (clichéd?) Canadian model of nationhood is, however, that of the "multicultural mosaic," a metaphor which acknowledges and actively promotes Tully's concept of the internal cultural difference rather than downplaying such differences. Such a model of Canadian nationhood sounds remarkably like that of Brasell's Queer Nation. Taken together, *Love and Human Remains*, *Kanada*, and *Zero Patience* can thus be seen to draw powerful parallels between the difficulties and narratives of Canadian nation-formation and that of queer nationalism, both affirming and complicating the idea of a national cinema. At the same time, each makes unique statements, focusing on different aspects of the intersections of sexuality and the Canadian nation-state. Emerging as they do from their own intersections of communities, genres, budgetary constraints, intended audiences, and marketing strategies—from the intercultural complexity of Canadian queer cinema—these films represent difference to each other as much as they do sameness. Arcand's character Kane has little place in the world of John Greyson; ACT UP does not exist in Hoolboom's Kanada. Canadian queer cinema is thus marked by a particularly intense form of intercultural difference.

Yet from an outside perspective, from the so-called dominant perspective, these films share a great deal, including CRTC-approved Canadian Content status, a Canadian setting, a certain openness to frank discussions of sex and sexuality, and, most obviously, a number of gay and lesbian characters. This simple fact of the visibility of these characters holds them and their films up for scrutiny as group. If, as Benedict Anderson asserts, cultural objects are used to create imagined communities, they are used by those both inside and outside those communities. Those within the GLBT community in Canada may use these films to imagine themselves, to portray themselves to themselves, to idealize themselves. But these films are also used by those "outside" the community to imagine it: they can be used as a window into the community, giving it a coherence that it might otherwise lack. The power of these external visions cannot be underestimated but neither can their potential distancing effects. [11]

Both Michel Foucault and Leo Bersani question the value of queer visibility, emphasizing the power of those who look. Foucault describes visibility in terms of surveillance, foregrounding the ways in which visibility allows the visible to be tracked, scrutinized, and judged by those in power (187). Bersani, focusing more specifically on gay men, asserts that the mainly heterosexual dominant group can happily watch Gay Pride parades and queer television characters because AIDS has promised the slow elimination of gay men from society. Hence, gay men's visibility is palatable to "straight society" only because of their absolute lack of power (Bersani, 24–25). I would complicate these critiques somewhat and suggest that different kinds of visibility are differently distributed among different queers. Those who do not publicly challenge accepted social and sexual mores and those with good demographics are much more likely to be visible in valorized and valorizing situations than those who cause trouble, who blur comfortable lines, who challenge sexual and gender norms: these queers are more likely to appear as demonized subjects of surveillance and social control. Yet both valourizing and demonizing moments of visibility may spread cultural information about queers and queerness: a newspaper article about men who are caught having sex in a public bathroom may ruin the lives of those who are arrested, but it may also open a world of possibilities, both sexual and social, for a reader feeling isolated and alone in his desires. And so while visibility cannot be supported as a wholly positive or activist goal, neither can it be fully dismissed as a worthless exercise. It must instead be carefully considered in each of its instances.

Moreover, although we can problematize concepts such as a queer nation or a Canadian queer cinema through questions about boundaries, borders, and intercultural complexity, such communitarian assumptions retain a tactical use value in certain political and social contexts. People use them every day. The CRTC continues to determine what is considered Canadian content—and what will represent Canada in the international film community—while various levels of Canadian government decide what homosexuals are and are not allowed to do in this country. And so the ways in which members of the queer/Canadian community attempt to define it *for themselves* remain important. As long as queer Canadians are gathered together as a group faced with various legal, social, and sexual challenges, some form of national queer community is necessary. Thus queer Canadian cultural production is also essential.

Many questions about this kind of cultural formation remain unanswered. What do queer Canadians actually watch and how do they view these moments of domestic cultural production? How do queer Canadian films and audiences change over time, since neither film production nor community formation is an ahistoric process? How do queer Canadian films compare with queer films drawn from other national film traditions? Such questions require careful consideration before we can fully understand the role of film in the formation of the queer Canadian nation. Yet, I hope the observations drawn from this study of these three films can present a starting point for further investigation, because academic writing is also a kind of cultural production that contributes to the project of nationhood. After all, any nation—queer, Canadian, or otherwise—is continually being imagined into existence.

NOTES

1. For a number of models for considering the transnational cultural economy, see Arjun Appadurai, "Disjuncture and Difference in the Global Cultural Economy." *Public Culture* 2.2 (Spring, 1990): 1–24.
2. "New queer cinema" was a label assigned to a loose collection of films that emerged in the early 1990s, including: *Paris is Burning* (Dir. Jennie Livingston; 1990); *My Own Private Idaho* (Dir. Gus Van Sant; 1991); *Poison* (Dir. Todd Haynes; 1991); *The Living End* (Dir. Gregg Araki; 1992); and *Swoon* (Dir. Tom Kalin; 1992).
3. According to Public Notice CRTC 2000–42, entitled "Certification for Canadian Programs—A revised approach," for a film to qualify as a Canadian production, the Producer must be the central decision-maker of a production from beginning to end and must be Canadian and the Production must earn at least six points using the following scale:

Director—2 points
Screenwriter—2 points
Lead Performer (or first voice)—1 point
Second Lead Performer (or second voice)—1 point
Production Designer—1 point
Director of Photography—1 point
Music Composer—1 point
Picture Editor—1 point

Notwithstanding the above, at least one of the director or screenwriter positions and at least one of the two lead performers must be Canadian. At least seventy-five percent of service costs must be paid to Canadians (with some exclusions), and at least seventy-five percent of post-production/lab costs must be paid for services provided in Canada by Canadians or Canadian companies.

4. It may seem that questions about the national status of cultural products are simply subjects for academic debate, or at most of interest only to industry professionals. But these matters can also resonate importantly with the national public. In September of 1991, the CRTC ruled that Bryan Adams' latest album, "Waking Up the Neighbours," was non-Canadian according to existing Canadian Content regulations. According to the regulations, Adams' album failed to qualify because, although Adams was Canadian, the album was produced outside the country, and Adams co-wrote the music with a producer, Robert John ("Mutt") Lange, who is not Canadian. When the news was made public, fans everywhere were outraged. B.C. Member of Provincial Parliament John Reynolds publicly asked Prime Minister Mulroney to intervene. Adams attacked the CRTC at press conferences and in an editorial he wrote for the *Toronto Star*; CRTC head Keith Spicer responded by attacking Adams, calling him ungrateful for the help that Canadian Content regulations provided him in his early years. In March of 1992, Gallup released a poll that found that seventy-six percent of Canadians disagreed with the CRTC decision to categorize Adams' album as non-Canadian content; only nine percent agreed with the decision. At the same time, Gallup also found that fifty-eight percent of Canadians believed that there should be Canadian Content on the radio. By January of 1993, the CRTC had revised its CanCon criteria to accommodate international co-productions more easily, thereby bringing Adams back into the fold.

5. This is an interesting reversal of a traditional notion of male bisexuality, in which the man usually seeks romantic/emotional involvements with women and quick, sexual satisfaction with men: here, Kane looks for romance with David, but quick sex with his girlfriend.

6. "The Beachcombers" was, of course, neither that simple nor that easily dismissed. Revolving around Nick Adonis, a Greek immigrant to Canada who lived and

worked in British Columbia, the series was remarkably popular for almost twenty years, and foregrounded Canada's multicultural diversity, while often dealing with topical and complex political issues in its later seasons.

7. Interestingly, a still photo of this shot appeared in the glossy-format gay periodical *Genre*, in a short article promoting the film: a photo of a straight character, in a gay magazine, promoting a somewhat ambiguous film. (*Genre*: No. 30, 1995)

8. In Hoolboom's *Kanada*, aging Prime Minister Jean Chrétien is replaced by superstar hockey player Wayne Gretzky as the leader of the centrist Liberal Party. "The Great One," as Gretzky was known when he played for the Edmonton Oilers, is selected by the Liberal party as the only figure who can unite a country that has grown tired of politics and politicians. Gretzky's campaign promise, "To do as little as possible for as long as possible," wins him the election in a landslide.

9. It is worth speculating about the names of Hoolboom's lesbian characters. The central figures of the film are a lesbian couple, whose masculine names, Charlie and Bobbie, both work as butch markers of lesbian culture and simultaneously evoke the idea of a male-male couple. Thus, although Hoolboom does not include any gay male romances in this film, the idea of gay male relationships does manage to enter the world of the film.

10. On December 6, 1989, a twenty-five-year-old man named Marc Lepine shot and killed fourteen women at L'Ecole Polytechnique in Montreal, before killing himself. He explicitly blamed feminists for ruining his life and left a suicide note that made his motives clear.

11. For example, the promotional "blurb" on the video-rental version of *Love and Human Remains* available at the national rental chain Rogers Video reads: "Set against a toxic nightscape of urban blight, David, social predator, and Candy stalk the remorseless wasteland of the 1990s, where sex is a body function and people are disposable" (Rogers Video Outlet: Serial No. 302041). This simple description, written by Rogers Video, paints a remarkably dark portrait of the characters and relationships featured in Arcand's film, one which seems to miss the film's point: amidst the dangers and uncertainties of contemporary life one's friends and lovers can be a powerful source of support. Moreover, the description assumes a great distance between the experience of the film's characters and that of its audience: the collection of Canadian queers featured in the film does not seem to be part of Rogers' vision of their customers.

WORKS CITED

Adams, Bryan. "'Real talent will always win out,' Adams says." *Toronto Star* (February 8, 1992), J1.

Anderson, Benedict. *Imagined Communities: Reflections on the Origin and Spread of Nationalism.* London: Verso, 1991.

Appadurai, Arjun. "Disjuncture and Difference in the Global Cultural Economy." *Public Culture*, 2.2 (Spring 1990): 1–24.

Berlant, Lauren and Elizabeth Freeman. "Queer Nationality." In *Fear of a Queer Planet: Queer Politics and Social Theory*. Ed. Michael Warner. Minneapolis: University of Minnesota Press, 1993. 193–229.

Bersani, Leo. *Homos*. Cambridge, MA: Harvard University Press, 1995.

Brasell, R. Bruce. "Queer Nationalism and the Musical Fag Bashing of John Greyson's *The Making of 'Monsters.'*" *Wide Angle*, 16.3 (February 1995): 26–36.

Butler, Judith. "Imitation and Gender Insubordination." In *The Lesbian and Gay Studies Reader*. Eds. Henry Abelove, Michele Aina Barale, and David M. Halperin. New York: Routledge, 1993. 307–320.

Canada. Canadian Radio-Television and Telecommunications Commission. Public Notice CRTC 2000–42: Certification for Canadian Programs—A revised approach, Ottawa, March 17, 2000.

Canadian Press. "PM asked to intervene in Adams controversy." *Toronto Star* (September 26, 1991), B11.

Canadian Press. "Poll finds 76 per cent disagree with CRTC ruling on Adams." *Toronto Star* (March 5, 1992), C7.

Canadian Press. "CRTC eases rule after Adams uproar." *Toronto Star*. January 30, 1993, A16.

Collins, Richard. *Culture, Communication & National Identity: The Case of Canadian Television*. Toronto: University of Toronto Press, 1990.

Foucault, Michel. *Discipline and Punish: The Birth of the Prison*. New York: Vintage Books, 1979.

Genre. "Genrepolitan." 30 (July-August 1995): 26.

Higson, Andrew. "The Concept of National Cinema." *Screen*, 30.4 (1989): 36–46.

Howell, Peter. "Bryan Adams' songs declared un-Canadian." *Toronto Star*, Final edition (September 12, 1991), A26.

———. "Spicer shoots back at Bryan Adams." *Toronto Star* (January 16, 1992), D1.

Kanada [motion picture]. Directed by Mike Hoolboom. Canada, 1993.

Love and Human Remains [motion picture]. Directed by Denys Arcand. Canada, 1994.

Mietkiewicz, Henry. "Adams blast falls out on record business." *Toronto Star (*January 15, 1992), F1.

Rice-Barker, Leo. "Love and Human Remains." *Playback*. September 13, 1993, F5, F13, F24.

Rogers Video Outlet. Promotional Blurb for *Love and Human Remains*. Serial No: 302041. Grant Park Plaza, 1847 Grant St., Winnipeg Manitoba.

Smith, Anthony D. "Ethnic Persistence and National Transformation." *British Journal of Sociology*, 35 (September 1984): 452–461.

Tully, James. *Strange Multiplicity: Constitutionalism in an age of diversity*. Cambridge: Cambridge University Press, 1995.

Warner, Michael. "Introduction." In *Fear of a Queer Planet: Queer Politics and Social Theory*. Ed. Michael Warner. Minneapolis: University of Minnesota Press, 1993. vii-xxxi.

Waugh, Thomas. "The Third Body: Patterns in the Construction of the Subject in Gay Male Narrative Film." In *Queer Looks: Perspectives on Lesbian and Gay Film and Video.* Toronto: Between the Lines, 1993. 141–161.

Wood, Robin. "The New Queer Cinema and Gay Culture: Notes from an Outsider." *Cineaction*, 35: 2–15.

Zero Patience [motion picture]. Directed by John Greyson. Canada, 1993.

the elephant, the mouse, and the lesbian national park rangers

bj wray

The relationship of nationalism to lesbianism has never been a monolithic one. Although it is easy to compile a lengthy account of the ways in which state-sanctioned nationalism has coerced, pathologized, and terrorized lesbians as sexual "deviants," and although it is easy to recount innumerable occasions on which the agents of national borders consistently police lesbian desire through the confiscation of sexually-explicit material, the ideology of nationalism has frequently and repeatedly been invoked as a paradigm for lesbian community-building. Nationalism—especially the sense of connectedness, unity, and commonality that its discourses convey—holds a certain appeal for an otherwise amorphous community whose members do not share a single geography, passport, or currency. In the succinct phrasing of legal theorist Carl Stychin, "[s]ocial movements . . . deploy the language of nation as a means of constituting and reinforcing their own identities" (7).

This vexed connection between national discourses of belonging and lesbian identity provides the backdrop for Shawna Dempsey and Lorri Millan's 1997 site-specific performance, *The Lesbian National Park Rangers.*[1] I have chosen *The Rangers* from Dempsey and Millan's extensive *oeuvre* because of the ways in which this performance demonstrates a complex interaction with, and intervention in, the operations of normative national and sexual discourses.[2]

Dempsey and Millan humourously interrogate the "unnaturalness" of lesbian sexuality from within the confines of the state-sanctioned "naturalness" of Banff National Park. The relationship between national citizenship and lesbian sexuality hinges upon an ever-shifting politics of representation, and Dempsey and Millan's strategies of lesbian representation, while cognizant of the pitfalls attached to visibility politics, employ parody and hyperbole to re-sight/site a lesbian subject within a national setting.

My examination of *The Lesbian National Park Rangers* is framed by contemporary discussions of rights discourses and sexual citizenship. Lesbian activism specifically and activist theory generally, within the Western nation-state, is most often driven by a desire for the rights that full and equal national citizenship promises. As one of the most tangible markers of belonging, full and equal citizenship is held up as a guarantor of minority recognition within the nation-state. Lesbian theorist Shane Phelan is representative in her assessment of the road to "democratic empowerment": "Clearly, new rights are needed if lesbians are to be full citizens" (129). Phelan's linkage of full citizenship with the procurement of rights characterizes contemporary mainstream sexuality activism. Both "rights" and "citizenship" are understood, in this equation, as concepts that must be expanded to include lesbian subjects. This form of mainstream activism takes for granted the liberating power of full and equal citizenship and fails to consider the ways in which the discourses of national citizenship actively materialize sexual identities, histories, and cultures.

As categories of identification, citizenship and sexuality engender certain representations of the identities at hand. The rights discourses associated with full and equal citizenship *compel* the narrativization of lesbian history, culture, identity, and desire along the homogenizing trajectory of national belonging. A rights discourse works to the extent that it both constitutes and articulates the existence of an identifiable, marginalized group of people. Calls for full and equal citizenship must grapple with the potential reiteration of normative notions of identity that are always already present in the national discourses at hand. Lesbian sexuality is imagined within the parameters of these activist calls for full and equal citizenship, and lesbian identity cannot be separated from discourses of national belonging. In other words, an analysis of the style in which identity is imagined—its discursive materialization—exposes the structuring power that national citizenship has on figurations of lesbian community and identity.

Critics of the power that citizenship wields over non-normative subjects and communities have tended to focus on the illusory nature of citizenship's apparent inclusivity. Specifically, the notion of "universal" citizenship has come under fire from feminist scholars for its implicit privileging of white, heteronormative subjects. Political theorist Iris Marion Young outlines the problematic foundation of conventional citizenship:

> Founded by men, the modern state and its public realm of citizenship paraded as universal values and norms that were derived from specifically masculine experience: militarist norms of honor and homoerotic camaraderie; respectful competition and bargaining among independent agents; discourse framed in unemotional tones of dispassionate reason. (266)

Citizenship is produced as a productive and disciplinary category that is regularly deployed within formal and informal relations of power. David Evans further clarifies this process: "Behind the rhetoric of universal rights of privacy, dignity, religious and cultural beliefs, there stands a citizenship machinery which effectively invades and corrals those who by various relative status shortcomings are deemed to be less than fully qualified citizens" (5). Non-normative sexual identities fall outside the realm of "universal" rights, and the "citizenship machinery" that Evans identifies actively curtails the representation and recognition of these identities within the nation-state.

In direct opposition to this process of delimitation, erasure, and exclusion, feminist and lesbian-rights activism often seeks to transform citizenship into an inclusive category of identification. On the other hand, separatist-based politics wants to be rid of the category altogether. In the words of Canadian historian Gary Kinsman, "[T]raditional concepts simply cannot be stretched to cover our experiences. We must step outside the dominant discourses—as must women and other oppressed groups—if we are to create a body of knowledge to help us in our struggle" (31). Rather than replicate either an assimilationist or a separatist approach towards imagining sexual citizenship and the new constitution of universality that these models tend to promote, I am interested in the types of citizenship that are forged where identification and misidentification overlap.

My usage of citizenship extends beyond state-sanctioned definitions and narrow legal and political applications. Rather, I understand citizenship as a malleable model of performed affiliations whose contours are discursively constituted and, therefore, continually reiterated within the nation-state, or as political theorist Terrell Carver notes, "citizenship is a movable metaphor of 'belonging' and 'inclusion'" (16). In the words of Lauren Berlant: "It [citizenship] is continually being produced out of a political, rhetorical, and economic struggle over who will count as 'the people' and how social membership will be measured and valued" (20). Citizenship, as we will see in *The Lesbian National Park Rangers,* is not a static delineation of national belonging, but is an active, ongoing performance that can never be fully or finally conferred. Conceptualized as performance, citizenship becomes newly accessible for resignification by minority subjects.

The Lesbian National Park Rangers begins this process of resignification through an exploration of the ways in which national identities come to be "naturalized." Dempsey and Millan's spectacular, hyperbolic performance transforms lesbian invisibility within discourses of Canadian nation-ness into a showy, campy display of "official" lesbian presence. The "naturalness" of national and sexual identifications is taken to task by Dempsey's and Millan's parodic invasion of a significant site of Canadian nationalism, Banff National Park. *The Lesbian National Park Rangers* interrogates the exclusionist operations of nation-making and exploits the signifiers of normative national belonging as the newly configured sites/sights of lesbian sexuality. Dempsey and Millan's performance does more, however, than simply expose the quotidian operations of nation-making. Instead of reiterating the representational difficulties associated with an oppositional approach to activism, the spectacle offered by *The Lesbian National Park Rangers* insists upon a mode of lesbian activism that critiques conventional discourses of national and sexual identification through *direct engagement* with these dominant paradigms.

Banff National Park is Canada's postcard to the world. Perhaps the most recognizable of Canadian scenery, Banff's wildlife, snow-capped mountain peaks, landmark hotels, European-inspired townsite, and five million tourists a year guarantee the international representational caché of this National Park. My academic home, the English department at the University of Calgary, banks on the allure of this National Park to entice guest lecturers and job candidates to our University: a day of lectures and a weekend in Banff, it sells well. Established in 1855, Banff is Canada's oldest National Park and the anchor in a countrywide chain of thirty-eight federally created and regulated "natural areas of Canadian significance" (www.parkscanada.pch.gc.ca/np/english/nptxt_e.htm).

Banff alone functions as Canada's Ur-Park. It acts, within an international

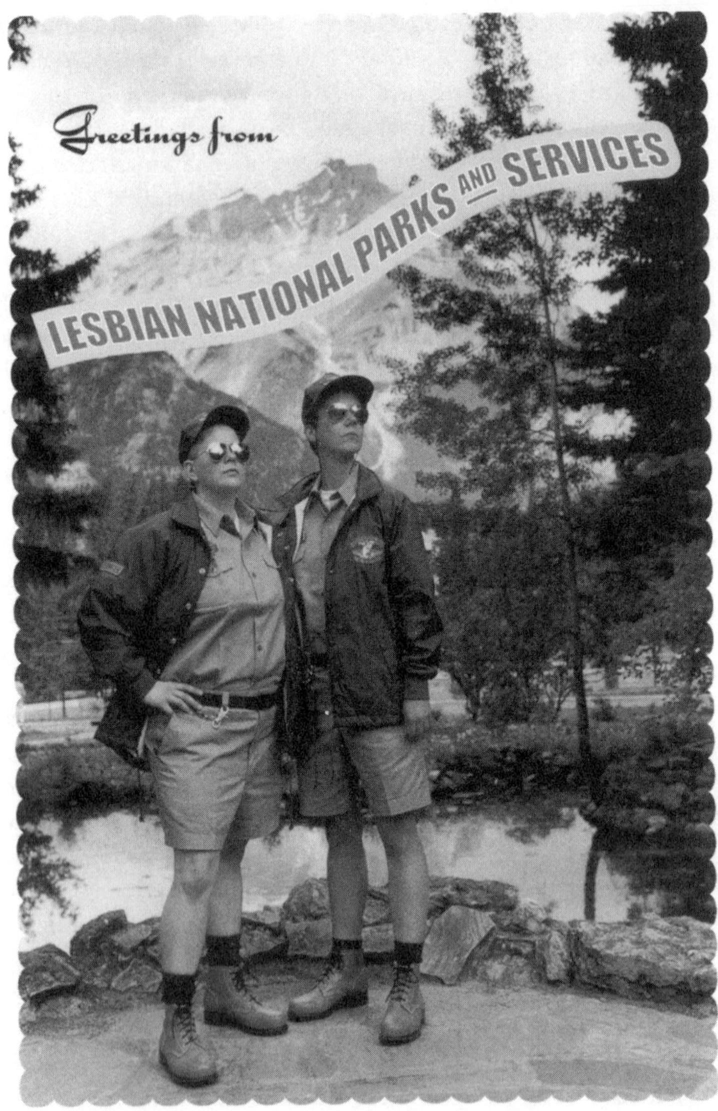

Figure 1. Lesbian National Parks and Services Postcard.
Photography Don Lee. Courtesy of Lori Millan and Shauna Dempsey.

and Canadian imaginary, as a tangible marker of Canadian geography and, more importantly, of Canadian identity. I hardly need remark upon the prestigious role ascribed to this so-called "wilderness" in the making of a Canadian national identity. Margaret Atwood's highly influential 1972 thematic guide to Canadian literature, aptly entitled *Survival*, informs readers that "[t]he central symbol for Canada . . . is undoubtedly survival. . . . For early explorers and settlers, it meant bare survival in the face of 'hostile' elements . . . . For French Canada after the English took over it became cultural survival. . . . And in English Canada now while the Americans are taking over it is acquiring a similar meaning" (32).[3] The commodification of Banff National Park into an irresistible tourist destination is a testament, then, to our triumphant "survival" in the wilds and, following Atwood's logic, while ignoring the Disney-like packaging of the Park, Banff's iconographic status also testifies to Canadian "cultural survival" in the face of what is commonly referred to in Canada as the threat of America.[4]

Canadian cultural commentator, Kyo Maclear, wryly summarizes Banff's contribution to Canada's "not-American" identity:

> Those Canucks who fear our very identity is in danger of obliteration by the juggernaut to the south—those who fear that McBanff burgers and Mount Rundle Dairy Queen sundaes are just around the corner—can leave Banff flush with local colour, "authentic" Indian curios and, perhaps most important, a sense of BIGNESS. (13)

"Bigness" is, indeed, most useful when the dominant trope of Canadian/American relations, first proposed by the late Pierre Elliot Trudeau, depicts Canada as the mouse asleep in the shadow of the American elephant. The precariousness of Canada's position within this analogy often extends into the academic realm where the ambivalence associated with this relationship is readily apparent. Linda Hutcheon remarks in the May 1999 issue of *PMLA*:

> For Canadians . . . the MLA, like the nation in which it is based, is perhaps not distant enough. Spatial and cultural proximity to the United States, a large and influential force, has had diverse effects on Canada-based academics, ranging from *fear* of what the media refer to as 'American cultural imperialism' to *pleasure* at participating in a larger professional context. (311–312, emphasis mine)

These simultaneous and contradictory responses to the American academy are symptomatic of the instabilities that characterize the ongoing production of English Canadian national identity. Coerced *and* seduced by the Americanization of our identity, the strength of the Canadian/American coalition does not depend upon a simplistic territorialization of the margin by the centre but, rather, this coalition holds because Canadian nationalist sentiment remains inextricably and complexly bound to a "not-American" status.

Marking and remarking upon differences (even, perhaps especially, where they do not exist) ensures the articulation of an English Canadian imaginary in the face of an otherwise invisible "otherness."

The complicated relationship between sameness and difference that defines Canada's link to America corresponds to the ambivalence that characterizes contemporary notions of sexuality. Andrew Parker comments that "if modern philosophies of the nation have had to negotiate between the contradictory requirements of sameness and difference, of universalism and singularity, these are also the (equally unstable) terms that have shaped modern conceptions of sexual orientation" (212). The concurrent existence of both universalizing and minoritizing discourses of homosexuality resonates with the tenuousness of national identities. The boundaries of Canada, like those of homosexuality, are internally and externally unstable. English Canadian national identity and homosexual identity share the structuration of incoherence, and activist identity-making strategies in each of these areas have frequently aimed to contain this incoherence by stabilizing, unifying, and rendering intelligible (therefore legitimate) a singular, monolithic paradigm of existence.

In particular, the grafting of lesbian identity onto a nationalist framework, as I have already touched upon, has proven to be a particularly durable as well as vexed linkage. Jill Johnston's now famous description of lesbian community as a "Lesbian Nation" first appeared in a 1971 *Village Voice* article and, since then, the association of nationalism with lesbian community building has been unshakable. The utopic ideals of Lesbian Nation continue to inform current mainstream activism in that lesbian identity is accorded legitimacy through an appeal to the nationalist rhetorics of citizenship. The belief in full and equal citizenship, and the attendant reliance on a discourse of rights, has permeated to the core of mainstream lesbian political organizing in North America. One's rightful place within the national body politic is delineated by asserting one's claim to certain rights.

Alan Sinfield astutely problematizes the agency assumed by rights advocates when he writes, "For it is not that existing categories of gay men and lesbians have come forward to claim their rights, but that we have become constituted *as gay* in terms of a discourse of ethnicity and rights" (271, emphasis in original). It is not that citizenship and equality rights legitimize pre-existing identities, but rather, the contours of identity are shaped by the demands of citizenship and rights models themselves. Sally Munt characterizes this process as the "Americanization of identity politics" (172). This Americanization signifies, for Munt, a non-reflective usage of national citizenship paradigms that, unwittingly, reinforces the homogeneity of identity politics. In other words, the tactic of shrouding sexual identity in a cloak of full and equal citizenship ignores the incoherencies at the heart of nationalism in favour of exploiting the legitimizing and coalitional-building powers of a nationalist rhetoric. In doing so, rights activism ironically mimics and upholds the means by which national incoherencies are sutured through the tactics of "othering" and coercion into "proper" citizenship.

Given the obvious pitfalls of working within national conceptions of sexual identity to obtain rights and establish coalitions, and the equally problematic refusal to engage in the struggle for full and equal citizenship, is it possible to transform this ambivalence into a critically reflective alliance with nationalism for activist ends? By way of answering this query, we must journey back to the rather unlikely site of lesbian activism: Banff National Park.

In July of 1997, the Banff Centre for the Performing Arts invited eight performance artists to participate in "Private Investigators," a three-week long exhibition that took place in and around the Banff townsite and at the Walter Phillips Gallery in the Banff Centre. Among the performers invited were Dempsey and Millan. For the "Private Investigators" exhibition, the Winnipeg-based video and performance duo created the fictitious organization, Lesbian National Parks and Services, and they donned the khaki uniform of the Lesbian National Park Rangers. For three weeks, the Lesbian National Park Rangers patrolled the streets of Banff politely handing out pamphlets on the Lesbian Flora and Fauna in Banff National Park while courteously dispensing directions and other Park information to unsuspecting tourists. The Rangers paddled the canoe routes and roamed hiking trails of the Park and they staged, in the centre of the townsite, a particularly successful Lesbian National Park Ranger recruitment day, complete with official induction ceremonies, pink lemonade for the Junior Rangers, and posters proclaiming: "Lesbian National Parks and Services WANTS YOU!"

With the splendour of the Banff scenery always in the background, Dempsey and Millan's performance offers a multi-layered commentary on the interlining of sexuality and nationalism in both state-sanctioned discourses *and* queer activist practices. Their parody of Canadian National Park Wardens is an insightful indictment of normative notions of identities. Kyo Maclear notes: "The first thing [Dempsey and Millan] want us to know is that nothing is what it seems: not the mythical 'lesbian' (demonized as a social threat, target and outsider), or the equally fictionalized 'ranger' (celebrated as a front-line guardian of the Canadian Wilderness)" (57). When these identities merge in the figure of the Lesbian Ranger, the signification process takes a very queer turn that requires a double- or triple-take on the part of the viewer. It is

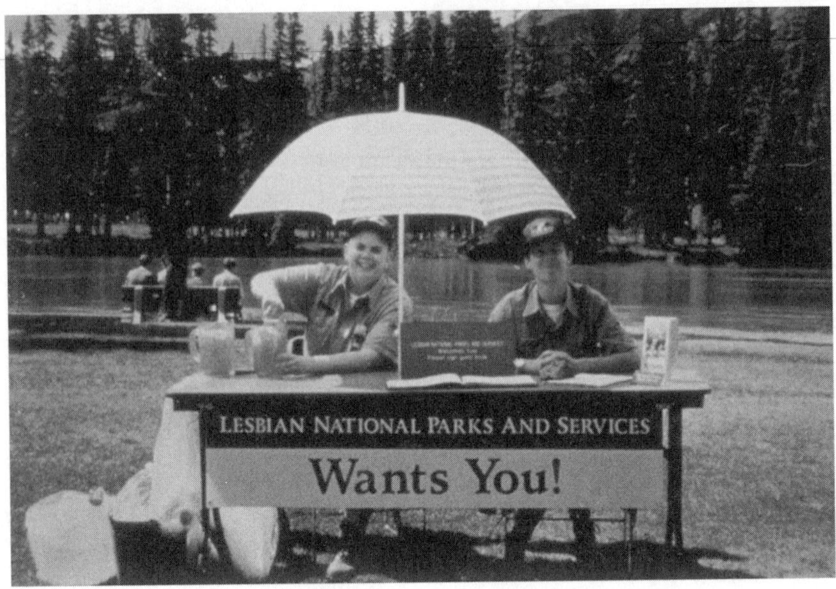

Figure 2. Ranger Recruitment. Courtesy Lori Millan and Shawna Dempsey.

in this momentary disruption that Dempsey and Millan's performance gently coaxes viewers out of the accepted, even expected, passive and unengaged consumption of the landscape that scenic tourism tends to promote.

The Lesbian Rangers' critique of tourist consumption continues in their information brochure where readers are assured that they will discover the uniqueness of the Banff Wilderness by hiking down Banff Avenue and trekking into Cascade Mall. The accompanying Banff street map directs tourists to such lesbian landmarks as the "Invisible Plaque Dedicated to our Founding Foremothers," the "Invisible Museum of Homosexual Mountain History," the "Invisible Lesbian Heritage House and Gardens," and of course the "Lesbian National Parks and Services Information" booth.

Attentive to what is hidden by national maps and histories, the Lesbian Rangers intervene in the production of a national imaginary by re-mapping "invisible" lesbian sites. That these places are marked as "invisible" suggests an unwillingness by Dempsey and Millan to replicate the problematics of representation often associated with mainstream visibility politics. This tongue-in-cheek depiction of lesbian activity in Banff crucially gestures towards the social amnesia encoded within the "happy trails mentality" (Maclear, 10) of Canada's National Parks System. Just as the "official" guidebooks to the area

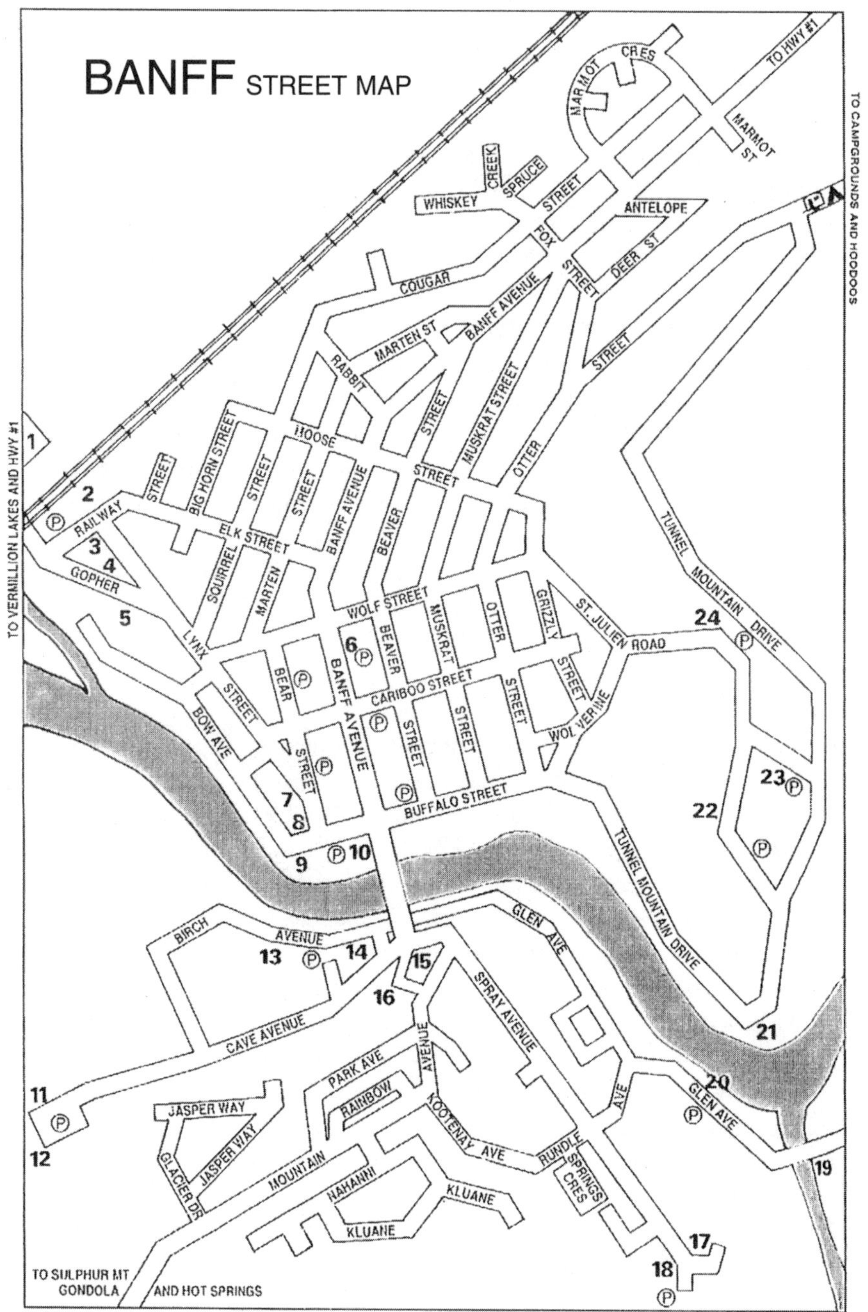

Figure 3. Townsite Map.

refuse to acknowledge anything but a heterosexual history so, too, they establish a specifically white-colonialist-national-narrative-of-progress by conveniently "failing" to mention that Banff National Park is part of a Siksika Nation land claim and that "the Canadian Rockies served as a physical and symbolic border for Japanese Canadians who were not allowed west of the mountains until the late 1940's" (Maclear, 10). Neither do these guidebooks mention that "the [mountain] peaks are unmarked graves for Chinese railroad labourers who died in the thousands" (Maclear, 10). Although the Lesbian Rangers expose the (hetero)sexual logic governing Banff National Park's "management" of the wilderness, their performance leaves intact the racial exclusiveness underpinning Canadian national belonging.

Arun Mukerjee powerfully sums up the exclusive operations of Canadian nationalism: "Canadian nationalism, for us nonwhites, is a racist ideology that has branded us un-Canadian by acts of omission and commission" (89). The ongoing production of Canadian nationalism in opposition to the threat of American domination reveals the exclusionary, racist practices perpetuated by an unexamined nationalist discourse. As Mukerjee continues, Canadian nationalists of the sixties and seventies "did not produce an ideology of national liberation that would include all Canadians on equal footing. Instead, they constructed a Canada that was being savaged by American domination. . . . Their Canada was an innocent victim" (89). This "innocent victim" mentality continues to dominate Canadian nationalist sentiment, especially in the realm of cultural nationalism. Dempsey and Millan intervene in the operations of this uncritical Canadian nationalism by hyperbolizing this traditional oppositional relationship to America, and by situating minority history within the parameters of a national institution. Their spectacular visibility within Banff National Park places lesbians at the heart of the nation-making process and begins to dismantle the binary of normative and non-normative sexual citizenship.

In a quirky homage to Lesbian Nation activism, Dempsey and Millan's performance takes up nationally inflected activist strategies. With their uniforms, slogans, maps, and historical information campaign, the Rangers exploit the material renderings of nationalism and, in doing so, they tap into the legitimacy, authority, and sense of respect that those trappings command. However, the parodic edge of their spectacle insists upon a self-reflective relation to the discourse of nationalism and, in particular, its impact on the style and content of lesbian mainstream political activism. Rather than strategize around lesbian minority status or assimilationist politics, the Rangers address and exploit those right-wing fears by explicitly confirming the existence of a "homosexual agenda."

Figure 4. Ranger Information Sheet.

The Rangers actively promote recruitment as well as the homosexualization of "the heterosexual wilderness" (55). In their daily Field Notes, they outline their goals and methodology for implementing an intensive homosexual overhaul of Canada's scenery and they note with much delight that "Ranger Envy" has inflicted many of their onlookers. In their Final Report, the Rangers conclude that: "The introduction of homosexual species to the area might also lead to exponential multiplication, transforming the gay-wasteland-that-is-Banff into a virtual Galapagos of homosexual wildlife" (55). With this hyperbolic flourish, the Rangers queer not just the nation but the entire ecosystem into a world-renowned site of oddities and "unnatural" creatures.

In their *The Rangers* performance, Dempsey and Millan appropriate a myriad of authoritative discourses. Margot Francis, in her review of *The Lesbian National Park Rangers,* assesses this tactic: "Throughout all the LNPS brochures, reports and performances, Dempsey and Millan inhabit the booming voice of the (white, male) 1950s 'expert'—and use it for their own ends. But never have we heard an expert talk about the desirability of achieving 'explosive homo growth'" (42–43). Dempsey and Millan's exploitation of "expert" voices works as an act of resignification that queerly inhabits these pathologizing discourses.

Dempsey and Millan also take on Canada's ambivalent relationship with America through a similar parodic appropriation of national registers. The often overwhelming presence of American cultural products in Canada and their subsequent influence on Canadian national identity, as either that which must be resisted *or* embraced, is, in Dempsey and Millan's performance, self-reflectively resisted *and* embraced. The resignification in their performance and literature of recognizably American slogans such as "The Lesbian National Park Rangers WANT YOU!," and "Wherever you go, whatever you do, ask not what lesbianism can do for you, but what you can do for lesbianism" is juxtaposed against the iconography of Banff National Park and the folk hero mythology accompanying the Park Wardens. This somewhat irreverent redeployment of American nationalist sentiment exposes the constructedness and yet pervasiveness of this American identity framework. The Rangers make use of these "Americanisms" to re-imagine Canadian ambivalence as a potentially playful, provocative national culture.

The critical cultural activism of Dempsey and Millan provides viewers with the opportunity to unravel the connections between national and sexual identities. The Lesbian National Park Rangers attack on several fronts at once and insinuate a lesbian presence into the quotidian operations of national culture. I want to remain mindful, however, of the extent to which the success of their performance hinges upon the "'benign,' white body of the ranger" (Francis, 41) that Dempsey and Millan each inhabit. Margot Francis situates the easy consumption of the Rangers performance by their Banff audience within the context of a "manageable, albeit risky, difference" (43). Francis reads Dempsey and Millan's whiteness as integral to the performance's reception:

> Importantly, the rangers' image of innocence, reminiscent of Girl Guides (or, Boy Scouts) only works for a majority white audience when it is materialized through whiteness, specifically Dempsey and Millan's white female bodies. Girl Guides, park rangers and many other icons can only be seen as benign, normative symbols if they are racialized as 'just people,' which, in a Canadian context, representations of people of colour have never been. (43–44)

There can be no question that Dempsey and Millan's whiteness, and the innocence—even dorkiness—of their appearance, lends legitimacy to their performance. However, Francis's analysis cannot account for the ways in which the Rangers resignify the whiteness they inhabit. The normative identities upheld by national citizenship (white, heterosexual, male, and so forth) are intimately linked and I would suggest that Dempsey and Millan's performance, through their historical revisions, parodic interventions, and focus on the *performativity* of nation-making, gestures towards the necessity of re-imagining *all* of these normative markers. The Rangers' interventions onto the "naturalization" process of national belonging have implications, then, for an explicitly anti-racist project.

The power of national discourses to materialize certain, acceptable bodies and elide "others" comes to the fore through their performance. *The Lesbian National Park Rangers* provides a critical commentary on the ongoing *processes* of nation-making, and although they do not literally embody a racialized other, Dempsey and Millan's performance initiates an examination of the operations of whiteness in national spaces. They reinvigorate the activist potentials of nationalism by reminding us that "whether you live in a large urban centre or a small rural community, on a mountainside or the vast, open prairie: Lesbian National Parks and Services depends on the commitment of all citizens to create an ecosystem better suited to the diversity of lesbian wildlife."

NOTES

1. At the time of this writing (October 2000), Dempsey and Millan are putting the final touches on a video "mockumentary" of their Lesbian National Park Ranger performance. Order inquiries may be directed to Finger in the Dyke Productions, 485 Wardlaw Ave., Winnipeg, Manitoba, R3L 0L9.
2. Dempsey and Millan have collaborated on feminist performance art since 1989. They are well known for pieces such as *Mermaid in Love*, 1990; *Mary Medusa*, 1993; the 1994 videotape *What Does a Lesbian Look Like*?, which played in rotation on MuchMusic; their film *Good Citizen, Betty Baker*, 1996; and their site-specific performance of *The Lesbian National Park Rangers*, 1997. Between 1989 and 1994 they completed a series of performances using the dress as metaphor: *Object/Subject of Desire*, 1993; *The Thin Skin of Normal*, 1993; *Arborite Housewife*, 1994; and *Glass Madonna*, 1994.
3. I invoke this outdated text by Margaret Atwood only to demonstrate the formative power of the "wilderness" within the historical constitution of a Canadian Literary Canon. Atwood's text solidified Canada's position as the colonized in relation to America, and this notion continues to permeate mainstream media discussions of Canadian identity. A number of Canadian writers have since provided excellent critiques of this hegemonic understanding of Canada. See, for instance, the writings of Arun Mukerjee, Fred Wah, Richard Fung, Thomas King, Dionne Brand, Roy Miki, and Marlene Nourbese Philip. In the words of Mukerjee, "Canadian literature, created, published, taught, and critiqued under the aegis of Canadian nationalism, promotes the settler-colonial view of Canada" (83).
4. The most recent discussion of this threat is found in *Maclean's Magazine* year-end poll on Canadian identity wherein fifty percent of Canadians surveyed fear we are becoming more like Americans (*Maclean's Magazine*, Dec. 20, 1999, 22).

WORKS CITED

Atwood, Margaret. *Survival: A Thematic Guide to Canadian Literature.* Toronto: Anansi, 1972.

Berlant, Lauren. *The Queen of America Goes to Washington City: Essays on Sexuality and Citizenship.* Durham, NC: Duke University Press, 1997.

Carver, Terrell. "Sexual Citizenship: Gendered and De-Gendered Narratives." In *The Politics of Sexuality: Identity, Gender, Citizenship.* Eds. Terrell Carver and Veronique Mottier. New York: Routledge, 1998. 13–24.

Dempsey, Shawna and Lorri Millan, perf. *Lesbian National Parks and Services.* Finger in the Dyke Productions, 1997.

———. "Lesbian National Parks and Services." In *Private Investigators: Undercover in Public Space* Eds. Kathryn Walter and Kyo Maclear. Banff: Banff Centre Press, 1999.

Evans, David T. *Sexual Citizenship: The Material Construction of Sexualities.* New York: Routledge, 1993.

Francis, Margot. "Unsettling Sights . . ." *Fuse* 22.4 (2000): 41–45.

Hutcheon, Linda. "Academic Free Trade? One Canadian's View of the MLA." *PMLA* 114.3 (1999): 311–17.

Kinsman, Gary. *The Regulation of Desire: Sexuality in Canada.* Montreal: Black Rose Books, 1987.

Maclear, Kyo. "The Accidental Witness." In *Private Investigators: Undercover in Public Space.* Eds. Kathryn Walter and Kyo Maclear. Banff: Banff Centre Press, 1999. 9–17.

Mukherjee, Arun. "Canadian Nationalism, Canadian Literature, and Racial Minority Women." *Essays on Canadian Writing* 56 (1995): 78–95.

Munt, Sally. *Heroic Desire: Lesbian Identity and Cultural Space.* New York: New York University Press, 1998.

Parker, Andrew. "Grafting David Cronenberg: Monstrosity, AIDS Media, National/Sexual Difference." In *Media Spectacles.* Eds. Marjorie Garber, Jann Matlock, and Rebecca Walkowitz. New York: Routledge, 1993. 209–31.

Phelan, Shane. *Getting Specific: Postmodern Lesbian Politics.* Minneapolis: University of Minnesota Press, 1994.

Sinfield, Alan. "Diaspora and Hybridity: Queer Identities and the Ethnicity Model." *Textual Practice* 10.2 (1996): 271–93.

Stychin, Carl F. *A Nation By Rights.* Philadelphia: Temple University Press, 1998.

Young, Iris Marion. "Polity and Group Difference: A Critique of the Ideal of Universal Citizenship." In *The Citizenship Debates: A Reader.* Ed. Gershon Shafir. Minneapolis: University of Minnesota Press, 1998. 263–90.

having a gay old time in paris: john glassco's not-so-queer adventures

Andrew Lesk

John Glassco's 1970 *Memoirs of Montparnasse* opens with an introduction not by the author, but by Leon Edel whose status as *the* biographer of Henry James arguably does much to raise the status of Glassco's book above many other reminiscences of the anglophone literati of 1920s Paris. Edel claims, "His book is more humane and "actual" than Hemingway's *A Moveable Feast*" (ix). He concludes with a comment about this "actual" which suggests a profound power:

> The graceful record illuminates many faces gone from this earth. We sit again at the Dome or the Select. We attend the parties *d'antan.* Was it all an hallucination provoked by an overdose of *omelette aux champignons*?

> Was it all a dream? Whatever it was, it is a delightful form of nostalgia—and of truth. *Optima dies . . . prima fugit.* (xi)

The *Memoirs* portrays the author's youthful escapades with various famous expatriates, including Robert McAlmon (his erstwhile lover), Gertrude Stein, and Man Ray, among others. And although Glassco's reputation in Canadian literary history is partly as poet, translator, and scandalous pornographer, none of those has received as much attention as the *Memoirs*, an outrageous account peopled by characters with rather flexible sexual desires.

Glassco's prefatory note states that he wishes "to impose a *narrative form* on everything that has happened since we left Montreal last February" (4, emphasis mine). Thus, regardless of Edel's claims about "truth," the issue of dissimulation in the writings—especially concerning Glassco's purported homosexual dalliances—becomes impossible to ignore. Of course, Glassco's coy manner in avoiding disclosing the actual character of his close male friendships is not without narrative precedent. Such ambiguity, embraced by early twentieth-century writers such as E.M. Forster and Henry James, was a veiled method of expressing what were then legally prohibited and psychiatrically proscribed same-sex desires.

But Glassco's veil was narratively drawn at a time when the injurious ramifications of the Oscar Wilde trials were decades in the past. With the revelation that much of the published recollections are factually misleading and were written not in 1929–1932 but in the late 1960s,[1] Glassco's deceptive impulses take on heightened importance. Most significantly, the autobiographical pact demanding unembellished truth, between the author and reader, breaks down.[2] Glassco's deceit is at least partly sexual. He chose to edit *out* his homosexual encounters and affairs, at a time when socially conservative views of libidinal bondings seemed to be breaking down in Canada.[3] Glassco's book was certainly not the first to shock Canadian readers: two notable examples which appeared on the Canadian literary scene just prior to Glassco's work are Leonard Cohen's *Beautiful Losers* (1966), a libidinal, metafictional free-for-all; and Scott Symons's *Combat Journal for Place d'Armes* (1967), a homoeroticization of the burgeoning Canadian nationalistic impulse.

Yet if the hostile reception to Symons's book[4] is the measure by which Glassco took his cue, it is perhaps unsurprising that Glassco encouraged the appellation of a Casanova-like "bad boy" of Canadian letters, and followed the path laid by Cohen rather than Symons, namely, using homosexuality as a provisional stance to embolden the need for a virile *heterosexual* nationalism. As Robert K. Martin writes, "Homosexuality is celebrated in Cohen, but only as a way of reinforcing heterosexuality" (*The Body Politic*, 29). Glassco's "straightened" (homo)sexual conduct encourages notice.

Glassco's desire for public fame, if not personal fortune, might be a partial motive for his revisions. This revised sexual past would not offend those for whom an ostensibly "flaunted" homosexuality would bar the author from serious recognition. I do not mean to assert unequivocally that Canada's purveyor of pornography (and one of the country's few public sexual obsessives) was a conformist, but it is at least arguable that he knew what might prevent entry into the canon of Canadian letters.

While much criticism has examined Glassco's fabulation, little attention has been paid to the social context of the author's struggles with homosexuality, both his own and others', and his subsequent "fictionalized" downplaying of it. The critical anxieties appear in any discussion of Glassco's lived existence and reveal much as to how the specter of homosexuality in his writing has been controlled by the broadly social need to keep him "straight," particularly in service of a national heterosexual literary tradition. And this need is something in which Glassco acquiesced.

Perhaps the most significant and recent challenge to the orthodoxy which asserts an unabashedly heterosexual Glassco is Richard Dellamora's recent essay on how the *Memoirs'* "queerness, both disavowed and acknowledged . . . marks it as a point of departure within Canada's recently formed national canon" (256–57). Dellamora forcefully argues that the text has been marginalized because of its queerness, that Glassco fails in his efforts to consolidate the interrelated arenas of literary, sexual, and national politics. Dellamora, however, eschews fixing Glassco's identity as homosexual since to do so would be "inaccurate given the variety of sexual contacts and relationships that he had while abroad. . . . His representation of homosexual relations, which more often than not are lesbian, are characterized by ambivalence" (259).

Dellamora's thoughtful staging of a conflicted Glassco, who searches for alternate possibilities of sexual/literary expression, makes an implicit argument that such quests are a move away from heteronormativity, when they are a move *toward* it. Glassco's multiple pursuits were not aimed at something so formidable as "queering the canon," in the manner of Scott Symons, but at suppressing any open declarations of avowed homosexual conduct (leaving aside for now the question as to whether such homosexuality involved simply genital acts or were something more emotively substantial). In writing of hidden homosexuality in autobiographical texts, such as Walt Whitman's *Leaves of Grass*, Dellamora states that "the existence of unacknowledged difficulties in these texts . . . block readers from receiving them as witnesses to an embodied existence" (256). Certainly, the stylized narratives that slyly skirt the issue of homosexuality encourage a double reading: You get it if you are looking for it. Yet to consider the (autobiographical) *Memoirs* as a similar text that encourages a nuanced reading is misleading, because Glassco leads his readers *away* from such suppositions.

The crux of the issue, in light of Dellamora's argument for a queer Glassco, is whether we should approach his written history with the rudimentary apparatus of what we now understand to be the queer, including its theoretical aspects.[5] While queer theory has done much to stretch the understanding of the multifaceted nature of desire, it does so at a cost, namely the denial of a homosexual "embodied existence," especially as it may have been lived out, by Glassco and others, in the early twentieth century.

Dellamora is correct in stating that Glassco "has bequeathed a contradictory set of representations of relations between literary ambitions and sexual and nationalist politics among Anglo-Canadians of his generation" (260). But according to Dellamora, these "representations" were wrought from Glassco's avoidance of the label "homosexual" in favour of a self-styled sexual imprecision which might undermine the (heterosexual) tradition of masculinist writing, exemplified by such men as Hemingway and Callaghan. In discussing queer subjects as people who both use and refuse the designation of homosexual, Dellamora positions Glassco as one of these queers who "critique, resist and reconfigure" homosexuality (Greg Bredbeck, qtd. in Dellamora, 260), adding that Glassco does so through perpetrated falsity; the result is "a performance that eschewed authenticity" (270). It appears, then, that Dellamora inadvertently conflates the homosexual's historical (and often necessary) need to fabricate and be ambiguous with his view of Glassco's active and ambitious plan to "reconfigure" what it meant (or means) to be homosexual in Paris in the 1920s (or as it was [re]viewed later in the 1960s).

This problematic—endowing the past and those who inhabited it with a non-binarized and sophisticated view of sexuality—is a key challenge to practitioners of queer theory, one that is apparently insurmountable because "queerying" either under-theorizes or discounts the relevant historical social contexts.[6] Glassco grew up in an era in which Freudian-influenced psychoanalysis produced homosexuality as the inferior binary opposite to the ideal: the gay man as a failed heterosexual. The judicial system criminalized those who did not succeed in "straightening out." The medical characterization of the homosexual, a relatively new identity, fixed sexuality not along a continuum of queer fluctuating desires but upon an axis of either/or hetero/homo, a binary which thus structured, or at least underscored, most modern Western social institutions. Glassco need not be read solely as resisting homosexuality to embrace heterosexuality, in the 1920s and/or 1960s. Yet social discourses—

whether they be the mutual interests of early twenthieth-century social reform and psychology or the fomenting English Canadian heteronationalism of 1967—still reveal much about the social temper of the era(s) at hand.

The Montreal literary sphere in which Glassco circulated reinforced binarized homophobic thinking. John Sutherland, a friend of Glassco's and a contributor to the journal *First Statement*, openly attacked the poet Patrick Anderson, in 1943, for his literary representation of "some sexual experience of a kind not normal" (4). [7] Anderson, of necessity, denied this, but as David Leahy notes, the attack serves as an important cultural marker "of the pervasive social phenomena and discourses that psychosexually interpellated, colonized, and regulated homosocial relations between men in Canada and the rest of the Western world in the 1940s and 1950s" (133).[8] A decade after beginning his memoirs, Glassco cannot have been ignorant of the censure of homosexuals, a contempt which had abated but little when, just prior to the completion of the *Memoirs*, the *Toronto Star* headlined Robert Fulford's review of Symons's *Place d'Armes* "A Monster From Toronto."[9]

Glassco cannot, then, be reduced to the mere textuality that constitutes the *Memoirs*, since the social sphere surrounding its production does not exist separately from the text. But in that he "queers the narrative" (Dellamora, 265), what are the implications of Glassco's textual performance, especially when the author disturbs the integrity of the 1920s'/1960s' heterosexual gender assumptions? Does Glassco's ambiguous sexuality follow culturally established modes of identity coherence, such as adherence to a sex/gender system marked by binary opposites? The reader must take Glassco at his word—for his words are all we have to define the events he experienced. His textual presentation may appear to disrupt the hetero/homo framework that orders what Stephen Seidman calls "fields of knowledge and cultural understandings which shape the making of subjectivities, social relations, and social norms" (156). But in Glassco's case, such disruptions are performance for posterity's sake.

In what Peter Dickinson calls "the national narrative of self-identification" (23), to be of national importance, one must subscribe to the governing and institutionalized narrative of heteronormativity. As Dickinson rightly asserts, Cohen abrogates his "sexual/textual 'response-ability' as yet another colonizing *gaze*, whereby the 'homosexual panic' of supposedly 'straight' characters is assuaged at the expense of the lived experience of self-identified gays" (24). Thus Cohen reflects the Canadian tradition which has often in the past anxiously and blindly (re)asserted the national refrain of regulatory heterosexuality, even when evidence to the contrary exists.

The reasons for this are not unsurprising. The nation-state, in promoting the interests of its (heterosexual) majority, must constantly revive in the minds of its citizens the need for an emboldening masculinity and attendant national self-assertion which cannot be found, seemingly, in an identification with what would be seen as the feminine (read: weak) or homosexual (read: weak men). Therefore, if evidence contrary to the national project is sensed, it must be rendered straight, and not just for and by Cohen and Glassco. Richard Cavell argues that Canadian scholarship on the sexually ambiguous Frederick Phillip Grove has been "unswervingly normatizing" (12) in its efforts to "nationalize" the author's literary status; the result is that "the overall thrust . . . displace[s] [Grove's] *sexual* difference onto his *national* difference, a difference that is then 'resolved'" (13). Glassco, writing in the frenzied centenary celebrations of English Canadian nationalism, resolved his own "homosexual problem" in advance of such doctrinaire critical verve by simply editing it out. The reward of belonging is, no doubt, certainly a compelling one.

Glassco's chronicle—his discreet self-awareness of his violation of literary, not to mention sexual, boundaries—reveals (albeit belatedly) a desire for self-importance. When, in the *Memoirs*, George Pol asks Glassco if he is already the Canadian avatar of someone else, Glassco responds: "So far I have not donned any mantle at all, but it was not easy" (32). His aspiration for recognition subtly parodies those successful men and women of Canadian letters who comprise, Glassco intimates, a highly unoriginal group. His own contribution, if recognized at all, will be original; he will be the avatar of himself.

However much agency Glassco thereby retains (enabling him to revisit and revise problematic sexual orientations), his resultant self-serving literary journal does not constitute a queer or queered text so much as, at most, an apolitically different one. His "imposition of narrative form" denotes agency, true, but he is quick to dispose of otherness when convenient, if his revisions to the original manuscript are any indication.[10] His play with boundaries and genre expectations, and his orchestration of narrative, is the kind of authorship of which Richard Dyer writes: "All authorship and all sexual identities are performance, done with greater or less facility, always problematic in relation to any self separable from the realization of self in the discursive modes available" (188). Dyer is careful, however, to insist upon the social waters in which such "selves" swim, highlighting the significance of the author's "material social position in relation to discourse, the access to discourses they have on account of who they are" (188). Obviously, Glassco's own social position, as a white male from a relatively wealthy family, afforded him access to a variety of social spheres, and he himself must have realized, if only intuitively, the privilege also accorded *heterosexual* authors.

When it came to the (re)writing and revising of his memoirs, Glasso knew, then, that Scott Symons was clearly not the one to emulate, if recognition in the Canadian literary canon would be at all forthcoming. Glassco's European adventures may seem risqué more than queer, given that in his *Memoirs* he plays upon rather than within the Paris literary *demi-monde*. A certain detachment from the goings-on at the *dancings* allows others to take the fall for the disgrace of being homosexual: the scribe-on-high comes across as worldly, not part of the provincial backwater that is Canada. Even if we are to believe that Glassco was indeed heterosexual (or bisexual), he in any event shows himself to be what Eric Savoy calls "queer straights . . . heterosexually privileged men and women whose investment in queer culture is both playful and entirely provisional" (134). Whatever the case may have been, Glassco nonetheless deflects the category of the "homosexual" in order to position himself as ambiguous, perhaps, but ultimately part of the (hetero)normative order.

Additionally, Glassco's silence on (or revision of) the nature of his (sexual) desires suggests that the revelation of (at least genitally) homosexual occurrences is akin to bad table manners.[11] Despite his disruption of the codes that keep hegemonic social structures in place, his expedient queerness, in the end, serves merely to reaffirm these structures. Even Eve Kosofsky Sedgwick's conception of "homosocial desire," which would place Glassco on a shifting plane of sexual desire, is not useful here.[12] The social and political utility inherent in identifying "the homosexual" is elided altogether. Any attempt at queering Glassco runs the risk of disregarding the binaries, sexual and societal and otherwise, that informed Glassco's text. His noted narrative "silences"—those expressions of indirection, coyness, and allusion—rewrite the extent to which he participated in the gay and lesbian societies of Paris circa 1929, and highlight the problems of his (later revealed) contradicting manuscript and professions of lying.

Indeed, when Timothy Dow Adams asks, "[H]ow can we begin to distinguish between metafiction and fraud, between docudrama and hoax, between a dishonest distortion, and authorial misrepresentation and lie?" (18), perhaps the most constructive response is to say that critics examining the *Memoirs* should not bother trying. Adams tries to circumvent the problems his question poses by asserting that the *Memoirs* is postmodern fiction "because of its constant concern with its own creation, its sense of self-reflexiveness" (18). Yet, Adams here mistakes self-aggrandizement for self-reflection or performativity. A text cannot be self-reflexive if it is constructed in anticipation of the reader, to mislead that reader. Glassco's achievement resides in his skill in confounding not only the reader's genre expectations but also critical certitude altogether.

Instructively, George Gusdorf writes that "In autobiography, the truth of facts is subordinate to the truth of the man, for it is first of all the man who is in question" (43)—and Glassco truly leaves many questions behind. Yet, even Gusdorf, in his assertion that "truth" should be the minion, suggests that there is indeed a true(r) story that can be told. That story, long thought to be the *raison d'être* of the genre of historical autobiography, has disappeared with the critical assertions of the disappearance of the author, especially authors of life histories who sidestep questions of veracity. Glassco's text is a staging of an unresolved identity wherein the author becomes the medium between private experience and literary and cultural expectations.

Of Glassco's dilemma, Gusdorf writes, "Choosing between enjoyment and achievement, between the demands of life and art" (144) is a rhetorical attempt to place himself within the realm of recognized artists who consider, presumably, serious questions. If the *Memoirs* are, to use Louis Renza's term, "*art*ifact" (269) and not genre, Glassco has resolved his dilemma of "choosing" by writing a modernist text that represents both art and achievement, though, in the end, his is a literary confession that seeks not to illuminate a life but to affirm an author's aspirations to reputation.[13] If, in recalling Foucault's assertion that confession was elicited to bring about the regulation of sexuality (63), Glassco's claims to sexual ambiguity do little to subvert that regulation. His reticent manner may disrupt the reader's ease in slotting him into easily recognizable categories, yet his alterity is, as I have stated above, ultimately appropriated by (hetero)normative structures of understanding, since it is these structures which will co-opt unregulated activity.

This conflict extends to his literary textuality wherein he confesses to lying. If it is no longer possible in a book to ascertain "truth," especially when the author admits to an absence of it, the same must be said for truth's opposite, falsity. Therefore, if this issue of truth were taken to its logic limits, the *Memoirs*, then, could be said to suffer from the weight of chronic relativity, that is, nothing in it can really be confirmed or denied. Thus, is it a parody of veracity when Glassco writes, "Here I must admit that I was always, though mainly in self-defense, a great practitioner of deceit. . . . [T]he constant need for lying had in fact sharpened my invention and contributed enormously to my enjoyment of the highest forms of poetry" (36)? We cannot know.

But we do know that, if we are to take his manuscripts as revealing something about the published version, beyond proof or disproof of veracity, Glassco did engage in sexual activity with men. This is somewhat contrary to *Memoirs'* self-portrait of a somewhat predatory heterosexual casually observing the life of Parisian gay aesthetes. His largely uncritical poise and social ease around homosexuals seem to indicate a personal neutralizing of hetero/homo oppositions and a disturbing of the comfort of rigid sexual definitions. But his characterizations of lesbians, for example, fold into misogyny, and it is difficult, leaving aside for now the disturbing nature of such comments, to determine if the barbs arise from an anti-homosexual sentiment, from distaste for certain women, or a convenient mixture of the two. Of Willa

Torrence and her friends, he writes: "[Their] faded asexuality was marked by the kind of fiercely possessive passion that is generally and more properly expended on cats and dogs." He describes the desires of middle-aged lesbians as a "cannibalistic selfishness, an appetite that has engrossed all the resources of their charm, brains, and conscious appeal as human beings" (40). The vituperative nature of the comment surpasses the bounds of ironic discontent, it seems to me. Does this go beyond misogyny to internalized homophobia and gay panic? If Glassco is at all attempting to queer the text—to confuse identity and neutralize opposition—his manner of doing so is definitely questionable; he seems, at the very least, to use homophobic comment to place himself above the maligned Other. There is nothing oppositional about any of this.

Glassco further carefully distances himself from the patrons of the *Falstaff* and the *Petite Chaumière*. He remarks quizzically on the butch/femme distinctions of the gay and lesbian communities he encounters. Furthermore, the *dancings* provide an opportunity to enumerate the garish appearances of the habitués and to comment upon their (dis)connection to society. Glassco's self-ascribed "profound thoughts" clearly re-inscribe borders, especially as they reinforce the distance between what he implies are criminally associated homosexuals and himself (54).

Glassco chooses, as another example, to highlight Robert McAlmon's homosexuality. He finds a way to be a genially unfaithful friend through a rhetorically subtle yet barbed jab at McAlmon's literary efforts. Not unlike the ruse performed with George Pol, Glassco mounts a complex, textual stage-managing. Putting his own surmises into the mouths of other characters, Glassco gives what were later proven to be his own thoughts a flattering credibility that he himself, an unknown writer, was unable to provide. Andre Breton, Ford Madox Ford, and Man Ray (Narwhal) each speak to an ultimately fascinated Glassco. He responds with awe to Man Ray: "This idea of Jane Austen as a kind of early D.H. Lawrence was new. Never had the value of her books been so confirmed as by this extraordinary interpretation of them: it was a real tribute" (95–6).

Glassco's deflection, which enables him to praise his own ideas through the mouths of others, allows him to avoid what he describes as McAlmon's pitfall, namely obvious self-regard and the kind of vicious self-absorption often associated with "cannibalistic" homosexuals. Glassco avoids claims of either self-aggrandizement or homosexually inflected narcissism, labels made common to the world-at-large by psychoanalytic views of sexual identity. This becomes manifest in Glassco's description of two of McAlmon's published works. He writes:

> They were obviously literal transcripts of things set down simply because they had happened and were vividly recollected. There was

> neither invention nor subterfuge; when the recollections stopped, so did the story, and one had the impression of a shutter being pulled down over the writer's memory as if in an act of self-defense against a *dénouement* either unformulated or too painful to remember. . . . He talked interminably, but to no effect or purpose for his ideas were not only negative and confused but expressed with such petulant incoherence they could hardly be taken seriously. (79–80)

Glassco evidently sets out to ensure that much of what passes as intellectual opinion, especially in the staged monologues, is not necessarily his own. The possibility that such monologues may be, rather, a parody of some author's presumed ability to recall long conversations word-for-word is undermined both by Glassco's admiration of the argument presented and by the way he situates himself in the scene, gathering up the limelight as he listens.

Glassco even goes so far as to provide his text with a "built-in" apologia. In his remarks on Casanova, Glassco appears to be hinting that if he himself is also faced with a Casanova-like literary rejection, one elicited solely by character defamation, he should be accorded understanding and should be accepted once again on his own terms:

> We end, in other words, by loving him as much for what he really was as for what he *tells* us he was, and discover that the two characters complement each other and make an intelligible whole. In this way we grasp the truth that man is not only a living creature but the person of his own creation. (188, emphasis mine)

Here, recalling Gusdorf, the emphasis on subjectivity tends to make any claims to the "truth" relative, leaving the reader with a performance that, despite its foundation in the genre of autobiography, may be merely and only a "recreation of the spirit of the times." Glassco's non-committal, fluctuating identity, that he is an elusive object of desire, is concomitant with the evasive nature of *Memoirs of Montparnasse* as a staged text of self-revelation.

At the end of the *Memoirs*, Glassco acknowledges the rules that govern literary acceptance and seeks to locate himself within the patterns created by such memoir writers as Rousseau; he writes: "These are the best we know of the life of individual man; from them alone we discern the probable pattern of our own lives" (236). Within the literary pattern established by his "forefathers," from Casanova to Cohen, Glassco realizes the possibility of agency and fame through performance, though it is, in the end, simply a self-serving performance that relies on the suppression of homosexual subjectivity, rather than an accomplishment that subverts heteronormative literary self-representation.

NOTES

1. See Kokotailo (1988) for a detailed comparison of Glassco's manuscript to the published *Memoirs*. The ruse was initially uncovered by Thomas Tausky and Stephen Scobie, in their essays in *Canadian Poetry: Studies, Documents, Reviews* 13 (1983).
2. For a discussion of the "autobiographical pact," see Philippe Lejeuene's *On Autobiography* (1989).
3. The Canadian federal government, for example, had introduced a bill, in 1969, decriminalizing same-sex acts, even before the advent of the (American) Stonewall Riots in that same year.
4. Robert K. Martin, in "Cheap Tricks in Montreal: Scott Symons's *Place d'Armes,*" details the withering criticism Symons faced. He writers that Symons's "anguished search for grace . . . was the product of a police and a sexual terrorism that we still have not fully left behind" (210, 1994).
5. Both within its projected aims and anti-identitarian stances, queerness (in at least its theoretical manifestations) shifts the play upon the libidinal field from an examination of homosexual subjectivity and its historical locations to a study of the universalization of all sorts of desires. The irony is that such rhetorical moves efface the "bodies" that lived (and live) with a formative understanding of the category of the homosexual, in favour of a sexual economy of lenient indistinction. This valorization of individual desire(s) over the material existence of self-identified gays and lesbians means that the measure of what counts is determined by the individual acting on his or her personal criteria, rather than on a larger group conscience or social cross-identification. The result often reveals a further irony, namely a reinforcement of the prerogative of a heterosexual understanding of all fields of desire, since unregulated domains will invariably fall to the dominant class's standards.
6. For a compelling analysis of the problems of the shortcomings of queer theory, see Steven Seidman. He writes that its theorists "have often surrendered to a narrow culturalism or textualism; they have not articulated their critique of knowledge with a critique of the *social conditions* productive of such textual figures. . . . The 'historical' is similarly reduced to an undifferentiated space" (160–61, emphasis mine). In other words, queer theorists place a marked emphasis on the potential play of the markers of meaning—quite often the literal words on the page—rather than on what it means when the entities (such as humans) that such markers signify circulate, and have circulated, in society.
7. For a brief overview of the relation of Glassco to Sutherland, see Fraser Sutherland, 1984. 11,59.

8. In his essay on the attack, Robert Martin writes that Sutherland makes use of medical categories, such as narcissism and abnormality, as code for homosexuality. The result was a denigration of the status of Anderson's "Poem on Canada" which, Martin writes, "readers could take as the definitive work of Canadian national expression of the 1940s were it not for Sutherland's allegations that it had personal qualities that made it . . . incapable of serving as a national poem" (1991, 199). It is clear that any deviation from the national body represented as aggressive and heterosexual (1991, 121) might be interpreted as psychologically or legally criminal.
9. Charles Taylor writes that most critics "not only attacked the book for its literary faults; they also emphasized its homosexual passages, and were explicitly offended by the author's broadsides against English Canadian society," adding that Fulford's review "rankled [Symons] the most" (217). Dennis Duffy, on the other hand, claims that Fulford's unsympathetic review "contains a just appraisal of Symons' strengths and weaknesses as a writer despite its lurid title" (155).
10. I do not mean to imply that the manuscripts should be understood as foundationally sound, as sources of "truth."
11. For an interesting accounting of Glassco's paradoxical feelings about homosexuality, especially as they are revealed in the manuscript, see Kokotailo, 96–103.
12. Eve Kosofsky Sedgwick writes that male homosociality is "the affective or social force, the glue, even when its manifestation is hostility or hatred or something less emotively charged, that shapes an important relationship" (2).
13. Kokotailo uses the term "artifice" in its late nineteenth-century sense, meaning "subterfuge," "a prominent feature of literary dandyism, aestheticism, and decadence" (115). Artifice is "both a means of defiance and a means of escape" (116).

WORKS CITED

Adams, Timothy Dow. "The Geography of Genre in John Glassco's Memoirs of Montparnasse." In *Reflections: Autobiography and Canadian Literature*. Ed. K. P. Stich. Ottawa: University of Ottawa Press. 15–25.

Cavell, Richard. "Felix Paul Greve, the Eulenburg Scandal, and Frederick Philip Grove." *Essays on Canadian Writing* 62 (Fall 1997): 12–45.

Dellamora, Richard. "Queering Modernism: A Canadian in Paris." *Essays on Canadian Writing* 60 (Winter 1996): 256–73.

Dickinson, Peter. *Here is Queer: Nationalisms, Sexualities, and the Literatures of Canada*. Toronto: University of Toronto Press, 1999.

Duffy, Dennis. *Gardens, Covenants, Exiles: Loyalism in the Literature of Upper Canada/Ontario*. Toronto: University of Toronto Press. 1982.

Dyer, Richard. "Believing in Fairies: The Author and the Homosexual." In *inside/out: Lesbian Theories, Gay Theories*. Ed. Diana Fuss. New York: Routledge, 1991. 185–203.

Foucault, Michel. *The History of Sexuality. Vol. 1: An Introduction.* Trans. Robert Hurley. New York: Pantheon, 1978.

Fuss, Diana, ed. *inside/out: Lesbian Theories, Gay Theories.* New York: Routledge, 1991.

Glassco, John. *Memoirs of Montparnasse.* New York: Viking, 1973.

Gusdorf, George. "Conditions and Limits of Autobiography." In *Autobiography: Essays Theoretical and Critical.* Ed. James Olney. Princeton: Princeton University Press, 1980. 28–48.

Kokotailo, Philip. *John Glassco's Richer World*: Memoirs of Montparnasse. Downsview, ON: ECW Press, 1988.

Leahy, David. "Patrick Anderson and John Sutherland's Heterorealism: 'Some Sexual Experience of a Kind Not Normal.'" *Essays on Canadian Writing* 62 (Fall 1997): 132–49.

Martin, Robert K. "Sex and Politics in Wartime Canada: The Attack on Patrick Anderson." *Essays on Canadian Writing* 44 (Fall 1991): 110–125.

———. "Cheap Tricks in Montreal: Scott Symons's *Place d'Armes.*" *Essays on Canadian Writing* 54 (Winter 1994): 198–211.

———. "Two Days in Sodom: or, How Anglo-Canadian Writers Invent Their Own Quebecs." *The Body Politic* 35 (1977): 28–30.

Olney, James, ed. *Autobiography: Essays Theoretical and Critical.* Princeton: Princeton University Press, 1980.

Renza, Louis A. "The Veto of the Imagination: A Theory of Autobiography." *Autobiography: Essays Theoretical and Critical.* Princeton: Princeton University Press. 268–95.

Savoy, Eric. "You Can't Go Homo Again: Queer Theory and the Foreclosure of Gay Studies." *English Studies in Canada* 20:2 (June 1994): 129–52.

Scobie, Stephen. "The Mirror on the Brothel Wall: John Glassco, *Memoirs of Montparnasse.*" *Canadian Poetry: Studies, Documents, Reviews* 13 (Fall-Winter 1983): 43–58.

Sedgwick, Eve Kosofsky. *Between Men: English Literature and Male Homosocial Desire.* New York: Columbia University Press, 1992.

Seidman, Steven. *Difference Troubles: Queering Social Theory and Sexual Politics.* Cambridge: Cambridge University Press, 1997.

Stich, K. P., ed. *Reflections: Autobiography and Canadian Literature.* Ottawa: University of Ottawa Press, 1988.

Sutherland, Fraser. *John Glassco: An Essay and Bibliography.* Downsview, ON: ECW Press, 1984.

Sutherland, John. "The Writing of Patrick Anderson." *First Statement* 1.19 (1943): 3–6.

Taylor, Charles. *Six Journeys: A Canadian Pattern.* Toronto: Anansi, 1977.

Tausky, Thomas E. "*Memoirs of Montparnasse*: A Reflection of Myself." *Canadian Poetry: Studies, Documents, Reviews* 13 (Fall-Winter 1983): 59–84.

redesigning wreck: beach meets forest as location of male homoerotic culture & placemaking in pacific canada

Gordon Brent Ingram

I think a lot about the qualities and designs of the public spaces that I visit regularly. I want to believe that this sensitivity to my environment, verging on an obsession, is rooted in some deep well of creativity. But my narratives of design and redesign are also part of a twentieth-century Canadian fag thing. I note escape routes from possible violence. I seek out screens for privacy and to avoid more obvious forms of hostility. I covet sites in which to have fun with my friends (new and old), natural stages on which to see and be seen. I am especially interested in the places where I find new forms of communality, which often is obscured by archaic notions of community. I take great pleasure in complex places that I can explore and in which I can

This is the more heavily visited portion of the southern end of Wreck Beach. This area is frequented by most of the gay and bisexual men who visit Wreck. Above the beach is the sprawling campus of the University of British Columbia with its Botanical Gardens, landscape architecture teaching studios, experimental fields, and dormitories. All the aerial simages in this essay are from the mid-1990s.

get lost. And I am not the only one. This preoccupation with homoerotic—often specifically homosexual—contact in public landscapes has a long history in Canadian gay male culture. Of such landscapes in the pantheon of Canadian male homosexual cultures, the West Coast's Wreck Beach, on the edges of the University of British Columbia and the City of Vancouver, is particularly symbolic and strategic.

Wreck comprises the southwestern shore of the peninsula west of central Vancouver. Here, nudists, including male homosexuals, are crammed into some of the last remaining habitat, in the centre of the metropolitan region, for bald eagles and great blue herons. On the cliffs are some of the few remaining ancient Douglas fir and Red Cedar trees in the area. On warm and sunny days, Wreck embodies the most expansive constellation of queer outdoor space that Vancouver has ever seen. Space, as in territory, becomes a kind of fetish in itself. In the summer, the southern portion of Wreck provides more area of homoerotic social space than the rest of such spaces in western Canada combined. Wreck is a mythic configuration of sites, a distinct location, of significance as well for neighbouring parts of Northwestern United States, and something of a lightning rod for the contradictions in contemporary West Coast homoerotic culture, aesthetics, social relations, and sexual expression.

In terms of space and daily visitors, Wreck is one of the largest, gay male nude beaches in the world. There are only a few other beaches in British Columbia, clothed or clothing optional, with extensive summering populations of sexual minorities. At Wreck, a diverse and idealistic erotic culture has taken root that at times reinforces consumerist body culture and at other times contests it. At this margin, many of the unresolved issues around gender, race, class, and physical ability are reiterated as Vancouver transforms itself in its second century. Perhaps Wreck can show us some new possibilities. The south end of Wreck is, in part, a clothing-optional queer theme park (with its share of married men) that warrants a closer examination. For those of us who find Vancouver society short of spaces for male nudity, this zone provides a much-loved refuge and space to re-create and think again about making a better (and more homoerotic) world. Nevertheless, Wreck is still a particularly conflicted Canadian landscape, a racialized arena where European corporeality is normalized and Asian, African, and Latin bodies remain exoticized and marginalized (Ingram 2000, "On the Beach," 217–238).

In revisiting Wreck, I want to explore some links between desire, communality, and conscious alteration of environments—what I argue is "design." But design, as conscious, collective, and co-ordinated, is relative. Places are only in part the result of conscious designs. Such designs are rarely sexual in overt terms and more often result from natural change or political or economic conflict. These tensions between identification with supposedly "wild" landscapes or with urban spaces and between found space and made place have been central elements in Canadian planning for over a century (Honorat and Collins 1999, 19). Within these dialectics, the roles of strategic sites for homoerotic social exchange and cultural expression have been poorly explored (Ingram 1997, 95–125). Even less understood has been the link between spaces of contact, cultural expression, and placemaking as forms of cultural production. In this essay, I examine the southern half of "Wreck," an area that on sunny days is inhabited almost totally by men comfortable with, and often engaged in, homosexuality.

On this "walk" of Wreck Beach, I pose four questions. How does a gay male social scene on a nude beach create the basis for a kind of rudimentary queer scape architecture? (Ingram 2000 "On the Beach," 108–123) How do the homoerotic bodies of naked men transform space? Besides these two questions, I also want to begin to unravel a disturbing paradox. Why are architecture and public art increasingly considered central in contemporary culture while queer desires in and designs for outdoor space, celebrating homoeroticism and disrupting notions of sexuality and gender, are still largely taboo in both academia and in planning decisions made about queer sites? Given that Wreck is a cultural landscape, still claimed by First Nations, can this space be used to "naturalize," or at least normalize, consensual homosexuality between adults? But before the theory, let's imagine a walk on a warm, sunny spring or summer day.

WALKING WRECK BEACH: FROM THAH'THUTLUM TO STSULAWH

In this shore route, walk southwest, then south, and then southeast in an arc that stretches around Point Grey. This landscape appears deceptively natural. Much of this walk is "clothing optional," and you may feel conspicuous, from April to October, if you choose to overdress. Various technologies and fetishes, however, complicate exposure of corporeal surfaces. From backpacks and boots to tattoos and piercing, even nakedness at Wreck is relative.

Begin above Spanish Banks, at the cliffs that look across to the North Shore, English Bay, and downtown Vancouver. These cliffs make up the area just east of the former village site of *Thah'thutlum* (shivering woman rock). This area was also an important site in the emergence of the West Coast counterculture in the dying embers of the Beats.

Moving southwest and along the bluffs, come to one of the most successful buildings designed by Arthur Erickson: the University of British Columbia Museum of Anthropology. Of concrete and glass, it houses an exceptional collection of historic Northwest coast artifacts, including ones from the Musqueam villages of the area.

Walking behind the museum, locate the steep stairs beyond the facsimile Haida long houses. Go down the cliffs near *Ka'wum* (howling dog rock), and walk south along the narrow beach.

Above: The Outer Limits, with older men, is on the left. The Oasis, with several hundred younger men at a time on sunny weekend days, is in the centre-right. The Flats, the major gay area from the 1970s, is on the right.

With a view of Vancouver Island, pass the western tip of Point Grey, *Ulksun*, and the former seasonal camp of *Thutsuleek* (always rough). This was the part of Wreck favoured by many lesbians for two decades.

Moving south along the beach, come to the site of the former seasonal camp, *Keekullukhum* (little stockade), on the site of today's main Wreck Beach.

Search through the thousands of naked people to find a little enclave where people of the same sex are lying down a little more closely together. This is the little queer pocket surrounded by the heterosexual and bisexual masses.

Stroll to the beginning of the swampy trail south of the bottom of the main trail. This was the centre of the pre-nude gay male cruising areas from the 1940s until the late 1960s. In the early 1970s, this muddy route signalled the shift from the (hetero)sexual revolution to still highly taboo public (homo)sex. Muddy feet on males on the main part of Wreck suggested at least bicuriosity.

Continuing on through the salt marsh and mud, come to The Flats, the former site of a stockade and camp, *Kullukhun*, where waterfowl, octopus, and shellfish were harvested offshore. This was the major gay male social space at Wreck in the 1970s and early 1980s.

The forest behind The Flats was an important area of public sex for two decades. Today, the well-worn trails are somewhat exhausted; the sites of homoeroticism have become diffused and diversified in the dense forests along the beach to the south.

Moving along muddy trails through the forest, come to what today is often referred to as The Oasis, a former Salish campsite called Humlusum (bending down to drink). The spring is still there but it has been polluted from the university campus on the cliffs above.

Out of the forest and on to the sandy beach below, search for a place to lie down. In the early 1990s, this tongue of sand was formed from a series of landslides. Alternatively called Glamour Beach and Attitude Point, on a sunny day, the beach sees hundreds of naked men, sleeping, chatting, and frolicking. Sometimes on particularly hot days, there is group sex just before sunset.

Going inland through a series of heavily eroticized side-trails and then south from the crowded beach area, find a series of quiet spots in the forest. This muddy shore supports only small groups of people in rich *topoi* of solitude, cruising, conversation, and sometimes a bit of sex.

Back on the main trail going south, come to a side trail up the slope and find a magnificent Douglas fir tree that is well over a hundred years old. At the base of the trunk is a slightly worn area sometimes littered with used condoms.

Further south, along the main trail, pass many naked men and occasionally a woman and come to several large boulders sacred to the Musqueam.

Continuing along the shore, as it shifts to the Southeast, come to the mouth of the stream, *Skeymukwalthtsa* (or devilfish [octopus] spring), at the bottom of Trail 7.

Struggle up the steep trail below the University's Botanical Gardens and go north on the side road to an area below Marine Drive with drive-by sex frequented by older males.

Down the trail again, meander south for another three kilometres along trails to find small clearings supporting intimate gay male scenes, often with more overt fetishists and older men. Moving southeast as the sea meets the great river, the Fraser, the Stalo, come to the still under-used area sometimes called The Outer Limits. After another hour of walking, come to the outskirts of what is left of two Musqueam villages, a cultural centre in the region for hundreds if not thousands of years.

WRECK AS THE TERMINAL CITY'S ALMOST-UTOPIAN QUEERSCAPE[1]

> In the artificially uncivilised areas of the cities, surveillance and detention threaten; in the externally uncivilised areas, nature threatens and—worse still—boredom. (Henning Bech 1997, 150)

Over the last century, beaches have been prime arenas for the homosexual outlaw and, more recently, for the gay consumer.[2] The emergence of nude beaches on public lands in twentieth-century North America has largely paralleled the emergence of the consciously homoerotic male. Nude beaches have

Above: On warm afternoons, several hundred men often enjoy The Oasis and Attitude Point, below.

often seen an effective tolerance of homoeroticism when homosexuality has been strictly forbidden. In the period since World War II, these nude beaches grew to tolerate some overt forms of queer, particularly male, communality and an innovative social order predicated on some co-operative and alternative relationships. But on Wreck, the social opportunities of nude beaches reached a more advanced phase. This large territory is seasonally queered with sites established by a range of relatively open networks, defined by social links and erotic desires.

In relatively new port cities such as Vancouver, beaches have become surrogates for purposefully designed forms of public space and the kinds of social discourses, from cruising to political demonstrations, that take place in such spaces (Berelowitz 1994, 32–37). Beaches with adjacent natural areas, and the regular warm-weather presence of networks of sexual minorities, can be particularly strategic sites. Such homoerotic beach spaces become institutions, or at least pre-institutions, though they remain vulnerable to homophobic planning decisions and outright attacks. Typically, such interzones support contradictory behaviour, from the communitarian to the atomized consumer, the hyper-commodified masculinity (Escoffier 1998, 66; Kinsman 1996, 304). Some behaviour at Wreck implies erotic alienation as "natural." Also, while the stereotypical gay consumer is present, the shaping of homoerotic pleasure by market forces is largely absent.

Like contemporary Vancouver, Wreck supports a blend of utopian and cynical views of the body, Eros, love, and community. Wreck, as a relatively wild area, an open space on the suburban edges of Vancouver, produces simmering conflicts between eroticized recreation and habitat protection (Rust 1995, 5–6). In these conflicts, the discussions of public sex, primarily between men, constitute a case in point. Public sex is a small part of a broad body of homoerotic practices, some of which are learned, and improved upon, in places such as Wreck. Even the term becomes questionable. The acts that comprise public sex are highly variable and diverge between groups, between networks and locales, and between decades. The lines between public and private sex, even between homosexual, bisexual, and heterosexual identities, are supple and beyond definition by the state, the market, and other ideologies. At Wreck, different homoerotic behaviours tend to overlap more than elsewhere in the city. Across such relatively large landscapes, the context of sex acts, their meanings and perhaps functions, can vary from site to site. All generalizations are problematic. At Wreck, as in this description of a case study from Montreal, "sexual relations in public, while they were supposed to be anonymous, silent, and quick, could sometimes be quite otherwise" (Higgins 1999, 194).

While the zone most frequented by gay males stretches for several kilometres along the south end of Wreck, lesbian sites, if they can even be called such, are small, scattered, and lie north of the main beach. There has been some discussion about the de facto segregation and domination of space by gay men at the south end of Wreck. Gay men have few public spaces in a region where they are close to being in a demographic majority but the south end of Wreck Beach is definitely one. Except for a few symbolic forays by young Amazons, this area has the "feel" of an all-male club on any sunny afternoon.[3] But the reality is that most of this framing of queer male space has been homophobic, defined by those who do not want to be in a homosexual space. Also, most other groups have little use for the area. Such thick forests and dark trails would be seen as dangerous by most women unless they were in groups. Heterosexual females and males have their scene at the main Wreck Beach area. In the cooler months, a few walkers and bird watchers enjoy the entire area. Yet, perhaps in a reaction to the homophobia from without, these social spaces have often been indifferent or vaguely hostile to women. At the same time, this vacuum and relative disorder are consistent with the arguments of Elizabeth Wilson on spaces where women have been able to find relative freedom in the city (Wilson 1991). For some older gay men, however, typically socialized by a patriarchal and repressive culture, women, by their presence, can still disrupt some experiences of freedom.

QUEER(ED) BY NATURE: SOME SHIFTING AESTHETICS OF BODIES & LANDSCAPE

> To view body as land or land as body has no essential meaning, yet neither can it ever be innocent. Its politics are always contextual; there are different kinds of looking. (Catherine Nash 1996, 167)

So far in this discussion, I have been attempting to appropriate an often deceptively apolitical discourse on the use of "wildland," and considered it in terms of a particular user group (homoerotic males). In this case, the "wilds" are relatively urban and the recreation is overtly erotic, whether people want to admit it or not. Whoever is at the south end of Wreck is affected by homoeroticism, whether or not they choose to participate. Social conflicts become evident in tensions within and between bodies and the physical land scape. Aesthetics mark broader cultural and political economic relationships. Aesthetics become an important factor in understanding social interactions. Aesthetics become the matrix for desire, motivation, and even constraints on behaviour. It might be possible to reflect on the broader implications of political economy on erotic desire and the tensions that emerge between divergent "user groups" and "stakeholders."

Naked corporeality-in-the-landscape, particularly in sites of marginalized sexualities, generates new individual and collective experiences with inevitable, often localized, cultural, political, and environmental impacts. These local cultures, in turn, engender new opportunities for individuals. For some, experiences at Wreck confirm that they and what they do are "natural," or at least are normalized. For others, they are queered through their new actions and communalities. This is not a subtle difference. But the recent dialectic, between essentialist ("nature") and constructionist ("nurture," through culture) notions of homoeroticism, emerges once more around bodies and landscapes. Wreck has become a large zone, a strip, of multiple overlaps of (queer) ambiguity, between sexual acts and identities that are both erotic and contaminated by political conflict. The milieu of Wreck does not constitute community, in any territorialized sense, but rather a shifting conclave of desire, aesthetics, and ecological sensibilities set on a beautiful but vulnerable cultural landscape. Wreck embodies the conflicting and co-operative (and self-disciplined) relationships of communities. Homoerotic sites at Wreck embody a range of relationships between desire and identity, from self-identified, unconscious, and often essentialized centres to queerer margins. The more marginalized the group, the more queer the site and the more it is relegated to the distant landscape. The most queer thus becomes part of the hinterland, the stereotype of the quintessentially Canadian.

Above: South of The Flats.

POSTCOLONIAL BODIES IN RACIALIZED LANDSCAPES; RACIALIZED BODIES IN POSTCOLONIAL LANDSCAPES

One of the locations where essential notions of race are both enforced and contested is on nude beaches. Wreck is one of the few locales in the region that offer an appearance of emphatic multiculturalism through the mingling of racial bodies and sexual identities. At Wreck, it is inevitable to be near and in visual contact with men with very different kinds of bodies. The playing field of the homoerotic gaze at Wreck has not been levelled but public sex and humour have disrupted hierarchies.[4] The forests behind the beach are used to stage fantasies that sometimes key on race, such as the jungle, and thus reinforce—and sometimes subvert—shifting castes of sex, social recognition, and consumerism.

Today, racialized body and landscape aesthetics are problematic, especially when they are defined by white perceptions of Asian, South Asian, and African groups in North America. On Wreck, three fetishized racial disparities tend to persist in public sex: the social invisibility of the Asian male and the exoticization of the dark, supposedly studly, male, primarily of African but at times South Asian heritage (Fung 1991; Mercer 1991 1994). The "black" presence sometimes disrupts the neo-colonial narrative of British Columbia being primarily white. In British Columbia, those of African heritage have often been mistakenly viewed as recent arrivals (Kanneh 1991; Ingram, "Mapping," 2000). The resulting exoticization of black male bodies functions to make them "out of place," fetish items rather than whole persons. Alternatively, the body of the Asian, in particular the south coast Chinese male, is too often ignored and treated as invisible in highly charged zones of male homoerotic contact (Wong 1991, 13). This is ironic given that men from the same regions have been so central to the construction of modern "British" Columbia. Most problematic, the Aboriginal body is largely absent. All of the exotic bodies are assumed to be recent transplants, new and thus in need of naturalization to a white and Eurocentric Canada. Like the playful, buff iconography in Bruce Weber's *Bear Pond*, attitudes too often support the myth that the northern landscape is primarily white territory.

The most valuable aspects of these sites of public sex, in terms of formation of new (Canadian) culture, are that at least men of a wide range of backgrounds and forms of racialization are attempting to take homoerotic space on their own constrained terms. The intimacy in the spaces in the forest behind Wreck operates through the tensions between a more race-blind body aesthetic and public sex that sometimes is intensely racialized. Racial fetishes at Wreck constitute a kind a map of the postcolonial world as played out in Pacific Canada, one more guide to more subtle inequities. The site, only selectively public with no direct cultural coding, is viewed as "natural habitat" (*Bear Pond* 1990, 171). But the queer naturalist aesthetic, and its associated fetishes, can obscure the reality that the opposite is closer to the truth. This "nature" consists of highly coded fragments inflected by both the adjacent campus and by heavy recreational use. But the indications of ecological degradation at Wreck are often detected less than the supposed "nature" of unabashed public homosexuality. This natural/unnatural dichotomy has emerged from centuries of obsessive attacks on homosexuality as a threat to the "natural" order of things. The obfuscation of the cultural landscape, created by the Musqueam, and the interracial encounter that came later, have yet to be considered fully "natural" in the cultures of the Canadian landscape.

DICKS IN PUBLIC SPACE

> Lesbian sex is not typically associated with public accessibility or lewdness. The mechanics of such exchanges usually required more room than any toilet stall, nature trail or BMW can furnish. . . . (Alison Dowsett 1998, 30)

At places such as in the wilds of the southern end of Wreck, the male member, both as a means to pleasure and a cultural icon, is effectively reinvented every three to five years. The phallus, the dick in space, is constructed out of more raw forms of desire (and place). The south end of Wreck is one of the least overtly commercial areas of queer, public Vancouver. In this public territory, the fully exposed gay and bisexual male body becomes part of a

Above: One of the more celebrated public sex areas—looking over The Oasis.

spectacle, an icon, competing with "consumer space" very near (Willis 1993, 263–264). But a homoerotic space outside of the more typical commercial and institutional constraints that limit eroticized contact remains vulnerable. Going into the third decade of the AIDS pandemic, Michael Brown states that "The viral focus [still often] reduces the already marginalized gay body to a mere vector for illness" (Brown 1995, 161). In this sense, exposed phalluses (and buttocks) at the south end of Wreck, showing signs of on-site contact, can still be sucked into both the medicalization of homosexuality and the homophobic project of refusing—or denaturalizing—the healthy gay body. For too many, the south end of Wreck remains more as a space where HIV is spread than for a wide range of relatively safe, social contact. The tensions in these views, between relative health and high risk of disease, sometimes determine the use of the physical environment and the identifications with and interactions in particular sites. Thus, the public sex zone behind The Oasis and those in The Outer Limits are perceived by individuals who like standing erotic contact as places for exploration and practice and for others as high anxiety locales of risk.

Through the exposure of male members within a still patriarchal apportionment of public space, Wreck was gendered before it was queered. Male nudity on the beach long preceded overt homosexuality. This old, neo-colonial dichotomy is slow to break down. The homoerotization of these areas, particularly along the southern trails, has been largely the result of an intensified masculinization rather than challenges to phobias around sex, homosexuality, group contact, and acts out of doors. If the body is the primary site for the construction of sexuality, an intersection of physicality, culture, and spirit, then this Canadian queerscape constitutes the location, the context, the environment, and the means of support for the supposedly "normative performance" of gender, race, and the social structures that they represent (Brod 1995, 15–19). The queerscape supports both sites of production of body-sex relations and arenas for contests over modes of both social intercourse and its selective restriction and repression.

Locations that support social space of the marginalized, and different constellations of public and private, have divergent functions in the reproduction of broader social relations. Parks and respective designs have relationships to this reproduction of political economic relationships through culture (Berrizbeita 1999, 196). On nude beaches throughout the twentieth century, gay men, as only partially willing defectors from heteronormative life, have frequently taken on the armour of hyper-masculinity. Fortunately, there has often been a high degree of parody and camp. On nude beaches, such as the southern half of Wreck, there is space for a body culture and aesthetic that can be playfully over-determined by primary and secondary sexual features. In this sense, the homoerotic sites of Wreck still function more as zones of heightened but temporary privileging of some male bodies. But that use of the male body, in the consumer market, has been going on anyway. If anything, serious "objectification" in places like Wreck is on the decline as it increases for heterosexual males in broader society. As society's preoccupation with the male body is on the rise, Wreck provides another key function: for s/m (standing and modelling)—for spaces of irony in which to play.

"NATURAL" QUEER SPACE AS CONTESTED SITES

Gay beaches in North America have repeatedly been the sites of conflict around sexual propriety, played out through explicit design or indirect controls on access and behaviour. In the late 1970s, in roughly the same period as visits from the homophobic Anita Bryant crusades, a would-be Vancouver TV evangelist led her flock along Wreck Beach to protest its nudity, drug use, godlessness, and perversity. The idea was to confront sinners and to shame them. This conscious attempt at destroying queer space constantly invoked "Sodom," that code word for anxieties over queer spatial appropriation and territorialization. However, on the day of the protest, there was a downpour and the nudists present taunted the group. The event was ridiculed in the local media, and the campaign was a failure. Since then, there have been continued, but less overt, efforts to control behaviour at Wreck. After two futile decades of harassment, the police agreed to allow the beach to become clothing optional in the late 1980s. By 1990, in the summer of the second Gay Games, there were dusk orgies on some of the more remote beaches. Over the

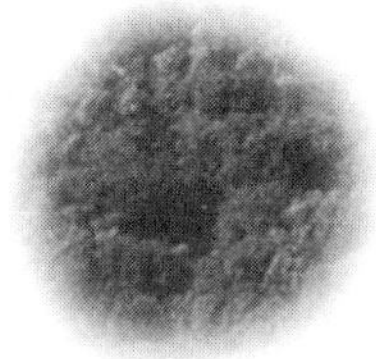

Above: Ancient Douglas fir tree, the base of which is frequented for stand-up sex.

last decade, the homoeroticism and summer presence of queer enclaves has been only a mild concern for police and the park managers of the Greater Vancouver Regional District (GVRD), who now have jurisdiction over management.[5] As late as 1999, however, males engaging in public sex were given warnings for being "blatant and in complete disregard for other beach-goers and so-called "public standards" (Yeung 1999,12). Yet there has been little exhibitionism in the southern parts of Wreck because most present have been involved in the sexual activity themselves.

In recent years, police sometimes appear suddenly to arrest beer sellers and drug dealers. In turn, targeted individuals usually disappear into the forest. Police entrapment for public sex has never been effective in the area. There have been court challenges arguing that consensual sex in a remote natural place, even on public lands, is essentially private and therefore legal. The quasi-privatizing functions of driftwood structures have also involved a complex legal discussion. Fortunately, cruising, on almost any warm day, allows for a sort of community surveillance of any policing.

The Wreck Beach Preservation Society formed two decades ago to protect the right to nudity and the natural landscapes of the area. Unfortunately, the organization has had only limited feminist and queer involvement and has tended to focus on the problems of the main beach. Every few years, there have been pressures and proposals that would effectively drive socially active gay men (and public sex) out of the area. An example of the unsuccessful attempts at homophobia by design occurred soon after the GVRD took over management of the area from the university over a decade ago. Wealthy residents complained that they could not enjoy their beach because it was overrun with perverts. A service road was proposed for the base of the cliffs. The result would not only have destroyed more natural habitat but would have further destabilised the cliffs and campus. In this case, the GVRD refused public funds for such closeted homophobia. But over the years, there have been more subtle efforts to block access to and to constrain the growth of the queer nodes.

CONCLUSIONS: CONFLICTING DESIGNS AS CANADIAN CULTURE

In returning to the four questions with which we embarked on in our walk along Wreck, some answers begin to emerge from this not-so-natural forest. For the sunny days of half the year, the gay male social scene on this nude beach generates a unique (Canadian) culture. There are virtually no other locations in the western half of the country in which to socialize in the same way. This culture is regional, national, and even international, by virtue of the citizenship and residence of the participants. These densities of homoerotic males, and their dense sets of homoerotic desires, transform the spaces in temporary and more indelible ways. Secondly, the freedom of this space is shaped by the expansive Canadian landscapes around it and the relatively tolerant society just beyond it. This freedom unleashes considerable energy that leads to both conscious designs, as in where people congregate, and effects. It remains difficult to have erotic desires without designs and without transforming locations: various tentative forms of queerscape architecture are shaped by culture. Thirdly, such "spontaneous" landscapes are ignored as culture (and any form of architecture) precisely because they challenge compartmentalized notions of culture, architecture, nature, sexuality, body, and landscape. Wreck is an exceptional and exoticized Canadian landscape and its culture remains marginalized even when homosexuality is no longer so marginal. Perhaps the least resolved question is whether this place, or any relatively wild Canadian landscape for that matter, can function to naturalize homosexuality and be "natural." There is the residue of over a century of Canadian cultural preoccupation with the natural landscape that often effectively celebrated the removal and marginalization of Aboriginals. With virtually all naked bodies still marked by discredited notions of race, desires, and relatively undisturbed habitat, no matter how marginal(ized), landscapes can never be transformed back to pristine states—conditions that may well have never existed anyway. To invoke other metaphors from adjacent parts of this landscape, Wreck is as much an arterial and expressway for a range of male homoerotic groups and an experimental station, with its share of toxic residues, as it is a rich and intact forest and shore ecosystem. As for the log booms, the mystique of the Canadian resource frontier and the fetish of export of "wood" from a hyper-masculine landscape have been all but exhausted.

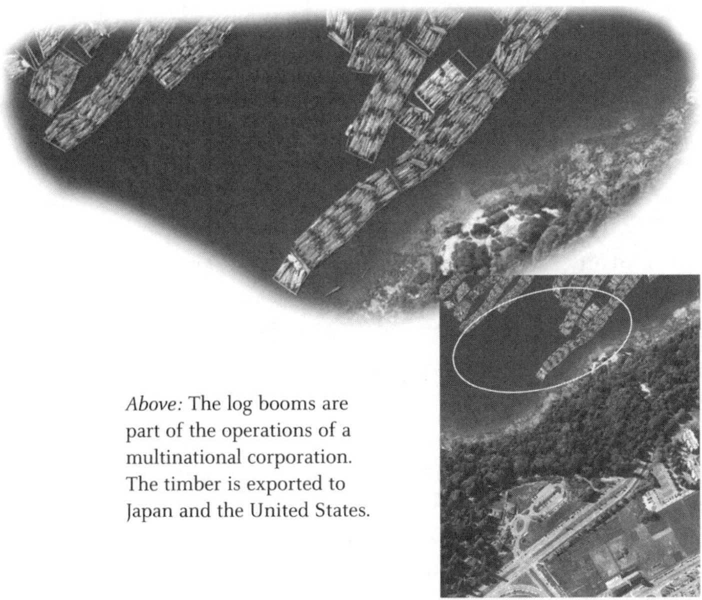

Above: The log booms are part of the operations of a multinational corporation. The timber is exported to Japan and the United States.

The future for Wreck, as a homoerotic space, is unclear. Wreck, as a queer space, could evaporate tomorrow. Another set of groups could come to dominate the south end rather quickly. Claiming of this public space by homoerotic males remains a contentious notion for heterosexual men, women of all orientations, and many gay men ourselves. New ways to assess and monitor sexual minorities and sexuality in public space are necessary. For example, the police use geographic information systems to track many crimes but more proactive tracking of vulnerability to homophobia and violence has yet to be envisioned. Out of more extensive forms of queer inventorying and surveillance, sex-positive forms of landscape design could produce new site plans and broader landscape architectures. But minority sexualities in general will probably continue to remain the poor (horny) cousins in the stakeholders of landscapes. Today, queer-positive landscape designs of public spaces in Canada will typically be met by covert hostility from both homophobes and liberals. The resistance by landscape design and management practitioners to acknowledge the entitlements of individuals engaged in public sex, socializing, and even romance will continue to constrain the recognition of the diversity of "recreational" needs and identification of conciliatory options. Without queer-friendly landscape architecture, it will be virtually impossible for the various groups, homosexual and heterosexual, women and men, Musqueam and newcomers, to enjoy these precious places together.

Without recognition of the homosexuality in this landscape, as long as authorities deny this meaning of this social and cultural "place," natural conditions will continue to be degraded. This situation is not a uniquely West Coast or Canadian condition but affects many such urban "wildlands" here and elsewhere in the world. Still, Wreck is our place, our opportunity to envision very different relationships between "man" (and woman) and "nature." In the Terminal City, queer "programming" of public landscapes will remain problematic and largely utopian, relegated to fantasy and culture rather than policy, for some time. Multiple pressures for more use compound the obstacles to queerscape architecture as a social project. Both "nature" and "natural homosexuality" are harmed by continued ecological degradation. In these arenas of cultural skirmishes around gender and sexual expression, the struggle for equal access and comparable comfort levels for women and ethnic minorities, with—rather than against—groups of particularly hardy and adventurous gay men, will remain difficult. In initiatives to better protect habitat, there is liable to be increased competition between low impact recreation activities, including sunbathing and sex, and the conservation of biological diversity. In this faux symmetry, assertion of Musqueam options for management and utilization of traditional resources remains enigmatic, "the wild card." Regardless of these current and potential conflicts, it will be increasingly difficult to ignore networks of sexual minorities as visitors engaged in valid recreational activities.

Is there a queer utopia emerging at Wreck? No, but Wreck comprises a set of locations that engender those impulses. There are intriguing opportunities for new ways to interact, to express ourselves, and to share. The open space, the forested cliffs, the big and ancient trees, and the beautiful bodies offer respite from a chaotic world and the global market place. But while on sunny days Wreck is a remarkable place of peace and tolerance, it has not escaped persistent pressures from only partially resolved colonialism, male domination, commodification of both nature and the body, and environmental degradation. I have posited some unresolved contradictions around the homoerotic body, desire, and landscape. I argue that some aspects of these tensions are particularly queer and Canadian. But other contradictions are more derived from the history of British Columbia and still others from the shifts towards globalization of political economies and (homo)erotic cultures.

Contradictions, by themselves, do not make culture or transform spaces as culture. But some such contradictions have prevented sexual minorities from intervening collectively to control their strategic landscapes, beyond the rather arbitrary influence of their spontaneous activities. Queer cultures remain half-formed even in this time of globalization. Experience of and interest in relatively natural landscapes may be one of the more common and stable elements of such cultures. A second element may be a conflicted attempt to remake sites formed by inequities around race, gender, and sexuality. In this Canadian context, notions of "naturalness," rather than indicating vital and diverse ecosystems, obfuscate social conflict. The feel of open space, of fewer social constraints, that is invoked by places such as Wreck is largely illusionary. It is open only in relation to the nagging claustrophobia of the growing state and urbanization.

At Wreck, different worlds strangely co-exist side by side and through bodies. Design proposals must recognize these tensions but refuse, which at least partially explains the lack of design, the illusion of nature conservation, in this Canadian landscape iconography. In ignoring conflict, even between eroticized male bodies, a false sense of freedom joins with new forms of cultural reproduction of social inequities. But Wreck remains one of my favourite places. For me, Wreck is a home in a larger culture that still often feels hostile to many homoerotic men and women. Even with all of the nagging tensions, the pleasure on a warm day of being with old and new friends naked on a beach or in a forest is indisputable.

Wreck transect: corporate log boom
(homo)sex beach and forest strand
cliff forest
drive-by public sex site
expressway
parking lot
experimental plot

NOTES

1. The label of "The Terminal City" for Vancouver goes back to the city's incorporation with a poem mentioned from 1887, in Roy, 1976.
2. Gay, nude, and semi-nude beaches have been strategic sites for gay and peace activism going back decades, as far back as, for example, the 1950s. See Hay, 1985/1996.
3. A trail and beach census by this author, on Sunday, August 12, 2001, between 3 and 5 p.m., yielded the following statistics: 6 women (all clothed and of European heritage) and 350 men. Of the men, most were completely naked with only 16 fully clothed and 57 nearly naked. Of the males, 313 appeared to have been primarily of European heritage, 26 of East Asian, 3 of South Asian, 2 of African, and 5 of Aboriginal. In that brief period, 34 of the men used public sex areas, and 14 were observed in sex or in states of sexual excitement.
4. The statements in this section about bodies are based on conversations on various parts of Wreck Beach, with men of a range of heritages, going back to the late 1970s.
5. In a mid-1998 statement, the police in charge of Wreck Beach indicated that they were not interested in enforcing laws against public sex as long as it was consensual and relatively discreet. See Zillich, 1998.

WORKS CITED

Bech, Henning. *When Men Meet: Homosexuality and Modernity.* Chicago: University of Chicago Press, 1997.

Berelowitz, Lance. "From Factor 15 to feu d'artifice: The Nature of Public Space in Vancouver." *a / r / c* 5 (1994/95): 32–37.

Berrizbeita, Anita. "The Amsterdam Bos: The Modern Public Park and the Construction of Collective Experience." In *Recovering Landscape: Essays in Contemporary Landscape Architecture.* Ed. James Corner. New York: Princeton University Press, 1999. 186–203.

Brod, Harry. "Masculinity as Masquerade." In *The Masculine Masquerade.* Eds. Adnrew Perchuk and Helaine Posner. Cambridge, MA: MIT Press, 1995. 15–19.

Brown, Michael. "Ironies of Distance: An Ongoing Critique of the Geographies of AIDS." Environment and Planning D: *Society and Space* 13 (1995): 159–183.

Dowsett, Alison. "No Knickers Needed: Lesbians Enjoy Public Sex but Don't Talk About It as Much as Men." *Xtra! West* 139 (December 10, 1998): 30.

Escoffier, Jeffrey. *The American Homo: Community and Perversity.* Berkeley: University of California Press, 1998.

Fung, Richard. "Looking for My Penis: The Eroticized Asian in Gay Video Porn." In *How*

Do I Look?: Queer Film and Video. Eds. Bad Object Choices. Seattle: Bay Press, 1991. 145–160.

Hay, Harry. "Remarks on Rude's Passing." In *Radically Gay: Gay Liberation in the Words of Its Founder*. Ed. Will Roscoe. Boston: Beacon Press, 1985. 313–318.

Higgins, Ross. "Baths, Bushes, and Belonging: Public Sex and Gay Community in Pre-Stonewall Montreal." In *Public Sex Gay Space*. Ed. William Leap. New York: Columbia University Press. 187–202.

Honorat, Yvan, and Daniel Collins. "Wild Reeds: An End-of-summer Salute to Queer Space." *Xtra! West* 158 (September 2, 1999): 19.

Ingram, Gordon Brent. "'Open' Space as Strategic Queer Sites." In *Queers in Space: Communities / Public Spaces / Sites of Resistance*. Eds. A.M. Bouthillette and Y. Retter. Seattle: Bay Press, 1997. 95–125.

———. "The Importance of Public Sex." *Xtra! West* 127 (June 25, 1998): 16–17.

———. "Mapping Decolonization in Male Homoerotic Space in Pacific Canada." In *De-Centering Sexualities: Representation and Politics Beyond the Metropolis*. Eds. Richard Phillips, Diane Watt, and David Shuttleton. London: Routledge, 2000. 217–238.

———. "(On the Beach): Practising Queerscape Architecture." In *Practice Practise Praxis: Serial Repetition, Organizational Behaviour and Strategic Action in Architecture*. Ed. Scott Sorli. Toronto: YYZ Artists Publishers, 2000. 108–123.

Kanneh, Kadiuta. "Place, Time, and the Black Body: Myth and Resistance." *The Oxford Literary Review* 13.1–2 (1991): 140–163.

Kinsman, Gary. *The Regulation of Desire: Homo and Hetero Sexualities*. Montreal: Black Rose Books, 1996.

Mercer, Kobena. "Skin Head Sex Thing: Racial Differences and the Homoerotic Imaginary." In *How Do I Look?: Queer Film and Video*. Eds. Bad Object Choices. Seattle: Bay Press, 1991. 162–210.

———. "Fear of a Black Penis." *Artforum* 32 (April, 1994): 80—81; 122.

Nash, Catherine. "Reclaiming Vision: Looking at Landscape and the Body." In *Gender, Place and Culture* 3.2 (1996): 149–169.

Roy, Patricia E. "The Preservation of Peace in Vancouver: The Aftermath of the Anti-Chinese Riots of 1887." *BC Studies* 31 (1976): 44–59.

Rust, Susan P. "The Urban Wilderness Park: An Oxymoron?" In *Proceedings of the Second Symposium on Social Aspects and Recreation Research*. San Diego, February 23–25, 1994. Berkeley: USDA Pacific Southwest Research Station PSW-GTR-156, 1995.

Weber, Bruce. *Bear Pond (for Donald Sterzin and His Blue Canoe)*. New York: Bulfinch Press, 1990.

Willis, Sharon. "Disputed Territories: Masculinity and Social Spaces." In *Male Trouble*. Eds. Constance Penley and Sharon Willis. Minneapolis: University of Minnesota Press, 1993. 262–281.

Wilson, Elizabeth. *The Sphinx in the City: Urban Life, the Control of Disorder, and Women.* Berkeley: University of California Press, 1991.

Wong, Lloyd. "Desperately Seeking Sexuality: A Gay Asian Perspective on Asian Men in Film." *Rites* (May, 1991): 13.

Yeung, Tom. "Wreck Beach Alert." *Xtra! West* 153. (June 24, 1999): 12.

Zillich, Tom. "Sex Acts Not Priority Target for New Wreck Beach Patrol." *WestEnder* (July 2, 1998): 9.

challenging canadian and queer nationalisms

Gary Kinsman

For Jim Egan (1921–2000), Canada's first gay activist

The title of the conference at which this essay was presented was "Queer Nation?" a term open to a number of different readings. One is that Canada is already a "queer nation," that the current form of the Canadian state, especially the equality rights section of the Charter of Rights and Freedoms, provides a vehicle through which our rights can be fully established. This is often combined with an English-Canadian defined Canadian nationalism. This intersection of Canadian and queer nationalism argues that the current Canadian state is the road to our liberation, a view which obscures the many problems of exploitation and oppression within Canadian state formation (Corrigan and Sayer 1985).

Queer legal theorist Carl Stychin suggests that Canada may be the first postmodern state. According to his insightful investigations of the intersections of nation, sexual identity, and rights discourse, Canadian state formation may be able to address social differences through its recognition of difference and toleration of diversity. He argues that "the Canadian national imaginary displays an instability which leaves it particularly open to contestation. The contingency of the national sign facilitates the articulation of competing identities deploying the use of nationalism" (Stychin 1995, 107).[1] Yet this obscures the racism, sexism, heterosexism, and class exploitation at the roots of Canadian state and social formation.

As a queer socialist activist opposed to Canadian *and* queer nationalism, and one who supports the national liberation struggles of the First Nations and the Québécois, I find these tendencies troubling. Canadian state formation has been an anti-queer project, a project of heterosexual hegemony (Kinsman 1996), in association with class, gender, race, national, linguistic, and other forms of hegemony (Gramsci 1971). This does not mean, however, that lesbians and gay men have been unable to exert agency and win gains within these state relations. Hegemony has never been total or secure. We have made important gains, but these gains have been limited

"Queer" is used here to identify with queer activism, which builds links between all those who engage in consensual, non-normalized practices of sexuality and gender, and to reclaim a term of abuse that has been used against us. I use queer as a broader term than lesbian or gay, which includes the experiences of people prior to the emergence of the current hetero/homo polarity, as well as people who have engaged in sexual practices that rupture heterosexual hegemony, but who would not see themselves as lesbian or gay (Kinsman 1996).

Queer nationalist activism in the early 1990s was an exciting wave that moved far beyond demands for limited human rights, stressing direct action against oppression and opposing "integrationist" strategies, which view lesbians and gay men as simply like heterosexuals except for what we do in bed. Yet it became trapped within an anti-homophobic analysis that focuses on individual bigotry and phobia and not on social practices and relations (Kinsman 1996, 33–34, 299–300) and also uses a nationalist discourse (Maynard 1991; Kinsman 1992) that constructs boundaries between those within and those without the "nation."

At the same time as the new queer activisms came a related but different use of the term, queer theory. This essay is in dialogue with and is a critique of queer theory, a literary and culturally derived theory that put in question the binary opposition between homo and heterosexualities (Sedgwick 1990; Butler 1990; Warner 1993; Seidman 1996; Jagose 1996; Hennessy 1994, 2000; McIntosh 1993; Namaste 1996, 2001). It contested heterosexual hegemony but is limited by the character of queer theory itself, which largely addresses only cultural and discursive terrains, rather than social practices. Its theory of language, drawn from poststructuralism, does not emphasize that language and discourse are produced by people located in various social positions

(D. Smith 1999; McNally 1997, 2001).[2] Canadian social and state formation cannot be analyzed simply as cultural or literary texts. The insights of queer theory must be given a firmer social, historical, and materialist grounding to make its insights relevant to social movement activism.[3]

QUEERS AS NATIONAL SECURITY RISKS

In high school I was constantly being called "commie," "pinko," "fag," words often scrawled on my locker. The sole basis for the "fag" (George Smith 1998) part was my refusal to laugh at anti-queer jokes. I was intrigued by this association between queers and commies. I now know much of it came from the national security campaigns against gay men and lesbians, as well as the actual connections between some queer activists and parts of the left. The claim that Canada is a queer nation is undermined quite dramatically by my and Patrizia Gentile's historical sociological research on those campaigns (Kinsman and Gentile 1998; Kinsman 2000, "Constructing"; Kinsman and Gentile, forthcoming). This research is based on interviews with gay men and lesbians who were directly affected by these campaigns and on critical textual analysis of the documents and policies through which these security campaigns were organized.[4]

Lesbians and gay men were constructed as security risks in the 1950s and 1960s because we were seen as fellow travellers of communists, violators of class and gender boundaries, and vulnerable to "blackmail" by "evil" Soviet agents (Kinsman 1996,148–212; J. Terry 1995, 1999). Designations of "national security risk" and "character weakness" mandated RCMP surveillance and interrogation of public servants, which led to the purges of hundreds of lesbians and gay men and to the collection of more than 9,000 names of suspected homosexuals in the Ottawa area by 1967 (Directorate of Security and Intelligence, 1967–1968). This also led to the "fruit machine" research to try to find an "objective" scientific technology that could determine sexual orientation. This technology was based on a pupillary response test that focussed on the impact of images of naked men and women on pupil dilation (Kinsman 1995; Kinsman and Gentile 1998). This relied on psychological assumptions of homosexuality as a sexual object choice or "deviant" sexual orientation and not as much on earlier notions of homosexuality as biological anomaly or gender inversion. The RCMP's task was to shift persons from "alleged" or "suspected" homosexuals to "confirmed" homosexuals, who could then be demoted or fired. The RCMP interrogations and surveillance asked "confirmed" homosexuals to identify others (Kinsman and Gentile 1998; Kinsman 2000, "Constructing"). These campaigns continued at a lower level in the public service in the 1970s and 1980s but with the previous intensity in the military

TOP SECRET

April 28, 1960.

TO: The Commissioner

Sir:

Homosexuality Within the Federal Government Service

This paper has reference to Security Panel document SP-199 dated May 12, 1959, particularly to the Conclusion wherein it is recognized that homosexuality constitutes a security threat, that certain homosexual characteristics -- instability, willing self-deceit, defiance towards society and a tendency to surround himself with other homosexuals -- do not inspire confidence, and that information obtained on homosexuals is often limited. Its purpose is to provide information on homosexuality obtained through recent investigations, to set out some of the problems encountered and anticipated in our investigations and to make certain recommendations regarding future investigations.

2. The paper is directed at the threat homosexuality constitutes to Canada from a security point of view and is not in any sense concerned with the moral issues involved in this problem.

3. Investigation over the past year has brought certain results and problems which, it is felt, could not have been fully anticipated when the subject of homosexuality was discussed by the members of the Security Panel and Security Panel Directive #199 drawn up. Firstly, our investigation to date which was limited because of its selectivity has revealed the names of over 700 proven, suspected or alleged homosexuals across Canada. More than 300 of these are, or were recently, residing in the Ottawa area where the investigation was concentrated. Of the 700 more than half are, or were recently, employed in federal government service. The investigation of necessity went beyond the government service in order that the most complete picture possible might be obtained. However, it is apparent that only a portion of the total number has come to light thus far.

Security documents declassified by CSIS.

and RCMP. In the seventies, lesbian and gay movements that fought against such policies became targets of RCMP surveillance as "gay political activists" and "radical lesbians" were seen as still greater security threats (Kinsman and Gentile, forthcoming).

WHOSE NATIONAL SECURITY?

Regarding the social construction of national security, we always need to ask which nation and whose security (Kinsman, Buse, Steedman 2000)? We need to critique the ideological concepts of "national security" and "character weakness," which were simply taken for granted within these confines.[5] "National security" first refers to the protection of state borders. As part of this external protection, a state defends the secrets that it accesses through security arrangements with other states. Secondly, it refers to "internal" security, the defence of the nation-state from enemies within. Certain groups or individuals are constructed as "other" and defined as threats to "national security."[6] Yet in Canada "internal security" threats get constructed through external security arrangements.

"National security" was defined in opposition to "threats" from communists, socialists, peace activists, trade unionists, immigrants, First Nation activists, supporters of Quebec sovereignty, Black activists, and "sex perverts," among others.[7] The concept of "national security" rests on notions of the interests of the "nation" (Enloe 1983; Enloe 1989; Parker 1992) which, in the Canadian context, is defined by capitalist, racist, heterosexist, and patriarchal relations. The Canadian state was formed through the subordination of the indigenous peoples, the Québécois, and the Acadians, first as part of the British Empire and later in alliance with U.S. imperialism.

As Les Moran suggests, during the post-war period "homosexuality was put into circulation in such a way that it produced the idea of homosexuality in opposition to the nation" (Moran 1991, 155). In the 1950s, homosexuals joined communists as primary security threats. Harold (a pseudonym), a gay man purged from the military during the national security campaigns, with whom I spoke in 1994, wrote in the early 1960s. " 'Security' is a sacred cow of a word in the name of which highly dictatorial and sweeping actions are possible for which no explanation can be forced" (Harold 1960–1961, 17).

"WHICH IS THE GREATER TREASON ... TREASON TO YOUR COUNTRY OR TREASON TO YOUR FRIENDS?"

In 1994, Harold said the RCMP would ask over and over again for the names of homosexuals. The two officers interrogating him would say, "'Look, you've got to know something, for god's sake tell us, tell us. We won't hurt anybody but tell us come on tell us.' [bangs on table] Boy you have no idea of how I hated them" (February 21, 1994). [8] Harold had described earlier:[9]

> This particular agency [the RCMP] does not operate with kid gloves. . . . It is true that to state the terms used by these agents were, mildly expressed, forceful but the method of attack was decidedly clever. . . . I was told that persons of my calibre are so much easier to handle than "drugstore cowboys." To my enquiry why, the answer was that I was an individual of responsibility, integrity, and background and could readily understand the terrible import of the question, "Which is the greater treason . . . treason to your country or treason to your friends?" Or, "A person like yourself must realize what a serious disservice you may do your country by withholding the names of people we must ensure are never exposed to treasonous blackmail." (Harold 1960–1961,12–13)

Loyalty to his friends meant he was a "traitor" to Canada.

INVERTING THE PROBLEM OF BLACKMAIL

Harold continued:

> They were, of course, applying a form of blackmail very difficult to resist. It contained an appeal to patriotism and reason, the pseudo-flattery of apparent recognition of integrity and a thinly veiled threat. . . . "We are not concerning ourselves, right now, with the criminal aspects of the situation." . . . To my sickened dismay, even the success I had achieved in keeping my professional and personal lives strictly separated was turned against me. I was told I MUST know quite a 'ring' of homosexuals in professional circles and my statement that I did not was immediately and emphatically rejected as a lie. . . . (Harold 1960–1961, 12–13)

Harold made a brilliant reversal of the national security discourse of "blackmail." Rather than blackmail from Soviet agents, the RCMP was trying to "blackmail" him into doing what he didn't want to do. They implied that they might lay criminal charges against him. Similarly, Hank stated that he was "only ever blackmailed by the RCMP" (February 20, 1995).

"National security" was defined by the security police and military of Canada and the American-led anti-Communist, anti-Soviet and anti-"third world" liberation alliance. In the U.S., homosexuality was sometimes portrayed as a virus sweeping across the continent (Geoff Smith 1992, 1994). Even for the private sector, the Americans set the standards for Canadian researchers and firms involved in defence and security-related research. Canadian public servants also often needed access to U.S. information and therefore had to conform to U.S. security standards. In 1948, the U.S. War Department was willing to share classified information with the Canadian Department of National Defence and other government agencies providing that "all personnel handling such material had been cleared from a security standpoint" (Robinson and Kimmel 1994, 325). The Security Panel recommended that full security precautions be taken in certain government branches to lead to this information transfer (Robinson and Kimmel 1994, 325–326). Of course, heterosexism in Canada has its own history: the criminalization of homosexuality, and prohibition from employment in the military and RCMP laid the ground for homosexuality as a national security threat (Kinsman 1996, 107–200).

The Royal Commission on Security report released in 1969 shows how national security works as an ideological practice. Even the report itself is not the version submitted to the Canadian government in October 1968: material had been omitted or amended in the public version "in the interest of national security." Regarding access to information, it states, "Neither does an individual have a right to confidence; on the contrary access to classified information is a privilege which the state has a right and duty to restrict" (*Report of the Royal Commission on Security* 1969, 28).

The Royal Commission was mandated to make a full inquiry into procedures having to do with the security of Canada as a nation and the rights and responsibilities of individual persons. The text places the "interests" of national security above individual rights wherever there is a conflict. Citizenship is defined not only by place of birth but also by loyalty to the state. This sanctions surveillance and interrogation of individuals and groups (Grace and Leys 1989, 62–85). A successful claim that an individual or a group is a threat to national security operates as a "cutting out" (Smith 1990, 30–32) device denying people their rights.

A flexible conceptualization of "subversion" contributes, as Grace and Leys argue, to expansive state definitions of "subversion":

> Many writers on subversion have complained that the term refers to a "grey area" and is difficult to define. Our view is that it has always referred to a fairly clear reality: legal activities and ideas directed against the existing social, economic and political order. . . . Any radical activity or idea with the potential to enlist significant popular support may be

> labeled "subversive" . . . [Subversion] is invoked . . . to *create* a "grey area" of activities that *are* lawful, but will be denied protection from state surveillance or harassment by being *declared* illegitimate, on the grounds that they *potentially* have unlawful consequences. In capitalist societies the targets of this delegitimation have been overwhelmingly on the left. (Grace and Leys 1989, 62–63, italics in original.

Under "Immigration and Security," the Royal Commission states that "Canada's requirement for immigrants must be balanced with the need to protect the safety and health of the state and its people by excluding certain classes of persons who appear to be undesirable" (*Royal Commission on Security* 1969, 45). This construction of the health of the state builds on public health policies (Sears 1992, 1995) which construct some groups as "vectors of infection" of the "general population" as well as on constructions of some people as "undesirable."

National security easily becomes just "taken for granted," the plain "common sense" which Antonio Gramsci pointed out is the way in which hegemony operates.[10] Those who identify with the powerful emotional and moral symbol of "Canada" therefore identify with Canadian "national security," a particular strategy of state formation and with a particular ideological project (Corrigan and Sayer 1985, 7–9). Differences of class, sexuality, gender, race, language, and nation, on which the Canadian state is actually built and which this unitary "national interest" suppresses, are deemed to be "other" and threats to national security. The 1960s saw the rise of social movements based on some of these differences, including Québécois nationalism, the organizing of Acadians and other francophone communities outside Quebec, anti-racist groups, associations for immigrant and refugee rights, and First Nations organizations. The Canadian state responded with various new strategies of management and containment, including bilingualism and multiculturalism. Such strategies have embodied gains for oppressed communities but they seldom address the social and economic roots of forms of oppression and exclusion (R. Ng 1995, 35–48; das Gupta 1999, 187–205; Bannerji 1995, 2000). As Bannerji argues, difference is beyond "cultural" (Bannerji 1995, 2000). We need to deal with more than difference understood as being only "cultural" in character and get to the social roots of the problem (Bannerji 1995; 2000).

Nation and national security are collecting categories combining a number of rather different social processes. [11] This brings together the interests of the "nation" with the maintenance of capitalist social relations, with participation in U.S. led security arrangements, with notions of "proper" politics, gender, family, sexuality, ethnicity, and race, i.e., coding Canadian as white. Canadians were constructed as white when national security was used against Japanese

Canadians in World War II, or when citizenship policies have been used against immigrants (Iacovetta 2000; Thobani 1999). The popular notion of the nation as "everyone" meets the construction of the nation is both an exclusion *and* an inclusion device. Some people are to be included while others are thrown outside the boundaries of the nation to become "threats" to the nation. Himani Bannerji locates a major tension in Canadian state formation between its colonial settler state history and present and its claim to be a "liberal democracy." As she puts it: "Viewed from the standpoint of indigenous peoples, the state of Canada is based on class, gender, and race, and it continues to administer these reserves as would a colonial state" (Bannerji 2000, 75). After introducing Benedict Anderson's useful distinction between the "official" nationalism of imperialism and "popular" nationalism (Anderson 1991, 86), which has a more progressive character, Bannerji argues that:

> This "popular nationalism" in my view is clearly not possible in Canada, whose context is the colonization and continued marginalization of the First Nations while seeking to build a liberal democratic state. In Canada, such "popular nationalism" contains legal/coercive strategies and the means of containment and suppression of all "others." (Bannerji 2000, 106)

Canada is anything but a queer nation. As for other oppressed groups, there is continuing employment discrimination and the labelling of queer workers as disloyal and unreliable. The exclusionary policies against queers in the RCMP and the military were only officially ended in the late 1980s and early 1990s. In 1998, a Canadian Security Intelligence Service (CSIS) spokesperson stated that security clearances can still be denied to closeted homosexuals because they have something to hide (Smith 1998; Sallot 1999). Consensual queer sexual practices continue to be criminalized and queer sexualities censored by state agencies (Kinsman 1996, 328–347, 356–359; Kinsman 2000, "Gays and Lesbians").

FROM EXCLUSION TO IDENTIFICATION WITH THE CANADIAN FEDERAL STATE

From the early 1970s on, other groups came to support gay and lesbian struggles, including feminists, trade unionists, and human rights activists. The limited human rights protection on the basis of sexual orientation won in Ontario in 1986 was a response to mobilizations and grass roots education by lesbians, gay men, and our supporters. The Canadian Charter of Rights and Freedoms (1982), and particularly Section 15 (the equality rights section), opened up a space to push forward our human rights claims (Rayside 1988, 62–91; Rayside 1998, 105–211; Herman 1994; Sanders 1994; Smith 1999; Lahey 1999). Governments were to bring their legislation into line with the Charter and laws which were not could be challenged. Section 15, which prohibited discrimination against a number of groups, did not explicitly mention sexual orientation, but it allowed gay and lesbian activists to argue that sexual orientation should be "read into" the charter.

This opened up possibilities for queer activists to make progress on the rights front, and this potential was seized by activists, individual lesbians, gay men, and their lawyers. At times, this has made it appear that legal cases involving lawyers and their clients have been enough to win our rights, but our struggles outside the courtrooms are still key to winning these victories even if they are won in a delayed and limited legal form. Section 15 created a much more favourable terrain of struggle and the basis for significant victories, but only in some areas. One important area where the Charter has so far been of limited use is in struggles against the criminalization of our consensual sexualities, sexual censorship, and the criminalization of prostitution related activities. Thus, the social stigmatization—and often the criminalization—of queer sexualities continue.

The May 25, 1995 Supreme Court Decision in the Jim Egan/Jack Nesbitt same-sex pensionable benefit fight was mixed. They lost their case, with four of the judges arguing that there was no discrimination in the denial of the benefit, and one arguing that there was, but that it was a "justified" form of discrimination (four judges argued that it was discrimination and it was not justified). At the same time, the Supreme Court decided that the equality rights section of the Charter should be read as including sexual orientation protection. Since then, further progress has been made on these fronts. There was a significant legal victory in the 1998 Rosenberg case involving two employees of the Canadian Union of Public Employees (CUPE) who challenged the federal income tax regulations that recognize only opposite-sex spouses for survivor benefits. CUPE supported the court challenge, and the court ruled that the federal Income Tax Act is unconstitutional and must be read to include coverage for some-sex partners. In the spring of 1999, the Supreme Court of Canada handed down a landmark decision in the *M. v. H.* spousal support case. After the relationship ended, M. attempted to seek support under the Ontario Family Law Act. She was denied the right to do so due to the exclusively heterosexual definition of "spouse" in the Act. The Supreme Court found that the Act violates the equality rights of lesbians and gay men by defining "spouse" as someone of the opposite sex. The Ontario government was given six months to correct the problem in its legislation (Barnholden 1999).

In October 1999, Bill 5 was passed in Ontario. The Tory government was not pleased with the legislation since it was forced into it by the Supreme Court decision and made it clear it does not consider lesbian and gay couples to be spouses. This amendment to 67 Ontario statues to include same-sex partners does not define same-sex partners as spouses or as families but does grant them the same rights as common-law heterosexual couples in a number of areas. While these changes are an important step forward, many activists are critical of the legislation for establishing lesbian and gay couples and our relationships as separate from, and secondary to, heterosexual spousal and family relations (Warner 1999).

In April 2000, the federal government adopted similar legislation. Even though the legislation was going to pass, the Liberal government added an interpretation clause affirming that marriage "is the union of one man and one woman to the exclusion of all others." What was supposed to be legislation affirming our rights now became legislation setting limits to our rights. While I, like many other queer activists, do not support the state institutionalization of marriage (Lehr 1999; Warner 1999) I oppose this addition to the legislation to reaffirm that lesbian and gay relationships are secondary to heterosexual marriage.

During the same period there has been an increase in forms of sexual censorship (for instance, in Little Sister's Bookstore's struggle against book and magazine seizures by Canada Customs) and a limited escalation of forms of sexual policing of consensual gay sex. These continuing forms of stigmatization and criminalization of queer sexualities hold back all our struggles (Kinsman 1996, *Regulation* and "Responsibility"; Kinsman 2000, "Gays and Lesbians"). While on an abstract and formal level, many state and social agencies now recognize that we should enjoy equal rights with heterosexuals, they are not willing to recognize our substantive social rights to equality and freedom from oppression. They are unwilling to be seen to endorse or to encourage the actual sexual practices and relationships in which we engage or to challenge the deeply rooted practices of heterosexual hegemony in Canadian state and social formation. Our rights as "private" individuals are recognized, while our real social and material differences—our erotic pleasures and the gender of those we love—are still not recognized as valid and equal. Also, while the lessening of the dependence of capitalist and state relations on the heterosexual family has led to a limited moral deregulation of lesbian, gay, and bisexual sexualities (Sears 1998), we are controlled more by market forces, professional agencies, and popular culture, which enshrine heterosexuality as the norm while opening up limited, ghettoized spaces for "queers."

This establishes the current contradictory situation we are in. On the one hand we have largely won our formal human rights (although major forms of social discrimination continue) but on the other hand our sexualities are often

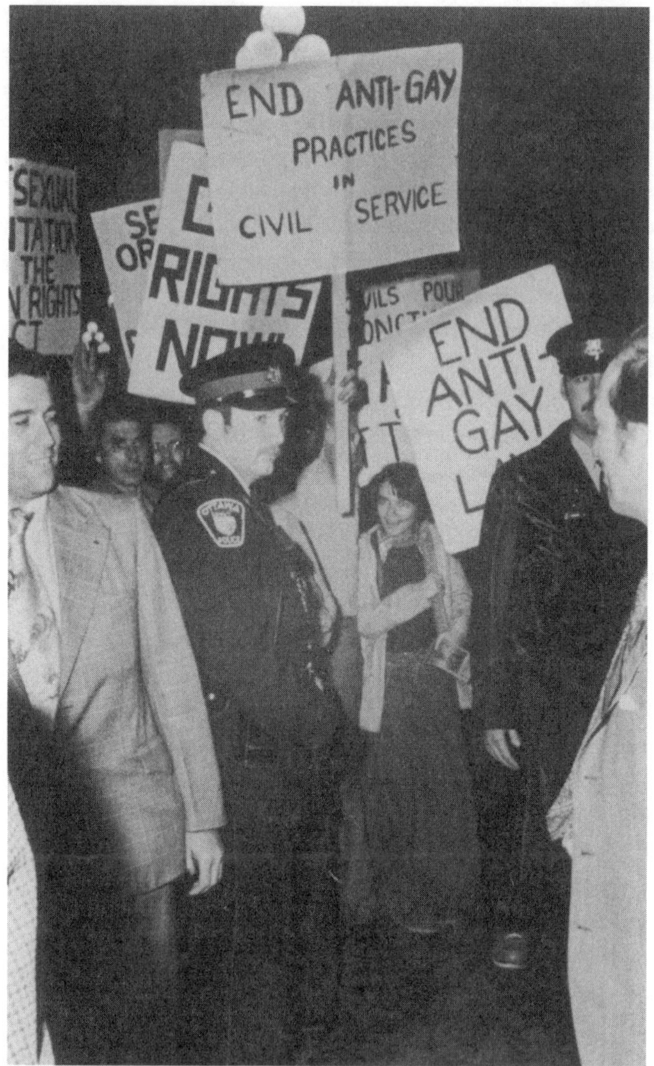

Figure 1. An early gay rights demonstration in the mid-1970s, with Prime Minister Trudeau in the foreground. From Paul-François Sylvestre. *Propos pour une libération (homo)sexualle. Montreal: Les Editions de l'Aurore, 1976;. p. 135.*

still criminalized and our relationships stigmatized. Our limited gains have led some gay, lesbian, and bisexual activists and lawyers to identify the existing federal state form as the avenue to further our rights. This has led some activists in the Canadian state outside Quebec and the First Nations to see such national liberation struggles, which put in question the federal state, as a threat to their rights. Thus, some gay and lesbian leaders supported the federalist Charlottetown Accord in 1993 despite the very legitimate opposition of the National Action Committee on the Status of Women, the Native Women's Association, and Quebec sovereignists to this Accord (Rebick 2000).

This perspective is now often shaped by class formation within gay and lesbian communities. Gay managers, administrators, professionals, and business people have risen to the top even though it was more left-wing and grass roots activists who created the social basis for them to do this and for them to be "out." Those who speak the same language as those who rule in our society come to mediate relationships between ruling agencies and lesbian and gay communities, often through strategies of "respectability" and "responsibility" that are associated with spousal benefit "we are family" and marriage struggles (Kinsman 1996, "Responsibility"). In Toronto, the Fraternity, an organization for gay male businessmen and professionals, has been building support for Julian Fantino, the chief of police who has a history of problems in his relations with gays and the black community. The Fraternity engages in these political initiatives without any democratic accountability to the broader gay and lesbian communities. Similarly, "out" gay Tories and Canadian Alliance members take up the same right-wing positions on most economic and social questions as other members of these right-wing political formations. This professional/managerial strata argues that an integrationist strategy will lead to our full acceptance in society. For some, achieving the right to marry is now presented as the end point of our struggle. Instead, I would argue that we need to contest social forms such as the state institutionalization of marriage and develop our relationships based on democracy, equality, and social justice (Sears 2001; Warner 1999). There are also many other aspects of oppression that we face other than the denial of our right to be married.

THE PAST AGAINST THIS PRESENT

A different perspective is provided by past queer organizing against federal state agencies and in support of Quebec's right to decide its own future. A more oppositional stance to the federal government and the sex police was adopted by activists in the 1970s, when the movement itself was under RCMP surveillance and there was also wider support for Quebec's right to self-determination. This was especially the case in the context of Quebec's passage of sexual orientation protection in 1977, many years prior to the Charter (Stychin 1998). This initial human rights victory was the result of massive rebellions in the streets of Montreal against the police raid on the Truxx bar, lobbying by the Association pour les droits des gais du Quebec (ADGQ) (M. Smith 1999, 55–57), and the election of the Parti-Québécois government.

In the mid- to late 1970s, there was a series of cross-country gay and lesbian rights coalitions (at one point called the National Gay Rights Coalition and later the Canadian Lesbian and Gay Rights Coalition) (M. Smith 1999, 57–63) that involved activists from Quebec and the rest of Canada. [12] These activists had to work together across the barriers of different national formations, since the Canadian state is a multinational state. After many years of contentious discussion, a decision was made in 1978, based on demands from Québécois gay and lesbian activists, to support the right to self-determination of Quebec. A connection was made between the self-determination of lesbians and gays to control our own bodies and lives and support for self-determination of the Québécois. This can be contrasted with the passage of the "Clarity Bill" in 2000, which denies Quebec's right to self-determination, and the weak opposition to it by the left and other activists outside Quebec (Krishnan 2000).

In 2001, Equality for Gays And Lesbians Everywhere (EGALE) is the only federal gay/lesbian rights lobby group, although the Foundation for Equal Families lobbies for spousal and family recognition rights. EGALE has a different organizing basis than earlier coalition efforts, particularly in being defined by a legal strategy predicated on the use of Section 15 of the Charter. It has become more difficult to organize in opposition to the federal state, against its continuing censorship and stigmatiziation of our lives. There are similarities here with the position of those who view the federal state as the only way that social programs and the remaining aspects of the welfare state can be defended (and perhaps extended in the future). This position forgets that many of these programs were fought for and won through the struggles of working-class and oppressed people across the Canadian state and are not some sort of essential feature of Canadian federalism. Also, this federal state form is being used as a central vehicle through which these social programs have been and are being dismantled by the current Liberal federal government (Krishnan 2000). This position also does not seem to notice the marginalizations that this federal state form was built upon, including the exclusion of immigrants and refugees and institutionalized racism (Thobani 1999; Bannerji 1995; 2000).

QUEER NATIONALISM

Some of my analysis stems from being in Toronto when Queer Nation was beginning to form in the context of broader organizing efforts against anti-queer violence in 1990. It was largely white and Anglo in character and, despite the intentions of its founders, excluded the experiences of many people of colour, as well as many working-class people. [13] In prioritizing queer identifications over other forms of oppression, it raises problems experienced by those in white, feminist organizing. Bannerji points to the problem of the "violence of abstraction" when gender is abstracted from race and class, and thus coded as white and middle-class (Bannerji 1995, 2000).

There are major problems when the "queer" aspects of someone's life is violently abstracted from the relations of gender, race, class, and sometimes national oppression. If queer is separated from these, it will be coded as white and Anglo in the English Canadian context. Bannerji's solution is that race, class, gender, and sexuality cannot be violently abstracted from each other and that we have to view these relations as having autonomy but also as having a mediated or mutually constructed character. Class is constructed through relations of gender, race, and sexuality, and sexuality is constructed through relations of class, gender, and race (Bannerji 1995; 2000). We have to avoid queer identifications that exclude the experiences of queers of colour and those; from oppressed national groups or two-spirited people, and that also do not challenge the social practices of white and English privilege that some queers live.[14]

There are problems with the "nationalism" of some Aboriginal leaders who construct a notion of "traditional" that excludes two-spirited people and queers from their national fabrics. Similarly, some currents in Québécois nationalism focus on the need to increase the birth rate of French-speaking Québécois and adopt an ethnic-based form of nationalism that opposes queers as non-reproductive. Still, there are also many nationalist currents in the left, and in union, feminist, and student movements that are more supportive of queers (Higgins 1999; Chamberland 1996; Stychin 1998).[15] Queers in "English-Canada" (for lack of a better expression) need to support struggles against the national oppression of the First Nations and the Québécois while at the same time supporting the struggles of queers in Quebec and the struggles of two-spirited people. Bannerji suggests that:

> The possibilities for constructing a radically different Canada emerge only from those who have been "othered" as the insider-outsiders of the nation. It is their standpoints which, oppositionally politicized, can take us beyond the confines of gender and race and enable us to challenge class through a critical and liberating vision. In their lives, politics, and work, the "others" hold the possibility of being able to expose the hollowness of the liberal state and to provide us with an understanding of both the refined and crude constructions of "white power" behind "Canada's" national imaginary. They serve to remind us of the Canada that *could* exist. (Bannerji 2000, 81, italics in original)

HISTORIES OF RESISTANCE

In this project of queer resistance and opposition to Canadian federal state formation there are very rich histories of resistance to learn from. The emergence of two-spirited groups is a sign of resistance to colonization and an attempt to reclaim and to transform previous Aboriginal practices that accomplished gender and sexual relations in very different ways than the current eurocentric regime of sexuality and gender (Gay American Indians and Roscoe 1988; Roscoe 1991, 1998; Cannon 1998; Kinsman 1996, 92–97; Adams 1999; Goodleaf 1993, 225–242; Obomsawin 1993). There are also important stories of queer resistance to, and non-cooperation with, the Canadian national security campaigns (Kinsman and Gentile 1998). As Sue put it when she was in the militia and at military camp in the late 1950s:

> [T]he deal was you were supposed to go out with men. So what we did was at military camp we went out with men in the early part of the evening, and then because we were very virtuous young women we said, "OK, we have to go home early." And the military being very accommodating said, "This is where the women sleep, this is where the men sleep." We said "Fine, that's cool, we'll go back with the women." . . . What we used to do, we dykes, we would want to go out and party. And we would take our bunk beads and we would fill them with pillows. And then we would ask the heterosexual women, and we would say to them, "We really want to meet Charlie." We would lie to them and they would cover cause they thought we were goin' out to meet men. We were goin' out to meet women. But we had it set up at the back of the barracks, and took over this room. We barricaded it from one side and then we had, had women on the other side guarding it, cause that's where we were with Charlie. But they never saw Charlie! So here we had all these straight women, guarding us and guarding our beds and making sure that the [authorities] never knew we were out. And we weren't supposed to be. So, we would be out with sergeants, staff sergeants, corporals, privates, lieutenants . . . no rank was untouched. . . . So we would be running all over camp. And the deal was you weren't allowed to leave the premises, so of course, we wanted wine, women, and song. So in order to get wine, women and song you had to leave the base. So you had to go out. But you weren't allowed to wear butchy clothing. You had to wear a *dress* [her emphasis]. So what we used to do was pull our pant legs up and hide them with our skirt. And you'd go out and through the gates in your skirt, right, lookin' all femmy and lovely. Well this one night we came home and we got a little too drunk. Well trust me that the pants were

> down. And we, we were up on charges the next day for being in some place we weren't supposed to be, improper attire, all kinds of things. So we learned that we shouldn't drink too much. (February 23, 1996)

The RCMP also encountered problems with non-cooperation from homosexual "informants." In 1962–1963, they reported that their campaign:

> . . . was hindered by the lack of cooperation on the part of homosexuals approached as sources. Persons of this type, who had hitherto been our most consistent and productive informers, have exhibited an increasing reluctance to identify their homosexual friends and associates. . . . (Directorate of Security and Intelligence, 1962–1963, 19)

The other side of this "lack of cooperation" is described by David, not a civil servant but drawn into the security campaigns when a friend gave the RCMP his name during a park sweep, a fairly common operation in the 1960s. According to David, the RCMP was far more interested in getting the names of homosexuals than in arresting people for "criminal" activities. David was interrogated by the RCMP, he was followed, and his place was searched. He described one situation involving the gay men who hung out in the tavern in the basement of the Lord Elgin:

> [W]e even knew occasionally that there was somebody in some police force or some investigator who would be sitting in a bar. . . . And you would see someone with a . . . newspaper held right up and if you . . . looked real closely you could find him holding behind the newspaper a camera and these people were photographing everyone in the bar. . . . We always knew that when you saw someone with a newspaper held up in front of their face . . . that somebody would take out something like a wallet and do this sort of thing [like snapping a photo] and then of course everyone would then point over to the person you see and of course I'm sure that the person hiding behind the newspaper knew that he had been found out. But that was the thing. You would take out a wallet or a package of matches or something like that . . . it was always sort of a joke. You would see somebody . . . and you would catch everyone's eye and you would go like this [snapping a photo]. And everyone knew watch out for this guy. . . . (May 12, 1994)

Michael, who worked for a while as a civilian employee of the Armed Forces, was interrogated by the RCMP in the 1960s. Other gay men had told him to say nothing to the RCMP and "if anybody did give anything they were ostracized." When he was left alone in the interrogation room, an RCMP officer said:

> "Is it true that you are a homosexual?" And I said, "Yes!" And he looked at me and I said, "Is it true that you ride side saddle?" and he laughed and that almost ended the interview. I mean, my intent was there, don't bother me any more, because I began to get the impression that it was a witch hunt. It was a real witch hunt. (July 15, 1994)

These narratives of resistance begin to flesh out the social organization of the "non-cooperation" the RCMP reports mentioned. The response in the bar suggests a way of not only exposing the officer or informant and saying they knew what he was up to—turning the tables on him so to speak. It also was a way of making fun of him and the security and police campaigns, using humour and camp as a way to survive them. [16] As David expressed it: "I think that the way people coped with the whole situation of surveillance and harassment was basically to make the best of it. And turn it as much as possible into a humorous situation. . . ." (May 12, 1994) Thus, the national security campaigns of the late 1950s and 1960s are not only a history of oppression and exclusion but are also a history of resistance and non-cooperation in very constraining circumstances. This non-cooperation of gays largely located outside the public service forced a shift in RCMP policy towards reliance on local morality squads and the extension of the surveillance net to provide other homosexual informants. Queer resistance, even in the early sixties, was able to reshape regulatory and policing strategies. In the 1970s, the emergence of the gay and lesbian liberation movements led activists to challenge, publicly and politically, these security practices. Today queer resistance in diverse forms continues, including among queer activists in anti-poverty, anti-racist, anti-police violence, the union, and other movements.

EXTENDING DEMOCRACY: CONTROL OVER OUR BODIES, GENDERS, AND SEXUALITIES

Like queer liberation, struggles for national self-determination of the First Nations and the Québécois and struggles against racism are struggles for social transformation, for democracy and equality between peoples, for a transformed socialism that addresses not only class exploitation but also all the forms of intersecting oppression (McNally 1997), including those directed against our communities, our bodies, our genders, and our sexualities.[17] For those of us in "English-Canada," this requires support for queer struggles in Quebec and also those of the two-spirited peoples but it also involves us in defining an "English Canadian" social project which is no longer based on the national or racial oppression of other people. It raises profound questions for us about how to develop cooperative and egalitarian relations with other nations and groups, through direct democracy that supports self-determination. Instead of queer nationalism, which like Canadian nationalism constructs some as "others," we need to construct new ways of organizing without queer, national, racial, or class oppression, a new queer-positive socialism. The struggle for control over our own bodies, genders, and sexualities is integrally bound up with struggles to end all forms of oppression.

These struggles bring us up against the Canadian federal state, which is an organizer of oppression and exploitation. In the end, we need to organize against the state form itself, which is based on constructing a series of relations that stand over and against people in our everyday lives, and that actively prevent us from gaining democratic control over the circumstances of our lives. Organizing for liberation requires the radical democratization of political and social decision-making, placing us in rupture with the project of state formation developed to manage national labour markets and to defend the interests of capital on a national and multinational level. Queer liberation needs to be part of a broader revolutionary transformation of social relations. As Karl Marx, in a rather different historical context, once put it, this kind of social revolution is:

> . . . a Revolution not against this or that, legitimate, constitutional, republican or Imperialist form of State Power. It [is] a Revolution against the State itself . . . a resumption by the people for the people of its own social life. It is [not] a Revolution to transfer it from one faction of the ruling class to another but a Revolution to break down this horrid machinery of class [and I would add gender, race, sexual, and national] domination itself. (qtd. in Corrigan and Sayer 1985, 207–208)

NOTES

1. See Carl F. Stychin, "Equality Rights, Identity Politics, and the Canadian National Imagination," in *Law's Desire, Sexuality and the Limits of Justice* (New York: Routledge, 1995), 102–116. Stychin's work is quite brilliant in pointing to the sexual character of nation building, and the relational character of national formation. At the same time his analysis tends to be insufficiently grounded in the social practices of state formation. Also see Carl F. Stychin, *A Nation By Rights, National Cultures, Sexual Identity Politics, and the Discourse of Rights* (Philadelphia: Temple University Press, 1998), 89–114.
2. Postructuralism is a broad theoretical approach that no longer believes in a

structuralist form of analysis in which the social is constituted and determined through social structures. Rather than unitary structures, poststructuralists focus on fragmentation and difference. There is usually an emphasis on psychoanalytical and literary deconstructive theory. In general, the subject—or subject positions—are seen as being constituted through discourse. Queer theory draws on poststructuralism and especially deconstructive literary theory for its inspiration.

3. I use materialist in a broad sense to include human sensuous practices. See Marx's thesis on Feuerbach, where a new social and historical notion of materialism can be seen as a synthesis of vulgar "materialism" and the active side of "idealism." See Derek Sayer, ed., *Readings From Karl Marx* (New York: Routledge, 1989), 7–10 and also Himani Bannerji, *Thinking Through, Essays on Feminism, Marxism and Anti-Racism* (Toronto: Women's Press, 1995).

4. On critical textual analysis see the work of Dorothy E. Smith including her "Textually Mediated Social Organization." In *Texts, Facts, and Femininity, Exploring the Relations of Ruling*, (New York: Routledge, 1990), 209–224.

5. "Ideology refers to all forms of knowledge that are divorced from their conditions of production (their grounds)." Roslyn Wallach Bologh, *Dialectical Phenomenology: Marx's Method* (London: Routledge and Kegan Paul, 1979), 19. Also see the work of Dorothy E. Smith including *The Everyday World as Problematic, A Feminist Sociology* (Boston: Northeastern University Press, 1987); *The Conceptual Practices of Power, A Feminist Sociology of Knowledge* (Toronto: University of Toronto Press, 1990); and her *Texts, Facts, and Femininity, Exploring the Relations of Ruling* (New York: Routledge, 1990), and the work of Himani Bannerji, including *Thinking Through: Essays on Feminism, Marxism and Anti-Racism* (Toronto: Women's Press, 1995); and her articles on the ideological construction of India: "Beyond the Ruling Category to What Actually Happens: Notes on James Mill's Historiography in *The History of British India*." in *Knowledge, Experience, and Ruling Relations*, Eds. Marie Campbell and Ann Manicom (Toronto: University of Toronto Press, 1995), 49–64; and "Writing 'India,' Doing Ideology," *Left History*, 2.2 (Fall 1994): 5–17.

6. One group defined as "other" in national security campaigns has been Arabs living within the Canadian state, especially in the context of the 1991 Gulf War, which led to a heightened surveillance and discrimination against Palestinians, Iraqis, Iranians, and others from the middle east. See Zuhair Kashmeri, *The Gulf Within, Canadian Arabs, Racism and The Gulf War* (Toronto: James Lorimer, 1991). "National security" has also been used against those opposed to capitalist globalization and trade pacts like the Asia Pacific Economic Co-operation, and the Free Trade Area of the Americas. On this see Karen Pearlston, "APEC Days at UBC: Student Protests in an Era of Trade Liberaliziation," in *Whose National Security?* Eds. G. Kinsman, D. Buse, and M. Steedman (Toronto: Between the Lines, 2000), 267–277.

7. On the diverse range of groups that were and are targeted by the national security

campaigns, see Kinsman, Buse and Steedman, eds., *Whose National Security?* (Toronto: Between the Lines, 2000).

8. For our research report, we interviewed twenty gay men and five lesbians who were directly affected by the national security campaigns. I draw upon a number of these interviews in this essay. The date designation in brackets at the end refers to when the interview took place.
9. I use "described" and "description" to refer to social relations and social practices that shaped people's experiences of the national security campaigns. See Dorothy E. Smith, "On Sociological Description: A Method From Marx," in *Texts, Facts and Femininity* (New York: Routledge, 1990), 86–119.
10. Antonio Gramsci referred to hegemony as uniting practices of coercion and consent. See Gramsci, *Selections From the Prison Notebooks* (New York: International Publishers, 1971).
11. Collecting categories are the headings through which a series of unrelated practices are regulated together through common administrative classifications. See Philip Corrigan, "On Moral Regulation" in *Sociological Review*, 29 (1981): 313–316.
12. Miriam Smith's 1999 account of cross-country lesbian and gay rights coalitions in the 1970s is very useful but is also limited by its inadequate analysis of the debate over fifty percent lesbian control in the NGRC/CLGRC and over the rupture of the CLGRC with the Saskatoon Gay Community Centre. On some of this see Bill Fields, "The Rise and Fall of the Fifty Per Cent Solution: Lesbians in the Canadian Gay Rights Movement," Faculty of Social Work, University of Regina, 1983; on file at the Canadian Lesbian and Gay Archives. Also see the chapter on the 1970s in our forthcoming *The Canadian War on 'Queers.'*
13. On the social construction of whiteness, see Roedigger, 1993 and Frankenburg, 1993.
14. I am not using the notion of "privilege" here as any sort of essential or inherent aspect of white or English people but rather as a social practice that allows white and English people to participate in relations of hegemony that are denied to those not socially constructed in this fashion. These social practices and relations can be transformed.
15. The Groupe interdisciplinaire de recherches et d'études: homosexualité et societé (GIREHS) held conferences on the "History of Gay and Lesbian Militancy in Quebec" on March 31, 1995, and a conference on "The National Question and Gays and Lesbians: Distinctions or Exclusions?" June 2, 1995.
16. Camp humour enables gay men to negotiate the contradictions between our particular experiences of the world and heterosexual social hegemony . It denaturalizes heterosexual normality by making fun of it. See, *The Regulation of Desire*, 226–227.
17. On this expansion of democracy and on participatory or direct democracy see Judy Rebick, *Imagine Democracy* (Toronto: Stoddart, 2000); my interview with

Judy Rebick,"Imagining Democracy, remaking the left: a conversation with Judy Rebick," *New Socialist*, 5.2 (May/June 2000): 10–13; and my review of her book "Participatory Democracy and a New Left," *New Socialist*, 5.3 (Sept./Oct. 2000): 28–29.

WORKS CITED

Adams, Howard. *Tortured People, The Politics of Colonialism.* Revised edition. Penticton, BC: Theytus Books, 1999.

Anderson, Benedict. *Imagined Communities.* London: Verso, 1991.

Barnholden, Patrick. "Does the 'Straight' Jacket of the Family Fit You?" *New Socialist*, 4.3 (1999): 22–23.

Bannerji, Himani. *Thinking Through, Essays on Feminism, Marxism and Anti-Racism.* Toronto: Women's Press, 1995.

———. *The Dark Side of the Nation, Essays on Multiculturalism, Nationalism and Gender.* Toronto: Canadian Scholar's Press, 2000.

Bologh, Roslyn Wallach. *Dialectical Phenomenology: Marx's Method.* Boston: Northeastern University Press, 1979.

Butler, Judith. *Gender Trouble: Feminism and the Subversion of Identity.* New York: Routledge, 1990.

Cannon, Martin. "The Regulation of First Nations Sexuality." *Canadian Journal of Native Studies* XVIII.1 (1998): 1–18.

Chamberland, Line. *Memoires Lesbiennes, le lesbianisme à Montreal entre 1950 et 1972.* Montreal: les editions du remue-menage, 1996.

Corrigan, Philip. "On Moral Regulation." *Sociological Review* 29 (1981): 313–316.

das Gupta, Tania. "The Politics of Multiculturalism, 'Immigrant Women' and the Canadian State." In *Scratching the Surface: Canadian Anti-Racist Feminist Thought.* Eds. Enakshi Dua and Angela Robertson. Toronto: Women's Press, 1999. 187–205.

Directorate of Security and Intelligence Annual Report, 1962–1963, RCMP.

Directorate of Security and Intelligence Annual Report, 1963–1964, RCMP.

Directorate of Security and Intelligence Annual Report, 1967–1968, RCMP.

Enloe, Cynthia. *Does Khaki Become You? Militarization and Women's Lives.* London: Pluto, 1983.

———. *Bananas, Beaches and Bases: Making Feminist Sense of International Politics.* London: Pandora, 1989.

Frankenburg, Ruth. *White Women, Race Matters: The Social Construction of Whiteness.* Minneapolis, MN: University of Minnesota Press, 1993.

Grace, Elizabeth, and Colin Leys. "The Concept of Subversion and Its Implications." In *Dissent and the State.* Ed. C.E.S. Franks. Toronto: Oxford University Press, 1989. 62–85.

Gay American Indians and Will Roscoe, eds. *Living the Spirit: A Gay American Indian Anthology.* New York: St. Martin's Press, 1988.

Goodleaf, Donna Kahenrakwas. "'Under Military Occupation': Indigenous Women, State Violence, and Community Resistance." In *And Still We Rise: Feminist Political Mobilizing in Contemporary Canada.* Ed. Linda Carty. Toronto: Women's Press, 1993. 225–242.

Gramsci, Antonio. *Selections from the Prison Notebooks,* New York: International Publishers, 1971.

Hannant, Larry. *The Infernal Machine: Investigating the Loyalty of Canada's Citizens,* Toronto: University of Toronto Press, 1995.

Harold. "A Case Study With Observations," 1960–1961.

Hennessy, Rosemary. "Queer Theory, Left Politics." *Rethinking Marxism* 7.3 (1994): 85–111.

———. *Profit and Pleasure: Sexual Identities in Late Capitalism.* New York: Routledge, 2000.

Herman, Didi. *Rights of Passage: Struggles for Lesbian and Gay Legal Equality.* Toronto: University of Toronto Press, 1994.

Higgins, Ross. *De la clandestine à l'affirmation: Pour une histoire de la communauté gaie montrealise.* Montreal: Cameaux and Nadeau, 1999.

Iacovetta, Franca. "Making Model Citizens: Gender, Corrupted Democracy, and Immigrant Reception Work in Cold War." In *Whose National Security? Canadian State Surveillance and the Creation of Enemies.* Eds. G. Kinsman, D. Buse, and M. Steedman. Toronto: Between the Lines, 2000. 54–167.

Jagose, Annamarie. *Queer Theory, An Introduction.* New York: New York University Press, 1996.

Kanehsatake: *270 Years of Resistance* [documentary]. Directed by Alanis Obomsawin. National Film Board. Canada, 1993.

Kashmeri, Zuhair. *The Gulf Within, Canadian Arabs, Racism and the Gulf War.* Toronto: James Lorimer, 1991.

Kinsman, Gary. "Queer 'Nations,' Queer Spaces: Academic Institutionalization and Queer Activism," given at the Canadian Association of Sociology and Anthropology Meetings, Charlottetown, June, 1992.

———. "'Character Weaknesses' and 'Fruit Machines': Towards an Analysis of The Anti-Homosexual Security Campaign in the Canadian Civil Service." *Labour/Le Travail* 35 (Spring, 1995): 133–161.

———. *The Regulation of Desire: Homo and Hetero Sexualities.* Montreal: Black Rose, 1996.

———. "'Responsibility as a Strategy of Governance: Regulating People With AIDS and Lesbians and Gay Men in Ontario." *Economy and Society* 25.3 (1996): 393–409.

———. "Managing AIDS Organizing: 'Consultation,' 'Partnership,' and 'Responsibility' as Strategies of Regulation." In *Organizing Dissent, Contemporary Social Movements*

In Theory and Practice. Ed. William K. Carrol. Toronto: Garamond, 1997. 213–239.

———. "Gays and Lesbians: Pushing the Boundaries." In *Canadian Society, Meeting the Challenge of the Twenty-First Century.* Eds. Dan Glenday and Ann Duffy. Toronto: Oxford University Press, 2000. 212–246.

———. "Constructing Gay Men and Lesbians as National Security Risks, 1950–1970." In *Whose National Security? Canadian State Surveillance and the Creation of Enemies.* Eds. Kinsman, Gary, D. Buse, and M. Steedman. Toronto: Between the Lines, 2000. 143–153.

Kinsman, Gary and Patrizia Gentile with the assistance of Heidi McDonell and Mary Mahood-Greer. "'In the Interests of the State': The Anti-Gay, Anti-Lesbian National Security Campaigns in Canada." A Preliminary Research Report, Sudbury, ON: Laurentian University, 1998.

———. *The Canadian War on "Queers": National Security as Sexual Regulation.* Forthcoming.

Kinsman, Gary, D. Buse, and M. Steedman eds. *Whose National Security? Canadian State Surveillance and the Creation of Enemies.* Toronto: Between the Lines, 2000.

Krishnan, Raghu. "The Clarity Bill: Icing on the Neoliberal Cake." *Canadian Dimension* 34.1 (July-August, 2000): 11.

Lahey, Kathleen A. *Are We Persons Yet? Law and Sexuality in Canada.* Toronto: University of Toronto Press, 1999.

Lehr, Valerie. *Queer Family Values: Debunking the Myth of the Nuclear Family.* Philadelphia: Temple University Press, 1999.

Maynard, Steven. "When Queer Is Not Enough." *Fuse,* 15.1/2 (Fall 1991): 14–18.

McIntosh, Mary. "Queer Theory and the War of the Sexes." In *Activating Theory: Lesbian, Gay and Bisexual Politics.* London: Lawrence and Wishart, 1993. 30–52.

McNally, David. *Socialism From Below,* New Socialist Group pamphlet, 1997.

———. "Language, History and Class Struggle." In *In Defence of History, Marxism and the Postmodern Agenda.* Eds. Ellen Meiksins Wood and John Bellamy Foster. New York: Monthly Review, 1997, 26–42.

———. *Bodies of Meaning, Studies on Language, Labor, and Liberation.* Albany, NY: State University of New York Press, 2001.

Moran, Leslie J. "The Uses of Homosexuality: Homosexuality for National Security." *International Journal of the Sociology of Law* 19 (1991).

Namaste, Ki. "'Tragic Misreadings': Queer Theory's Erasure of Transgender Subjectivity." In *Queer Studies: A Lesbian, Gay, Bisexual and Transgender Anthology.* New York: New York University Press, 1996, 83–203.

Namaste, Viviane K. *Invisible Lives.* Chicago: University of Chicago Press, 2001.

Ng, Roxana. "Multiculturalism as Ideology: A Textual Analysis." In *Knowledge, Experience, and Ruling Relations, Studies in the Social Organization of Knowledge.* Eds. Marie Campbell and Ann Manicom. Toronto: University of Toronto Press, 1995, 35–48.

Parker, Andrew, et. al. *Nationalisms and Sexualities.* New York: Routledge, 1992.

Pearlston, Karen. "APEC Days at UBC: Student Protests and National Security in an Era of Trade Liberalization." In *Whose National Security? Canadian State Surveillance and the Creation of Enemies*. Toronto: Between the Lines, 2000, 267–277.

Rayside, David. "Gay Rights and Family Values, The Passage of Bill 7 in Ontario." *Studies in Political Economy* 26 (Summer, 1988): 62–91.

———. *On The Fringe, Gays and Lesbians in Politics*. Ithaca, NY: Cornell University Press, 1998, 105–211.

Rebick, Judy. *Imagine Democracy*. Toronto: Stoddart, 2000.

Report of the Royal Commission on Security. Abridged version. Ottawa: Queen's Printer, 1969.

Robinson, Daniel, and David Kimmel. "The Queer Career of Homosexual Security Vetting in Cold-War Canada." *Canadian Historical Review* LXXV.3 (September 1994): 319–345.

Roedigger, David. *The Wages of Whiteness: Race and the Making of the American Working Class*. London: Verso, 1993.

Roscoe, Will. *The Zuni Man-Woman*. Albuquerque: University of New Mexico Press, 1991.

———, ed. *Changing Ones, Third and Fourth Genders in Native North America*. New York: St. Martin's Press, 1998.

Sallot, Jeff. "The Spy Masters' Talent Hunt Goes Public." *The Globe and Mail* (June 22, 1999): A1, A14.

Sanders, Doug. "Constructing Lesbian and Gay Rights." *Canadian Journal of Law and Society* 9.2 (Fall, 1994).

Sayer, Derek, ed. *Readings From Karl Marx*. New York: Routledge, 1989.

Sayer, Derek and Philip Corrigan. *The Great Arch, English State Formation As Cultural Revolution*. London: Basil Blackwell, 1985.

Sears, Alan. "'To Teach Them How To Live': The Politics of Public Health from Tuberculosis to AIDS." *Journal of Historical Sociology* 5.1 (1992): 61–83;

———. "Before the Welfare State: Public Health and Social Policy." *The Canadian Review of Sociology and Anthropology* 32.2 (May, 1995), 69–188.

———. "Queer Times?" *New Socialist* 3.3 (June-July, 1998): 12–13; 25.

———. "Can Marriage Be Queer?" *New Socialist* 29 (March/April, 2001): 31–33.

Sedgwick, Eve Kosofsky. *The Epistemology of the Closet*, Berkeley: University of California Press, 1990.

Seidman, Steven, ed. *Queer Theory/Sociology*, London: Basil Blackwell, 1969.

Smith, Brian K. CBC Radio News, April 14, 1998.

Smith, Dorothy E. *The Everyday World as Problematic, A Feminist Sociology*. Toronto: University of Toronto Press, 1987.

———. "K Is Mentally Ill." In *Texts, Facts and Femininity: Exploring the Relations of Ruling*. New York: Routledge, 1990, 30–32; 43.

———. "Textually Mediated Social Organization." In *Texts, Facts and Femininity*. Ed. Dorothy E. Smith. New York: Routledge, 1990, 209–224.

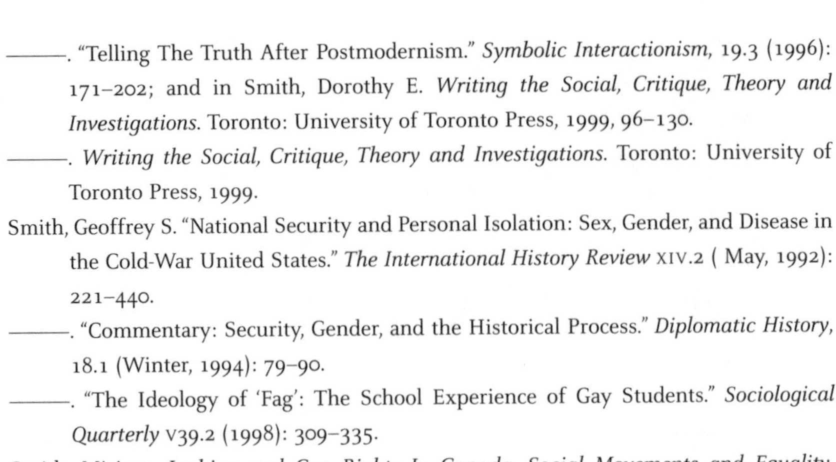

———. "Telling The Truth After Postmodernism." *Symbolic Interactionism*, 19.3 (1996): 171–202; and in Smith, Dorothy E. *Writing the Social, Critique, Theory and Investigations*. Toronto: University of Toronto Press, 1999, 96–130.

———. *Writing the Social, Critique, Theory and Investigations*. Toronto: University of Toronto Press, 1999.

Smith, Geoffrey S. "National Security and Personal Isolation: Sex, Gender, and Disease in the Cold-War United States." *The International History Review* XIV.2 (May, 1992): 221–440.

———. "Commentary: Security, Gender, and the Historical Process." *Diplomatic History*, 18.1 (Winter, 1994): 79–90.

———. "The Ideology of 'Fag': The School Experience of Gay Students." *Sociological Quarterly* V39.2 (1998): 309–335.

Smith, Miriam. *Lesbian and Gay Rights In Canada, Social Movements and Equality-Seeking, 1971–1995*. Toronto: University of Toronto Press, 1999.

Stychin, Carl F. "Equality Rights, Identity Politics and the Canadian National Imagination." In Stychin, *Law's Desire, Sexuality and the Limits of Justice*. New York: Routledge, 1995.

———. *A Nation By Rights, National Cultures, Sexual Identity Politics and the Discourse of Rights*. Philadelphia: Temple University Press, 1998.

Terry, Jennifer. "Momism and the Making of the Treasonous Lesbian," unpublished paper presented at the Canadian Historical Association, Montreal, Quebec, 1995.

———. *An American Obsession, Science, Medicine, and Homosexuality in Modern Society*. Chicago: The University of Chicago Press, 1999.

Thobani, Sunera. "Changing the Nation's Ranks, Canadian Immigration Policy in the 21st Century." In *Reclaiming the Future, Women's Struggles for the 21st Century*. Ed. Somer Brodribb. Charlottetown, PEI: gynergy, 1999, 75–96.

Warner, Michael, ed. *Fear of a Queer Planet*. Minneapolis: University of Minnesota Press, 1993.

———. "Beyond Gay Marriage." In *The Trouble With Normal: Sex, Politics and the Ethics of Queer Life*. Ed. Michael Warner. Cambridge, MA: Harvard University Press, 1999, 81–147.

———. "Bill 5: 'Same-Sex Partner Law,'" *Outwards, Coalition for Lesbian and Gay Rights in Ontario* (November, 1999): 1–2.

Weeks, Jeffrey. *Sexuality and Its Discontents*. London: Routledge and Kegan Paul, 1985, 5–10.

Whitaker, Reg. *Double Standard: The Secret History of Canadian Immigration*. Toronto: University of Toronto Press, 1987.

Whitaker, Reg, and Gary Marcuse. *Cold War Canada: The Making of a National Insecurity State*, Toronto: University of Toronto Press, 1994.

siting lesbians: urban spaces and sexuality

Catherine Nash

INTRODUCTION

Most major North American cities contain an area referred to as the gay "ghetto," "village," or neighbourhood. These districts typically can be found in the downtown core and, although there is usually a lesbian presence, most are dominated by gay men. These areas are purportedly the centre of the "gay life," containing the offices of the local gay organization and community centre, bars, restaurants, bookstores, and other businesses catering to gays and lesbians.

It has been in only the last ten years that distinctly lesbian areas have been documented in several American, British, and Canadian cities (Sy Adler and Johanna Brenner 1992; Gill Valentine 1993; and Anne-Marie Bouthillette 1997). However, the majority of the research on the urban spatial organization of lesbians has emerged as a secondary or peripheral issue in research on gay men.[1] This essay sets out the research findings of a case study examining a lesbian neighbourhood in a mid-sized Canadian city. The purpose of the research was to develop an understanding of the emergence of a lesbian community as a distinct developing and functioning urban spatial formation.[2]

THE HISTORICAL FRAMING OF GAY AND LESBIAN SPACE: DISCIPLINARY LITERATURE

However clandestine the "gay life" was thought to be, the emergence of gay and lesbian spaces has not gone unnoticed. Since World War II, a veritable explosion of research—arriving at conclusions as numerous as the disciplines framing the research—has examined and diagnosed "the homosexual," and, by extension, homosexual meeting places.

In the post-war period, a burgeoning concern over the apparent increase in homosexual activity (stemming in large part from the findings of Alfred Kinsey's reports of 1948 and 1953) galvanized medical doctors, psychologists, and psychiatrists to produce a huge body of contradictory and generally uncomplimentary research on homosexuals (Beiber 1962; Bergler 1957; Cappon 1965; Socarides 1968). Almost all were aware of gay spaces and districts and saw them as an unfortunate outgrowth of an expanding and annoyingly unrepentant group of deviants. The fact that such places existed only compounded the problem of homosexuality, allowing people who were "mentally ill" to have a false sense of normalcy and safety in numbers. Such social groupings were, in and of themselves, feeble reflections of normal social relations. As Daniel Cappon states:

> [A] person may live within the protective confines of a small, esoteric, social group which tolerates homosexual behaviour; within a sphere or orbit of life with remarkable sameness: same sex, same bars, same bohemianism or dandyism, same abstract painting, same delicate interior decoration, same "beat" music, "beat" poetry, same sporty cliques, same gossip." (10)

As the discipline of sociology came into its own in the 1960s and early 1970s, the focus on gay spaces changed. In considering "deviant behaviour," sociologists argued that agents of social control "labelled" certain actions or behaviours as "deviant," saddling the individual with a stigmatized persona and causing him to seek others of his own kind. This solidified what might have been occasional behaviour into a deviant identity (Becker 1963; Lemert 1967; Gagnon and Simon 1967). In examining "deviance" as a label, sociologists began to consider broader questions about the "normalizing" of certain historically and culturally specific values that, they argued, reflect not that which is inherently deviant but the power of some to define and exert social control over the behaviours of others.[3] By the mid-1980s, sociologists, psychologists, and others were suggesting that there was little difference between homosexuals and their straight counterparts, in terms of mental health, social interaction, contribution to society, and that perhaps the true difficulties for homosexuals arose from society's misguided condemnation and bigotry (Levitt and Klassen 1974; Plummer 1975).[4]

Interest in the study of these "deviant subcultures" prompted a re-evaluation and reformulation of the nature and purpose of homosexual spaces. Research, undertaken in an ethnographic format, portrayed such spaces as part of a broader coping strategy resulting from assuming the homosexual role assigned through the labelling process, a tactic successfully employed by deviant groups to protect themselves from mainstream censure (Achilles 1964; Hooker 1965; Leznoff and Westley 1956).[5]

This research acknowledged that gay places were dominated by gay men. First, regardless of homophobia, society completely accepted large groups of men congregating in the absence of women. Women unaccompanied by men were constrained by what society deemed appropriate for potential wives and mothers, an assumption that was applied to all women. The few women who did circulate in the gay social world had to break various taboos (Gagnon and Simon 1967; Warren 1976). Secondly, homosexuals themselves saw these spaces as "sexual market places" and thus for men, an environment which was purportedly not of interest to lesbians who, as women, craved romance and long-term relationships (Cory 1964; Hoffman 1968).

In earlier years, the bars were represented in the literature as haunts or hangouts predominantly for the lower-class homosexual. Homosexuals holding "good" jobs could not afford to frequent these spaces for fear of exposure (Leznoff and Westley 1956). For medical experts, however, valiant coping strategy or not, homosexual subcultures (and by extension, their meeting places) were but a pale imitation of the truly healthy ethnic minority groups. As Gagnon and Simon point out, "In contrast to ethnic and occupational subcultures, the homosexual community, as well as other deviant sub communities, has very limited content. . . . The important fact is that the homosexual community is itself an impoverished cultural unit" (in Dinitz et al 1969, 342–349).

In the early 1980s, the maturing gay and lesbian political movements were hitting their stride, and novel academic research, focusing on political and new social movement theory, recast gay spaces as representing the tactical appropriation or colonization of space as part of political action by an "oppressed" minority (Adam 1979). Gay and lesbian scholars sought to counter mainstream research that saw both gay and lesbian groups as something less than legitimate "communities" and their spaces as something impoverished and makeshift. Manuel Castells and Karen Murphy (1983) saw the domination of certain neighbourhoods by gay men as marking the emergence of a new social movement that became a powerful political force "through the spatial organization of a self-defined cultural community" (138). Local gay political involvement impacted at the neighbourhood level through gentrification, and the formation of business associations and community groups, which, through their spatial manoeuvering, reordered space within a broader political context (Knopp 1990). As gay "liberation" activism gave way to gay "assimilation" politics, the framing of the gay population as an ethnic "minority" meant that gay spaces symbolized the physical territory of a culturally distinct social group (Epstein 1987, 9–54).

The urban concentrations that received academic attention and public notoriety at the time were clearly dominated by gay men and, although lesbians were present, they did not figure prominently nor did they seem to have their own distinct areas. In considering why this might be so in San Francisco, Castells and Murphy reasoned that the inherent differences between men and women structured their relationships to space. "[W]omen rarely have these territorial aspirations: their world attaches more importance to relationships and their networks are one of solidarity and affection. In this, gay men act first and foremost as men and lesbians as women" (139).

While there was some appeal in the argument that men and women have innate gender differences in their relationships to urban spaces, contrary opinions began to appear. Lawrence Knopp and Mickey Lauria (1985) rejected Castells "innate territoriality theory" and explained the lack of lesbian spaces as a measure of the fact that society reacts to and treats gay men and lesbians differently. "[G]ay males, whose sexual and emotional expressiveness has been repressed in a different fashion than lesbians, may perceive a greater need for territory" (158).

As research on women in cities developed, challenges to Knopp and Lauria's explanation for the lack of lesbian-defined territories emerged, one that focused on how men and women, in general, operate in different economic and social circumstances. Lesbians operating outside the accepted gender roles of wife and mother may find themselves, as women, less able to compete economically and socially. Gay men, as men, are more financially and socially capable of organizing spatially and upgrading neighbourhoods (Holcomb 1986). In a 1990 investigation of an ill-fated attempt by some gay developers and real estate agents to establish a gay neighbourhood in New Orleans, Knopp argued that "[L]esbians' ability to cope with oppression through entry in the housing market (and hence the middle class) is more limited than gay men. Residential concentrations of lesbians tend to resemble the patterns and processes of segregation that characterize other marginalized groups more than they do gay men (349)." Thus, the lack of development of a spatially-based lesbian community may have had less to do with lesbians being "less territorial" than gays, and more to do with the gendered economic realities of the marketplace. These realities include limited access to capital and other resources.

Yet, with the passage of time, lesbian concentrations had begun to materialize, and with them came the seemingly inevitable comparisons with gay male districts. Using a methodology similar to that of Castells and Murphy, Sy Adler and Johanna Brenner conducted, in 1992, one of the first detailed studies of a lesbian neighbourhood in an unidentified city in the United States. Their express purpose was to compare their findings against Castells and Murphy's statements about why lesbians fail to dominate any urban spaces. They were particularly interested in considering whether the absence of a publicly identifiable lesbian neighbourhood reflected inherent gender differences in interests, needs, and values, or reflected differences in the resources available to gay men and lesbians. They concluded that it was a little of both.

Adler and Brenner's research, in fact, demonstrated that an identifiable lesbian residential neighbourhood did indeed exist but without an associated lesbian-controlled, commercial focal point. The lesbian neighbourhood was located in a section of the downtown core considered to be a countercultural or alternative neighbourhood. By comparison, it was much less visible than similar gay male areas and did not have the degree of territorial control and affiliated political and social activism. This did not lead Adler and Brenner to conclude, however, that lesbians were less "territorial" than gay men. Their study demonstrated that lesbians, as women and as primary caregivers for children, had different concerns about the kinds of areas that they occupied. City centres were not, in general, attractive locations for women because of safety concerns for both themselves and their children; however, economically the downtown was more attractive, containing as it did, lower-cost housing, reduced need for a car, and ease of access to social services. In addition, women did not have the financial capability to be involved in the gentrification process—a specifically gendered and class-related reasoning unrelated to questions of sexual preference or orientation—to the same extent as gay men.

While the lesbian concentration scrutinized by Adler and Brenner had some similarities to gay residential areas, it had an even lower proportion of owner-occupied housing than Castells' gay male territory. Overall, the lesbian area had lower rents, less expensive homes, and was not a prime area for gentrification. Adler and Brenner concluded that lesbians were not gentrifiers in the traditional sense, nor did they wish to control space through the aggressive visibility of gay men, out of concern for their personal safety and that of their children (but see Rothenberg 1995).

While Castells and Murphy concluded that gays (as men) were acting within the existing political structure to gain power and political clout, Adler and Brenner argued that lesbians operating with a feminist agenda appeared to have other concerns. Given that lesbian politics has been closely allied with the women's movement, their ideological leanings were more global and less restricted to representation in the existing political system. In their words, "Lesbians who created lesbian culture and urban communities in the 1970's did so in connection with a movement against male domination whose critique went far beyond simple demands for incorporation into existing society" (33). Women were less focused on controlling space for political power and more interested in addressing broader theoretical issues outside of the existing social structure. This, combined with differing gendered relations to space, seemed to explain the later evolution of lesbian neighbourhoods and their distinctive characteristics.

One can conclude from the literature that gender and sexuality are important factors in considering a group's relationship to space or their locational choices. Gender is important in both the historical evolution of lesbian areas and the emerging characteristics. Historically, women have had a difficult and more constrained relationship with urban space than men. In the late 1960s and early 1970s, gay men were building institutional spaces in central city locales to serve their communities. At the same time, social mores and expectations suggested that "nice, proper" women did not frequent bars or taverns unescorted, let alone start businesses, form private clubs, or wander downtown streets in the evenings.

The relationships between spaces and identities also varied across class and racial lines. Working-class lesbians may have found it easier, and more socially acceptable, than middle- or upper-class women to frequent taverns and restaurants where lesbians were known to meet. Research that looked at lesbian spaces in the 1950s and 1960s found working-class bars to be the only known or at least somewhat visible gathering places (Davis and Kennedy 1993; Chenier 1996). At the same time, women's employment opportunities were also more restricted, limiting access to the economic resources needed for home ownership or business start-up. As women's social and economic positions changed in the 1970s and early 1980s, possibilities for lesbian areas emerged. While research confirmed the presence of lesbian residential concentrations, these areas did not support an overtly visible lesbian commercial and/or institutional space similar to gay male areas (Castells and Murphy 1983).

Most recently, some academics have begun to rethink their approach to understanding the evolution of distinctly lesbian spaces. They have started with the basic premise that gay and lesbian spaces have evolved through completely distinctive processes and function in distinctive ways (Bouthillette 1997). The purpose of this case study was to examine the evolution of a distinctly lesbian area through interviews with those living and participating in that neighbourhood to determine how and why this area became the physical location of a part of the lesbian population.[6] More work is required on the distinctive particularities of lesbians' interrelationships with urban spaces, without comparison with gay spaces.

THE CASE STUDY

The research examined the spatial organization and locational characteristics of a particular lesbian community in a mid-sized city (population approximately 125,000) in central Canada between 1993 and 1995. It was well known within the city's lesbian and gay community that a particular residential area had a reputation as a lesbian enclave. [7]

One aspect of the study's approach was to use various definitions of lesbian space. Spaces can be conceptualized not only within the traditional urban planning categories based on "use" (residential or commercial), but as spaces which are much more ambiguous and unstable. Spaces may have temporary distinct users such as a bar that is heterosexual by day and homosexual at night. Other spaces are more "mixed": patronized by both straights and gays although perhaps without the knowledge of the straight users.

Space can also be thought of as "public" or "private." For the purposes of the case study, private spaces were those to which access could be restricted. (The most obvious example of this sort of space is one's private residence.) Public spaces were those to which all members of the public had access. These included streets, businesses, and public property such as community centres, libraries, and public parks. However, lesbians have used various means to partially control access to spaces. These included membership requirements or spaces reserved for women-only or lesbian-only activities. (The resulting spaces are referred to as "semi-public" and may be either temporary or permanent.) For the purposes of the case study, temporary spaces included those that, for a particular time, were reserved for women-only or lesbian-only activities, including dances held in a local community centre or the once-a-month dinners held at a local restaurant. Permanent spaces included those spaces that were women-only or lesbian-only at all times.

In order to gather information about the perceived existence of areas of lesbian concentrations, I approached various organizations providing both spaces and/or services to lesbians specifically or to women in general (with lesbians as a recognized component).[8] A total of eleven organizations were identified as delivering services, in whole or in part, to lesbians. The names of these organizations have been changed in order to avoid identification of the study area. They included: International Women's Day Committee (IWD); Gay Pride Day Committee (GPD); Women's Activities Committee (WAC); Gay/Lesbian/Bi-Association (GLBA); Circles and Squares (hairdresser); Women's Mail Order Book Service (Women's Books); a Lesbian Dance Collective (Sapphistry); Women's Music Festival (Music Festival); Gay/Lesbian Newspaper (GLN); Women's Bookstore (Mrs. Gaskill's); Women's Restaurant and the Meeting Place (Meeting Place). (A summary of these organizations and their characteristics is found in Appendix A.)

These organizations, by providing services to lesbians, were reasonably expected to have knowledge about the lesbian population, places where lesbians frequented, lesbian or lesbian-positive businesses or areas of lesbian concentration. Principal members of these organizations were interviewed about the nature and location of the local lesbian population, lesbian organizations, and businesses and were asked to identify any area(s) they recognized as lesbian areas of concentration. In four cases, the participants also lived in the areas identified as having a lesbian concentration.

The presentation of the results of the study is divided into two parts: institutional/commercial spaces and residential spaces. First, participants described those types of institutional spaces (either public or semi-public in nature) used or frequented by lesbians such as bars, restaurants, community centres, and bookstores. These spaces were further classified as either temporary or permanent spaces and their location characteristics described. Secondly, participants described two residential areas and the characteristics identified these as areas of lesbian concentration.

INSTITUTIONS/COMMERCIAL SPACES

A large number of the activities within the lesbian community(ies) took place in public or semi-public spaces that were usually perceived as heterosexual in nature. Within the study area, WAC and IWW events were generally held in local community centres, public libraries, or school gyms and auditoriums. For short periods of time, these places were dominated by women-only or lesbian-only events and generated a sense of safety and control of semi-public space that was unusual. It may also have been disconcerting for the usual users of such facilities to find "their," usually heterosexual, space co-opted and designated as lesbian space. Conflict was always possible but rarely occurred.

In other circumstances, the taking over or occupying of public space was a deliberate action designed as a political act to raise awareness of gay and lesbian or women's issues. Within the study area, there was an annually organized Gay Pride march down the main street of the city, a deliberate (and temporary) appropriation of public space as a political gesture. The Take Back the Night March was another annual event in the study area where women asserted their right, through sheer force of numbers, to walk the streets at night without harassment or fear.

Other public spaces such as restaurants, bars, and movie theatres became known as places that were safe and/or tolerant of lesbians. Within the study area, there were three or four downtown restaurants that were seen as lesbian-friendly, places where lesbians could go without concerns about the owner, staff or other patrons causing them difficulty. Ascertaining which spaces were likely to be supportive or at least safe for lesbians was usually determined by trial and error. Several participants noted:

> You don't even realize that you are testing a place but you are testing the atmosphere . . . it's not as if you could give your partner a big hug and see how they go for that. It's much more subtle than that but it's . . . a certain level of awareness usually with the staff. Do these people know that gay people exist and that they're like people they know. . . ? (008:8)

> So there are several places in town that it is really no problem, they are quite gracious and you are not tolerated, you are welcomed. (002:28)

Other spaces mentioned included the repertory movie theatre that screened alternative movies, certain health food stores, and several other downtown shops. Most of these businesses also had community bulletin boards that were used by the various organizations to advertise upcoming events and were described as "alternative" or "non-mainstream" businesses. One downtown church, the local chapter of Metropolitan Community Church (now defunct), and the community centre were also identified as resource or information centres about lesbian activities. Knowing safe places to get information about community events was a critical point for a majority of the participants.

> I think we need to know or have places where we can go and find out about different kinds of information. People or facts. It's like knowledge is power and the more knowledge you have the more powerful you are. (007:29)

Several organizations provided permanent space for lesbians, although only one was lesbian-only space. The GLBA, in some form or another, had provided space and services to the lesbians and gays in the study area for some fifteen years. The space was shared with other groups but offered private areas for meeting, a phone line serviced by volunteers, an information centre, and a library. The space was situated on the edge of the downtown area and had a somewhat restricted user base.

The Meeting Place was originally conceived to provide permanent space for lesbians and other women to meet, hold different events for and by women, such as art exhibits, concerts, and literature readings, and to be used as a drop-in place to have lunch and chat. The space was essentially semi-private in nature as users were required to obtain a membership. It was located in the downtown core a block from the main street. It came into being because of a perceived need within the women's community for a place for women to meet. One of the original owners noted:

> There was nothing in the community, not even a bookstore—a women's bookstore. So nobody had any way of making contact with other feminists and [for] that we needed space. It was felt that space was needed for people to get together and talk and we could have guest speakers and that sort of thing. (002:1)

The Meeting Place closed its doors after only a year and a half of operation after struggling with the all-too-common economic difficulties experienced by such organizations and unresolved and painful conflict between member factions. Difficulties arose between so-called "straight" women and "radical" lesbians over how the space should be used. Two main issues brought the matter to a head. First, straight women expressed an interest in bringing male friends to certain events, which was unacceptable to other women. Secondly, certain lesbian entertainers made pointed and less than flattering comments about straight women. The resulting split in the membership remained unresolved years after the Meeting Place's demise and the hurt and resentment continues to run deep amongst certain groups within the community.

Circles and Squares offered the only lesbian-only space and was located in one of the neighbourhoods identified as a lesbian area. The owner of Circles and Squares was able to restrict access to only people within the community through an appointment and referral process.

The women's bookstore, Mrs. Gaskill's, was acknowledged by all participants as one of the most important, permanent spaces within the study area for providing a safe meeting place in which to socialize and get information on local events. Although men are not overtly barred, the bookstore was an example of a public space almost exclusively used by women. It was recognized as an important institutional space for any lesbian community, one commonly found in most North American urban centres. It was acknowledged by all participants as a primary institution for the local community. Its closure was considered a major loss.

> We used to have a women's bookstore and we don't any more. Very clearly that was a place where you could go if you were a woman coming into town or new to town or a student . . . you could go to the women's bookstore and I think it was a common thing amongst communities. (001:6)

All of the organizations interviewed, with the exception of the Music Festival, used spaces in or near the downtown core. Mrs. Gaskill's and the Meeting Place were located in the central business district of the study area. The WAC sports-oriented recreational events were usually booked into public schools located near or in the downtown core. All of these different spaces were accessible on foot or by bus from one of the two neighbourhoods identified as having a lesbian concentration. The gathering point for participants in the Gay Pride march was in a local park at the edge of this neighbourhood. The march proceeded from there down the main downtown street. The remaining businesses, which were viewed as lesbian-friendly, were also located in the downtown area.

RESIDENTIAL CONCENTRATIONS

Participants identified two residential areas thought to have a concentration of lesbians. The first, and the one perceived as being "known" as a lesbian neighbourhood, was located north of and within walking distance of the downtown core. It is referred to here as the North Residential Area (NRA). The second area, referred to here as the Second Residential Area (SRA), was somewhat removed from the city core.

The participants distinguished the two residential neighbourhoods predominantly by "class." The NRA was described as more working-class, with smaller houses, a more transient population, and a greater diversity of people and housing types. In the SRA, housing and rental prices were higher than in the NRA, and the neighbourhood was perceived as having larger and more expensive homes. However, the housing stock was still quite mixed in nature with single- and multiple-unit buildings dispersed throughout, a number of which were rental properties. The participating residents felt that this was the area where lesbians with higher incomes would choose to live:

> It's more working class and it's more . . . how do I describe it? The houses [in the NRA] are generally smaller, they are not so well kept, you know, as the houses on the [other side] . . . quite often the [NRA] is fairly

> run down. . . . Its population is more a mix, I think, of transient populations. (006:20)

> I think there are more owner-occupied houses in this area. The houses are larger on the whole or quainter or more historic. There's a whole bunch of things that make them a bit more expensive. It tends to be a middle-class area. It is better kept and large. The taxes are higher. (006:21)

In order to cross-check the perceptions of the participants about the nature and characteristics of the neighbourhoods, I examined the census tracts for the two areas with respect to housing type, ownership/rental, household type, and various population characteristics. The results are set out in Appendices B and C. Each area or district characteristic was compared to the overall data for the city (census agglomeration [CA]). With respect to the NRA, the participants' observations are borne out by the census data. Both the population characteristics and housing types were more diverse than the CA as a whole with a more diverse and older housing stock, a high proportion of renters, and less traditional household composition. However, the census data for the SRA is inconclusive. While the NRA was more congruent with census-tract boundaries, the SRA was part of a larger census tract, which precluded more specific analysis. Physically, the SRA was separated from the remaining census tract area and formed a distinctly bounded residential neighbourhood.

REASONS FOR LOCATIONAL CHOICE

Economic Reality

The participants were asked to consider the appeal of both the NRA and SRA as places for lesbians to live. All participants felt that economic factors militated against the development of a lesbian territory consisting of a residential and commercial component. This included limited access to the capital resources necessary to finance home ownership and business start-ups by women. With respect to the evolution of the residential areas alone, economic realities were also the strongest factor. The NRA was described as a more economically depressed part of town containing more affordable housing. Affordability included the notion of accessibility to local amenities by walking:

> If they [lesbians] are going to buy homes, they have to be affordable so it has to be in an area, I think, that has the amenities of downtown, that has affordable housing, so not really high-cost housing. (001:9)

> I think it's a cheap area to rent and a cheap area to buy. . . . We would not have been able to buy a house anywhere else. . . . We like to be able to walk downtown . . . income factors in again because a lot of lesbians don't have cars so they have to go where they can get groceries, they can get services . . . they can go places, they can meet people. . . . (008:11)

Perceptions of Safety

The need to blend into a neighbourhood for safety reasons was also a factor for those participants living in both areas. "Safety" seemed to be comprised of two discreet features. In the more general sense, the participants found both the SRA and NRA to be comfortable areas to walk in at night, the parks comfortable and well-lit, and neighbours friendly and quiet. More broadly, "safety" also meant blending into the area rather than standing out.

> . . . [I]f you moved [to the suburbs] where it is very stable, family oriented . . . you know, you stand out because you are two women or two women who do not have a family. I mean, you don't fit in. [In the NRA] I think people, generally speaking, do not take much note of each other in the first place and there is a high tolerance of differences. (006:22)

The NRA and SRA were perceived as equally safe at the physical level and diverse enough that non-traditional households would not stand out.

Castells' "Innate Territoriality" Theory

A majority of the participants felt that women were territorial but were uncertain that this was for the same reasons as gay men. Several participants saw gay men as males who were controlling territories for political purposes: to field political candidates, develop power bases through business associations, and to control land for their own benefit, all the while working within the existing power structures. Participants were certain that lesbians operated within a different framework, perceiving economic concerns and collective safety and security issues as paramount.

For lesbians and women in general, to be "visible" is quite risky, which raises questions about the criteria used by Castells and Murphy. They employed Adler and Brenner (1992) to determine whether an area could be labelled "gay territory." Castells and Murphy (1983) argued that several criteria must be met in order for a group to claim or control urban space. The group must have a certain visibility through obvious retail businesses and services run by and for gays. This visibility is enhanced by a certain amount of community activity in the form of fairs or block parties representing some kind of public, collective affirmation of control by the people who live in the neighbourhood. Such areas should also have some business or residential organization to defend the neighbourhood's interests, relate to the city government, and financially support the community activities that create and maintain the urban subculture.

These "control" criteria, in whole or in part, are obviously limited in determining lesbian concentrations. The issue of visibility is a difficult one for the lesbian community as it is for women, in general, in urban areas. Advertising the existence of lesbian neighbourhoods and businesses is often dangerous. Circles and Squares, for example, received numerous threats for several years prior to its relocation in the NRA. The Music Festival was disrupted by local males at its rural location and was forced to hire security for its events. It is unlikely that lesbians would want to advertise or overtly demonstrate their control of urban space in the same fashion as gays.

> If there was a neighbourhood where a lot of lesbians were living I would expect to see the odd pink triangle or an above average number of women's symbols dangling in stained glass . . . but I think lesbians would be pretty confident in recognizing each other . . . why would they bring trouble among themselves by putting lavender bands around telephone poles? (008:13)

The NRA was visible to those "in the know" through the use of signs and symbols related to the lesbian community. The ability to control space does not necessarily depend on its being visible to others outside the community. Outsiders are more vulnerable and less able to interfere in activities if they are unaware of what is going on around them. Lesbians would know each other and could act in concert to protect and claim space without displays of overt domination.

> We have a rainbow flag in our backyard and it's up a fairly high pole and you can see it from, you know, a fairly large area. People who would know the rainbow flag would probably say, "Oh, hey that's neat!" . . . Other people might not know what it was or what it means. (001:22)

Most participants felt that lesbians were quite circumspect and unlikely to overtly or publicly declare control over urban spaces. However, participants felt that lesbians would indicate lesbian spaces or households in ways that would identify such spaces to each other or others familiar with the signifiers.

CONCLUSION

The case study demonstrates that lesbians in a mid-sized Canadian city concentrate in residential areas similar in nature to those described in current research literature and for similar reasons. American and British research demonstrates that lesbian concentrations are usually found in countercultural neighbourhoods, containing a higher number of non-traditional households, a lower proportion of owner-occupied housing, and lower rents (Lockard 1985; Winchester and White 1988; Adler and Brenner 1992; Rothenberg 1995). However, while one could conclude that lesbians settle in areas similar to those of gay men, this conclusion would only be a superficial assessment; lesbians move into different areas for different reasons.

Gay commercial areas developed in the parts of town that would tolerate more disapproved-of activities, such as bars and bathhouses, and that were also located within reasonable proximity of popular public parks and outdoor cruising areas. Since lesbians were not engaged in such activities, such spaces were not central to their community. Secondly, with the urban restructuring in the 1970s and 1980s, residential neighbourhoods in the downtown core experienced a resurgence, with construction of new accommodation geared to the single person and the refurbishing of older housing stock (Weightman 1980; 1981; Knopp and Lauria 1985). For gays, locating in these areas appealed to them as they contained those institutions central to their social lives.

For lesbians, this economic structuring had a distinctly different impact. The selection of a residential neighbourhood was not generally linked to access to the bar or bathhouse scene. As for women in general, especially in the Canadian context, downtown neighbourhoods provided affordable housing within a reasonable distance of transportation and services. Residential neighbourhoods with a higher number of women overall seemed to reflect women's increasing employment in the service sector of the labour market and their relocation from the suburbs to neighbourhoods closer to places of employment (Pratt and Hanson 1988; Rose and Villeneuve 1993). The findings in this case study support these conclusions. Economic and safety concerns dominated the reasons given for locational choice. While participants felt some comfort in knowing other lesbians lived in the area, they did not need to dominate or control a territory in the fashion suggested by Castells and Murphy (1983).

It is reasonable to conclude then that gender and class are of far more analytic weight than sexuality in understanding lesbians' residential locational choice. Histories of the evolution of gay and lesbian spaces tend to start with gay male spaces and then treat lesbian spaces as an extension, a reflection, a modification, or even a fine tuning. Instead, the evolution of lesbian spaces requires a separate study, with independently developed models that fit the distinct sites of lesbian communities.

This essay is based on my Master's research at the School of Urban and Regional Planning, Queen"s University, Kingston, Ontario. My thanks to Susan Fitzgibbon for her review of this paper and our spirited discussions.

NOTES

1. The usual caveat: I use the term "gay" when referring to men engaged in same-sex activity and the term "lesbian" when referring to women engaged in same-sex activities. When referring to both gays and lesbians as a group, I use the term "homosexuals" and the term "queer" to refer to all those sexualized minorities falling outside the heterosexual/homosexual categories, including "bisexuals," "transgendered," and "transsexual" individuals.
2. This research did not deal with the question of the meaning or existence of lesbian "community" in the sociological sense. For research pertaining to the evolution or existence of gay and lesbian "community," see Lee 1979; Levine 1979; Winters 1979; and Lockhard 1985.
3. The medical profession continued to speak about the homosexual as an individual case study while sociologists and others, with their focus on social organization and interaction, began to speak of "subcultures," communities, and finally "minorities." The subsequent reconceptualization of the gay deviant subculture as an "ethnic minority" had a profound influence on both mainstream perceptions and gay and lesbian politics (Humphreys 1979; Yearwood and Weinberg 1977).
4. With specific reference to Canadian sociological work see, for example, Crysdale and Beattie 1979; Foster 1972; Sacco 1988.
5. In some cases, the police in various cities saw homosexual bars as ways of containing deviance for surveillance and control purposes (Hoffman 1968).
6. The city selected was unique in two aspects. First, this city is considerably smaller than those examined in previous research. Secondly, the lesbian community had a considerably higher profile than the more modest and "subdued" gay male community, an unusual situation.
7. The participants in the study were adamant that the city itself and its identifying characteristics be kept confidential. All interviews were recorded and transcribed and copies were provided to the participants for review and comment. A draft copy of the thesis was also provided to participants for their review and suggestions.
8. Semi-structured interviews were done with key informants for each organization identified, a total of eleven interviews, lasting two to three hours each. Again, participants were asked to review the material.

WORKS CITED

Achilles, Nancy. "The Development of the Homosexual Bar as an Institution." In *Sexual Deviance*. Eds. John H. Gagnon and William Simon. New York: Harper and Row, 1967. 228–224.

Adam, Barry D. "A Social History of Gay Politics." In *Gay Men: The Sociology of Male Homosexuality*. Ed. Martin P. Levine. New York: Harper and Row, 1979. 165–181.

Adler, Sy and Brenner, Johanna. "Gender and Space: Lesbians and Gay Men in the City." *International Journal of Urban and Regional Research* 16.1 (1992): 24–34.

Becker, H.S. *Outsiders: Studies in the Sociology of Deviance*. New York: The Free Press, 1963.

Bergler, Edmund. *Homosexuality: Disease Way of Life?* New York: Hill and Wang, 1957.

Bieber, Irving et al. *Homosexuality: A Psychoanalytic Study*. New York: Basic Books, 1962.

Bouthillette, Anne-Marie. "Vancouver's Lesbians." In *Queers in Space: Communities/public Places/sites of Resistance*. Eds. Gordon Brent Ingram, Anne-Marie Bouthillette, and Yolanda Retter. Seattle: Bay Press, 1997. 213–232.

Cappon, Daniel. *Toward an Understanding of Homosexuality*. Englewood Cliffs, NJ: Prentice-Hall, 1965.

Castells, Manuel and Karen Murphy. "City and Culture: The San Francisco Experience" In *The City and the Grass Roots: A Cross Cultural Theory of Urban Social Movements*. London: Edward Arnold, 1983. 19–35.

Chenier. Elise. *Tough Ladies and Troublemakers: Toronto's Public Lesbian Community*. Masters Thesis, Department of History, Queens University, Kingston, Ontario, 1995.

Clinard, Marshal B. *The Sociology of Deviant Behaviour*. New York: Holt, Rinehart and Winston, 1995.

Cory, Donald Webster. *The Lesbian in America*. Citadel Press: New York, 1964.

Crysdale, Stewart and Christopher Beattie. *Sociology Canada: An Introductory Text*. Toronto: Butterworths, 1973.

Davis, Madeline D. and Kennedy, Elizabeth Lapousky. *Boots of Leather, Slippers of Gold: The History of a Lesbian Community*. New York: Penguin, 1993.

Dinitz, Simon, Russell R. Dynes, and Alfred C. Clarke. *Deviance: Studies in the Process of Stigmatization and Societal Reaction*. New York: Oxford University Press, 1967.

Epstein, Steven. "Gay Politics, Ethnic Identity: The Limits of Social Constructionism." *Socialist Review* 17 (1987): 9–54.

Foster, Marion. *A Not So Gay World: Homosexuality in Canada*. Toronto: McClelland and Stewart, 1972.

Gagnon, John H. and William Simon. eds. *Sexual Deviance*. New York: Harper and Row, 1967.

———. "Homosexuality: The Formulation of a Sociological Perspective." In *Deviance: Studies in the Process of Stigmatization and Societal Reaction*. Eds. Simon Dinitz,

Russel R. Dynes, and Alfred C. Clarke. New York: Oxford University Press, 1967. 342–349.

Hoffman, Martin. *The Gay World: Male Homosexuality and the Social Creation of Evil.* New York: Basic Books, 1968.

Holcomb, Briaval. "Geography and Urban Women." *Urban Geography* 7 (1986): 448.

Hooker, Evelyn. "The Adjustment of the Male Overt Homosexual." In *The Problem of Homosexuality in Modern Society.* Ed. Hendrik M. Ruitenbeek. New York: Dutton, 1963. 141–161.

Humphreys, Laud. "Exodus and Identity: The Emerging Gay Culture." In *Gay Men: The Sociology of Male Homosexuality.* Ed. Martin P. Levine. New York: Harper and Row, 1979. 134–147.

Ingram, Gordon Brent, Anne-Marie Bouthillette and Yolanda Retter, eds. *Queers in Space: Communities/public Places/sites of Resistance.* Seattle: Bay Press, 1997.

Kinsey, Alfred, W. B. Pomeroy and C. E. Martin. *Sexual Behaviour in the Human Male.* Philadelphia: W. B. Saunders, 1948

———. *Sexual Behaviour in the Human Female.* Philadelphia: W.B. Saunders, 1953.

Knopp, Lawrence and Lauria, Mickey. "Towards an Analysis of the Role of Gay Communities in the Urban Renaissance." *Urban Geography* 6 (1985): 152–69.

Knopp, Lawrence. "Social Theory, Social Movements and Public Policy: Recent Accomplishments of the Gay and Lesbian Communities in Minneapolis, Minnesota." *International Journal of Urban and Regional Research* 11 (1987): 243–61.

———. "Some Theoretical Implications of Gay Involvement in an Urban Land Market." *Political Geography Quarterly* 9 (1990): 333–380.

Lee, John Allen. "The Gay Connection." *Urban Life* 8.2 (July): 175–198.

Lemert, Edwin. *Human Deviance, Social Problems and Social Control.* Englewood Cliffs, NJ: Prentice-Hall, 1967.

Levine, Martin P., ed. *Gay Men: The Sociology of Male Homosexuality.* New York: Harper and Row, 1979.

Levitt Eugene E. and Albert D, Klassen. "Public Attitudes Towards Homosexuality." In *Gay Men: The Sociology of Male Homosexuality.* Ed. Martin P. Levine. New York: Harper and Row, 1974. 19–35.

Leznoff, Maurice and William A. Westley. "The Homosexual Community." In *The Problem of Homosexuality in Modern Society.* Ed. Hendrik M. Ruitenbeek. New York: Dutton, 1963. 184–196.

Lockard, Denyse. "The Lesbian Community: An Anthropological Approach. *Journal of Homosexuality* 11 (1985): 83–95.

Plummer, K. *Sexual Stigma: An Interactionist Account.* London: Routledge and Kegan Paul, 1975.

Pratt, Geraldine and Susan Hanson. "Gender, Class, and Space." In *Environment and Planning Dept.: Society and Space* 6 (1988): 15–35.

Rose, D. and P. Villeneuve. "Work, Labour Markets and Households in Transition." In *The Changing Social Geography of Canadian Cities.* Eds. L.S. Bourne, and D.F. Ley. Kingston: McGill-Queen's University Press, 1993. 153–174.

Rothenburg, Tamar. "And She Told Two Friends: Lesbians Creating Urban Social Space." In *Mapping Desire: Geographies of Sexuality.* Eds. David Bell and Gill Valentine. London: Routledge, 1995. 165–181.

Ruitenbeek, Hendrik M. ed. *The Problem of Homosexuality in Modern Society.* New York: Dutton, 1963.

Sacco, Vincent F. ed. *Deviance: Conformity and Control in Canadian Society.* Toronto: Prentice-Hall, 1988.

Socarides, Charles W. *Overt Homosexual.* New York: Grune and Stratton, 1968.

Valentine, Gill. "(Hetero)sexing Space: Lesbians Perceptions and Experiences of Everyday Places." *Environment and Planning Dept.: Society and Space* 11 (1993): 395–413.

———. "Negotiating and Managing Multiple Sexual Identities: Lesbian Time-space." *Transactions* 18 (1993): 237–248.

Warren, Carol A. B. "Women Among Men: Females in the Male Homosexual Community." In *Gay Men: The Sociology of Male Homosexuality.* Ed. Martin P. Levine. New York: Harper and Row, 1996. 222–238.

Weightman, Barbara. "Gay Bars as Private Places." *Landscape* 24 (1980): 9–16.

———. "Towards a Geography of the Gay Community." *Journal of Cultural Geography* 1 (1981): 106–112.

Winchester, H.P. and P.E. White. "The Location of Marginalised Groups in the Inner City." *Environment and Planning Dept.: Society and Space* 7 (1988): 37–54.

Winters, Chris. "The Social Identity of Evolving Neighbourhoods." *Landscape* 23 (1979): 8–14.

Yearwood, Lennox and Thomas S. Weinberg. "Black organizations, gay organizations: Sociological parallels." In *Gay Men: The Sociology of Male Homosexuality.* Ed. Martin P. Levine. New York: Harper and Row, 1977. 301–316.

APPENDIX A: PARTICIPANT ORGANIZATION CHARACTERISTICS

Organization	Lesbian	Women Only	Permanent Space	Temporary Space
1. IWW	no	yes	no	yes
2. GLBA	yes	no	yes	yes
3. GPD	no	no	no	yes
4. Sapphistry	yes	no	no	no
5. Music Festival	no	yes	no	yes
6. GLN	no	no	n/a	no
7. Meeting Place	yes	no	yes	no
8. WAC	no	yes	no	yes
9. Circles and Squares	yes	no	yes	no
10. Women's Books	no	yes	n/a	n/a
11. Mrs. Gaskill's	no	no	yes	no

Source: Author's research 1995–1996

APPENDIX B: SELECTED POPULATION CHARACTERISTICS

	Census Agglomeration	Northern Residential Area	Second Residential Area
	% of total	% of total	% of total
Percentage of total population			
Female	50.08	53.3	51.42
Household size (persons per household)			
1	23.85	40.83	34.12
2	33.92	34.02	38.09
3	17.5	13.46	13.09
4	24.64	11.68	14.68
Household type[1]			
Census family[2]	69.53	45.86	55.55
Non-family houshold[3]	29.74	53.55	43.25
2 or more census families	0.73	0.73	0.79
Census family breakdown			
Husband/wife	86.4	76.26	83.33
Single parent male	1.99	2.85	2.08
Single parent female	11.16	20.89	15.27
Marital Status			
Single	30.15	41.55	38.5
Married	53.8	31.7	41.42
Separated, widowed or divorced	16.76	26.9	20.07
Average income per household (20% sample)	47,101	43,196.5	40,113

1 Household—the basic division of private households in the census between family and non-family households.

2 Family household—is a household, which contains at least one census family. A census family consists of a now-married couple and common law couples (heterosexual and with or without children) and lone-parent families.

3 Non-family household—all households which are not census families.

Source: Statistics Canada, 1991 Cat. No. 95–344 (100% Data) and 95–345 (20% Data).

APPENDIX C: SELECTED DWELLING UNIT CHARACTERISTIC

	Census Agglomeration	Northern Residential Area	Second Residential Area
	% of total	% of total	% of total
Tenure			
% owned	59.35	31.26	52.99
% rented	40.64	68.74	47.01
Dwelling type (private)[1]			
% single	55.66	21.46	41.66
% multiple dwellings[2]	14.78	25.85	19.68
% Apartments >5 units	12.32	7.68	16.93
% Apartments <5 units	16.63	41.35	21.65
% other[3]	0.61	11.9	0.03
Age of dwelling			
% pre 1946	19.3	50.05	22.26
%1946 - 1970	34.52	26.07	53.96
% 1971 - 1985	31.76	17.93	21.83
% 1986 - 1991	14.41	5.93	1.59

1 Private Dwelling—refers to a separate set of living quarters with a private entrance from the outside or a common hall, lobby, vestibule or stairway inside a building and satisfies three conditions for year-round use.
2 Multiple dwelling—refers to a semi-detached, house, a row house and a duplex. These are listed separately in the census but are consolidated here.
3 Other—refers to other single-attached houses and moveable dwellings including trailers and mobile homes.

Source: Statistics Canada, 1991 Cat. No. 95–344 (100% Data) and 95–345 (20% Data).

wear it with pride: the fashions of toronto's pride parade and canadian queer identities

Andrea N. Frolic

Toronto's annual Lesbian, Gay, Bisexual, Transsexual and Transgender Pride Week is billed as "Canada's largest, most fun-filled and Queerest cultural festival" (festival press material). The festivities culminate in the Pride Parade on the last Sunday in June, the anniversary of the 1969 Stonewall Rebellion, which is heralded as the symbolic birth of the contemporary gay and lesbian rights movement. In 2000, over three-quarters of a million people converged around Church Street to watch and participate in this showcase of Canadian "queer culture."[1] To the uninitiated, it is a bewildering sight, a cross between a beauty pageant, a biker rally, a political march, a leather bar, a nudist camp, and a Mr. Universe contest. The pride it expresses is not egotism or haughtiness; it is more akin to an anti-assimilationist romp, a dance of joyful defiance. The parade is a corporeal map of the ideological and sexual terrain of the contemporary Canadian queer scene.[2] This photo essay attempts to read this map by focusing on the fashions of the parade and their various functions in the context of Toronto's Pride Week. Unpacking the diverse sexual and political strategies encoded in these fashions will also facilitate an appraisal of the notion of a Canadian "queer nation."

CONFRONTATION, ASSIMILATION, AND AMBIGUITY: THE HISTORY OF PRIDE PARADES IN NORTH AMERICA

According to Richard Herrell, confrontation was the primary strategy of early American gay and lesbian liberation efforts (231). The Pride parades of the 1970s aimed at overcoming the invisibility of this subculture and opposing mainstream heteronormative ideology.[3] The most visible and controversial factions of the subculture dominated these parades: leather men, drag queens, and butch lesbians.

Things changed in the mid-1980s as the AIDS crisis swept over the gay community and gay activists lobbied the media and medical institutions to help contain the epidemic and to find a cure. In order to evoke compassion in mainstream society for the victims of AIDS and to combat the homophobic backlash and hysteria that attended the initial outbreak, the "in your face" confrontational tactics of the preceding decade were largely dropped in favour of an assimilative approach. Rather than emphasizing sexual deviance, the community began to redefine itself as one based, not on acts of sex, but on acts of love. American Pride parades of this era highlighted similarities between the queer community and the mainstream, rather than showcasing deviant sexualities. Contingents of lesbian and gay sports leagues, clubs, professional associations, religious organizations, and support groups dominated these events. American Pride parades became, as one journalist lamented at the time, "rituals of normalcy," portraying the queer community as similar to the mainstream in everything except sexual behaviour, and evidence of this one exception was virtually erased from the Chicago Pride festivals of the 1980s (Herrell, 230–33, 235).

While a clear ideological shift from confrontation in the 1970s to assimilation in the 1980s may have marked some American Pride parades, Toronto's Pride celebrations were historically less politically homogeneous.[4] The first festivities were associated not with the Stonewall rebellion, but with a Canadian legislative landmark. They were held at the end of August to commemorate the August, 1969 federal decriminalization of homosexual acts for consenting adults over the age of twenty-one, when then-Justice Minister Pierre Trudeau uttered his famous "the state has no place in the bedrooms of the nation" statement. The Pride events of the early 1970s tended to be overtly political, as in 1974 when more than 100 people marched to the Ontario legislature in an effort to include sexual orientation in the Ontario Human Rights Code. No Pride events took place in Toronto from 1975 to 1980. Then, in 1981, the first legally incorporated Lesbian and Gay Pride Day was held in Toronto on Sunday, June 28, just three weeks after the Metro Toronto Police raided various bathhouses and arrested 400 men. In spite of the politically charged atmosphere that year, the day was billed as a nonconfrontational event, "an afternoon of fun and frolic." A confrontational agenda was revived, however, in the theme of the 1984 Pride Week: "We Are Everywhere: 150 Years of Faggots and Dykes." A more assimilative approach was evident in the 1986 Pride theme "Forward Together." This was also the first year in which the Pride program and logo focussed on AIDS. In 1987, sexual orientation was included in the Ontario Human Rights Code, prompting another assimilative Pride theme for that year: "Rightfully Proud."

Over the course of the 1990s, the political ideologies of Toronto's Pride festivals, as encapsulated in the Pride week themes, have varied. The Pride themes of the early 1990s were overtly confrontational ("By All Means Necessary"-1990; "Breaking the Silence"-1992; "Come Out"-1993). In celebration of the 25th anniversary of Stonewall, the 1994 parade Grand Marshals were drag kings and queens. A more assimilative approach was adopted in 1995 with the theme, "Remember, Celebrate, Make a Difference." The parade Grand Marshals that year were Jim Egan and Jack Nesbit, the gay couple from British Columbia who had won a spousal benefits ruling in the Supreme Court. Another assimilative legislative landmark was heralded in the 1996 Pride theme, "We Are Everyone's Family," which featured as Grand Marshals four lesbian couples, each of which had won the right to adopt their partner's children. Pride themes toward the turn of the century were more ambiguous ("Queer by Nature"-1997; "MegaPride"-1998; "One Pride Fits All"-1999; "Heroic Past, Proud Future"-2000) and could be read as assimilative, confrontational or apolitical. This political ambiguity is also reflected in the diverse fashions of millenial Pride parade participants.

IDENTITY, REPRESENTATION, AND FASHION

Diana Fuss's identification theory, outlined in her book *Identification Papers*, is a useful starting point for decoding the relationship between fashion and identity as it was reflected in the Pride parades of the late 1990s. Fuss operates within a psychoanalytic model, drawing on both Freud and Lacan. The influence of these theorists is apparent in her working definition of identification. She states that, "Identification is an embarrassingly ordinary process, a routine, habitual compensation for the everyday loss of our love-objects." Simply put, identification is "the detour through the other that defines a self" (1–2). Knowledge of the self is predicated on knowledge of the ever elusive other; thus, self-knowledge is perennially unstable and fraudulent, a psychic phantom. One must emphasize, however, that identification and identity are not synonymous. Identity is "identification come to light," the individual's conscious attempt to bring order to the chaos of the self, to put a face on the phantom (2). This face is not fixed, however, because it correlates to some extent with the fluctuating features of identification. As Fuss puts it, "Identity is continually compromised, imperiled ... even *embarrassed* by identification" (10, emphasis in original). She argues, further, that our understanding of politics and relationships might be radically altered if we recognized "that every identity claim ('I am not another') is based upon an identification ('I desire to be another')" (10).

Even more disconcerting is the question of representation. Fuss does not address this problem; however, building on her theoretical framework, representation may be conceptualized as the public face of identity. Identity-formation is a conscious but private production (the inner self), while representation is the well-packaged product an individual markets to the rest of the world (the public self). One key to successful social interaction is the representation of a coherent identity. Thus, one's public self is, by necessity, more stable than one's identity, although the details of one's representation do differ depending upon the context of an interaction, the relative power of the actors, etc. While representation may be less elastic than identity and less erratic than identification, it has its own pitfalls, hermeneutically speaking. An individual might interpret her own representation in one way, while an observer might interpret it completely differently. Thus, the relationships between identification, identity, and representation are reciprocal. Social interactions facilitated by representation can influence identity, which in turn may affect the identification process.

The vocabulary of representation is metaphoric and allusive, subtly hinting at the psychic mechanisms at its root. One primary mode of representation is fashion, which, as Malcolm Barnard writes, "represent[s] something like a border or a margin between a public, exterior persona and a private, interior identity" (173). While clothing has a pragmatic dimension, it is a particularly poignant mode of representation because it forms a diaphanous boundary between self and other. As Kaja Silverman argues, "Clothing and other kinds of ornamentation make the human body culturally visible ... clothing is a necessary condition of subjectivity ... in articulating the body, it simultaneously articulates the psyche" (qtd. in Steele, 186).

In his book *Fashion, Culture, and Identity,* Fred Davis explores how this particular mode of representation functions as a system of communication about the self. He argues that there are no fixed formulas for interpreting fashion, so precise meanings cannot be assigned. In his words:

> Perhaps [fashion] can best be viewed as an incipient or quasi-code, which, although it must necessarily draw on the conventional visual and tactile symbols of a culture, does so allusively, ambiguously, and inchoately, so that the meanings evoked by the combinations and permutations of the code's key terms (fabric, texture, colour, pattern, volume, silhouette, and occasion) are forever shifting or "in process." (5)

The source of the intentions that give meaning to fashion rest not with the designer or wearer or spectator exclusively. Rather, meaning is affixed to fashion through negotiations between these roles (Barnard, 31). Because of its allusive quality, it is difficult to get people to interpret the same garment in the same way. Interpretations vary markedly between persons of different classes, genders, ages, regions, ethnicities, and taste subcultures.

Fashion is also highly context dependent. As Davis says: "What some combination of clothes or a certain style 'means' will vary tremendously depending upon the identity of the wearer, the occasion, the place, the company and even something as vague and transient as the wearers' and the viewers' moods" (8). Fashion, as a mode of representation of the self, involves the intersection of psyche, corporeality, and culture; its meanings are entangled with the desires, fantasies, behaviours, social circumstances, politics, and aesthetics of both the wearer and the observer of fashion.

Fashion is a particularly revealing mode of representation in the queer community. Most other subcultures in Canada are based on ethnicity, language, religion, or geography and while in some cases "clothing," such as the hijab or turban, is important or even paramount, most rely just as much or more on other symbols, such as common foods, myths, or rituals to express their distinctiveness. The queer community, however, cuts across all nationalities, regions, faiths, classes, politics, and languages so other cultural metaphors do not unify its members. Rather, this diverse group is linked by sexual practices or gender identities that deviate in some way from the compulsory heterosexuality encoded in the discourses of mainstream society. Since it lacks other cohesive cultural metaphors, and the desires of the body are its focus, what is closest to the body—clothing and other forms of adornment—naturally becomes a locus of representation in this community.

THE FASHIONS OF PRIDE

Although the relationships between fashion, identity, and sexuality are enormously complex and subtle, an analysis of the fashions of the Pride parade may yield some insights into Canadian queer culture.[5] For the purposes of this essay, fashion is defined very broadly to include not only clothing, but also hairstyles, makeup, jewelry, and accessories. The aim of this analysis is not to assign precise meanings to Pride fashions. Indeed, such precision is impossible. Rather, by grouping the fashions into genres, their various possible meanings may be explored, producing general matrices of interpretation. Dividing them into six categories may elucidate the bewildering array of contemporary Pride fashions: Leather-lovers, Exhibitionists, Blenders, Gender-benders, Drag Kings and Queens, and Associates.[6] Of course, these categories are not mutually exclusive. Many styles fit into multiple categories, demonstrating the provisional nature of any fashion analysis and the complexity of queer identities.

Leather-lovers

Leather clothing has existed since before the Neolithic period. In the nineteenth century, leather became a fetish material, and in twentieth-century North America, it acquired associations with motorcycle gangs, cowboys, and sadomasochistic (S/M) sexual practices. By the 1950s, the motorcycle itself had accumulated several symbolic meanings. According to Valerie Steele, it had become a sexual symbol, a vehicle with "thrusting" pistons and a revving engine, which the rider "mounts" in order to be "transported" (176). For Daniel Harris, the gay leather subculture was spawned in part by the 1953 Marlon Brando cult film classic, *The Wild One*, in which the motorcycle was both a counter-cultural symbol (the embodiment of unfettered individuality and rebellion against social mores), and a symbol of the industrial economy. During the 1950s and 1960s, Harris argues that gay men gravitated towards motorcycle culture and its fashions as a way to "subvert the prevailing stereotypes of effeminate homosexuals by creating a hyper-masculine environment in which members could cultivate the machismo of their heterosexual heroes" (181). The "cult of leather" gradually replaced its emphasis on motorcycles (a mantle that has been taken up by the "Dykes on Bikes" who lead the Toronto Pride Parade), and leather itself became a way for gay men (and increasingly lesbian women) to identify themselves with others and to establish social and political networks (Harris, 183–4). Thus, in the words of Steele, "[a]lthough leather functions as an international sign for sadomasochism, it has also come to signify homosexuality" (157).

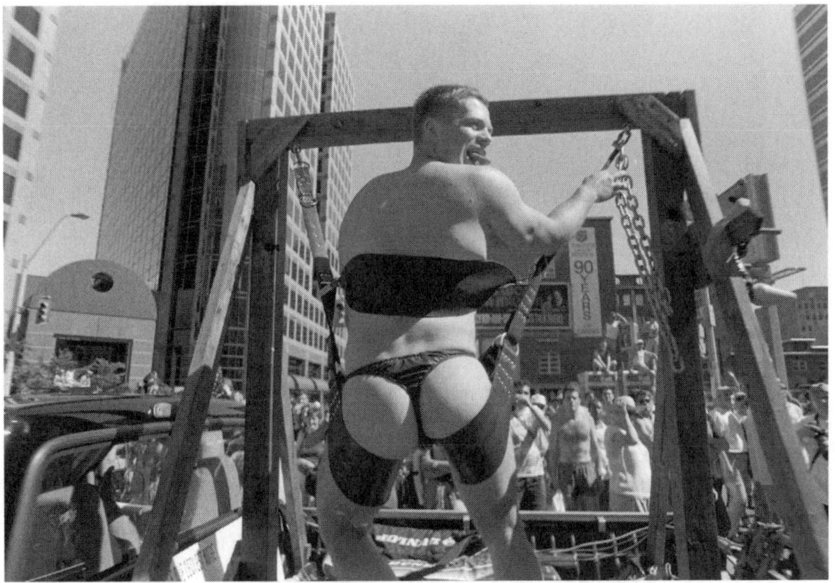

Figure 1.

Almost anywhere leather appears in our culture, from upholstery to saddles, it is charged with an aura of eroticism. "Nothing else feels like leather next to your skin," said fashion designer Donna Karan. "It's the ultimate sensuality!" (qtd. In Steele, 158). While elements of S/M and motorcycle styles have been incorporated into some *haute couture* (particularly the designs of Vivian Westwood, Gianni Versace, and Thierry Mugler) and have even trickled down into some mainstream fashions, Leather-lovers do not wear the soft, slinky outfits of the fashion runways. The leather of the Pride parade is explicitly fetishistic, including caps, chaps, harnesses, boots, vests, and corsets (see Figure 1).[7] The meanings of these head-turning fashions are bound up with Leather-lovers' constructions of desire and sexuality. Some parade participants in the late 1990s wore explicit indicators of S/M role-play, such as whips, paddles, collars, and masks.[8] Others encoded their sexual preferences in their fashions more discreetly. For example, by wearing handkerchiefs of different colours in various locations on their bodies, S/M practitioners signal their sexual preferences to potential partners.[9] Through either cryptic signs, like handkerchiefs, or obvious signals, like whips, the fashions of many Leather-lovers function to make public their "deviant" sexualities. Thus, Leather-lovers continue to embody a confrontational political strategy in contemporary parades. Their willingness to flaunt their social and sexual rebellion may account for the uneasiness they evoke in outsiders.

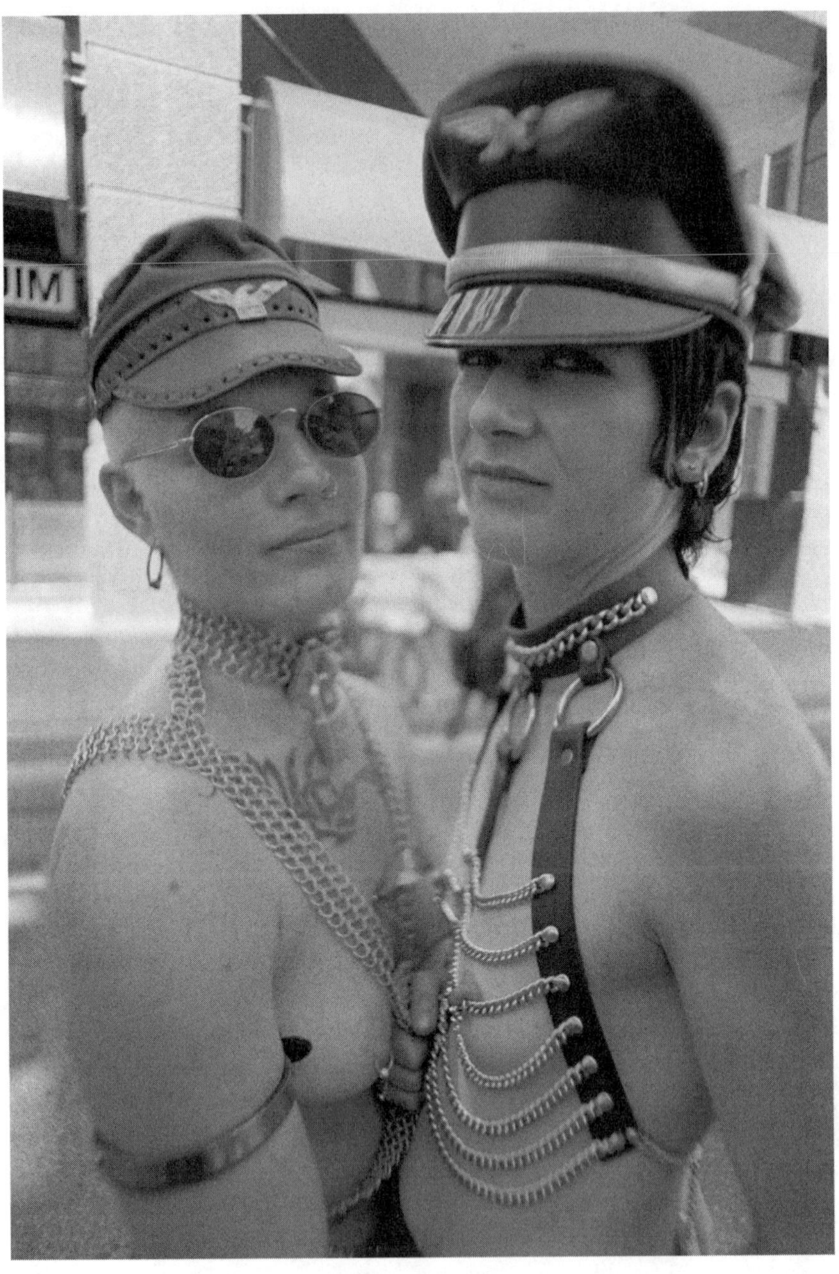

Figure 2.

Because S/M sexualities are predicated upon "top" and "bottom" role-playing, rather than heteronormative gender roles, Leather-lovers also challenge the queer community itself. They include some male-female pairings (see Figure 2), transgressing the conventional same-sex definition of "queer." Thus, leather fashions have come to signify a cluster of meanings, including: gay political liberation, unorthodox sexual practices, social rebellion, the masculinization of gay subculture, and the social networks that leather bars have historically facilitated within these communities (Harris, 183). The fashions of Leather-lovers function to both attract others inside the leather community (same sex *or* opposite sex), and to exclude outsiders, including effeminate gay men.

Exhibitionists

Another group whose attire (or more accurately, lack of attire) attracted attention in Pride parades of the late 1990s was the Exhibitionists. Unlike Leather-Lovers, however, the fashions and ideologies of Exhibitionists appear sharply divided along gender lines.

For male Exhibitionists, the purpose of clothing is not to cover the body, but to accentuate its contours. Most are topless or decked out in body-hugging T-shirts or tank tops, with cycle shorts, thongs or other apparel with a high "crotch consciousness" on the bottom (see Figure 3). While there are some slim and "beefcake" Exhibitionists, the vast majority conformed to the muscular, hairless physiques which came into vogue in the early 1980s when photographer Bruce Weber and fashion designer Calvin Klein collaborated to produce the first openly erotic men's underwear advertisements.[10] These ads depicted "god-like men clad only in their underwear; an affront to the Puritanism and homophobia of American society" (Steele, 129). Male exhibitionists are almost uniformly young, although a wide spectrum of ethnicities is represented. Reminiscent of Michelangelo's David, they simultaneously embody luxurious sensuality, strength and discipline, as this body type can only be achieved by spending hours in the gym.

The fashions of male Exhibitionists also expose two current trends in some quarters of gay culture. First, there is a revival of desire in the community after almost two decades of caution following the outbreak of the AIDS epidemic. Their revealing apparel courts lustful stares, teasing the libido of the viewer. Secondly, these fashions herald the gay cult of the sculpted body. While perhaps gay men were historically more body-conscious than most straight men, today there seems to be enormous pressure to conform to a hypermasculine body type, perhaps in part as a reaction against the stereotype of the effeminate gay man.[11]

In sharp contrast, it seems that female Exhibitionists bare all in defiance of mainstream society's impossible demands on women's bodies. They are typically topless, wearing ordinary shorts or jeans on the bottom. Very few conform to the current idealized female form. Rather, topless women of all shapes and sizes participate in the parade (See Figure 4). A broad spectrum of ages is also represented among female Exhibitionists, from teenager to middle-ager, although there tend to be more Caucasians than visible minorities. Their fashions (or lack thereof) might be interpreted as a celebration of women's real bodies, not the adolescent, liposuctioned and airbrushed versions depicted by popular media.

Their dress also takes aim at the prudery of mainstream society and the sexism of the law, which, up until February 1997, made going topless in public a crime for women in Ontario. On the whole, female Exhibitionists' fashion choices appear to be politically, rather than sexually or aesthetically, motivated.[12] Even if inviting desire is part of their agenda, it still has a political edge as they endeavour to rewrite the discourses of desire (predicated upon a particular body type) imposed on women by mainstream society. Female Exhibitionists have a defiant, righteous, and playful air about them, confident in their natural beauty and their right to dress, or undress, as they please. As Steele has noted: "[c]lothing itself is generally associated with power, and nakedness with its lack" (171). However, while the tactics encoded in the fashions of male and female Exhibitionists may be the inverse of one another (sensual vs. political; the glorification of the idealized male form vs. the vilification of the idealized female form), in both cases nakedness is donned as a mantle of power.

Blenders

Unlike Leather-lovers and Exhibitionists, Blenders do not court double takes or politely averted eyes.[13] Blenders are not visibly queer and thus blend into mainstream society. Female Blenders, commonly identified by the somewhat pejorative label "lipstick lesbians," wear conventional feminine fashions, including long hair, makeup, blouses, skirts or dresses. This attire theoretically enables the wearer to pass as straight. The same holds true for male Blenders who don mainstream masculine clothing in modest colours. For some gays and lesbians, blending might simply be a survival tactic—the proverbial path of least resistance. However, the politics of blending into the mainstream has been a site of contention within the queer community for many years. Some deplore blending, asserting that it depoliticizes homosexuality by portraying it as a lifestyle choice rather than a radical sexual and ideological

Figure 3.

Figure 4.

identity. Others embrace blending as a confrontational political strategy, arguing that by appearing conventional, Blenders challenge homophobic stereotypes and the compulsory heterosexuality associated with traditional gender roles and fashions.

The controversy surrounding the politics of blending may be rooted in the different values assigned to masculine and feminine appearances in mainstream culture. Within a heteronormative framework, feminine fashion positions women as the passive objects of the male gaze. According to Sue-Ellen Case, however, this was not the case for the femmes of the 1940s and 1950s. Using a psychoanalytic framework, Case highlights the performative nature of butch and femme fashions of that era. The butch donned male attire in order to possess (symbolically) the penis (and its attendant power and payoffs), with the intention of attracting other women. The femme adopted the compensatory attributes of womanliness, but in "playing up" her femininity to the butch (another woman), she revealed the masquerade of conventional female gender roles and liberated femininity from its heterosexual shackles. The posturings of the butch-femme aesthetic were always "acknowledged as roles, not biological birthrights, nor any other essentialist poses" (Case, 193–4). Thus, their fashion-performances challenged the conventional view of gender roles (and their associated heterosexual couplings) as "natural."[14]

Today, feminine lesbian fashions are largely detached from the butch-femme binary. Many female blenders don feminine attire to attract not butch lesbians but other lipstick lesbians, transgendered or transsexual lesbians. In some ways, this deployment of the feminine aesthetic is even more radical. Viewed through the lens of straight society, a stereotypical, feminine appearance functions primarily as a means of evoking male desire, but when traditional symbols of femininity are employed to attract another (conspicuous) female, the symbolic code of heterosexual desire is destabilized.

Since the time of the suffragettes, feminists have raised concerns about the negative impact conventional fashions may have on women's bodies, psyches, and political aspirations. Thus, despite their potential to challenge heterosexism, feminine lesbians are often criticized by other factions of the lesbian community who argue that mainstream feminine standards of beauty are constructed by and for men.[15] Because of the potential harm women may do to themselves in attempting to achieve this idealized female form, some argue that lesbians should not conform to these standards. As well, according to Carole-Anne Tyler, the "female female impersonation" of the lipstick lesbian tends to reify a particular type of femininity—namely white, Anglo, and bourgeois—excluding the feminine aesthetics of working-class women and women of colour (384).[16]

For gay men, the debate over the politics of blending is less contentious.

While some of the same arguments for and against blending could apply to both lesbian women and gay men, there seems to be less tension between gay identities and mainstream masculine fashion than there is between lesbian identities and mainstream feminine fashion. This may be due in part to gay men's pervasive influence in the fashion industry (Smith, D. 1–2). As well, less emphasis is placed on men's appearance in mainstream society, making the politics of blending less problematic for gay men.

Finally, it must be acknowledged that blending is an essentially fluid process because the ability to blend is so context dependent. Wearing the same fashions, one might either blend in or stick out, depending on the occasion, the setting, and the other people present. In addition, the wearer's attitude and accessories, in conjunction with a culture's codes and stereotypes, may transform separate straight-looking articles of clothing into an undeniably queer outfit. For example, many male Blenders wear traditional masculine attire while displaying their queerness through some detail of their appearances, particularly jewellery, body language, hair styles or even the "fit" of their clothing. The line between straight and queer appearances is constantly shifting and never definitive and it depends on the identities of the viewer and the wearer, as well as the circumstances. Blenders walk closer to this line than those whose fashions are explicitly queer.

The more radical factions of the community, who feel that all queers should be "out" in everyday life, will undoubtedly continue to criticize Blenders. Within the context of the Pride parade, however, Blenders' fashions combat homophobic and heterosexist stereotypes by revealing that, contrary to public perception, not all queers are queens and Leather-lovers. Blenders make it difficult to distinguish the boundary between the queer Pride participants and the straight supporters or tourists who come to watch this "exotic" spectacle. Ostensibly, Blenders' message to the mainstream is: If someone as normal looking as me can be queer, anyone can be queer.

Gender-benders

By manipulating the appearance of their bodies, gender-benders challenge mainstream assumptions about the link between biological sex, gender roles, and sexual orientation. In her autobiography, *Gender Outlaw,* Kate Bornstein, who describes herself as a transsexual lesbian, outlines the eight commandments of gender in our culture:

1. there are two and only two genders (male and female);
2. one's gender is invariant;
3. genitals are the essential sign of gender (vagina = female, penis = male);

4 any exceptions to the two-gender rule are not to be taken seriously (they are jokes, pathology, etc.);
5 there are no transfers from one gender to another except ceremonial ones (like masquerades);
6 everyone must be classified as one gender or another;
7 the male/female dichotomy is a natural one and,
8 membership in one gender or another is natural and innate (46–50).

These rules are rarely spelled out, but they are so deeply enmeshed in our social norms and rituals that they seem inherently true. Bornstein further asserts that once the culturally constructed commandments of gender are exposed, they can be defied. In her words:

> So there are rules to gender, but rules can be broken. On to the next secret of gender—gender can have ambiguity. There are many ways to transgress a prescribed gender code, depending upon the worldview of the person who's doing the transgressing: they range from preferring to be somewhat less than rigidly gendered, to preferring an entirely non-definable image. Achievement of these goals ranges from doing nothing, to maintaining several wardrobes, to full surgical transformation. (51)

Recognizing the ambiguity of gender challenges compulsory heterosexuality, premised as it is on the existence of a binary gender system. One more gender rule exists that is not explicitly identified by Bornstein. This rule posits that the two genders are opposite but complementary, thus personal and sexual fulfillment can be found only in heterosexual relationships. Without a rigidly defined gender system the whole facade of heterosexual normativity crumbles. Therefore, when Gender-benders challenge the cultural constructions of masculine and feminine, they also destabilize heterosexuality as a compulsory (and "natural") sexual practice.[17]

Fashion is a powerful weapon in the armory of Gender-benders. Susan Kaiser has shown that we first learn to identify gender through clothing. Children, as young as two years of age, use clothing to classify people according to conventional rules of gender years before they understand the biological differences between the sexes (56). Through their fashions, Gender-benders consciously challenge and subvert gender cues. They reveal that gender is culturally constructed and inherently ambiguous, and, thereby, open to deconstruction, manipulation, and play. The Gender-benders of the Pride parade encompass two subgroups: neo-butch lesbians, and transsexual and transgendered people.

Neo-butches

Like Exhibitionists, Gender-benders tend to be divided along gender lines. The majority of female Gender-benders may be categorized as Neo-butches. In the context of the Pride parade, a typical Neo-butch sports black lace-up boots or sneakers, cut-off jeans, a black bra or T-shirt or tank top, and cropped hair. Like their predecessors of the 1940s and 1950s, Neo-butch lesbians reject traditional feminine apparel. However, these women are also the intellectual, political, and sexual heirs of the second wave of feminism and the fashion heirs of 1970s punk culture. Their aggressive, unaesthetic fashions signify a radical ideology, rather than a preference for a specific kind of sexual practice. Their attire symbolizes their renunciation of society's historical imagination of women as dependent, chaste, vain, and fragile by connoting attributes of power, independence, sexual prowess, freedom, and invulnerability—traditionally masculine qualities.

Neo-butch fashions are not usually about trying to pass as a man or rejecting the female self. As Steele observes: "It is not that women want a penis, but that, like men, they want the power that patriarchal society has attributed to the phallus, and that is symbolized by phallic clothing" (184). While the articles of clothing themselves might be masculine, they are often worn in a manner that emphasizes the female contours of the body, particularly the hips, breasts, and backside. They function to attract the gaze of other women, who may or may not be Neo-butches themselves.

Most women today wear unisex clothing for their function and comfort. In the Pride parade, Neo-butch fashions are gender bending because they are part of a conscious strategy to subvert the customary semiotics of femininity. As June Reich points out: "Once the split between anatomy and the semiotic is recognized in the process of interpretation—the economy of desire for an Other does not have to follow a heterosexist matrix" (264). The fashions of the Neo-butch depict an alternative femininity, one that enshrines the subjectivity and autonomy of the wearer and which is liberated from heteronormative discourse.

Transsexual and Transgendered People

Transsexuals are conventionally defined as individuals whose gender has been changed through sex re-assignment surgery. Transgendered people, sometimes called non-operative transsexuals, are individuals who possess the genitals of one gender, while living out their lives (or portions of their lives) as the other gender. With this in mind, one might guess that transsexual and transgendered people generally endeavour *not* to stand out in the Pride parade (see Figure 5). Both transsexual and transgendered people typically wear fashions that allow them to pass as their chosen gender in everyday

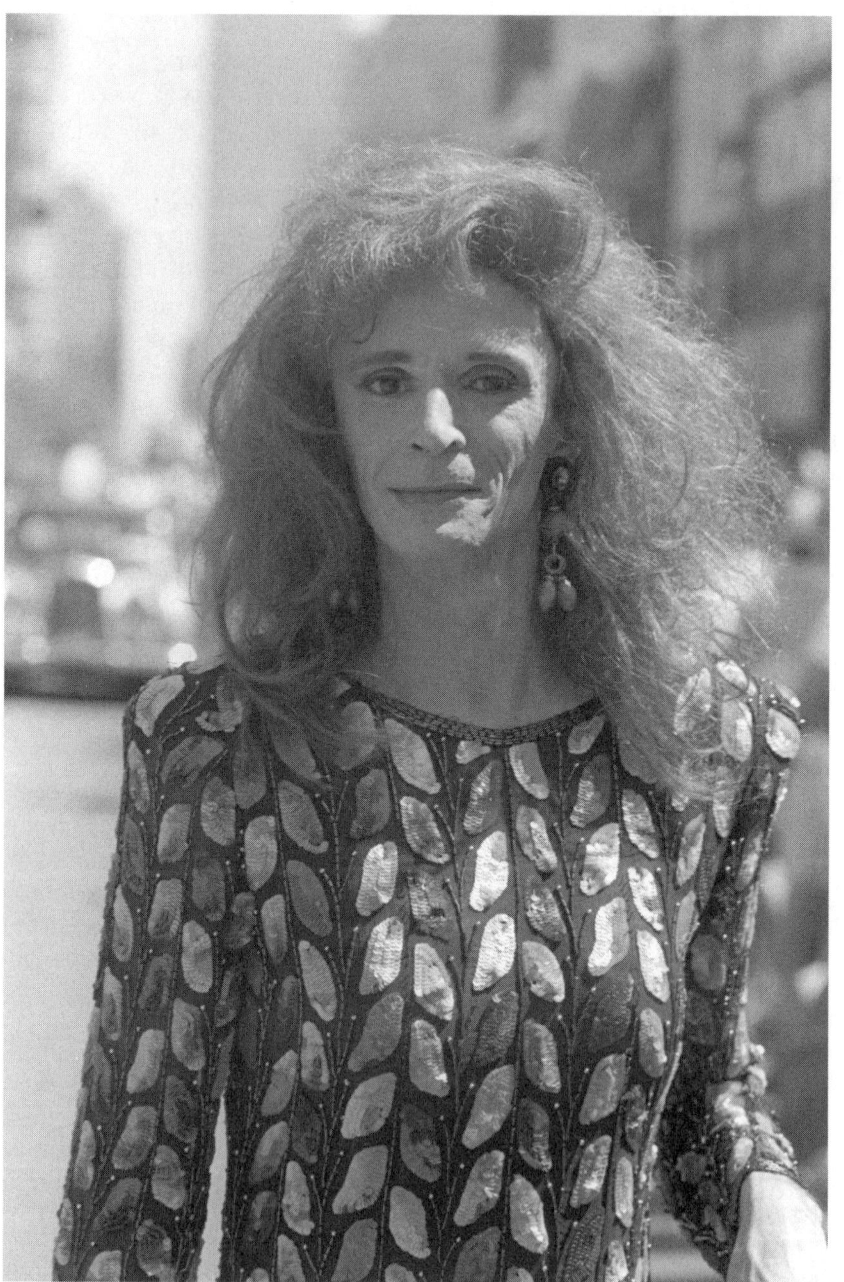

Figure 5.

encounters. In fact, they may be the quintessential Blenders. In the context of the Toronto Pride Parade, however, some transsexuals and transgendered people flaunt their gender-bending identities, perhaps because it is a relatively safe environment to do so. Some consciously challenge the relative invisibility of transsexual and transgendered people by boldly proclaiming their transgressive gender tactics. One transgendered participant in the 1996 Pride parade wore a T-shirt proclaiming, "I've become my mother!"

Some members of the queer community are ambivalent about the extreme gender-bending strategies of transsexual and transgendered people. Reich, for example, argues that transsexuality "works to stabilize the old sex/gender system by insisting on the dominant correspondence between gendered desire and biological sex" (260). However, even the stereotypical transsexual who feels "like a woman trapped in a man's body" transgresses Bornstein's gender commandment number eight: that membership in one gender or another is natural and [biologically] innate. As well, many transsexuals, like Kate Bornstein, are gay or lesbian identified post-transformation. Thus, it is difficult to determine how different a surgically constructed penis (or vagina) is from Reich's "genderfucking" dildo, on an ontological level.

Transsexuals and transgendered people are also accused by some of trafficking in traditional gender stereotypes, reifying our culture's rigid demarcation between male and female attributes and appearances (Steele, 189). This argument is rather flimsy as their successful deployment of gender stereotypes implicitly detaches these attributes from a particular sex. Transsexual and transgendered people are living proof that one's gender is not invariant, that genitals are not the essential sign of gender, and that membership in one gender or another is not natural or inherent. By highlighting the fluidity, performativity, and ambiguity of gender, transsexual and transgendered people challenge not only heterosexuality, but also sexual orientation as a definitive category. After all, if male/masculine and female/feminine are only provisional categories, so are lesbian, gay, bisexual, and even transsexual and transgendered.

Drag Queens and Kings

Daniel Harris argues in *The Rise and Fall of Gay Culture in America* that transsexual/transgendered people and drag queens and kings are entirely dissimilar, both aesthetically and psychologically. The former generally prefer unobtrusive clothing that blends and is unlikely to draw attention to the imperfections of their "disguises." The stylistic ideal of the drag queen, however, is "screaming vulgarity": the "drag queen doesn't flee from his gender but actually incorporates it into his costume. Nor does he fear disclosure as the transvestite does; he invites it" (203–4). The instant recognizability of the drag queen is due in part to a hangover of the exaggerated styles, shimmering fabrics, loud colours, and stylized shapes of the vaudeville stage, where drag was a standard in the early part of the twentieth century. This stage quality is evident in the Las Vegas showgirl bikini and headpiece in Figure 6. The nostalgic quality of many contemporary drag fashions also stems from the fact that, in Harris's words: "In all but the most formal contexts, the distinctions in clothing between the sexes have become so amorphous, so ill defined, that it is almost impossible to do drag of contemporary women's daily wear" (208).

For this reason, drag kings are often more difficult to recognize than drag queens because so much masculine clothing has crossed over into mainstream female apparel. To be recognized in drag, a woman must wear specialized male clothing, such as a uniform, or formal attire, or imitate a male celebrity. Similarly, drag queens often resort to sporting feminine fashions worn by women in ceremonial or performative contexts where the differences between the sexes are more clearly demarcated, such as weddings, beauty pageants, proms, and debutante balls. Harris observes that the androgynous fashions of today are far more transgressive in their blurring of gender boundaries than contemporary drag, which is regressive: "The sartorial prison has already been unlocked. We have escaped it. Drag knocks to be let back in" (209).

While this "nostalgic drag," with its exaggerated femininity/masculinity, may not be transgressive in its deployment of conventional gender cues, it may be subversive on another level. Drag is imbued with irony and "camp." According to Susan Sontag, camp is a dual sensibility that vacillates "between the thing as meaning something, anything, and the thing as pure artifice" (57). Camp is particularly evident when drag queens imitate celebrity icons such Lucille Ball, Mae West, and the Royal family. If all it takes to be recognized as the Queen of England is a frumpy dress, a crown, a pair of white gloves, and a back-handed wave, this performance calls into question the substantiality and stability of the identity of the real Queen. The unspoken challenge of nostalgic drag fashion is: "If I woke up a man, and I am the Queen this afternoon, what will I be tonight? What is the real me, the essential self?" As one queen puts it, in Rosamond Norbury and Bill Richardson's *Guy to Goddess: An Intimate Look at Drag Queens*, "We [queens are] cousins to clowns. We shake things up. We hide our surface selves with makeup, and let what's beneath come out. In drag, I feel like I'm something more than myself" (94). Through imitation and parody, drag queens and kings disrupt any notion of a real or fixed identity. They reveal that all identities are constructed, and therefore changeable. The public self is ever and always a representation, persona or

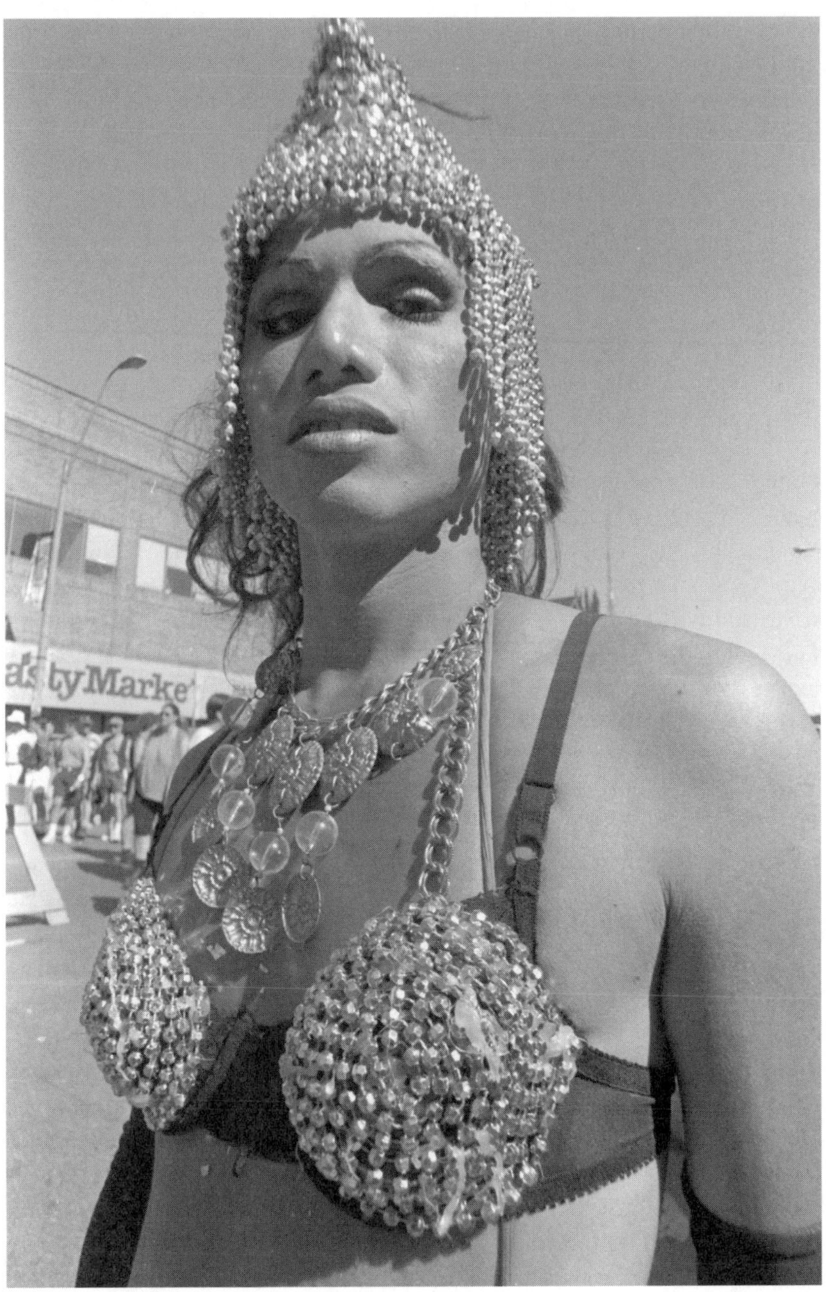

Figure 6.

role. On their bodies, queens and kings write the mantra of post-modernism: nothing is essential, all is provisional, illusive, an act (including the binary gender roles they perform). It is this admission and challenge that gives drag queens and kings their power to entertain and to horrify.

Another ideological undercurrent was visible in some of the drag fashions of Toronto's Pride Parades in the 1990s. According to Harris, after Stonewall, "Drag was embraced by large sectors of the gay community as the ceremonial costume of the new militant homosexual, and thus the uniform of the burgeoning gay rights movement" and the "flaming assertiveness of this quasi-militaristic figure ironically began to masculinize a hyperfeminine aesthetic." Furthermore, Harris asserts that the politicizing of drag and the masculinization of gay culture during the 1970s ultimately led to a disowning of the effeminate qualities of historical drag. At this time, queens began to display more masculine traits, thus leading to a bizarre hybrid: half-transvestite, half man (208–212). In "rough drag" a queen may sport traditional feminine attire along with a full facial beard. Rough drag often performs a wicked dissection of heterosexual tastes by donning the trashy fashions of suburban housewives and trailer park girls. By literally airing the dirty laundry (and fashion *faux pas*) of the mainstream, this type of drag functions as one of the weapons in the modern homosexual's arsenal of resistance against homophobia. In Harris' words: "The aesthetic of drag has thus come full circle, so that the traditional spectator of drag, the heterosexual, becomes its new subject, and the drag queen herself becomes the source of the 'gaze' " (214).

While Harris implies that rough drag has almost entirely displaced nostalgic drag in contemporary American queer celebrations, this was not the case in the Toronto Pride parades of the late 1990s, where both were present. The co-existence of these two forms of drag demonstrates the ideological and sexual diversity of the Canadian queer scene. Tyler argues that the "denigration of [nostalgic] drag queens in gay culture may be a rejection of the heterosexist stereotype of the effeminate invert, who is contrasted with the 'real thing,' the gay-identified masculine man, but it also may be a misogynist rejection of the feminine" (372). Rough drag may indeed reify masculinity and the binary gender system, as there is never any question of the "real" gender of the wearer. However, while rough drag may be "in bed" with the mainstream's views of gender, its concomitant excoriation of the tastes and prejudices of the straight world are definitely confrontational. Nostalgic drag, while reinforcing some gender stereotypes, is also confrontational in its own way, highlighting the performativity of all self-representations. Thus, the political strategies of both forms of drag are somewhat ambiguous.

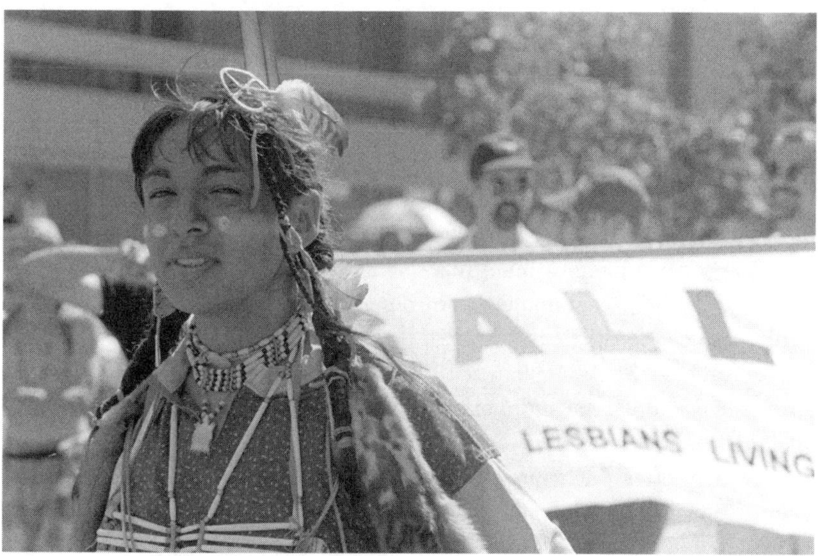

Figure 7.

The Associates

The fashions of Associates inevitably overlap with the other four categories. However, their distinguishing feature is their association with groups in the queer community or broader society, including religious, ethnic, recreational, support, professional, and political organizations. Typically, T-shirts, placards or banners announce their affiliations. Many employ the traditional symbols of the community—black and pink triangles, red ribbons and rainbow flags—in their logos. A uniform, like a choir robe, may also proclaim membership.

In the Pride parades of the late 1990s, Associates with confrontational *and* assimilative agendas were represented in almost equal numbers. Corporate queers in suits followed hard on the heels of left-wing activists carrying a model of the head of Mike Harris (the conservative premier of Ontario) on a platter. Sports teams and churches, whose presence had a normalizing effect on the parades of the 1980s, walked in tandem with groups lobbying for legislative changes. While politics remains a priority for some members of the queer community, it is apparently not the *forte* of most Associates at the turn of the millennium. Instead, many prefer to focus on their own recreational interests such as swimming, clubbing, and music.

This category was not only politically and socially varied but also racially and ethnically diverse. While most visible minorities in the Pride parades fit into other fashion categories, some drew particular attention to their ethnicity through their association with groups representing their segment of the population. These Associates portrayed the intersection of their ethnic and queer identities in a variety of ways. While some sported mainstream fashions (perhaps out of a desire to minimize their ethnic distinctiveness), others highlighted their differences, expressing resistance to cultural assimilation by donning ethnic attire (See Figure 7). Still, others wore unique Pride apparel which was neither mainstream nor exclusively ethnic, signaling perhaps an abandonment of the ethnic/Western binary in order to forge an alternative, hybrid sexual and cultural identity of their own.

Collectively, the Associates demonstrate that queers are everywhere—in all regions, professions, religions, political parties, and ethnic subcultures—and that they seek fellowship with other like-minded people. However, they also overtly betray the heterogeneity of queer "culture," which is in fact a conglomeration of myriad micro-communities with disparate agendas.

UNDRESSING THE CANADIAN QUEER COMMUNITY

As this analysis demonstrates, multiple political and sexual identities were represented in the fashions of Toronto's Pride Parade in the late 1990s. The overtly confrontational factions (namely, Gender-benders, Leather-lovers, Drag Queens and Kings, and Exhibitionists) visually dominated the landscape of these parades. Although assimilative tactics by nature do not garner as much attention, Blenders and Associates made up for their unobtrusiveness through sheer volume. The deployment of both strategies in these parades perhaps demonstrates the ambivalent relation queers have to mainstream Canadian society at the turn of the millennium. While several legislative policies and rulings in the 1990s provided gay and lesbian couples with some of the protections and rights enjoyed by heterosexual couples, queer people, particularly those who are non-monogamous, are still marginalized politically and socially. Thus, some Pride parade participants aimed to provoke the mainstream with in-your-face tactics, while others preferred to emphasize the similarities between themselves and their straight neighbours.

Assimilation vs. confrontation was not the only controversy inscribed on the bodies of Pride parade participants. Some Pride fashions also revealed a theoretical debate between identity politics and Queer politics. Advocates of identity politics believe certain aspects of a person's identity, particularly sexual orientation, are fixed—some would even say innate. Thus, people do not choose to be gay/lesbian/bisexual/transsexual/transgendered; they are either born this way or their orientation is set early in life through a combination of biology and socialization. Some activists use this rationale to combat homophobia and heterosexism, arguing that queer people should not be discriminated against because their sexual orientation is "not their fault." Many supporters of identity politics, including many Associates, seem to advocate creating a distinct queer community, while simultaneously embracing the distinct niches (gay, lesbian, transsexual, transgendered, S/M, bisexual, etc.) within it.[18]

In contrast, those who support Queer politics argue that people *have* identities, that is, identities are possessed by people, and therefore can be chosen, manipulated and discarded at will, rather than *are* identities, which implies that identities are innate and fixed. According to Rosanne Kennedy, Queer ideology:

> . . . rejects the notion of a gay or lesbian identity because identities inadvertently support the binary logic of compulsory heterosexuality; in opposition to a binary logic of homosexuality/heterosexuality, queer emphasises that which disturbs the complacency of the opposition itself. Queer shifts the focus from sexual identity to sexual performativity, and claims that queers are everywhere rather than on the margins. . . . Queer should disturb all sexual boundaries and create sexual mayhem, so that any individual may occupy or perform any sexual or gender identity, rather than have a true identity; in this way, queer undermines the very notion of a truth of sexuality. (139–140)

The Pride fashions of Gender-benders, and to some extent drag queens and kings, are corporeal representations of Queer politics. Queer rhetoric embraces postmodern discourse regarding the transience, fluidity, and performativity of all signs, including identities. Thus, Queer advocates employ labels such as lesbian and gay only provisionally. They consciously subvert these designations in order to upset the mainstream belief in the innateness of gender, sexual orientation and other modes of identification. In a Queer world, people would be free to don, alter, and cast-off selves as easily as they do clothes because there is no "real" self, only performances of self.

The assimilation/confrontation and identity/Queer politics debates will no doubt continue to rage in the fashions of Pride parades as well as the pages of academic books for years to come. The amazing variety of Pride fashions reflects the community's willingness over the past three decades to embrace an increasingly diverse population. The message written on the collective bodies of parade participants is: "In this community, anything goes: anonymity or celebrity, monogamy or promiscuity, traditional gender roles or gender bending, the political or the sensual." The official rhetoric surrounding Toronto's Pride festival has followed suit, advocating a discourse of heterogeneity. This was evident in the theme of the 1996 Pride Week: "We are Everyone's Family."

In Toronto's official Pride *Guide,* this theme was interpreted as reflecting "in a non-political way, the fact we come from all racial, cultural, linguistic, and religious backgrounds. It is because we encompass the diversity of families in this nation that *we truly are Everyone's Family."* In other words, queers are fundamentally different among themselves, and, therefore, the queer community mirrors mainstream Canadian society in its diversity.

While the discourse of heterogeneity is nice in theory, in practice it does not always work.[19] Tensions bubble beneath the festive surfaces of Pride parades. The contradictory discourses embodied in the fashions of Pride participants are never actually negotiated. Rather, the parades are comprised of contiguous components. Women and men rarely walk shoulder to shoulder in the parades, unless they are part of a political or recreational organization. Gender-benders, Exhibitionists, Leather-lovers, Drag Queens and Kings, Blenders, and Associates all tend to travel along the parade route in discrete groups, rather than in an integrated mass. It is debatable whether the emotional and ideological climate is one of mutual acceptance, or merely mutual tolerance for the span of a few hours, for the sake of the show. In 1996, a Dyke March was added to the schedule of annual Pride Week festivities. Presumably women would not take to the streets independently if they felt their political and ideological needs were adequately met in the Pride Parade.

If the Pride parades of the 1990s tell us anything about Canadian queer culture, it is that it is not a unified culture at all. In some measure it is like Benedict Anderson's "imagined community." Participants obviously feel that they "belong" in the Pride parade; however there are no obvious practices, objects, or ideologies that unite them into a community. Each individual identifies with one or more particular micro-community (the S/M community, the lesbian-feminist community, etc.), imagined as a piece of a larger, amorphous whole. These micro-communities have their own distinct politics, tastes, and relationships, and exist quite independently of one another. As the official Pride Toronto Website touts, Pride week "is a vital political statement for our *communities,* with more than three quarters of a million people coming together to celebrate *individuality, diversity, and freedom of sexual expression"* (emphasis mine). This slogan indicates that there is in fact no one "queer community" but many communities, and Pride week is really not about queer solidarity at all. It is a festival of personal autonomy.

In times of crisis, these micro-communities can effectively work together, as they did at the outset of the AIDS crisis, but their differences never dissolve. Once the crisis is past, they migrate happily back into their separate corners. "Queer culture" is simply a convenient label for a nebulous, expansive, organic collection of subcultures that can never be wholly defined or delineated. It exists as a concept in our collective imaginations, but not as a tangible reality.

This radically fragmented portrait of the Canadian queer community raises some disconcerting questions. For instance, if "we are everyone's family," is there anyone we don't include? By including heterosexual S/M and bisexual subcultures, same-sex sexual practices are no longer the defining feature of this imagined community. So what is? Who can rightly call themselves queer? When pushed to define "queer," people tend to begin in the negative: "queer is not straight, queer is not mainstream." Come to think of it, it's a lot like asking someone to define what it means to be Canadian; inevitably the initial answer is "not American."

This analogy between the queer community's identity crisis and that of Canadian society in general is not so far-fetched. Canada is also an imagined community of sorts, with its own menagerie of linguistic, religious, political, and cultural micro-communities. Canadian nationalism is currently imperiled by many forces: Quebec nationalism, American cultural domination, economic globalization, and—as witnessed by the results of the 1997 federal election—regionalism. Arguably the only thing all Canadians share is a protracted quest for a coherent national identity.

Predictably, there is very little in Toronto's Pride Parade that is distinctly Canadian, aside from its heterogeneous quality and the occasional reference to specific Canadian political figures or policies. In fact, the parade bears a striking resemblance to Herrell's description of Chicago's Pride Parades.[20] Perhaps the Canadian nation and the Canadian queer community are on parallel tracks. Their survival requires more than showy, but superficial, signs of solidarity. Canada's unity crisis will not be resolved through the vacuous flag waving and fireworks of Canada Day. In the same way, Canadian queers need more than annual parades to be a nation.

NOTES

1. In this essay, I use the word "queer" as a general term encompassing the entire spectrum of the contemporary community, including lesbian, gay, bisexual, transsexual, and transgendered people. In the paper's conclusion, where it is assigned a particular ideological meaning, Queer is capitalized.
2. I acknowledge that the Toronto Pride Parade does not encompass the whole spectrum of Canadian queer culture. For example, the length of the parade route, the pace, and the long hours in the hot sun prohibit many disabled and elderly people from participating in the parade. I use the parade only as a general gauge, not as a definitive representation of the entire community.
3. Confrontation was apparently a cross-border strategy in the 1970s as some speakers generated controversy at the 1978 Gaydays celebration in Toronto by supporting intergenerational sex and S/M ("Pride Toronto" website).

4. This brief history of Toronto's Pride Week is drawn from the official "Pride Toronto" website (www.pridetoronto.com/weekhistory) and the Canadian Lesbian & Gay Archives.
5. Keeping in mind the context-dependency of fashion, I acknowledge the fashions of the Pride Parade are unique and not necessarily representative of the everyday wear of most queers. On Pride Day, the community puts itself on display. Thus, it is a great opportunity for analyzing the relationship between queer fashions and ideologies.
6. Special thanks to A. Noack for her contributions to the Leather-lovers, Blenders, and Gender-benders sections.
7. Patrick Wey (www.patrickwey.com) took all of the photographs at the 1996 Pride Parade, a public event; a place to see and be seen. Many participants carried cameras or video recorders. The majority of the photographs here were taken with the knowledge and consent of the subjects. I have not included pictures of people who objected to being photographed.
8. Daniel Harris argues, however, that much of the sting has been taken out of the gay leather community since its inception. Through the 1970s and 1980s the leather community sanitized itself of its violent, counter-cultural elements by casting S/M role play as an expression of individuality, freedom, and sexual and emotional fulfilment, largely setting aside the traditional S/M narrative of dominance and submission (Harris, 197).
9. For example, a lavender handkerchief worn on the right side of the body indicates a bottom or submissive who enjoys group scenes. For more information on men's and women's handkerchief codes, see the book *Coming to Power* produced by the California-based lesbian S/M organisation SAMOIS.
10. The undershirt was historically associated with working-class men. Thus the garment came to connote virility, especially since it also delineated the musculature of the male torso (Steele, 128).
11. However, this trend, like so many in the queer community, is crossing over to the mainstream. Witness the increasing popularity of bodybuilding and the prevalence of "buffed" male bodies in popular culture.
12. Their scanty fashions also highlight how the environment influences fashion. On Pride Day 1996, when these pictures were taken, it was over 30 degrees Celsius, prompting some women to take off their shirts in an effort to keep cool.
13. The use of the term Blenders in this context is not intended to connote any value judgment; it is simply the most accurate way to describe this group in relation to the other parade participants.
14. Recent accounts of the butch-femme subculture have also indicated that the choice between butch and femme may have been closely linked to preferred sexual practices. For a historical discussion of butch-femme culture, see Lillian Faderman's *Odd Girls and Twilight Lovers.* For anecdotal accounts of lesbian butch-femme relations, see Joan Nestle's *A Restricted Country* and Leslie Feinberg's *Stone Butch Blues.*

15. This political rejection of normative feminine beauty may partially explain the appearance and acceptance of a range of body sizes and shapes within lesbian subculture.
16. Debates surrounding the politics of blending for lesbian women were fuelled by the rise of 'lesbian chic' in popular culture in the late 1990s. While some welcomed the attention lavished on lesbian women, others argued that the mainstream media only represented a small segment of the lesbian community: those who conform, at least partially, to traditional feminine standards of beauty.
17. June Reich calls performances which foreground the gap between sex and gender "genderfuck": "the effect of unstable signifying practices in a libidinal economy of multiple sexualities" (Reich: 264).
18. This is similar to the racial equality movement that advocates equity for all 'people of colour,' and yet conceptualizes individuals as members of distinct ethnic groups.
19. Witness the demise of the organization Queer Nation, which virtually collapsed under the weight of its own diversity.
20. The influence of America is confirmed by the fact that Toronto's Pride week no longer marks the anniversary of a Canadian event (as it did at its inception), but an American event, the Stonewall Rebellion.

WORKS CITED

Anderson, Benedict. *Imagined Communities: Reflections On the Origin and Spread of Nationalism.* 2nd ed. London: Verso, 1991.

Barnard, Malcolm. *Fashion as Communication.* New York: Routledge, 1996.

Bornstein, Kate. *Gender Outlaw: On Men, Women and the Rest of Us.* New York: Routledge, 1994.

Case, Sue-Ellen. "Toward a Butch-Femme Aesthetic." In *Camp: Queer Aesthetics and the Performing Subject.* Ed. Fabio Cleto. Ann Arbor, MI: University of Michigan Press, 1999. 185–199.

Davis, Fred. *Fashion, Culture, and Identity.* Chicago: University of Chicago Press, 1992.

Faderman, Lillian. *Odd Girls and Twilight Lovers.* New York: Columbia University Press, 1991.

Feinberg, Leslie. *Stone Butch Blues.* Ithaca, NY: Firebrand Books, 1993.

Fuss, Diana. *Identification Papers.* New York: Routledge, 1995.

Harris, Daniel. *The Rise and Fall of Gay Culture.* New York: Hyperion, 1997.

Herrell, Richard K. "The Symbolic Strategies of Chicago's Gay and Lesbian Pride Day Parade." In *Gay Culture in America.* Boston: Beacon Press, 1992. 239–42.

Kaiser, Susan B. *The Social Psychology of Clothing.* New York: Macmillan, 1990.

Kennedy, Rosanne. "The Gorgeous Lesbian in LA Law: The Present Absence?" *The Good, the Bad and the Gorgeous: Popular Culture's Romance With Lesbianism.* London: Pandora, 1994. 132–141.

Nestle, Joan. *A Restricted Country*. Ithaca, NY: Firebrand Books, 1987.

Norbury, Rosamond and Bill Richardson. *Guy to Goddess: An Intimate Look at Drag Queens*. Vancouver: Whitecap Books, 1994.

Reich, June L. "Genderfuck: The Law of the Dildo." In *Camp: Queer Aesthetics and the Performing Subject*. Ed. Fabio Cleto. Ann Arbor, MI: University of Michigan Press, 1999. 237–254.

Smith, Leslie. "Not So Strange Bedfellows." *The Globe and Mail* (January 9, 1997), D 1–2.

Sontag, Susan. "Notes on "Camp." In *Camp: Queer Aesthetics and the Performing Subject*. Ed. Fabio Cleto. Ann Arbor, MI: University of Michigan Press, 1999. 53–65.

Steele, Valerie. *Fetish: Fashion, Sex, and Power*. New York: Oxford University Press, 1996.

The Lesbian, Gay, Bisexual, Transsexual, Transgender Pride Committee of Toronto. "Pride Guide '96: Toronto Edition." Toronto: Alternate Sources, 1996.

The Lesbian, Gay, Bisexual, Transsexual, Transgender Pride Committee of Toronto. Pride Toronto. 2000. Website. Date of Last Access: September 8, 2000 <www.pridetoronto.com>.

Tyler, Carole-Anne. "Boys Will Be Girls: Drag and Transvestic Fetishism." In *Camp: Queer Aesthetics and the Performing Subject*. Ed. Fabio Cleto. Ann Arbor, MI: University of Michigan Press, 1999. 369–392.

fairy tales of two cities: queer nation(s)—national cinema(s)

Thomas Waugh

CLAUDE (*voice off*): And now everything is changed, for that driving desire that was never satisfied, that torment, has taken the form of a ray of hope.

From *À tout prendre* (1963)[1]

BEV: Why, Doug, you'd almost think that you guys were —
DOUG: Oh come on, cut it out, Bev.

From *Winter Kept Us Warm* (1965)

SANDRA: Hormones! Isn't life exciting on the Main![2]
MAURICE (club owner) (to protégé): If [the Chez Sandra Club] didn't pay so much, I would have got rid of this fucking rabble

> long ago. . . . You don't know if they're men or if they're women. . . . And they spend their lives making dumb jokes about it. . . . That's all they talk about, try to get them talking about anything else! Goddamn gang of lunatics. Give me straight people any day, who go to straight clubs, see straight shows. To look at cunt, dammit, real cunt, not imitation rubber ones. . . . When you come here, dammit, the men smell like cunt and the girls are built like trucks. But what can you do? It pays. . . .
>
> From *Il était une fois dans l'Est* (1973)

> SOCIAL WORKER: Have you been sleeping with this roommate?
> LIZA: Oh no, Robin and I sleep in different worlds.
>
> From *Outrageous!* (1977)

Claude, Bev, Doug, Liza, the Social Worker, Sandra, and Maurice are all talking about identities and desires, but only Maurice is talking about the bottom line, the economics of sexual marginality.

My objective in this essay is to sort out the interface of cultural texts and a certain "habitation/nation system," namely the precarious political entity called Canada, and to factor in a "sex/gender system," or certain overdetermined queer corners of it, to flesh out, as it were, Maurice's analysis.[3] Furthermore, my endeavour is to historicize this interface within our so-called national cinema, or more properly—since it is not possible to speak of a monolithic national cultural apparatus any more than it is possible to speak of a Canadian queer identity—our national cinemas. Although no one would deny that the 1960s and 1970s were key to the transformation of national feelings, sexualities, and cinemas within the state called Canada, both queerness and Canada were largely invisible in Canadian cinemas during that critical period. Nevertheless, let's look at a few representative cinematic texts from this period of invisibility and transformation, in fact, the four key feature films whose dialogue I have already offered for tasting, to see if confronting invisibilities makes them less invisible, more material.

To do so representatively is of course to straddle geographical, chronological, and political borders. It means keeping one foot in both of the bicultural camps of private sector Canadian film production of those decades, Montreal and Toronto, as well as before and after the chronological watershed of the late sixties, the historical divide around 1968–69 that partitions the period.[4] (Perhaps, as an Anglo Montrealer by adoption, I am especially qualified to do so, a straddler by history, geography, culture, and choice. . . .) This somewhat artificial time and space border straddling can be visualized as a grid, no doubt too neat, in order to highlight the symmetries and oppositions through which our four films partook of the material constructs of nation, sexuality, and cinema, and to illuminate retroactively these constructs in that formative historical period that began with the Quiet Revolution and ended with the first Referendum of 1980.[5]

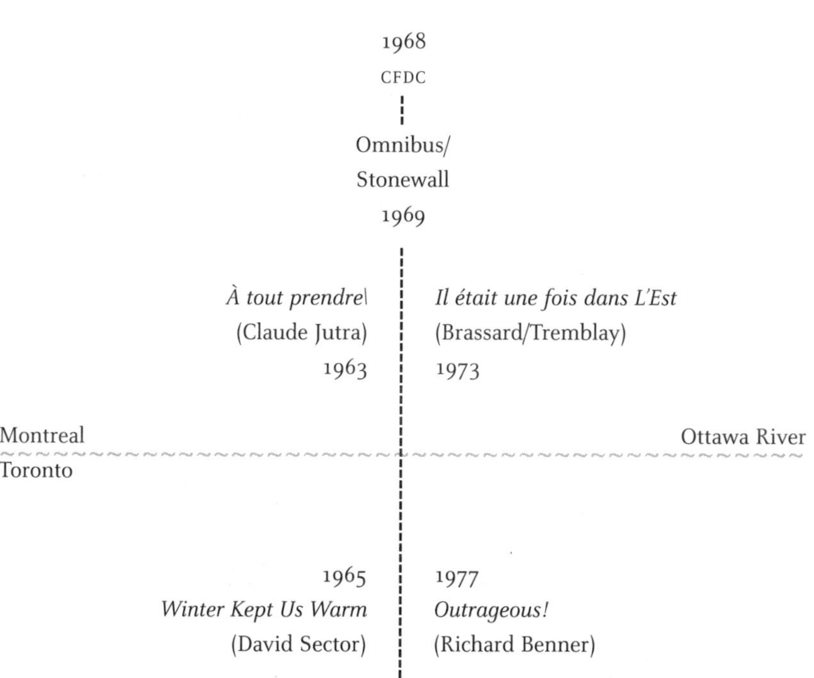

The dividing line of 1968–69 marks both the founding of the Canadian Film Development Corporation (CFDC) and the Omnibus Bill, and therefore the official transition from an artisanal cinema to an industrial one, and from underground sexual subcultures to decriminalized sexual constituencies, a political minority.[6] Geographically speaking, though the 1960s were the age of the Trans Canada Highway and the St. Lawrence Seaway, these east-west vectors scarcely spanned at all the huge chasm between the two metropoles of French and English Canada, nor between the two national cinemas and the two sexual and political cultures they (coyly?) embraced.

Our corpus of four feature fiction films—two from Toronto and two from Montreal, two from the sixties and two from the seventies: *À tout prendre*

(1963), *Winter Kept Us Warm* (1965), *Il était une fois dans l'Est* (1973), *Outrageous!* (1977)—are stuck schematically but symptomatically within the four quadrants of this grid, texts particularly and materially fraught with the queer, national, and cinematic identities being formed within the borders of this federal state and this formative period. The four films, and the symptomatic critiques that I have selected, resonate with echoes, symmetries, and divergences in every direction, across both geographical and chronological borders. They allow us to trace tandem trajectories of queer identities and desires through a cinematic sifting of class, economic, geographical, cultural, linguistic, and sexual variables, onscreen and off, in the two urban locales in the era of Expo '67 (Montreal) and the Spadina Expressway (Toronto). The films are representative of the queer-authored fiction features that emerged from these spatial and chronological quadrants: they had to be, they were virtually the only ones, and they thus acquired a disproportionate historical weight, dialoguing with each other like an epochal chorus.[7]

À tout prendre ([*Take It All*], Dir. Claude Jutra, Montreal, 1963, Best Canadian Feature Film Award). This semi-autobiographical experimental narrative shows a privileged young filmmaker named Claude passionately involved with a black model, named Johanne, who suddenly guesses that he likes boys. He strolls with her up the Mountain, the famous gay cruising area, where he fantasizes that he and Johanne are attacked by a leather biker straight out of 1963's epochal gay biker film, *Scorpio Rising*. Johanne gets pregnant, Claude dumps her, and the relationship dissolves in narcissism, rejection, and bitterness.[8]

Winter Kept Us Warm (Dir. David Secter, Toronto, 1965; Semaine de la critique, Cannes). This University of Toronto student production, a realist social melodrama, impressed international critics at Cannes in 1966. Doug, big man on campus, meets Peter, a shy young Finnish Canadian theatre major from Capreol, and discovers that his friendship is more than male bonding and even more than frolicking in the snow on the grounds of the U of T's residences compound. Doug is jealous of Peter's girlfriend, and Doug's girlfriend is jealous of Peter; Peter loses his virginity to his girlfriend, Doug suddenly can't get it up with his, and their friendship dissolves in narcissism, rejection, and bitterness.

Passing across my grid's vertical watershed of 1968–69, we find *Il était une fois dans l'Est* ([*Once Upon a Time in the East*], Dir. André Brassard, Montreal, 1973; Official Canadian Representative, Cannes), a downbeat melodrama based on characters from the plays of the brilliant young stage sensation Michel Tremblay. Hosanna the Queen of the Main is planning the greatest transformation of history as Elizabeth Taylor Queen of the Nile, but her rival, Sandra, hostess of a club modelled after the landmark club *Cléopâtre*—still in existence as of this writing—plots to steal both Hosanna's thunder and her boyfriend, Cuirette, in the same big night of revenge on the Main. This story, and the other plots woven in and around the universe of the Duchesse de Langeais, drag queens, waitresses, lesbians, housewives, and drunks of the "East," dissolve in rejection, bitterness, and rage.

Meanwhile, in the shadow of the new Toronto Dominion Centre, *Outrageous!* (Dir. Richard Benner, Toronto, 1977; Silver Bear, Berlin Film Festival), an upbeat hybrid of backstage musical and melodrama, tells the story of a hairdresser named Robin, a refugee from a closety salon, and his roommate Liza, a refugee from schizophrenia and psychiatry. Robin is the best female impersonator in town but can only make it as a diva impressionist in New York. His triumph is qualified because Liza's baby is stillborn, but hey, everyone has "a healthy case of craziness," and let's dance.

The films must first be situated within three intersecting discursive and material frameworks: cinema/culture; sex/gender; and space, or habitation/nation system.

CINEMA/CULTURE

Along with the passage from artisanal feature fiction to industrial state-financed cinema is the parallel passage from the gay subtext—not so much the voice of the other as the voice from under—to the gay spectacle, from innuendo to performance, from acting to acting out. The cinematic cultures of the two regions are diametrically opposed: in the sixties Cocteau and Truffaut, plus Hitchcock and Anger, are the presiding geniuses of cinephilic Montreal, but in Toronto we are still colonial English and Drama Majors fixated on Ibsen, Eliot . . . and Harry Belafonte. In the seventies, Montreal cross-fertilizes Genet and Elizabeth Taylor, but Toronto counters with erratic dreams of Hollywood and New York. Despite different genres and cultures, all four films embody a cinema of alienation and despair, the sublimated desire and self-directed violence that struggling new wave cinemas by thirty-year-old male, would-be auteurs have embodied in many national cultures. In Montreal, this means Jutra's three surrogate suicide fantasies and Brassard's heavy theatrical screaming in rainy nocturnal streetscapes. In Toronto, Secter's recourse is to fistfights and poetry, and Benner's to a climactic disco dance party that can scarcely disavow the traumatic stillbirth. All four films are fragile creations, enlivened by their autobiographical authenticity (both *À tout prendre* and *Outrageous!* star their real-life protagonists), anomalous even within the self-financed auteur moviemaking of the sixties and the erratic early years of CFDC financing of the seventies. None was ever really part of a continuum of film culture, despite their respectable critical and commercial success. Even *Outrageous!*, which the CFDC seemingly couldn't believe was a hit, despite rave reviews—from *Variety*, Rex Reed, Judith Crist, and others—and sellouts in New York, was a flash in the pan (notwithstanding an uneven sequel a decade later produced shortly before the AIDS-related deaths of star Craig Russell and director Benner [*Too Outrageous!*, 1987]). Their lonely marginality and intense sincerity makes all four films seem so vital and enduring today.

SEX/GENDER

Heterosex abounds in these queer films, but Claude's passion leads to a payoff for an implied abortion and Doug's passion to impotence. Tremblay/Brassard's characters are too stressed or drunk or mad to fuck, except in flashback, and in any case it would lead, in the story's pre-legalization period setting, to the devastating botched abortion of the film's *dénouement*. Liza's male pickup just doesn't understand anything—women, queer roommates, or schizophrenia—and their bad sex leads to the corpus's third fruitless pregnancy! Do these images of sterility cast a metaphoric shadow over the films' same-sex fucking? Perhaps, for queer love happens only in the loose sense, in surrogate, oblique, and off-screen forms. *Outrageous!* is the exception, but even there Robin has to pay for its begrudging enactment by trade. Both of these sixties films displace the homoerotic onto the erotic exoticism of ethnicity, on otherness as a space of sexual liberation (Claude's deluded Haitian fantasies of Johanne and their dalliance at the famous black jazz club Rockhead's; Doug's delectation of Peter's Finnish pastries, folksongs, and—wink, wink—sauna). The breezy homosociality of Jutra's *café-terrasse* and Secter's university residence clearly masks the fissures of taboo desire and sadistic initiation. In the seventies films, images of erotic expression may be more outspoken and upfront but are also no less disturbed, banished to the idyllic country of the past by Brassard's stylized flashbacks, or restricted to the glittery artifice of masks and performance in both films.

In general, from the sixties to the seventies, the transitions are telling: from closeted isolation to a collectivity (for better or worse); from intense moments of private confession to spectacular outbursts of public acting out; from conflictual triangles of girlfriends and boyfriends (in which the girlfriends get the short end, it goes without saying) to supportive circles of gay male-female solidarity that transcend biological gender; from the surrogate homosocial intimacy of bathing, drinking, and sports to the heterosocial claustrophobia of the dysfunctional family kitchen, workplace, and playspace. In the sixties, the dream of bursting through the shells of repression animates the films, while the seventies are the decade of deferred utopias and bad sex,

Hosanna's betrayals, the Duchesse's delusions, Robin's humiliations, and Liza's bone crunchers, where everyone knows how little salvation can be found in the flesh but keeps looking for it anyway.

SPACE, OR HABITATION/NATION SYSTEM

All four films claim the urban geography of their cities, undertaking the pleasurable bricolage of fictional worlds through on-location shooting and community-recruited extras, seducing audiences with the boosterish recognition of naming and familiarity. The pairs of films from Montreal and Toronto follow surprisingly similar trajectories through this space. For one thing they follow instinctively the political agendas of gay politics of their respective periods. Jutra and Secter prophetically inhabit the anxious bedrooms where, according to Trudeau, author of the Omnibus Bill, the state has no business. Yet in the private space of Claude's ground floor bachelor pad and Doug's dormitory room, privacy doesn't really exist, and even when beer buddies aren't crowding through the doors and windows, hidden looks and hovering innuendos can erupt at any moment into the violence of flouted desire (Claude's masochistic fantasy of street urchins shooting through his apartment windows at him; Doug beating up Peter in his dorm room because he can't fuck him). Brassard and Benner, in tune with their decade's slogan, "Out of the closets and into the streets," literally have their queens stop the traffic on rue Ste Catherine and Yonge Street, respectively. Urban public nightlife and street life are the settings for tumultuous climaxes of both seventies films, as well as the refuges from all that bedroom bad sex.

The sixties camera also explores the ambiguous haunts of the middle-class intelligentsia as they play out their high cultural alibis on the Radio-Canada film set or at the University of Toronto drama club rehearsal space. The seventies see a shift to rawer subaltern regions: the working-class bathroom and kitchen; the vocational ghettos of hair salons, snack bars, and liquor stores, tacky in Montreal, more sanitized in Toronto. The sixties are also charged with the furtive eroticism of the unorganized sexual undergrounds of Mount Royal (the cruising area to which Claude climbs with Johanne) and the Hart House shower room (where Peter—flirtatiously? sadistically?—commands Doug to scrub his back!). Both films seem to have one spatial mythology strategized for "national" audiences, and another for private recognition by queer audiences, knowing surveys of *our* undergrounds, *our* ghettos and *our* liminal spaces. This territory is replaced by the organized public visibility and commodification of the seventies, the profit and spectacle of the Main's *Club Cléopâtre,* and the gleaming Manatee Club at the centre of Toronto's emerging Wellesley Street gay ghetto. (As Maurice says, it pays.) The two seventies

Figure 1. À tout prendre: Director Claude (right) his eye on his actor and plays out his middle-class ambiguity and high culture alibi on the film set. Courtesy Cinémathèque québécoise.

films brazenly and defiantly proclaim gay public geography, but the problematical and provisional status of this declaration remains discernible, whether in Brassard/Tremblay's garish misanthropism or in Benner's overstated cheerfulness and escapes to elsewheres. If Claude seemed unaccountably at home in Montreal's tony, Anglo West End downtown (which, incidentally, housed the embryonic gay ghetto of the sixties), a decade later Brassard embraces the red light district and *balconvilles* further east, the at once tolerant and intolerant crucibles of marginalities of every kind (where housewives may scream "*bibite*" [loosely, "creepy-crawly"] at the "butch" [lesbian] in the "*ruelle*"[alley], despite there being an outcast in every family). [9] The Torontonians are more into urban renewal than slumming, moving up from Secter's seedy beverage rooms of the Yonge Street hetero tenderloin towards the domesticated and gay-friendly strip that Benner frequents in the seventies (skating at City Hall rink, anyone?). In short, all four films are shaped by the volatile urban dialectic of private and public intrinsic to the metropoles of the sixties and seventies, the cyclical tunnelling and emancipation, taming and commoditization of the zones of the forbidden.

Despite, or perhaps because of, their inextricable centrality to collective discourses and material frames of cinema/culture, sex/gender and habitation/nation, the four films are seldom revived and have resisted canonization, thus maintaining their invisibility within the official boundaries of "national" cinemas of both Quebec and English Canada. Only the name-brand auteur label of *À tout prendre* merits an occasional flash out of oblivion.[10] Yet, all four films were situated as "national" texts by heterosexual critics upon their initial release, a legitimation withdrawn by subsequent tastemakers in each case.

Of *À tout prendre*, Denys Arcand, wearing his film critic hat, for *Presqu'-Amérique*, was quick to draw connections between film, sexuality, and (French Canadian) nation:

> Why can Claude have a valid relationship only with this foreign Johanne whom he wants to make even stranger? There are after all "everyday" Québécois women all around him . . . both onscreen and psychologically. *À tout prendre* doesn't succeed in getting close in tenderness and satisfaction to real everyday women. And in that, the hero is like lots of 30–year-old French Canadians, sensitive and cultivated, who have to have women who are black, yellow, or red, in any case "foreign," in order to have their intoxicating affairs. There is here, it seems, an unconscious refusal to coincide with his collective self, at the same time as an unquenchable thirst to perfect oneself in *a mythic exteriority* that arises from the global situation of our people . . .
>
> *. . . Nothing very surprising that at that point the film seems to claim the right to homosexuality. . . . Nothing very new or very immoral in that. The only question is to know to what extent homosexuality is a solid form of sexual activity and in what manner it has a special state of self-affirmation, given our global context of existence in relation to artistic expression.* [11]

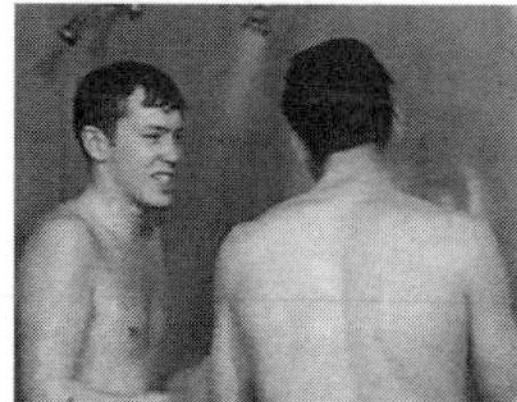
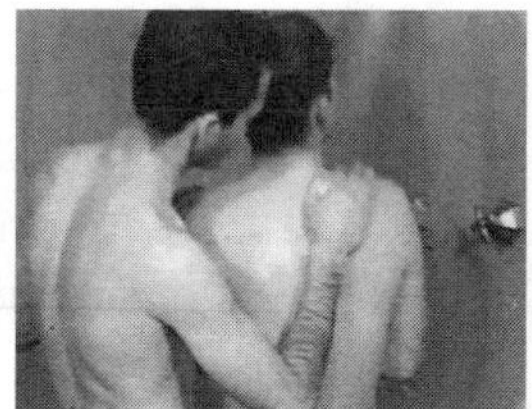
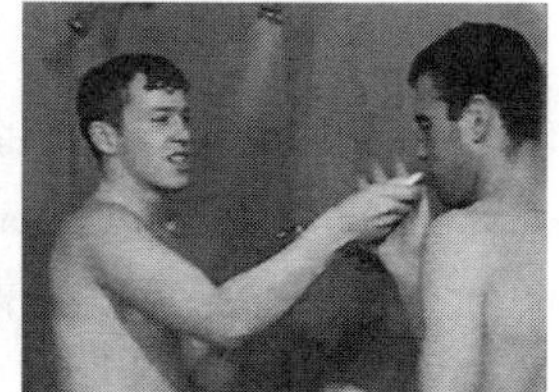

Figure 2. Winter Kept Us Warm: The University of Toronto shower room as unorganized sexual underground: Peter flirtatiously? sadistically? commands Doug to scrub his back! Courtesy CFMDC.

Figure 3. Il était une fois dans l'Est: The Chez Sandra club on the Main as crucible of marginality: Sandra (*right*) plots to steal Hosanna's butch boyfriend, Cuirette, while castoff waitress, Pierrette, responds drunkenly to his flirtation. Courtesy Cinémathèque québécoise.

Of *Winter Kept Us Warm,* a more sympathetic French critic, Louis Marcorelles, started with a comparison of this "very very beautiful film" to J.D. Salinger's *Catcher in the Rye.* Hinting at rather than sermonizing sexual marginality, he was no less ready and sweeping than Arcand with ethnic and national sexual stereotypes, matching them perceptively to Secter's cinematic style. Marcorelles then went on prophetically to decipher the rivalry across the linguistic divide, of which the Winnipeg-born Jew, Secter, couldn't have been more oblivious:

> A literature of the heart in the best sense: emotions, Anglo-Saxon style, without infinite nuances, but with strong feelings, an unconscious cruelty. The joy of living, of loving, of hurting . . . frantic egoism. The little beast in you and me.
>
> *Winter Kept Us Warm* has above all the quality of being Anglo-Saxon to the extreme: its little dose of humour, skin-deep, *its tenderness that doesn't dare declare itself,* of unconscious cruelty. . . .
>
> *Winter Kept Us Warm* is beyond everything else a Canadian film: Canadian as one breathes, according to the strange mixture which has

> created a nation that is comparable to no other, a misaligned door opening on the edge of history. David Secter knows nothing of the National Film Board (NFB), has vaguely heard the name of Michel Brault, is unaware of Groulx and Perrault and Macartney-Filgate. Who cares as long as the Canadian "grace" . . . remains. This freedom of tone, this camera as tall as a man, stopping on a whim to follow a squirrel, frolicking in the snow among the flakes. . . .[12]

Il était une fois dans l'Est had beat out *The Apprenticeship of Duddy Kravitz,* as well as other films, to represent Canada at Cannes in 1973. In response, in Jean Leduc's review in *Cinéma Québec,* the phobic political undercurrents beneath Arcand's feigned sophistication, came out into the open. Leduc started out with a valid question, but then lined up drag queens, intellectuals, and Tremblay himself (marginalized to the point of the "infinitesimal") for the firing squad:

> In what sense can a work of fiction really represent a national reality with its network of socio-economic-cultural implications. . . . Did the criterion of representativeness ever play a role at any level? Is the milieu of drag queens on the Main strongly representative of the reality of Canada, of Quebec, of Montreal? What infinitesimal proportion of this reality does it represent? In any case is the image *Il était une fois dans l'Est* offers faithful to this supermicroscopic reality? (I am told that it is not.) And does the reality of drag queens on the Main differ noticeably from the reality of drag queens in London, Hamburg, Berlin and Rome? *Il était une fois dans l'Est* gives the impression of being focused principally on this reality even if other elements dredged up from other Tremblay theatre play a part. There remains the general feeling from the whole of the film of great despair.
>
> Is this a true image of Quebec reality or would it be an image equivalent to those favoured by certain intellectuals who need this security in order to disguise their inability to really grasp Quebec reality? [13]

Outrageous!, the Canadian sleeper success story of the 1970s, merited three pieces in *Cinema Canada,* a rave, a pan, and a production story. John Locke's rave began with an anecdote of a New York moviegoer's praise for its non-national generic spectacle value and then led in to a dissection of its un-Canadian Canadianness:

> "It's the best show you've ever seen." This is not a typical reaction to Canadian films . . . *Outrageous!* . . . is the best Canadian narrative film I

> have seen, and forgetting about nationalism for a moment, it is a very good film indeed in 1977 international terms. . . .
>
> The acting is so uniformly excellent that it is positively "un-Canadian." . . . *Outrageous!* is un-Canadian in this specific sense: all the performers say their lines in a believeable fashion. . . . Canadian films often seem to disguise their nationality. Actors and actresses never say "aye." Canadian artifacts like money and license plates never appear. . . . *Outrageous!* breaks these conventions usually followed by Canadian films looking for U.S. distribution, and it makes the broken conventions work in its favour. . . .
>
> Thank you Richard Benner whoever you are, I have been waiting for years to see a really good Canadian narrative film. [14]

These national linkages to our four "really good Canadian narrative" films call for several observations. The fact that the two Quebec films were marked as negatively national by nationalist critics, that is, as nationally unrepresentative, is an indicator of two things: the ways problematical questions of sexuality and class were postponed or papered over by the nationalist consensus of the intelligentsia and the left, and the way cinema was assumed to be the privileged medium of national expression in the sixties and pre-Parti Québécois seventies. The struggle to end film censorship during the Quiet Revolution had been, in every way, a "national" struggle, yet Quebec filmmakers were called into line when they diverged from some undefined but sentimentally monolithic fantasy of the young *pure laine* heterosexual couple. (Paradoxically, Arcand's ideal couple rarely appeared in Quebec narrative of the period other than in *Valérie* [Dir. Denis Héroux, 1968] or *Deux femmes en or* [Dir. Claude Fournier, 1970]—certainly not in his own films!) On the other side, significantly, both *Winter* and *Outrageous!* were tagged as essentially and positively Canadian through the objective outside eyes of a French champion of Québécois nationalist cinema, and an American expatriate critic who saw the film in New York, respectively.

Interestingly, of the four films, only *Outrageous!*, directed by an American expatriate and resolved in New York, explicitly claims, in onscreen textual terms, the national as boldly as it does the queer. I am referring not only to the jingoistic flaunting of Toronto's cosmopolitan urban monuments in the very decade when Toronto was bypassing Montreal in size and representative aspirations: the TD Centre; the CN Tower; Nathan Phillips Square; Union Station; and the streetcars. I am referring also to the famous and all too symptomatic jokes about the Canada Council and "making it in New York" (whose absorption by audiences effectively inoculated them against a film about a Canadian impersonating American divas and brain draining to New York).

Outrageous! was thus participating in the simultaneous and interconnected awakening of nationalism and cinephilia in English Canada—later crystallized beginning in 1983 at the "Perspectives Canada" series at the Festival of Festivals—a full generation after Quebec had seen the same phenomenon. In comparison with the queer Montrealers' unexamined assumption of national belonging, was Benner protesting a bit too much?

Naming the nation is one thing, but what about naming sex? How do the thematics of sexual marginality that retroactively seem so central enter the critical discourse? As we have seen, the practice and politics of naming in criticism is as tortuous as in the films themselves. Arcand's slur on *À tout prendre*'s "claim" to the "non-solid" activity of homosexuality is as disingenuous as Claude's coming out is courageous, and as obscured by his irrational logic as Claude's claim is by narrative intricacy. Marcorelles' Wildean euphemism about tenderness is as graceful as *Winter*'s oblique sincerity. (One Canadian review of Secter's film explicitly named the "homosexual" thematic only to declare it "not really necessary," just as the *New York Times* was opining that Jutra was throwing in homosexuality simply to be avant-garde.)[15] Leduc's pseudo-sociological scapegoating exceeds even Tremblay's characters' gutter vilification—sampled in my epigraph above—of women, queers, and most significantly of themselves. Locke hiply avoids commenting directly on the queer thematics, and, though *Outrageous!* is actually the first of the four films to use the g-word, the critic prefers "raunchy," "leather," and "unique" to "gay." (But the magazine's accompanying pan makes up for this delicacy with the, by now, very unhip "homosexual" and decries the addition of all the "lamentable" drag stuff to Margaret Gibson's source story.)[16] It goes without saying that none of the four critics identified the films as queer, gay, or homosexual cinema, and it would be anachronistic to expect otherwise, even in the seventies, all the more so with the avoidance and innuendo that invested criticism as much as it did the cinema itself. In sum, all reviews referred to the sexual marginalization of the film's diegetic world, either naming to disavow or avoiding to tolerate. But only the Québécois reviewers connected sexuality with the collectivity, negatively in both cases of course, even if the filmmakers conspicuously didn't dare. Needless to say, Benner's grafting of gay pride onto English Canadian nationalism was unique for 1977—something that perhaps only an immigrant director would have dared in the days when the "national" gay newspaper, *The Body Politic*, was spending more time in court than in the press room, and something no native critic dared to do in any way whatsoever, gay or straight. [17]

By 1977, however, we can finally speak properly of the existence of gay criticism and its engagement with our corpus. One discreetly gay critic, the late Jean Basile, had warmly welcomed *À tout prendre* in *Le devoir*[18], and the late festival impresario Richard Roud, also discreetly gay, had provided one of *Winter*'s most glowing raves, a coy but retroactively lucid recognition of a "something":

> . . . a [stunning] moment when all of a sudden one realises that one has got it all wrong, that something quite different is happening up there on the screen, but that that something is nevertheless completely convincing and right. [19]

But only *Outrageous!*, a dozen years later, was received and assessed—and in fact hotly debated—by a gay critical constituency, both in Toronto and abroad. Interestingly, *The Body Politic* hated it, printing a long denunciation of the film by Michael Riordan, acknowledging only indirectly the film's momentous historical place as the first Toronto explicitly gay feature by virtue of the unusual three-page length of the piece and the generous photo spread. Riordan's grounds for his savagery were political:

> Will one heterosexual, even one heterosexual parent, march with us because of it, fight on our side, vote us into power, grant us custody, let us teach her/his children what it is to be gay? Will one heterosexual be changed by it—not comforted but changed, challenged, moved to original thought? . . . What is there in its images for us? Will it make us stronger in any way? What does it contribute to our view of ourselves or of the world? Does it challenge any of the learned misconceptions that weigh us down? Most important, does it move us closer to a fresh non-heterosexist way of dealing with each other? [20]

This eloquent but conventional invocation of the "positive image" problematic and its instrumentalist conception of cultural effect reflects a common—and no doubt tonic—slant in early feminist and gay liberation criticism. Riordan's failure to recognize other politics of representation was offset by his forceful statement of a political contextualization that is decidely local: his fury against the enthusiastic embrace of *Outrageous!* by the local tabloid the *Toronto Sun*, that more than any other medium had actively led the campaign against both the beleaguered *The Body Politic* and the inclusion of sexual orientation in Ontario's human rights code. Gay criticism was even more deluded then than now about the ideological coherence of right wing media, and even more conspiratorial about the one-dimensional effectivity of media images. Riordan's only reference to the "national" stature of the film was indirect, an acknowledgment of the director's New York roots and the film's boffo reception in the American media and *Variety*. He also pointedly

Figure 4. Outrageous! Toronto hairdresser Robin (Craig Russell) impersonating American diva Carol Channing and making it in New York. Courtesy Cinémathèque québécoise.

referred to a gushy notice in an "American" gay paper, not naming Boston's *Gay Community News* (GCN) as the source of the rave.

GCN, the most prominent American gay and lesbian community paper and that closest in spirit to *The Body Politic*, had indeed run both an uncharacteristically superficial and positive review by David Holland, stating:

> From the gay liberation point of view, the film is far ahead of almost anything that has come before. . . . four star rating. [One wants Benner to give us] even more of his vision, now that he has furthered the image of gays as human beings on film. . . . In *Outrageous!*, gayness is a normal ordinary feature of life and neither the characters nor director Benner give it a second thought. . . . It's a bravissimo accomplishment. [21]

GCN had followed up with a long glowing interview with Russell, by Gregg Howe, a few months later, featuring the star's pouting observations that straight audiences were preferring the film to gay audiences.[22] However, judging from Russell's reference to a pan in the *Chicago Gay News* that had particularly stung him, it seems that Riordan's views were not isolated and that the gay reception of *Outrageous!* was at least mixed. The GCN coverage, like most American notices then as now, mentioned the Canadian label only in passing if at all, and this clearly signified a "non-Hollywood" sensibility rather than an expression of a national culture. The queer critical debates about *Outrageous!*, then, all assumed its utmost pertinence to their constituency but the relevance of its "national" origins never entered the picture, regardless of how overstated its "Canadianness" was on the screen. Overwhelmed by the pan-national constituency for the emergent gay and lesbian cinema, late seventies gay criticism overlooked other political contexts and frameworks for the new films, local and national, regardless of the fact that the local and the national were the arenas where the politics of sexuality were being hammered out.[23]

In conclusion, I have shown how these four muffled but haunting voices of the sexual other in the Montreals and Torontos of the sixties and seventies offer symmetrically parallel stories probing the intersection of sexual identity and collective space before and after the 1969 critical watershed of gay urban histories in the West. Queer nation? Perhaps. But do the important synchronicities between the two pairs of films add up to Canadian nation, our national cinema? Perhaps only in one sense, in their combined "otherness" in the face of the American models rooted in their respective decades. The queer-friendly, avant-garde films of sixties New York (*Flaming Creatures*, 1962–63) and California (*Scorpio Rising*, 1963) had celebrated figures of defiant marginality as the prophets of the impending gay revolution, but the flaming creatures of Toronto and Montreal in the sixties are the worried young men in conservative suits and narrow ties learning folk songs and dating girlfriends. Interestingly, a ghost from Kenneth Anger's *Scorpio Rising* makes an appearance in *À tout prendre* as the motorcycle leather boy who attacks the heterosexual couple, but this is Claude's masochistic fantasy, not a "real" character. [24] In the seventies, American models of post-Stonewall "positive image" realism proliferated in both documentary (*Word is Out*, 1978) and fiction (*A Very Natural Thing*, 1974), the latter of which Riordan had referred to, but also went un-seconded north of the border. The Toronto and Montreal equivalents now seem to have been our very own politically incorrect flaming creatures, Hosanna and Robin. These two proletarian transvestite hairdressers, I posited in an earlier publication as spectacular bipolar emblems of interfacing queer nationality and schizophrenic "Canadian" cultural identities in the post-Stonewall decade, acting up and acting out, screaming, singing, performing delayed-reaction multiple-identitied marginalities on Yonge Street and the Main, while their American cousins were aspiring to a respectable aesthetic of national belonging and centrality. [25] It may seem only that the sixties took a decade to reach north of the border, but it is doubtful that the felicitous synchronicity of this parallel "otherness" of the Montreal and Toronto myths and icons constitutes a national consensus, queer or Canadian.

What is visible, rather, in these two sets of magnificently anomalous and uncanonizable films, these four fairy tales of two cities, is neither one nation or two nations or two solitudes or four *auteurs* but two queer metropoles and two distinctly lived and felt inhabitations of those metropolitan spaces, two cultural geographies, two geographical cultures of desire. The four films' respective mythologies and materialities of desire and identity are distinct, overdetermined by their distinct authorial sensibilities and cinematic heritages, and their two distinct socio-political cultural and historico-spatial environments. Among other things they are legible in retrospect also as the origins of two peripatetic historical trajectories in which Montreal queer cinema would one day most characteristically explore the perils of private intimacy (*À corps perdu* [Dir. Léa Pool, 1988], *Quand l'amour est gai* [Dir. Laurent Gagliardi, 1994], *L'Escorte* [Dir. Denis Langlois, 1996]) and Toronto's the assertion of public rights (*Urinal* [Dir. John Greyson,1988], *Out: Stories of Lesbian and Gay Youth* [Dir. David Adkin, 1993], *Skin Deep* [Dir. Midi Onodera, 1995]). (And what better way to view the delirious incoherence of *Lilies* (1996), that Torontonian's English-language adaptation of a Montreal French-language play celebrating a shared queer past in an imagined rural hinterland, except as the merger of these two trajectories?) In any case, the grid of *À tout prendre* and *Il était une fois dans l'Est, Winter Kept Us Warm,* and *Outrageous!* reminds us squarely of how cities, their communities both imagined and demographic, their crowds and their outcasts, their infrastructures and their networks, their cultures, their economies, their geographies have been the motors, crucibles and canvases of our cinemas . . . [26] So let's bracket the national for a while, please, either queer or Canadian, and in fact let's use these fairy tales of two cities to refocus on the metropolitan and the material, both the subnational and the supranational, the transnational and the postnational, the local and the global, in short, to reclaim the urban.

NOTES

1. Cited dialogue excerpts are from VHS versions of *À tout prendre, Winter Kept Us Warm, Outrageous!,* and from the published scenario in *Il était une fois dans l'Est: Un film de André Brassard* (Montreal: L'Aurore, 1974) (translations mine). I am grateful to the Social Sciences and Humanities Research Council of Canada and to Concordia University for funding this research, and to Terry Goldie for inviting

me to develop it for initial keynote presentation at York University's "Queer Nation?" conference, March 1997. A different version of this essay appears in the *Canadian Journal of Film Studies* 10.2 (2001).

2. The "Main," or Boulevard St-Laurent, is Montreal's traditional north-south dividing line between the anglophone West and the francophone East; in addition the area around the intersection of the "Main" and rue Ste-Catherine, the main east-west artery of the city, is the traditional red-light district, as well as a site of the club Cléopâtre and other gay nightlife in the pre-Stonewall period evoked by *Il était une fois dans l'Est.*

3. The two "system" formulations belong respectively to Eve Kosofsky Sedgwick, "Nationalisms and Sexualities in the Age of Wilde," In *Nationalisms and Sexualities*, Eds. Andrew Parker et al. (New York: Routledge, 1992) and Gayle Ruben, "Thinking Sex: Notes for a Radical Theory of the Politics of Sexuality." In *Pleasure and Danger: Exploring Female Sexuality.* Ed. Carole S. Vance (London: Routledge and Kegan Paul, 1984).

4. With regard to the public sector, institutional cinema of this period, I have written elsewhere of its deeply buried transgressive undercurrents and of *Some American Feminists* (1977), the single film that approaches any degree of explicitness towards a queer (in this case lesbian) thematic. If it is an urban fairy tale, it is one of New York, and it is of course no accident that the first queer film to see the light in the National Film Board (NFB) desert should be one of exile. See my "Nègres blancs, tapettes et butch: images des lesbiennes et des gais dans le cinéma québécois." *Copie zéro* (1981): 12–29.

5. The "Quiet Revolution" or "Révolution tranquille" refers in Quebec history to the period of radical social, political, and cultural modernization ushered in by the Liberals under Jean Lesage, following the death of old guard premier, Maurice Duplessis, in 1959. The sovereigntist Parti québécois was first elected to head the provincial government in 1976, under René Lévesque, and it offered its referendum on "sovereignty-association" four years later, in which the "No" vote prevailed.

6. The Omnibus Bill reforming sexual offenses portions of the criminal code, including the removal of clauses dealing with "buggery" and "gross indecency" (but not the full removal of the State from the bedrooms of the nation) was passed by Parliament on May 14, 1969, giving the modern period of Canadian queer/sexual politics its symbolic start. Six weeks later, Greenwich Village drag queens and other queers rose up against police harassment at the Stonewall Tavern, giving the symbolic start of modern American queer politics a more dramatic and revolutionary flavour—at least in comparison with a partial reform handed down by paternalistic, homophobic politicians in colonial imitation of a British reform law from two years earlier. See Gary Kinsman, *The Regulation of Desire: Sexuality in Canada* (Montreal: Black Rose Books, 1987).

7. The exceptions come from Quebec, of course, and consist of a couple of Anglo-Montreal ambiguities, *Montreal Main* (Dir. Frank Vitale, 1974) and *The Rubber Gun* (Dir. Allan Moyle, 1977), and a couple of Trois-Rivières obscurities by Michel Audy (for example, *La maison que empêche de voir la ville*, 1975). For a comprehensive inventory of the Quebec gay films and filmic representations of this period see my "Nègres blancs."
8. *Scorpio Rising* (1963), a prophetic California avant garde film by gay pioneer Kenneth Anger, whose influence on Claude Jutra is a promising issue for further research.
9. In fact Brassard shot *Il était une fois dans l'Est* in the West, in the then-empty Hawaiian Lounge on Stanley Street, which ended its twenty-five-year intermittent vocation as a gay-welcoming space in the 1980s when it became a hetero strip club catering to NHL hockey players. For more of the evolution of Montreal queer geography, see Irène Demczuk and Frank Remiggi, eds., *Sortir de l'ombre. Histoires des communautés lesbienne et gaie de Montréal* (Montreal: VLB éditeur, 1998).
10. Peter Morris has commented on the odd resistance of *À tout prendre* to canonization but does not attribute this to Jutra's discourses of sexual marginality. See "In Our Own Eyes: The Canonizing of Canadian Film," *Canadian Journal of Film Studies* 3.1 (Spring 1993): 27–44.
11. Denys Arcand, "Cinéma et sexualité." *Presqu'Amérique* 1.3 (translation and emphasis mine).
12. Louis Marcorelles, "La semaine de la critique." *Cahiers du cinéma* 179 (juin 1966): 47–48 (translation mine).
13. Jean Leduc, "Il était une fois dans l'Est, The Apprenticeship of Duddy Kravitz: La représentation d'un milieu donné." *Cinéma Québec* 3.6/7 (avril/mai, 1974): 43–44.
14. John W. Locke, "A Healthy Case of Craziness." *Cinema Canada* 41 (October, 1977): 17–18; 20–21.
15. Respectively, see Joe Medjuck, "*Winter Kept Us Warm*," *Take One* 1.1 (Sept.–Oct. 1966): 24, and Bosley Crowther, "Screen: 'Take It All' Opens at the Plaza," *The New York Times*, April 26, 1966.
16. See Ted Fox, "Richard Benner's *Outrageous*." *Cinema Canada* 41 (October 1977): 21.
17. *Outrageous!* even goes to bat for biculturalism, incorporating in its pan-national allegorical frieze a nasty and hyperfeminist Québécois dyke in exile a full decade before a more elaborate version of the same character appears in *I've Heard the Mermaids Singing* (Dir. Patricia Rozema), a film that shares Secter's taste for T.S. Eliot inspired titles. *Mermaids* is similar to *Winter* in other ways as well, with its post-Stonewall exploration of ambiguous borders between homosociality and homosexuality. *Outrageous!*'s nasty dyke is a far cry from the brave, strong, and sexy lesbian couple in *Il était*.
18. Jean Basile, "*À tout prendre*, de Jutra, au Festival." *Le devoir* 12 (août, 1963). Basile

does not mention Jutra's queer confessional, but certain suggestive keywords and phrases appear: "Narcissus," "adolescent," "too personal" . . . "even exposes himself bravely—here is everything!—in all his complexity" (translation mine).

19. Richard Roud, "The Cannes Festival." *Sight and Sound* 35.3 (Summer, 1966): 154.
20. Michael Riordon, "Outrageous!" How Can You Argue with Success?" *The Body Politic*, 37 (October, 1977): 15.
21. David Holland, "Honest, Beguiling, 'Outrageous' Step Forward." *Gay Community News* (August 27, 1977): 8.
22. Gregg Howe, "Craig Russell: The Sweet Smell of Success." *Gay Community News* (April 1, 1978): 8–9.
23. One of the most detailed and measured "positive image" critiques of *Outrageous!* also came from abroad, from Richard Dyer, British pioneer of gay film studies whose groundbreaking *Gays and Film* (BFI) came out in 1977, the same year as the film. Dyer mentioned the Toronto locale only in passing and focused instead on comparing *Outrageous!* with the U.S. *Word is Out—Stories from Some of Our Lives* (Mariposa Film Group, 1978) in terms of discourses of realism, utopia, and gender categories. Richard Dyer, "Out! Out! Out!: A Review of *Outrageous!* and *Word is Out.*" *Gay Left: A Gay Socialist Journal* 9 (1979) : 27–30.
24. Jutra probably saw *Scorpio Rising* (1963) in a preliminary version since he had clearly been following Anger's career since its beginning, having echoed Anger's *Fireworks* (1947) in his own *Mouvement perpétuel* (1949).
25. Thomas Waugh, "Cultivated Colonies: Notes on Queer Nationhood and the Erotic Image," in *Canadian Journal of Film Studies* 2.2/3 (Fall 1993): 145–178.
26. I am not denying the existence of Canadian rural and regional cinemas, at least I don't think I am, though there may not be many very queer ones.

WORKS CITED

À corps perdu [motion picture]. Directed by Léa Pool, Canada, 1988.

À tout prendre [motion picture]. Directed by Claude Jutra, Canada, 1963.

The Apprenticeship of Duddy Kravitz [motion picture]. Directed by Ted Kotcheff, Canada, 1974.

Basile, Jean. "À tout prende, de Jutra, au Festival," *Le devoir* 12 (août, 1963).

Crowther, Bosley. "Screen: '*Take It All*' Opens at the Plaza," *The New York Times* (April 26, 1966).

Demczuk, Irène and Frank Remiggi, eds. *Sortir de l'ombre. Histoires des communautés lesbienne et gaie de Montréal.* Montreal: VLB éditeur, 1998.

Deux femmes en or [motion picture]. Directed by Claude Fournier. Canada, 1970.

Dyer, Richard, ed. *Gays and Film.* London: British Film Institute, 1977.

———. "Out! Out! Out!: A Review of *Outrageous!* and *Word is Out!.*" *Gay Left: A Gay Socialist Journal* 9 (1979): 27–30.

Fireworks [motion picture]. Directed by Kenneth Anger. United States, 1947.

Flaming Creatures [motion picture]. Directed by Jack Smith. United States, 1962–63.

Fox, Ted. "Richard Benner's *Outrageous!*" *Cinema Canada*, 41 (October, 1977): 21.

Il était une fois dans l'Est [motion picture]. Directed by André Brassard. Canada, 1973.

I've Heard the Mermaids Singing [motion picture]. Directed by Patricia Rozema. Canada, 1987.

Kinsman, Gary. *The Regulation of Desire: Sexuality in Canada.* Montreal: Black Rose Books, 1987.

La maison que empêche de voir la ville [motion picture]. Directed by Michel Audy, Canada, 1975.

L'Escorte [motion picture]. Directed by Denis Langlois. Canada, 1996.

Lilies [motion picture]. Directed by John Greyson. Canada, 1996.

Medjuck, Joe. "*Winter Kept Us Warm,*" *Take One* 1.1 (Sept.-Oct, 1966): 24.

Montreal Main [motion picture]. Directed by Frank Vitale. Canada, 1974.

Morris, Peter. "In Our Own Eyes: The Canonizing of Canadian Film." *Canadian Journal of Film Studies* 3.1 (Spring, 1993): 27–44.

Mouvement perpétual [motion picture]. Directed by Claude Jutra. Canada, 1949.

Out: Stories of Lesbian and Gay Youth [documentary]. Directed by David Adkin. Canada, 1993.

Outrageous! [motion picture]. Directed by Richard Benner. Canada, 1977.

Quand l'amour est gai [motion picture]. Directed by Laurent Gagliardi. Canada, 1994.

The Rubber Gun [motion picture]. Directed by Allan Moyle. Canada, 1977.

Rubin, Gayle, "Thinking Sex: Notes for a Radical Theory of the Politics of Sexuality." In *Pleasure and Danger: Exploring Female Sexuality.* Ed. Carole S. Vance. London: Routledge and Kegan Paul, 1984.

Salinger, J. D. *Catcher in the Rye.* New York: Little, Brown, 1951.

Scorpio Rising [motion picture]. Directed by Kenneth Anger, United States, 1963.

Sedgwick, Eve Kosofsky. "Nationalisms and Sexualities in the Age of Wilde." In *Nationalisms and Sexualities.* Eds. Andrew Parker, et al. New York: Routledge, 1992.

Skin Deep [motion picture]. Directed by Midi Onodera. Canada, 1995.

Urinal [motion picture]. Directed by John Greyson. Canada, 1988.

Valérie [motion picture]. Directed by Denis Héroux. Canada, 1968.

A Very Natural Thing [motion picture]. Directed by Christopher Larkin. United States, 1974.

Waugh, Thomas. "Nègres blancs, tapettes et butch: images des lesbiennes et des gais dans le Cinéma québécois." *Copie zéro* (1981): 12–29.

———. "Cultivated Colonies: Notes on Queer Nationhood and the Erotic Image," *Canadian Journal of Film Studies* 2.2/3 (Fall, 1993): 145–178.

Winter Kept Us Warm [motion picture]. Directed by David Secter. Canada, 1965.

Word is Out—Stories from Some of Our Lives [documentary]. Mariposa Group. United States, 1978.

INDEX

NOTES ON CONTRIBUTORS

JAMES ALLAN has an MA from McGill University of Montreal and is currently working on his doctorate in the Department of Communications at the University of Massachusetts. He has previously written on Montreal's gay club culture, misogyny in mainstream gay-themed films such as *In & Out* and *The Adventures of Priscilla, Queen of the Desert*, and on the political ramifications of the Chelsea gym-queen. His latest project, for which he was awarded a GLAAD Dissertation Fellowship, investigates forty years of film and television texts that naturalize and politicize relationships between gay men and straight women.

WESLEY CRICHLOW holds a Ph.d. from the University of Toronto/Ontario Institute for Studies in Education with a focus on Critical Pedagogy and Cultural Studies. His doctoral thesis, "Buller Men and Batty Bwoys: Hidden Men in Toronto's and Halifax's Black Communities," was the first post-graduate work on this topic in Canada. He is also active in consultation and volunteer work with government and non-profit organizations on race and the law, human rights, and social justice issues.

LYNNE FERNIE is a Vancouver-born, multi-disciplinary artist, filmmaker, song lyricist, cultural activist, and day-job worker who has lived in Toronto since the 1970s. In the 1980s, she lived in a scruffy loft on Queen Street West, co-founded the feminist journal, *Fireweed*, edited the art magazine, *Parallélogramme*, and exhibited art in galleries across Canada. In the 1990s, she wrote and co-directed two Genie Award-winning documentary films: *Forbidden Love*: *the Unashamed stories of Lesbian Lives* (1993) and *Fiction and Other Truths: A Film about Jane Rule* (1996). With the National Film Board of Canada, she is currently working on a short documentary-with-animation on homophobia for children.

ANDREA N. FROLIC is a doctoral student in Cultural Anthropology at Rice University in Houston, Texas. Her research interests include the cultural dimensions of illness, medical ethics, and gender studies. Patrick Wey, whose work accompanies Frolic's essay, is a freelance photographer and artist located in Waterloo, Ontario.

PAULINE GREENHILL is Director of Women's Studies at the University of Winnipeg. Her most recent book, co-edited with Diane Tye, is *Undisciplined*

Women: Tradition and Culture in Canada (Montreal: McGill-Queen's University Press, 1997).

PAULINE GREENHILL is Dominatrix of Anti-Christ Studies at the Perversity of Winapig. Her most recent book, co-edited with Demon Ties, is *Disciplining Women: Vultures in Perdition in Canadada* (Montreal: McKill-Queen's Undiversity Press, 1997).

GORDON BRENT INGRAM is from Vancouver Island and has a doctorate in environmental planning from the University of California, Berkeley. He has taught at Antioch College, the Santa Cruz and Berkeley campuses of the University of California, the University of British Columbia, and most recently at the International Institute for Aerospace Survey and Earth Sciences. He was an editor of the Lambda Award-winning *Queers in Space* and is author of the *On the Edge of a Great Forest: The Construction of Public Space by Sexual Minorities in Pacific Canada*; *terminal city hard love*; and *Building The Terminal City*, to be published in 2002–2003.

GARY KINSMAN is a gay liberation, global justice and socialist activist who teaches sociology at Laurentian University in Sudbury. He is the author of *The Regulation of Desire: Homo and Heterosexualities* and many book chapters and articles on sexual politics. He is co-editor (with Dieter Buse and Mercedes Steedman) of *Whose National Security? Canadian State Surveillance and the Creation of Enemies* and co-author (with Patrizia Gentile) of *The Canadian War on "Queers": National Security as Sexual Regulation* (forthcoming).

ANDREW LESK recently completed his doctorate at the Université de Montréal, with a dissertation on the gay Canadian writer Sinclair Ross. He has published on Ross, Leonard Cohen, Chinua Achebe, Jack Hodgins, and Willa Cather, as well as on literary criticism and queer theory. He resides in Toronto.

CATHERINE NASH is currently finishing her Ph.d in urban geography at Queen's University, Kingston, where she is studying the evolution of the Toronto's "gay ghetto." She has a Master's in Urban and Regional Planning from Queen's University, a law degree from the University of Ottawa and, in a past life, spent eight years practicing municipal and land development law.

ZOË NEWMAN recently completed her Ph.d in Sociology and Equity Studies, at the Ontario Institute for Studies in Education, University of Toronto. She is currently a Social Sciences and Humanities Research Council of Canada postdoctoral fellow at York University in Toronto. Her current research looks at how racial and sexual hierarchies are sustained through the organization of urban space.

MICHELLE K. OWEN is an Assistant Professor at the University of Winnipeg in the Department of Sociology. Sections of her dissertation, "We Are Family?": The Struggle for Same-Sex Spousal Recognition in Ontario and the Conundrum of "Family." (University of Toronto, 1999) have been previously published in *RFR:* Special Issue on Feminist Practice in Qualitative Research (28:1/2) and *Inter/National Intersections: Law's Changing Territories* (UBC Press, 1998), edited by L. Campbell. Her current research interests include bisexuality in the Canadian context and the construction of gender in cyberspace.

ELAINE PIGEON is a Ph.d candidate at the Université de Montréal, where she is completing her dissertation on queer aspects of Henry James's fiction.

THOMAS WAUGH has been teaching film studies at Concordia University in Montreal since 1976, and has also developed curricula on HIV/AIDS and in queer studies. He is the author of *Hard to Imagine: Gay Male Eroticism in Photography and Film from their Beginnings to Stonewall* (Columbia University Press, 1996), *The Fruit Machine: Twenty Years of Writings on Queer Cinema* (Duke University Press, 2000), and *Outlines: 200 Underground Erotic Graphics from Before Stonewall* (Arsenal Pulp Press, Forthcoming). He is also a critic, public lecturer, and festival programmer.

BJ WRAY currently holds a Social Sciences and Humanities Research Council of Canada Postdoctoral Fellowship at the University of California, Davis. She is working on a book-length project, *Performing Sexual Citizenship*, which examines the relationship between national and sexual identities in contemporary American and Canadian lesbian performance art. Publications include "Choreographing Queer" in *Dancing Bodies, Living Histories* (Banff Centre, Press 2000) and "Structure, Size and Play: The Case of the Talking Vulva" in *Decompositions: Postdisciplinary Performance* (Indiana University Press, 2000).

TERRY GOLDIE is a professor of English at York University in Toronto and author of *Fear and Temptation: the Image of the Indigene in Canadian, Australian and New Zealand Literatures* (McGill-Queen's University Press, 1989) and *Pink Snow: Homotextual Possibilities in Canadian Fiction* (Broadview Press, forthcoming in 2002). He is co-editor, with Daniel David Moses, of *An Anthology of Canadian Native Literature in English* (Oxford University Press, 1998) and also, with Robert Gray, of a special issue of *Ariel*, entitled "Postcolonial and Queer Theory and Praxis" (April 1999).